The Data Lakehouse Revolution

Harnessing the Power of Databricks for Generative AI and Machine Learning

Rajaniesh Kaushikk

Foreword by Scott Hanselman

Apress®

The Data Lakehouse Revolution: Harnessing the Power of Databricks for Generative AI and Machine Learning

Rajaniesh Kaushikk
Green Brook, New Jersey, USA

ISBN-13 (pbk): 979-8-8688-1720-5   ISBN-13 (electronic): 979-8-8688-1721-2
https://doi.org/10.1007/979-8-8688-1721-2

Copyright © 2025 by Rajaniesh Kaushikk

This work is subject to copyright. All rights are reserved by the Publisher, whether the whole or part of the material is concerned, specifically the rights of translation, reprinting, reuse of illustrations, recitation, broadcasting, reproduction on microfilms or in any other physical way, and transmission or information storage and retrieval, electronic adaptation, computer software, or by similar or dissimilar methodology now known or hereafter developed.

Trademarked names, logos, and images may appear in this book. Rather than use a trademark symbol with every occurrence of a trademarked name, logo, or image we use the names, logos, and images only in an editorial fashion and to the benefit of the trademark owner, with no intention of infringement of the trademark.

The use in this publication of trade names, trademarks, service marks, and similar terms, even if they are not identified as such, is not to be taken as an expression of opinion as to whether or not they are subject to proprietary rights.

While the advice and information in this book are believed to be true and accurate at the date of publication, neither the authors nor the editors nor the publisher can accept any legal responsibility for any errors or omissions that may be made. The publisher makes no warranty, express or implied, with respect to the material contained herein.

> Managing Director, Apress Media LLC: Welmoed Spahr
> Acquisitions Editor: Smriti Srivastava
> Development Editor: Laura Berendson
> Editorial Assistant: Jessica Vakili

Cover designed by eStudioCalamar

Cover image designed by Pixabay

Distributed to the book trade worldwide by Springer Science+Business Media New York, 1 New York Plaza, New York, NY 10004. Phone 1-800-SPRINGER, fax (201) 348-4505, e-mail orders-ny@springer-sbm.com, or visit www.springeronline.com. Apress Media, LLC is a Delaware LLC and the sole member (owner) is Springer Science + Business Media Finance Inc (SSBM Finance Inc). SSBM Finance Inc is a **Delaware** corporation.

For information on translations, please e-mail booktranslations@springernature.com; for reprint, paperback, or audio rights, please e-mail bookpermissions@springernature.com.

Apress titles may be purchased in bulk for academic, corporate, or promotional use. eBook versions and licenses are also available for most titles. For more information, reference our Print and eBook Bulk Sales web page at http://www.apress.com/bulk-sales.

Any source code or other supplementary material referenced by the author in this book is available to readers on GitHub: https://github.com/Apress/The-Data-Lakehouse-Revolution. For more detailed information, please visit https://www.apress.com/gp/services/source-code.

If disposing of this product, please recycle the paper

To Kallpana, my wife, your belief made this possible.

To Aarnna, my daughter, may you always dream boldly.

To Casper—thank you for keeping me company through it all.

Table of Contents

About the Author xv

About the Technical Reviewer xvii

Foreword xix

Introduction xxi

Chapter 1: Getting Started with Databricks 1
   Overview of Databricks 2
      A Unified Data Life Cycle Platform 2
      Flexibility and Scalability 2
      Collaboration Capabilities 3
      Cloud-Native and Open by Design 3
      Support for All Data Personas 3
      Real-Time Analytics and AI-Driven Discoveries 3
      Governance and Security 4
      Data Ecosystem Integration 4
      Business Use Cases and Industry Applications 4
      Databricks Unique Proposition 5
   Key Features and Benefits of Databricks 5
      Lakehouse Architecture: Bridging Data Warehouses and Data Lakes 5
      Collaborative Notebooks 11
      Managed Compute Clusters 12
      AI and Machine Learning Integration 13
      Security and Governance: Safeguarding Data with Confidence 15
      Cloud Integrations 17
      Delta Sharing for Data Collaboration 19

TABLE OF CONTENTS

    Support for Diverse Workloads 21

    Cost and Performance Optimization 23

    Monitoring and Logging capabilities 25

Key Components of Databricks 27

    Notebooks: Your Interactive Development Environment 27

    Databricks Clusters 28

    Databricks Jobs 29

    Databricks Workflows 29

    Navigating the Interface: Step-by-Step 30

Creating the Databricks Account 33

    Step 1: Choosing the Cloud Provider: Finding the Right Fit for Your
    Databricks Environment 33

    Step 2: Registering Your Databricks Account 35

    Step 3: Configuring Your Workspace 37

    Step 4: Configuring Compute Clusters 38

    Step 5: Managing User Access and Roles 40

    Step 6: Integrating Data Sources 42

    Workspace Deployment in Action 42

Tips and Best Practices for Efficient Navigation in Databricks 43

    Organize Your Workspace for Clarity 43

    Master Keyboard Shortcuts 44

    Optimize Cluster Usage 44

    Leverage Search and Filtering Tools 45

    Collaborate Effectively 45

    Monitor Jobs and Clusters 46

    Use Workflows to Automate Repetitive Tasks 46

    Keep Your Environment Clean 47

    Databricks Navigation in Action 47

Hands-On Lab: Setting Up and Navigating Databricks 48

    Logging into Databricks 48

    Setting Up Your Workspace 49

Configuring Compute Clusters	50
Working with Notebooks	51
Summary	54

Chapter 2: Introduction to Machine Learning and Data Lakehouses ... 55

Overview of Machine Learning	56
Why Machine Learning Matters	56
Key Concepts in Machine Learning	57
Types of Machine Learning	60
Supervised Learning: Learning with a Teacher	60
Unsupervised Learning: Finding Hidden Patterns	61
Reinforcement Learning: Learning Through Rewards	62
Comparing the Three Types of Machine Learning	63
Real-World Examples and Use Cases	64
Hands-On Lab: Practical Exercises on Basic ML Concepts	66
Exercise 1: Supervised Learning—Predicting Housing Prices	66
Exercise 2: Unsupervised Learning—Customer Segmentation	85
Summary	106

Chapter 3: Data Preparation and Management ... 107

Introduction to Data Ingestion	108
Batch Ingestion	108
Streaming Ingestion	111
Batch vs. Streaming Ingestion	114
Standard Data Ingestion Tools and Methods	115
Data Cleaning and Transformation	118
Techniques for Data Cleaning and Preprocessing	119
Forward/Backward Fill (Time-Series Data)	120
Tools and Libraries for Data Transformation	132
Open Source Libraries	132
Data Integration Platforms	132
Cloud-Native Solutions	133

TABLE OF CONTENTS

    Specialized Transformation Tools 133

    Machine Learning-Driven Transformation Tools 134

    Governance and Catalog Integration 134

    Best Practices for Data Transformation 135

Managing Data with Unity Catalog 135

    Key Problems Unity Catalog Solves 136

    How Unity Catalog Works 138

    Best Practices for Data Organization and Governance 139

Hands-On Labs 141

    Exercise 1: Batch Processing with Databricks 141

    Exercise 2: Streaming Data Processing in Databricks 146

    Exercise 3: Handling and Cleaning Batch Data in Databricks 148

    Exercise 4: Managing Data with Unity Catalog in Databricks 154

Summary 157

Chapter 4: Building Machine Learning Models 159

Fundamentals of Machine Learning Models 160

Introduction to MLflow 162

    Key Features and Components 162

    Step-by-Step Guide to Creating an MLflow Project in Azure Databricks 165

Choosing the Right Algorithm for Model Training 167

    Why Is Choosing the Right Algorithm Important? 167

Scenario: Choosing the Right Algorithm for Customer Churn Prediction 173

    Identifying the Type of Problem 173

    Considering the Data Characteristics 173

    Balancing Interpretability vs. Accuracy 174

    Computational Requirements 174

    Choosing the Right Algorithm Based on Data Type 174

Model Training and Hyperparameter Tuning 175

    What Are Hyperparameters? 175

    What Is Hyperparameter Tuning? 176

    Why Is Hyperparameter Tuning Important? 176

Evaluating Model Performance	180
Key Metrics for Evaluating Model Performance	180
End-to-End Example: Evaluating Model Performance and Logging with MLflow	185
Train a Classification Model	186
Make Predictions and Compute Evaluation Metrics	186
Log Metrics with MLflow	186
Interpret the Metrics	187
Viewing MLflow Logs in Databricks	187
Experiment Tracking with MLflow	188
Why Experiment Tracking Is Important	189
Recording and Managing Experiments	189
Hands-On Labs	191
Lab 1: Hyperparameter Tuning with MLflow and Hyperopt	191
Lab 2: Training a Random Forest Model with MLflow	194
Lab 3: Loan Default Prediction Lab	198
Summary	213

Chapter 5: AutoML and Model Optimization 215

Introduction to AutoML	216
What Is AutoML?	216
Why Use AutoML?	216
Use Cases of AutoML	217
How AutoML Improves Fraud Detection?	218
How AutoML Works?	218
Benefits and Limitations of AutoML	221
Benefits of using AutoML	221
Challenges and Limitations	222
Why Choose Databricks AutoML?	224
Key Advantages of Databricks AutoML	224
Using Databricks AutoML	225
Setting Up and Running AutoML Experiments	225
Interpreting AutoML Results	229

TABLE OF CONTENTS

Model Optimization Techniques 231
Techniques for Improving Model Accuracy 231
Performance Tuning and Optimization Strategies 234
Hands-On Lab 1: AutoML Experiment for Housing Price Prediction 238
Scenario 238
Prerequisites 238
Generating the Sample Dataset 239
Running AutoML in Databricks 239
Interpreting AutoML Results 246
Databricks AutoML Python API 250
Why Use the AutoML Python API? 251
Running AutoML Using Python API 251
Evaluating and Deploying the Best Model 251
Retrieving AutoML Results 251
Loading and Testing the Best Model 252
Hands-On Lab 2: Predicting Loan Defaults Using Databricks AutoML (Python API) 253
Generate Sample Loan Application Data 254
Run AutoML for Loan Default Prediction 255
Evaluate AutoML Results 255
Deploy and Test the Best Model 256
Summary 257

Chapter 6: Deploying Machine Learning Models 259
Model Deployment: What It Takes to Go Live 260
Deployment Strategies and Considerations 265
Batch Deployment 266
Real-Time Deployment 269
Edge Deployment 271
Deployment Considerations 274
Model Serialization 275
Computational Resources 277
Integration Requirements 279

Compliance and Governance	281
Cloud-Based Deployment	283
On-Premises Deployment	287
Hybrid Deployment	289

Deploying Models in Databricks ... 292
    Using MLflow for Model Deployment and the Deployment Challenge ... 293
    Understanding MLflow's Approach to Deployment ... 296
    Common Deployment Patterns Supported by MLflow ... 300
    MLflow Model Registry: Your Model's Home in Production ... 303
    MLflow Deployment Quick Checklist ... 304
    Best Practices for Deployment in Production ... 305
    Troubleshooting Model Deployment Issues ... 307

External Integration Patterns ... 318
    REST API Integration ... 318
    Webhook Integration ... 319
    Message Queue Integration ... 319
    Mobile Application Integration ... 319
    Integration Best Practices ... 320

Monitoring and Maintaining Deployed Models ... 322
    Setting Up Monitoring and Alerting ... 323
    Managing the Model Life Cycle and Updates ... 326

Hands-On Exercise: Predict Customer Churn and Serve the Model via REST API ... 327

Summary ... 333

Chapter 7: Advanced Topics in Machine Learning ... 335

Overview of Explainability Techniques: SHAP, LIME, and Beyond ... 336
    SHAP ... 337
    LIME ... 338
    Partial Dependence Plots ... 338

Ethical Considerations in Machine Learning ... 340
    Recognizing and Addressing Bias ... 340
    Ensuring Fairness and Accountability ... 342

TABLE OF CONTENTS

  Regulatory Implications and Compliance 343

 Future Trends in Machine Learning... 345

  Emerging Technologies and Architectures 345

  Future Trends in Machine Learning 346

  Emerging Technologies and Architectures 346

  Real-Time and Continual Learning 348

  ML in the Age of Generative AI 349

 Hands-On Lab: Explainability and Governance for Loan Default Risk Prediction 350

  Create a Realistic Loan Default Dataset 351

  Train a Binary Classification Model 355

  Generate SHAP Explanations 357

  Log SHAP Artifacts with MLflow 362

  Register the Model and Enrich with Unity Catalog Metadata 364

  Train a New Model Version and Compare Interpretability 366

 Summary 371

Chapter 8: Lakehouse AI and Retrieval-Augmented Generation (RAG) 373

 Introduction to Lakehouse AI 374

  Key Features and Capabilities 375

  Benefits of Lakehouse AI 377

 Retrieval-Augmented Generation (RAG): A Foundation for Enterprise LLMs 379

  What Is RAG and Why Does It Matter? 380

  RAG Architecture and Components 381

  Model and Tooling Options 383

 Building RAG Pipelines with Lakehouse AI 385

  Implementing RAG with Delta Tables and Vector Search 386

  Implementing Governance on RAG Pipelines 391

  Prompt Engineering and Guardrails 392

 Real-World Use Cases and Industry Applications 395

  Healthcare: Clinical Note Summarization 395

  Finance: Fraud Detection and Document Analysis 396

  Retail: Intelligent Product Recommendations 397

TABLE OF CONTENTS

Lab: Building a Vector Search-Powered HR Chatbot on Databricks 397
    Step 1: Install Required Libraries 398
    Step 2: Restart the Python Kernel 399
    Step 3: Create Catalog and Schema Using PySpark 399
    Step 4: Load HR Policy Sample Data into a Delta Table 400
    Step 5: Verify HR Policy Data in SQL 402
    Step 6: Create and Validate Vector Search Endpoint 402
    Step 7: Create and Sync Vector Search Index 404
    Step 8: Perform Semantic Search on the Vector Index 407
    Step 9: Define LangChain Configuration for the HR Chatbot 408
    Step 10: Constructing the Retriever Pipeline with LangChain and Vector Search 410
    Step 11: Building the LLM Chain to Generate HR Answers 413
    Step 12: Enable MLflow Autologging for LangChain 415
    Step 13: Building the Full RAG Chatbot Pipeline with LangChain, Vector Search, and Databricks LLM 416

Summary 420

Chapter 9: Conclusion and Next Steps 423

Recap of Key Concepts 424
    Getting Started with Databricks 424
    Introduction to Machine Learning and Lakehouses 425
    Data Preparation and Management 426
    Building ML Models with MLflow 427
    AutoML and Model Optimization 428
    Deploying Models 429
    Responsible AI and Governance 430
    Lakehouse AI and Retrieval-Augmented Generation (RAG) 431

Resources for Further Learning 432
    Official Databricks Resources 432
    Books and Technical References 433
    Online Courses and Certifications 433
    Communities and Forums 434
    GitHub Repositories and Templates 434

TABLE OF CONTENTS

Next Steps in Your ML Journey 435
Build and Operationalize Your Own Projects 435
Join or Lead a Data Project Team 435
Contribute to Open Source and Community 436
Seek Feedback and Reflect on Impact 436
Plan Your Career Growth 436
Summary 437
Key Takeaways 437
Looking Ahead 438
Final Words 438
Call to Action 438

Index 439

About the Author

Rajaniesh Kaushikk is a globally recognized leader in the field of data and artificial intelligence, with over 23 years of experience transforming complex technological challenges into intelligent, scalable solutions. His career has been defined by a passion for exploration, a drive to build, and a deep commitment to sharing knowledge. Throughout his professional journey, Rajaniesh has helped organizations across industries and continents harness the full potential of technologies like generative AI, machine learning, Apache Spark, and Data Lakehouse Architecture. He believes in designing solutions that not only solve technical problems but also empower people.

Rajaniesh's contributions have earned him Most Valuable Professional (MVP) awards from both Microsoft and Databricks, along with the distinguished title of Databricks Champion—a recognition that places him among a select group of experts celebrated for their technical leadership, community impact, and commitment to knowledge sharing. These honors reflect his passion for making cutting-edge technologies accessible, practical, and simplified.

Rajaniesh is a sought-after speaker at Microsoft, Databricks, and global tech events, where he shares insights on generative AI, cloud-native solutions, and scalable data platforms. Known for his clear and engaging style, he makes even the most complex topics accessible across audiences—from boardrooms to classrooms.

Beyond the stage, he reaches a worldwide community through his blog at www.RajanieshKaushikk.com and YouTube channel https://www.youtube.com/@RajanieshKaushikk, where he shares practical tutorials, industry trends, and hands-on guidance. He's driven by a belief that open, accessible learning is essential to growing the next generation of technology leaders. Rajaniesh thrives where technology, creativity, and community meet—bringing curiosity, purpose, and heart to everything from mentoring to enterprise strategy.

Outside of work, Rajaniesh enjoys cooking, music, and spending time with his wife, daughter, and their curious dog. These personal passions help him stay grounded and fuel his drive to build and inspire with purpose.

About the Technical Reviewer

Kasam Shaikh is a prominent figure in India's artificial intelligence landscape, holding the distinction of being one of the country's first four Microsoft Most Valuable Professionals (MVPs) in AI. Currently serving as a Senior Architect, Kasam boasts an impressive track record as an author, having authored five best-selling books dedicated to Azure and AI technologies. Beyond his writing endeavors, Kasam is recognized as a Microsoft Certified Trainer (MCT) and influential tech YouTuber (@mekasamshaikh). He also leads the largest online Azure AI community, known as DearAzure | Azure INDIA, and is a globally renowned AI speaker. His commitment to knowledge sharing extends to contributions to Microsoft Learn, where he plays a pivotal role.

Within the realm of AI, Kasam is a respected subject matter expert (SME) in generative AI for the cloud, complementing his role as a Senior Cloud Architect. He actively promotes the adoption of No Code and Azure OpenAI solutions and possesses a strong foundation in hybrid and cross-cloud practices. Kasam Shaikh's versatility and expertise make him an invaluable asset in the rapidly evolving landscape of technology, contributing significantly to the advancement of Azure and AI.

In summary, Kasam Shaikh is a multifaceted professional who excels in both technical expertise and knowledge dissemination. His contributions span writing, training, community leadership, public speaking, and architecture, establishing him as a true luminary in Azure and AI. Kasam was recently awarded as the top voice in AI by LinkedIn, making him the sole exclusive Indian professional acknowledged by both Microsoft and LinkedIn for his contributions to artificial intelligence!

Foreword

We stand at an extraordinary moment in the evolution of technology, a moment where data, machine learning, and generative AI are no longer just tools for data scientists but essential building blocks for the intelligent systems that define our world. The question is no longer "Can we build it?" but "Should we, and if so, how do we build it responsibly?"

Rajaniesh Kaushikk's *The Data Lakehouse Revolution* arrives at exactly the right time with exactly the right message. This isn't just a book on Databricks or AI models. It's a guidebook for the next generation of builders, thinkers, and technologists who want to harness data not only for performance but for purpose.

I've spent my career helping developers and technologists thrive across changing platforms, and one truth always holds: abstraction is powerful, but understanding is empowering. This book doesn't just teach you how to use a Lakehouse. It helps you understand why the Lakehouse matters. Rajaniesh doesn't shy away from the tough parts. He leans into them, tackling explainability, fairness, bias mitigation, and compliance with evolving global regulations. He reminds us that building with empathy, traceability, and accountability is not optional. It is the only way forward.

You'll find practical insights here, from SHAP and LIME to MLflow, Unity Catalog, and Retrieval-Augmented Generation. These concepts are woven into a framework that is both technically robust and ethically grounded. You'll learn how to bring generative AI to life using your organization's real data, how to scale responsibly, and how to audit and govern models that operate in the real world.

But more than that, this book inspires confidence that the tools of tomorrow are in the right hands—yours.

So to every data scientist, ML engineer, developer, and leader reading this: let *The Data Lakehouse Revolution* be more than a reference. Let it be a call to action. Use this knowledge to build systems that are not only intelligent but just. Architect platforms that amplify insight, not inequality. Design for transparency, auditability, and inclusion from the start.

The future of AI is not inevitable. It must be intentional. Let's build it together, and let's build it right.

Scott Hanselman
VP of Developer Community
Microsoft

Introduction

In today's data-driven world, organizations face the dual challenge of managing massive datasets and converting them into actionable intelligence. As the demand for real-time insights, scalable infrastructure, and responsible AI increases, so too does the need for a unified approach to building, deploying, and governing data and machine learning solutions. This book addresses that challenge through the lens of **Databricks and the Lakehouse Architecture**, providing a hands-on, end-to-end guide for modern data and AI practitioners.

Whether you are a data engineer, data scientist, ML practitioner, or analytics leader, this book is designed to help you confidently navigate the evolving landscape of scalable machine learning and AI systems. Through a progression of chapters, you'll learn how to transform raw data into intelligent, production-ready applications—without sacrificing security, governance, or performance.

Who This Book Is For

This book is ideal for professionals working at the intersection of data engineering, analytics, and machine learning, particularly those seeking to build end-to-end pipelines in Databricks. Readers with foundational experience in Python, SQL, or data platforms will benefit the most, although the book also introduces advanced concepts in a beginner-friendly, step-by-step format.

Whether you're exploring ML for the first time, deploying production-grade systems, or transitioning into a role that bridges AI and business strategy, you'll find practical value here. The book also speaks to leaders responsible for operationalizing AI while ensuring responsible governance and regulatory alignment.

INTRODUCTION

What This Book Covers

This book follows a structured, cumulative approach to modern machine learning workflows on Databricks. Each chapter builds upon the last to simulate real-world projects, from ideation through deployment and monitoring. Here's what you can expect:

- **Chapter 1: Getting Started with Databricks** introduces the Lakehouse Architecture, unified analytics workflows, and foundational Databricks capabilities, including collaborative notebooks, autoscaling compute, and cloud-native security.

- **Chapter 2: Introduction to Machine Learning and Data Lakehouses** explains core ML concepts—including supervised, unsupervised, and reinforcement learning—and explores how Lakehouse Architecture simplifies feature access, governance, and model iteration.

- **Chapter 3: Data Preparation and Management** focuses on ingesting, cleaning, and transforming data at scale using tools like Auto Loader and Delta Lake. You'll also learn to apply best practices in schema enforcement, deduplication, and metadata governance with Unity Catalog.

- **Chapter 4: Building Machine Learning Models** introduces MLflow and demonstrates how to structure experiments, track metrics, and register models. You'll train, evaluate, and version models in a collaborative, traceable environment.

- **Chapter 5: AutoML and Model Optimization** explores how to use Databricks AutoML for rapid prototyping, then moves toward hyperparameter tuning and performance enhancement strategies for more customized models.

- **Chapter 6: Deploying Machine Learning Models** covers deployment strategies (batch, real-time, and edge), environment packaging, CI/CD integration, and how to monitor model behavior over time for drift, latency, and SLA violations.

- **Chapter 7: Advanced Topics in Machine Learning** delves into explainability (SHAP, LIME), algorithmic fairness, and ethical AI practices. You'll learn to build systems that are auditable, accountable, and aligned with emerging regulatory frameworks.

- **Chapter 8: Lakehouse AI and Retrieval-Augmented Generation (RAG)** takes you into the frontier of generative AI. You'll build intelligent assistants using vector search, embeddings, and large language models (LLMs) grounded in your enterprise data, governed, and scaled via the Lakehouse.

- **Chapter 9: Conclusion and Next Steps** recaps key concepts and offers guidance for extending your skills, building production-grade systems, and integrating Databricks ML practices into your organization.

How to Use This Book

This book can be read linearly as a hands-on progression or nonlinearly as a reference. Each chapter features practical examples, architectural insights, and real-world use cases across various industries, including finance, healthcare, and ecommerce. You'll gain not only technical fluency but also a deeper understanding of how to design scalable, trustworthy AI systems.

Whether you're building your first model or designing an enterprise-scale ML platform, this book equips you with the tools, workflows, and mindset required to succeed in the era of governed, scalable, and responsible AI.

Let's get started.

CHAPTER 1

Getting Started with Databricks

In an era where data is the new currency, companies are increasingly relying on insights gleaned from vast amounts of data to make informed decisions, innovate, and stay competitive. However, as data grows more complex, organizations encounter significant challenges in managing, processing, and analyzing it. These include handling diverse data formats, integrating information from multiple sources, and enabling seamless team collaboration.

To overcome these challenges, businesses require a unified platform that simplifies the data life cycle and empowers teams to innovate without being constrained by traditional systems. **Databricks** rises to meet this need. More than just a data platform, Databricks is a transformative solution that redefines how organizations approach big data, analytics, and artificial intelligence (AI). Developed by the original creators of Apache Spark, Databricks combines the power of distributed computing with user-friendly tools and a collaborative environment.

Why is Databricks indispensable in today's data landscape?

- **It streamlines the entire data life cycle, from ingestion to analysis, eliminating** the need for multiple tools.

- **It enables real-time insights:** A critical asset for businesses in dynamic markets.

- **It fosters collaboration:** By bridging the gap between data engineers, scientists, and analysts, Databricks ensures that all stakeholders make meaningful contributions to data-driven initiatives.

CHAPTER 1   GETTING STARTED WITH DATABRICKS

This chapter explores the core principles and capabilities of Databricks, from its platform architecture to hands-on engagement with its user interface. By the end, you'll understand why Databricks transforms industries and how you can leverage its capabilities to advance your data projects.

Overview of Databricks

Databricks provides a unified platform for managing, analyzing, and processing vast volumes of data. In the data landscape where businesses grapple with increasing data volumes, fragmented workflows, and disconnected tools, Databricks bridges these gaps through its scalable, collaborative, and cloud-native platform capabilities. It enables organizations to unlock the full potential of their data.

A Unified Data Life Cycle Platform

Databricks supports the entire data life cycle, from ingestion and storage to processing and deployment, ensuring seamless operations within a single environment. This unified approach eliminates inefficiencies associated with switching between tools, reduces complexity, and accelerates time-to-value.

Flexibility and Scalability

Built on **Lakehouse architecture**, Databricks combines the flexibility of data lakes with the performance of data warehouses. This architectural advantage enables businesses to

- Store large volumes of structured, semi-structured, and unstructured data without sacrificing accessibility.
- Perform advanced analytics and machine learning directly on raw or curated data.
- Eliminate data duplication typically required in separate data lake and warehouse systems.

Databricks also scales to meet the demands of modern data-driven enterprises, allowing organizations to process **terabytes** to **petabytes** of data without performance bottlenecks.

Collaboration Capabilities

Databricks facilitates cross-functional collaboration, enabling data engineers, scientists, and business analysts to work seamlessly together. The platform's interactive notebooks serve as shared workspaces, where teams can write code, share visualizations, and document results in real time. This collaborative environment breaks down silos, fostering innovation and agility.

Cloud-Native and Open by Design

One of Databricks' advantages is its cloud-native architecture. Running on leading cloud platforms such as **Azure**, **AWS**, and **Google Cloud**, Databricks exploits the cloud's scalability, reliability, and global reach. Its foundation in open source technologies, such as Apache Spark and Delta Lake, ensures compatibility and minimizes **vendor lock-in**. This openness enables integration with tools such as Power BI, Tableau, Informatica, and Talend, thereby enhancing adaptability across diverse ecosystems.

Support for All Data Personas

Databricks caters to a wide range of roles within an organization:

- **Data Engineers**: Use advanced ETL capabilities to create robust pipelines for data ingestion, transformation, and enrichment.
- **Data Scientists**: Experiment with machine learning models using integrated libraries like TensorFlow, PyTorch, and Scikit-learn.
- **Business Analysts**: Execute SQL-based queries to derive insights without requiring extensive programming knowledge.

Real-Time Analytics and AI-Driven Discoveries

The ability to process and act on data in real time is essential in today's business environment. Databricks leverages the power of **Apache Spark** to process **batch** and **streaming data**, enabling businesses to simultaneously

- React to events as they occur, such as detecting fraud or delivering personalized recommendations.

- Extract actionable insights from a combination of historical and real-time data.
- Build and deploy machine learning models that dynamically adapt to changing data patterns.

Governance and Security

As data privacy concerns and security threats grow, Databricks provides critical features to ensure data governance and protection:

- **Role-Based Access Control (RBAC)**: Restrict access to sensitive information based on user roles.
- **Delta Sharing**: Facilitate secure and scalable data sharing with internal and external stakeholders without duplication.
- **Unity Catalog**: Centralized governance with fine-grained access controls, auditing capabilities, and metadata management.

Data Ecosystem Integration

Databricks integrates very well with existing tools and technologies, enhancing its versatility:

- **ETL and Data Pipelines**: Integrates with tools like **Apache NiFi**, **Talend**, and **Informatica** to simplify data ingestion and transformation
- **Business Intelligence**: Supports BI tools like **Power BI**, **Tableau**, and **Looker** for visualization and reporting
- **Machine Learning Operations**: Includes tools like MLflow to streamline the tracking, management, and deployment of machine learning models

Business Use Cases and Industry Applications

Databricks is a platform used across a range of industries:

1. **Retail**: Deliver personalized shopping experiences with AI-driven recommendation systems.

2. **Finance**: Detect and prevent fraud in real time using streaming analytics.

3. **Healthcare**: Accelerate drug discovery and enhance patient care with predictive analytics.

4. **Manufacturing**: Optimize supply chain operations through IoT data and machine learning.

Databricks Unique Proposition

Databricks offers a built-in capability to simplify complex workflows and drive innovation by uniting disparate teams and technologies. Databricks enables organizations to

- Accelerate data-driven decision-making.
- Minimize operational overhead through automation and scalability.
- Foster innovation using advanced analytics and machine learning capabilities.

Key Features and Benefits of Databricks

Databricks offers various features designed to streamline data management and analysis. Its technical approach bridges the traditional gaps between different data systems, enabling organizations to achieve greater value from their data. This section explores Lakehouse Architecture, a key feature that enhances Databricks' unified and efficient data processing capabilities.

Lakehouse Architecture: Bridging Data Warehouses and Data Lakes

Traditional data systems operated under a split paradigm for decades: **data lakes** for storing massive volumes of raw, unstructured data and **data warehouses** for managing structured, query-optimized datasets. While effective for their respective purposes, this division often led to inefficiencies. Organizations had to duplicate data, maintain complex synchronization pipelines, and manage siloed teams for these disparate environments. This duplication resulted in **higher costs, slower innovation, and a fragmented view of data**.

Before we dive deeper into the benefits of data lakehouses, it's essential to understand why traditional data architectures—data lakes and data warehouses—often fall short on their own. Table 1-1 highlights their differences and limitations.

Table 1-1. Comparison Between Data Lake vs. Data Warehouse

Feature	Data Lake	Data Warehouse
Data Type	Stores all data types: structured, semi-structured, and unstructured.	Primarily stores structured data organized in tables.
Storage Cost	Low-cost storage using systems like Amazon S3 or Azure Blob Storage.	High-cost storage due to optimized and indexed formats, which enable faster queries.
Schema Enforcement	Schema-on-read: Data is stored as-is, and structure is applied when accessed.	Schema-on-write: Requires data to be structured before it is ingested.
Performance	Slower query performance, especially for analytics on large datasets.	High-performance queries designed for business intelligence (BI) and reporting.
Data Processing	Ideal for batch processing and large-scale analytics, but lacks real-time capabilities in many cases.	Optimized for fast transactional processing and reporting.
Governance	Limited governance, with challenges in access controls, data versioning, and quality checks.	Strong governance, with built-in access controls and data quality mechanisms.
Machine Learning Support	Directly supports ML and AI workflows by allowing access to raw data.	Limited support for ML, requiring extensive preprocessing to fit structured formats.
Key Limitation	Lacks performance, governance, and reliability for real-time analytics.	Expensive and inflexible for handling diverse or rapidly growing unstructured data.

By addressing these limitations, data lakehouses provide a **unified solution** that combines

- The **scalability and flexibility** of a data lake
- The **performance and governance** of a data warehouse

Databricks provides the solution with its **Lakehouse Architecture**, which combines the **scalability and flexibility** of data lakes with the **performance and reliability** of data warehouses. By unifying these two systems into a single architecture, the **Lakehouse** eliminates traditional bottlenecks, reduces operational overhead, and enables teams to work more efficiently with diverse data sources.

Key Characteristics of Lakehouse Architecture

Lakehouse Architecture offers several distinct features that help with data management.

Unified and Versatile Data Storage

The Lakehouse Architecture offers a revolutionary approach to data management by combining **structured, semi-structured, and unstructured data into a single, unified repository**. This unification eliminates the inefficiencies of traditional systems, which require maintaining separate infrastructures for different data types, thereby helping organizations analyze and utilize their data holistically.

Breaking Down Data Silos

In traditional systems, data is typically managed in silos based on its structure and use case. **Structured data**—like tables and relational databases—was stored in data warehouses optimized for querying and reporting. Meanwhile, **semi-structured** (e.g., JSON logs or XML files) and **unstructured data** (e.g., videos, images, and audio) resided in data lakes designed for raw storage and long-term archiving.

This division created **costly data silos**, resulting in

- **Duplication Across Systems**

    Data often had to be duplicated between lakes and warehouses to perform advanced analytics. For example, an ecommerce company might store transaction logs in a data lake for archival purposes but duplicate the same data in a warehouse for real-time reporting. This approach unnecessarily doubled storage costs.

- **Complex Synchronization Workflows**

    Maintaining data consistency across systems necessitated complex ETL (Extract, Transform, Load) workflows. These workflows were resource-intensive and prone to errors, often resulting in delays. For instance, if customer order data updated in the warehouse wasn't synchronized with the data lake, it could result in conflicting reports across departments.

- **Fragmented Insights**

    Data silos fractured the organization's ability to generate unified insights. Analysts frequently needed to manually integrate data from multiple systems, which slowed innovation and decision-making. For example, a healthcare provider might struggle to correlate structured patient records from a warehouse with unstructured medical images stored in a lake, limiting their ability to make timely, data-driven decisions.

Unified Solution with the Lakehouse Architecture

The **Lakehouse Architecture** solves these challenges by integrating all data types into a centralized platform. This consolidation eliminates duplication, reduces synchronization complexity, and enables teams to access and analyze all data in a single location. Whether working with customer transactions, IoT sensor logs, or multimedia files, enterprises can now streamline their analytics workflows.

By breaking down silos and enabling unified storage, the Lakehouse simplifies data management, empowering organizations to achieve faster and more accurate insights while reducing operational overhead.

Flexibility Across All Data Formats

The Lakehouse can handle diverse data formats:

- **Structured data**, such as tables or relational databases
- **Semi-structured data**, like sensor logs or web clickstreams
- **Unstructured data**, including rich media like videos, audio, and images

This versatility allows enterprises to **retain data in its original form**, avoiding time-consuming conversions and maintaining fidelity. Whether analyzing sales records, customer behavior, or multimedia assets, teams can work directly with their data with efficiency and speed.

For example, an **ecommerce platform** stores structured transaction histories, semi-structured user activity logs, and unstructured product videos in a single location. Analysts can then correlate data across formats to identify trends, such as which product images or videos drive the highest engagement and sales.

Elimination of Data Duplication

One of the benefits of the Lakehouse Architecture is its ability to eliminate data duplication, a common issue in traditional data management systems. Previously, organizations replicated data between data lakes for storage and data warehouses for analytics, leading to increased costs and operational inefficiencies.

Challenges of Duplication in Traditional Systems

- **Increased Costs**: Maintaining multiple copies of the same data inflated storage expenses.

- **Complexity**: Teams relied on error-prone ETL (Extract, Transform, Load) workflows to move data between lakes and warehouses.

- **Data Inconsistencies**: Delays in synchronization often cause discrepancies between systems, leading to inaccurate reports or analyses.

With Lakehouse, all data is stored once in a unified repository and made accessible for various use cases, including analytics, machine learning, and reporting. For example, a retail company can centralize sales data in Lakehouse and utilize it for both historical analysis and real-time dashboarding, eliminating the need for multiple copies.

By consolidating all data into a unified repository, the Lakehouse Architecture delivers several key advantages:

- **Operational Simplicity**: No more juggling with multiple platforms to manage different data types.

- **Enhanced Collaboration**: Cross-functional teams can access and analyze data without barriers.

- **Cost Savings**: Eliminates the need for data duplication, reducing storage and processing expenses.

- **Faster Insights**: Integrated data allows for real-time analysis across structured, semi-structured, and unstructured formats.

- **Improved Data Accuracy:** Ensures teams consistently access the most up-to-date data.

- **Streamlined Workflows:** Removing the need for synchronization simplifies the overall workflow.

High-Performance Queries

The Lakehouse Architecture helps organizations with **advanced caching, partitioning, and query optimization**, providing warehouse-like performance for analytics queries while preserving the flexibility of a data lake. This unification enables faster, more actionable insights that drive real-world outcomes. For example, a financial organization leveraging the Lakehouse Architecture can store structured transaction data, semi-structured behavior logs, and unstructured customer service audio recordings in a single repository. By querying this unified system, analysts can efficiently detect patterns indicative of fraud. These capabilities reduce the operational complexity of fragmented systems and enable real-time responses to emerging risks, offering a significant competitive edge.

Delta Lake for Transactional Capabilities

Delta Lake serves as the backbone of the Lakehouse, bringing robust **ACID (Atomicity, Consistency, Isolation, Durability)** transactional capabilities. These capabilities ensure that all data operations, such as inserts, updates, or deletes, are reliable and consistent, even when multiple users or systems access the same data simultaneously.

For instance, an ecommerce company processing millions of customer orders daily benefits from transactional integrity, ensuring that sales data is accurate, even during high-traffic events like Black Friday. By eliminating common issues such as partial updates or duplicate records, Delta Lake helps maintain clean and reliable data pipelines.

Data Versioning and Time Travel

Delta Lake's **data versioning** and **time travel** capabilities allow users to query historical versions of their data. This feature is critical for maintaining data integrity during audits, debugging workflows, or comparing different periods for analysis.

For example, a financial institution may need to investigate discrepancies in quarterly reports. With time travel, analysts can access and analyze the exact dataset used to generate the quarterly report by revisiting the version of the data before processing. This feature also enables rollback functionality, allowing teams to revert to a previous data version in the event of errors or unintended modifications.

Collaborative Notebooks

Successful data initiatives rely on effective team collaboration. However, data engineers, scientists, and analysts often juggle separate tools for coding, documentation, and visualizing results. These issues lead to miscommunication, duplicated efforts, and missed opportunities for insight.

Databricks helps overcome these challenges with Collaborative Notebooks, which bring teams together. These notebooks help interaction and improve productivity across roles by enabling real-time collaboration, rich visualization, and multi-language support.

Key Features of Collaborative Notebooks

Real-Time Multiuser Editing

Collaborative Notebooks allow multiple users to write, edit, and execute code simultaneously. This capability eliminates workflow bottlenecks, enabling teams to work harmoniously on complex tasks.

For instance, while data engineers fine-tune ETL pipelines, analysts can generate visualizations of real-time results—all within the same shared environment. This synchronous workflow reduces delays and fosters innovation.

Enhanced Communication Tools

Collaborative Notebooks streamline communication and documentation:

- **Markdown cells** enable users to annotate code, share insights, and clearly explain workflows.

- Embedded **graphs and charts** provide instant visual feedback, making complex data more accessible to stakeholders.

- A built-in **version history** ensures that every change is logged, enabling teams to track progress, revert to earlier stages, and maintain accountability.

This combination of features bridges the gaps between technical and nontechnical stakeholders, ensuring everyone stays aligned.

Multi-language Support

Databricks' Collaborative Notebooks can support multiple programming languages in a single notebook. With simple commands, users can transition between

- **Python** for advanced machine learning workflows
- **SQL** for querying structured datasets
- **R** for statistical analysis
- This flexibility helps teams to leverage diverse skill sets without switching tools, maximizing productivity, and reducing friction in multidisciplinary projects.

Managed Compute Clusters

Modern data workloads often require substantial computational resources, primarily as businesses handle increasingly large datasets and complex analytics. Misconfigured or static clusters can lead to performance bottlenecks, underutilized resources, and escalating costs. Databricks addresses these challenges with **Managed Compute Clusters**, which automate resource allocation to ensure performance and cost efficiency.

Key Features of Managed Compute Clusters

Autoscaling for Dynamic Workloads

One of the features of Databricks' Managed Compute Clusters is that they scale dynamically. Clusters automatically adjust their size in response to workload demands, ensuring optimal resource utilization without requiring manual intervention.

For example, an ecommerce platform preparing for Black Friday sales can scale up its clusters to handle the surge in customer activity. Once the sales period ends, the clusters scale down during low-traffic times, saving costs without sacrificing performance.

Cost Efficiency Through Resource Optimization

Databricks can prevent unnecessary expenses by deallocating idle nodes when no longer needed. This proactive approach ensures organizations pay only for the resources they actively use, optimizing their budget allocation and eliminating waste.

For instance, a media streaming company running analytics on viewership trends can keep costs low by deactivating clusters during off-peak hours while maintaining high performance during prime time.

Preconfigured Environments for Simplicity

Setting up distributed systems, such as Apache Spark, can be time-consuming and prone to errors. Databricks eliminates this complexity by offering preconfigured environments tailored to best practices. These ready-to-use clusters enable teams to focus on their workflows without worrying about setting up infrastructure.

For example, a healthcare research team analyzing genomic data can quickly deploy a Spark-optimized cluster without specialized IT knowledge.

Streamlined Management and Monitoring

The Databricks interface simplifies cluster management with tools to start, monitor, and stop clusters. Detailed performance logs allow users to troubleshoot issues efficiently, ensuring uninterrupted operations.

For instance, a logistics company monitoring real-time delivery data can rely on Databricks' intuitive dashboard to quickly track cluster performance and resolve bottlenecks.

AI and Machine Learning Integration

The journey from building machine learning models to deploying them is often fragmented and time-consuming, involving multiple tools and disjointed workflows. Databricks simplifies this process by offering an end-to-end solution that combines experimentation, tracking, and deployment within a single, unified platform. By integrating powerful tools like MLflow and preconfigured libraries, Databricks reduces friction in the machine learning life cycle, enabling faster and more reliable insights.

Key Features of AI and Machine Learning Integration

MLflow Integration

Databricks includes native support for MLflow, a robust open source framework that centralizes the machine learning life cycle. With MLflow, data scientists can track experiments, monitor hyperparameters, and evaluate results—all in one place. Teams can compare models based on metrics such as accuracy or latency, ensuring the best-performing version is deployed. It makes it easier to replicate and scale successful experiments.

For example, a marketing team might use MLflow to fine-tune a recommendation engine, comparing multiple algorithms and configurations before deploying the most effective model to enhance personalized user experiences.

Preconfigured Libraries

Databricks optimizes popular machine learning frameworks, such as TensorFlow, PyTorch, and XGBoost, within its environment. These libraries come preinstalled and preconfigured, allowing data scientists to focus on experimentation without worrying about setup and compatibility issues. This approach supports rapid iteration and scalability, whether building predictive models for customer behavior or training neural networks for image recognition.

For example, a healthcare provider can use TensorFlow within Databricks to build deep learning models that analyze medical images for early disease detection, significantly accelerating research timelines.

Simplified Deployment

Deploying machine learning models to production can be a significant bottleneck, often requiring additional infrastructure and custom engineering. Databricks simplifies this process with one-click deployment capabilities. Once validated, a model is integrated into production environments, reducing the complexity of infrastructure management. This ease of deployment ensures that organizations can operationalize insights faster and at scale.

For example, a logistics company could deploy a predictive maintenance model built in Databricks directly into its operational systems, enabling real-time monitoring of vehicle health and minimizing downtime.

Security and Governance: Safeguarding Data with Confidence

Data security is a top priority for modern organizations. Databricks provides tools to ensure data protection, including **role-based access control (RBAC)**, **Unity Catalog**, and **end-to-end encryption**. These features secure sensitive information and facilitate compliance with regulations such as **GDPR** and **HIPAA**.

Key Features of Security and Governance

Role-Based Access Control (RBAC)

Role-based access control (RBAC) is a system that defines and enforces access to specific data or resources based on an individual's role within an organization. Instead of granting unrestricted access to everyone, RBAC enables administrators to assign permissions tailored to an individual's specific responsibilities, ensuring that users can only access the information they need to perform their tasks effectively.

For example, engineers responsible for building fraud detection algorithms may need access to detailed transaction logs to refine their models in a financial institution. On the other hand, business analysts may only require summarized and anonymized data to create reports without needing to see personally identifiable information. RBAC makes this distinction possible by assigning different permissions to engineers and analysts.

This approach protects sensitive information and reduces the risk of accidental or malicious misuse. Moreover, RBAC helps organizations comply with regulations like GDPR by ensuring that only authorized personnel can access sensitive customer data.

Unity Catalog

Unity Catalog is a centralized data governance solution in Databricks that simplifies how organizations manage access, metadata, and data lineage across their datasets. Think of Unity Catalog as a control tower for your data—it provides a single point of management for who can access your data, tracks its usage, and audits changes over time.

Core Functions of Unity Catalog

1. **Centralized Metadata Management**

    Metadata refers to data about your data, such as the dataset's source, format, and purpose. Unity Catalog brings all this information into one place, making it easier for teams to understand the context of their data. For instance, a marketing team analyzing customer behavior logs can quickly use metadata to identify which dataset contains the latest clickstream data.

2. **Lineage Tracking**

    Data lineage tracks the journey of your data—where it originates, how it's transformed, and where it ends up. For example, a global retailer using Unity Catalog can trace sales data from the point of collection (e.g., point-of-sale systems) to its use in dashboards and reports. This lineage tracking is particularly helpful when troubleshooting issues or auditing compliance with data regulations.

3. **Fine-Grained Access Controls**

    Unity Catalog allows organizations to assign precise access permissions to datasets. For example, a healthcare provider might enable doctors to access sensitive patient records while administrative staff can only view anonymized data. This fine-grained access control ensures the right people see the right data without exposing sensitive information unnecessarily.

4. **Streamlined Compliance**

    With Unity Catalog, organizations can quickly generate audit logs that show who accessed data and when, ensuring compliance with laws such as HIPAA or GDPR. These logs are invaluable during audits or investigations, as they demonstrate that data governance policies are being adhered to.

Now, let's understand how the Unity catalog works in practice with an example. Imagine a company using Unity Catalog to manage its sales data. The marketing team requires access to anonymized customer insights for campaign targeting, while the data science team requires access to raw data to train predictive models. Unity Catalog enables the company to grant specific access to these teams, ensuring they only see the data relevant to their work. At the same time, the IT team can monitor and audit who accessed what data, ensuring compliance and security.

Data Encryption

Databricks utilizes advanced encryption techniques, including AES-256, to safeguard data both in transit and at rest. These encryptions ensure that sensitive information remains secure, even during storage or network communication. Consider a healthcare provider managing patient records: encryption safeguards these records as they are processed or transferred between systems, ensuring compliance with regulations such as HIPAA and protecting patient privacy. This protection level builds stakeholders' trust and minimizes the risk of data breaches.

Cloud Integrations

In today's fast-evolving business environment, leveraging cloud platforms such as Azure, AWS, and Google Cloud is a cornerstone of modern data infrastructure. These platforms offer the scalability, reliability, and flexibility necessary to manage vast amounts of data. However, integrating analytics and machine learning workflows with these ecosystems can become complex and time-consuming. Databricks addresses these challenges by offering seamless cloud integration, allowing organizations to utilize their existing cloud resources without additional overhead.

Databricks is designed as a cloud-native platform to work harmoniously with cloud storage, compute resources, and other services. This deep integration enables businesses to deploy, manage, and scale workloads efficiently, whether for regional operations or global enterprises with distributed architectures.

Key Features of Cloud Integration

Native Support for Cloud Storage

Databricks works natively with leading cloud storage solutions, including **Azure Blob Storage, Amazon S3, and Google Cloud Storage**. This tight integration eliminates the need for complex configurations, enabling users to quickly connect Databricks to their existing data lakes and start analyzing data immediately.

Let's understand it with an example: An ecommerce company centralizes its customer purchase data in Amazon S3, leveraging Databricks on AWS to analyze this data. By forecasting purchasing trends, the company optimizes inventory levels, ensuring products are stocked appropriately for peak seasons, all without needing additional data pipelines.

Scalability Across Cloud Regions

Databricks supports multi-region scalability, enabling organizations to distribute their workloads across multiple regions globally. This capability ensures low-latency access to data while meeting compliance requirements such as GDPR or regional data residency laws. It's particularly beneficial for multinational companies operating in diverse geographic markets.

For example, a global logistics company deploys Databricks clusters across multiple AWS regions to analyze delivery performance in real time. By processing local data closer to its source, the company improves route optimization and reduces delivery delays, enhancing customer satisfaction.

Collaboration with Cloud-Native Services

Databricks integrates with various cloud-native services to expand its functionality. For example:

- **Google BigQuery** for serverless, large-scale analytics.
- **Azure Data Factory** is used to create and orchestrate ETL (Extract, Transform, Load) workflows.
- **AWS Lambda** for serverless computing, enabling dynamic and event-driven processing.

This flexibility enables businesses to design workflows that cater to their specific needs while leveraging the best features of their cloud ecosystem.

For example, a media company uses Azure Data Factory to automate data pipelines, feeding video metadata into Databricks. Here, machine learning models analyze viewer preferences and generate real-time recommendations, creating a personalized experience for each user.

Elastic Compute Resources: Adapting to Dynamic Workloads

Databricks leverages the elastic nature of cloud platforms to scale dynamically compute resources based on workload demands, ensuring operational flexibility and cost efficiency.

- **Dynamic Scaling:** During high-demand periods, such as peak shopping events or real-time data analysis, Databricks automatically scales up clusters to handle increased workloads. Conversely, during low-demand periods, clusters scale down to prevent resource wastage.

- **Cost Efficiency:** Elastic scaling eliminates the need for over-provisioning by ensuring organizations pay only for the computing resources they use. Features like auto-termination further reduce expenses by shutting down idle clusters.

For example, an online retailer hosted on Azure Databricks scales up compute clusters during Black Friday to process real-time sales data and scales down during off-peak hours, thereby optimizing performance and costs.

This capability enables organizations across various industries, such as retail, healthcare, finance, and entertainment, to adapt their infrastructure seamlessly, meet fluctuating demands, and focus on deriving insights without worrying about resource management.

Delta Sharing for Data Collaboration

Traditional data-sharing methods, such as exporting static files or creating duplicate datasets, have long been a source of inefficiency, high costs, and security risks. These methods often result in sharing outdated information and creating significant overhead for maintaining synchronization across systems. **Delta Sharing**, an innovative feature of Databricks, addresses these issues by enabling secure, real-time access to live data without duplication or physical transfers.

Delta Sharing enables organizations to collaborate seamlessly across internal departments and external partners while maintaining complete control over their data. It combines scalability, efficiency, and regulatory compliance, making it an essential tool for modern data-driven workflows.

Key Features of Delta Sharing

Real-Time Access to Live Data

Delta Sharing provides instantaneous access to live data, eliminating the delays and inaccuracies associated with copying data to separate locations for sharing. This ensures that collaborators always work with the latest and most accurate datasets.

For example, a logistics company uses Delta Sharing to provide its delivery partners with live shipment data. This real-time access enables dynamic tracking and better decision-making without requiring time-consuming file exchanges or manual updates.

Fine-Grained Access Control

Delta Sharing allows data owners to specify detailed permissions for who can access specific datasets, tables, or even individual columns. This ensures sensitive information is protected while granting collaborators the data they need.

For example, a retail organization shares aggregated sales data with suppliers to help them manage inventory efficiently. However, it restricts access to individual customer purchase histories to maintain privacy and comply with data protection regulations.

Open Standard for Interoperability

Delta Sharing is built on open source technology, enabling compatibility with various tools and platforms. Users can access shared data directly through popular programming languages, such as Python, SQL, and R, or analytics tools like Excel, Tableau, and Jupyter Notebooks, regardless of whether they use Databricks.

For example, a research institution collaborates with external academic partners by sharing datasets through Delta Sharing. Partners can analyze the data using their preferred tools, ensuring accessibility without requiring specialized infrastructure.

Scalable for Growing Demands

Delta Sharing is designed to handle high-frequency access and large-scale datasets. This scalability ensures that Delta Sharing can seamlessly adapt without compromising performance as organizations grow or their data-sharing requirements increase.

For example, a multinational enterprise uses Delta Sharing to distribute live sales data to regional offices during high-demand events, such as Black Friday. With thousands of concurrent users querying data in real time, Delta Sharing ensures uninterrupted access and reliable performance.

Built-In Security and Compliance

Delta Sharing minimizes the risk of data breaches and unauthorized usage by providing access to live data without creating physical copies. Comprehensive logging ensures that every data request is auditable, helping organizations comply with regulations like GDPR and HIPAA.

For example, a financial services firm shares live market data with investment partners, logging every query to meet stringent regulatory requirements while maintaining data security and integrity.

Delta Sharing in Action

A global fashion retailer leverages Delta Sharing to share real-time inventory data with suppliers. Suppliers can dynamically adjust restocking schedules with live updates on stock levels, thereby reducing inefficiencies such as overstocking and stockouts. This seamless collaboration fosters better supply chain management, enhances operational efficiency, and builds stronger partner relationships.

Support for Diverse Workloads

Modern organizations face various data workloads, including Extract, Transform, Load (ETL) operations, machine learning model development, and SQL-based business intelligence queries. Historically, these workloads were distributed across multiple specialized tools, resulting in inefficiencies, increased costs, and fragmented workflows. **Databricks** addresses this challenge by providing a unified platform that supports diverse workloads seamlessly, enabling organizations to focus on innovation instead of managing disparate systems.

Comprehensive ETL Pipelines

ETL workflows are the backbone of any data-driven organization, ensuring that raw data is cleansed, transformed, and ready for analysis. Databricks streamlines this process with advanced tools for fault-tolerant and efficient pipelines, leveraging **Delta Lake** to handle large-scale data transformations with ease.

For example, a retail company processes clickstream data from its ecommerce platform, removing duplicates and enriching it with customer segmentation. This pipeline directly feeds into a real-time marketing dashboard, enabling targeted promotions that drive sales.

Integrated Machine Learning Capabilities

Databricks streamlines the machine learning life cycle by enabling data scientists to build, train, and deploy models on a single platform. Preinstalled libraries, such as TensorFlow, PyTorch, and MLflow, facilitate experimentation and model tracking, thereby reducing the friction between development and production.

For example, a transportation company leverages Databricks to train predictive models for delivery delays. By analyzing historical and live traffic data, the company enhances operational efficiency and customer satisfaction.

SQL for Business Intelligence

Business analysts can leverage the power of Databricks without requiring advanced programming skills. With SQL support and seamless integrations with tools like **Power BI**, **Tableau**, and **Looker**, Databricks bridges the gap between technical and nontechnical users.

For example, a hospital analyzes patient appointment data using SQL queries in Databricks, identifying patterns to reduce no-shows and optimize resource allocation.

Unified Batch and Streaming Data Processing

Managing batch and streaming data within the same environment is a critical advantage of Databricks. Organizations no longer need separate tools for historical analysis and real-time processing, streamlining workflows and reducing complexity.

For example, an IoT-enabled factory analyzes live sensor data to detect equipment anomalies in real time while conducting historical trend analysis to predict maintenance needs. This dual capability helps minimize downtime and enhance operational efficiency.

Advanced AI Workflows

Databricks extends beyond traditional machine learning to support advanced AI workflows, such as natural language processing (NLP), image recognition, and recommendation systems.

For example, a media company utilizes Databricks to analyze both historical and real-time user behavior, thereby building a recommendation engine that delivers personalized content and enhances user engagement and retention.

Unified Workload Management in Action

Organizations across industries are leveraging Databricks to unify their diverse workloads and achieve operational excellence. For example, a logistics company utilizes Databricks to address critical challenges, including cleansing GPS data through efficient ETL pipelines, developing predictive models to forecast delivery delays, and processing real-time traffic data to optimize routes dynamically. This integration reduces delays, enhances customer satisfaction, and streamlines operations.

Similarly, an international manufacturing firm utilizes Databricks to ingest IoT sensor data from factories worldwide, using Apache Kafka, and stores the results in **Delta Lake** for real-time anomaly detection. Data scientists build predictive maintenance models with **PyTorch**, while engineers visualize insights using **Power BI** dashboards. This unified approach minimizes downtime, increases production efficiency, and enables data-driven decision-making at scale.

By consolidating these diverse workloads onto a single platform, Databricks helps organizations to overcome fragmented workflows, accelerate innovation, and enhance their competitive edge.

Cost and Performance Optimization

Balancing performance and affordability is critical for businesses managing large datasets and complex workloads. Inefficient resource utilization drives up costs, while suboptimal performance can slow operations and hinder decision-making. Databricks addresses this dual challenge through advanced performance optimizations and cost-saving features, helping organizations streamline their data infrastructure while maximizing efficiency.

Key Features of Databricks for Cost and Performance Optimization

Photon Engine for Accelerated Queries

Databricks' **Photon Engine** significantly enhances SQL query performance, delivering up to 20 times faster execution on modern hardware. This enhancement enables real-time analytics on vast datasets, a capability critical for industries like retail during peak sales seasons.

For example, a global retailer reduced query times on large-scale sales data from hours to minutes, enabling near-real-time monitoring of top-performing products during Black Friday.

Autoscaling Compute Clusters

Dynamic autoscaling ensures that cluster resources are allocated based on workload demands. This prevents over-provisioning, ensures high availability during traffic surges, and reduces costs during off-peak hours.

For example, an online streaming platform dynamically scaled its clusters during a global event to handle real-time user interactions, scaling down afterward to save costs while maintaining performance.

Adaptive Query Execution (AQE)

Adaptive Query Execution adjusts query execution plans dynamically at runtime to optimize performance based on data volume and structure. This reduces execution times and resource usage for varying workloads.

For example, a telecom company analyzing call records saw a 30% reduction in query execution times by leveraging AQE, which seamlessly adapted to their changing data patterns.

Cloud-Native Cost-Saving Features

Databricks leverages discounted computing options like AWS Spot Instances and Azure Low-Priority VMs for non-time-sensitive tasks, such as batch processing and archival.

For example, a financial services company reduced computing costs by 40% by running nightly data cleansing tasks using Spot Instances.

Delta Lake for Optimized Storage

Delta Lake optimizes storage through **file compaction** and **Z-Ordering**, enhancing disk utilization and accelerating query performance.

For example, a healthcare provider grouped fragmented medical records in Delta Lake, improving query speeds and reducing storage costs while maintaining efficient access to critical data.

Cost and Performance Optimization at Scale

During its annual sales event, an ecommerce company turned to Databricks to optimize performance and minimize costs. Key improvements included

- **Photon Engine**: Accelerated SQL queries provided real-time insights into top-performing products.

- **Autoscaling Clusters**: Dynamically adjusted resources to manage demand surges and scaled down post-event to reduce expenses.

- **Spot Instances**: Saved 35% on compute costs by allocating noncritical ETL tasks to discounted resources.

- **Delta Lake**: Consolidated transaction logs, reducing storage requirements and accelerating query times.

These optimizations enabled the company to operate efficiently at scale, delivering fast insights to drive sales strategies while maintaining cost-effectiveness.

Monitoring and Logging capabilities

In today's fast-paced, data-driven world, large-scale systems demand robust monitoring and logging to maintain reliability, optimize resource utilization, and ensure compliance with industry standards. Databricks addresses these needs by offering comprehensive tools that provide real-time insights, proactive issue management, and performance optimization. These capabilities empower businesses to operate efficiently, even in the most complex environments.

Key Features of Databricks Monitoring and Logging

Real-Time Job Dashboards

Interactive dashboards deliver actionable insights into job progress, execution times, and data flow. They allow teams to identify bottlenecks and address them before they escalate quickly.

For example, a banking firm uses real-time dashboards to monitor reconciliation jobs, ensuring immediate intervention to prevent delays in financial reporting.

Cluster Performance Metrics

Databricks tracks critical metrics such as CPU usage, memory consumption, and disk I/O, providing a detailed view of resource utilization. These insights enable teams to fine-tune their systems for better performance.

For instance, a healthcare provider analyzing imaging datasets optimizes cluster configurations to balance performance with cost efficiency.

Detailed Logs for Debugging and Compliance

Comprehensive logs capture every detail, from query plans to error messages, supporting debugging and compliance audits.

For example, a telecom company resolved an ETL pipeline error caused by a schema mismatch by analyzing these detailed logs, ensuring continuity in downstream analytics.

Alerts and Notifications

Automated alerts notify teams of workflow anomalies or failures, integrating seamlessly with tools like PagerDuty and Slack.

For instance, an online retailer sets alerts for data ingestion failures during peak sales, allowing teams to resolve issues quickly and maintain uninterrupted analytics.

Audit Trails and Compliance

Databricks maintains extensive audit trails, recording data access, transformations, and updates. These trails ensure accountability and compliance with regulations like GDPR and HIPAA.

For example, a biotech firm demonstrated FDA compliance using audit logs to track data changes during clinical trials.

Historical Metrics for Trend Analysis

Historical data allows teams to analyze trends and predict future resource demands, ensuring readiness for seasonal or cyclical workloads.

For instance, a media company uses trend analysis to pre-scale clusters for streaming demand spikes during the holiday season.

Monitoring and Logging in Action

A global logistics company processes millions of delivery records daily using Databricks. Real-time dashboards help track ETL pipelines that process GPS data, while cluster metrics optimize configurations for memory-intensive tasks. Detailed logs resolve delays caused by network congestion, and alerts notify teams of potential issues with analytics jobs. Historical metrics enable the company to prepare for high-demand periods, such as Black Friday, ensuring seamless operations during these peak times. These features collectively empower the organization to maintain reliability, minimize downtime, and optimize processes for peak performance.

Key Components of Databricks

Databricks contains key components, including Notebooks, Clusters, Jobs, and workflows, all accessible from the main menu. These interconnected tools enable you to streamline your data operations and focus on generating insights. Let's understand what these tools are and why they are important.

Notebooks: Your Interactive Development Environment

Notebooks are at the core of the Databricks experience, providing an interactive workspace for writing and executing code, documenting findings, and visualizing results.

- **What Are Notebooks?**

    A Databricks notebook is a multipurpose document that combines code execution, text explanations, and visualizations in a single, interactive interface. It supports multiple programming languages like Python, SQL, Scala, and R, making it versatile for various use cases.

- **Features**
  - **Code Cells**: Write and execute code in blocks, enabling iterative development.
  - **Markdown Support**: Add explanations, notes, and annotations alongside your code for better documentation.
  - **Visualization Tools**: Generate graphs and charts directly in the notebook for instant insights.
  - **Multi-language Support**: Use magic commands like %sql or %python to switch between languages within the same notebook.
- **Example Use Case**

  A data scientist uses a notebook to preprocess a dataset, train a machine learning model in Python, and visualize performance metrics—all in one place.

Databricks Clusters

Clusters are the engines that power your data operations in Databricks, enabling you to run everything from small-scale queries to large-scale machine learning workflows.

- **What Are Clusters?**

  A cluster is a group of virtual machines (VMs) that provide the computational resources needed to execute your code. Clusters are fully managed by Databricks, eliminating the need for manual provisioning, maintenance, or scaling.

- **Features**
  - **Autoscaling**: Dynamically adjusts the number of nodes in your cluster based on workload demands.
  - **Preconfigured Environments**: Comes with preinstalled libraries optimized for Spark workloads.
  - **Cluster Types**: Choose between interactive clusters (used for development), job clusters (for running jobs), or high-concurrency clusters (used by multiple concurrent users).

- **Example Use Case**

    A data engineer configures a job cluster to deploy jobs and uses interactive clusters for development.

Databricks Jobs

Jobs allow you to schedule and automate recurring tasks, such as data ingestion, transformation, and analytics, without requiring manual intervention.

- **What Are Jobs?**

    A job is a scheduled workflow that executes a series of tasks, such as running a notebook, querying data, or triggering a machine learning model. Jobs can be configured to run on a set schedule or in response to specific events.

- **Features**
    - **Task Scheduling**: Automate tasks to run at specific intervals, such as hourly or daily.
    - **Job Dependencies**: Define dependencies between tasks to ensure they execute in the correct order.
    - **Alerts and Monitoring**: Get notified of job failures or performance issues to ensure reliability.

- **Example Use Case**

    An analyst sets up a job to run an SQL query every morning, generating a sales report emailed to stakeholders.

Databricks Workflows

Workflows are used to design and execute complex, multistep data pipelines that involve multiple tasks and dependencies.

- **What Are Workflows?**

  A workflow is a sequence of interdependent tasks executed in a specific order. Workflows in Databricks allow you to combine notebooks, scripts, and data processing tasks into cohesive pipelines.

- **Features**

  - **Task Orchestration**: Define the sequence of tasks, including dependencies, retries, and branching logic.

  - **Integration with Other Tools**: Connect workflows to external systems via APIs or triggers.

  - **Scalable Execution**: Run workflows on large-scale data with distributed compute power.

- **Example Use Case**

  A retail company builds a workflow to ingest sales data from an S3 bucket, clean and transform it using a notebook, and then load the processed data into a Snowflake database for reporting.

Navigating the Interface: Step-by-Step

1. **Main Menu**

   - Access key components, such as Notebooks, Clusters, Jobs, and Workflows, from the navigation pane on the left.

   - Use the search bar to locate resources quickly, as shown in Figure 1-1.

CHAPTER 1   GETTING STARTED WITH DATABRICKS

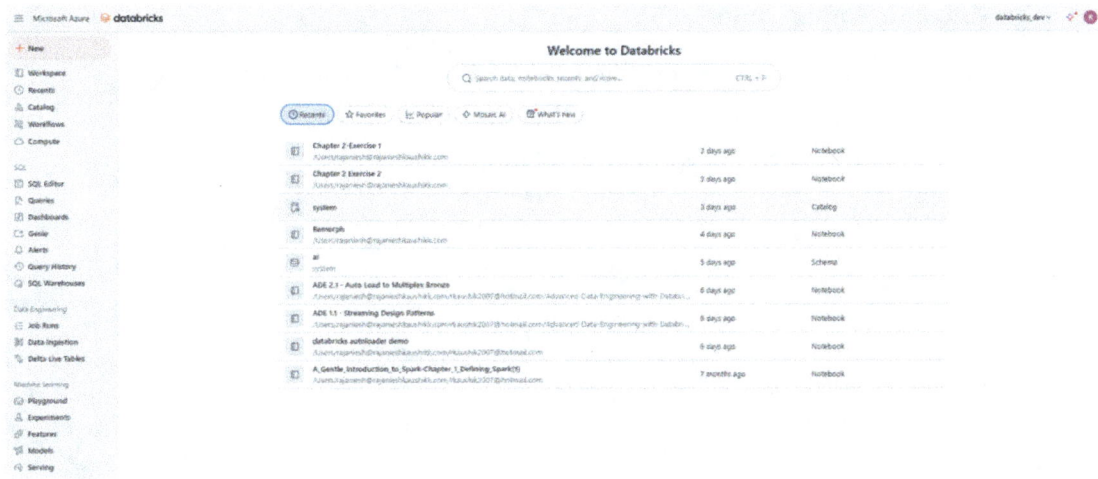

Figure 1-1. *Search bar to locate the resources in Databricks*

2. **Workspace View**

    - Organize your resources into folders and projects for better management. Please refer to Figure 1-2 for an illustration of the workspace view.

    - Collaborate with team members by sharing notebooks and other assets directly from the workspace.

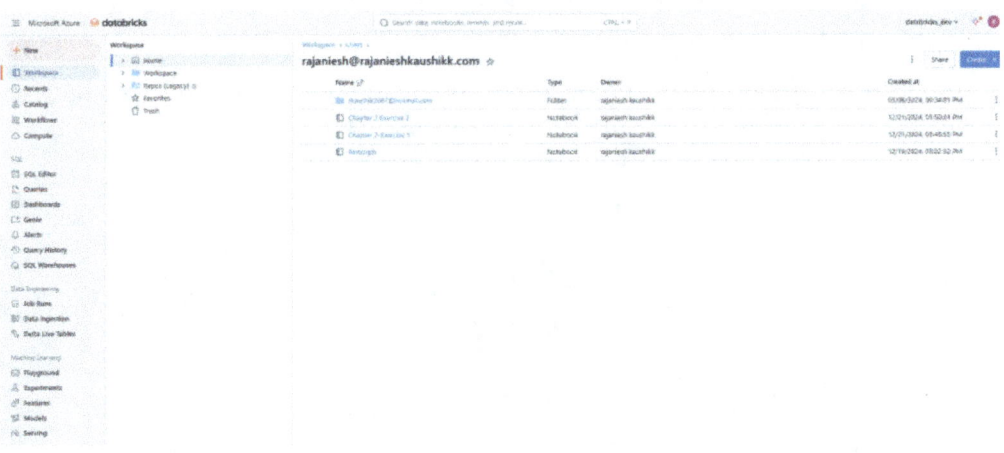

Figure 1-2. *Workspace view in Databricks*

31

CHAPTER 1   GETTING STARTED WITH DATABRICKS

3. **Cluster Management**

    - Monitor active clusters, view performance metrics, and manage configurations directly from the Clusters tab. See the list of clusters in the Compute tab in Figure 1-3.

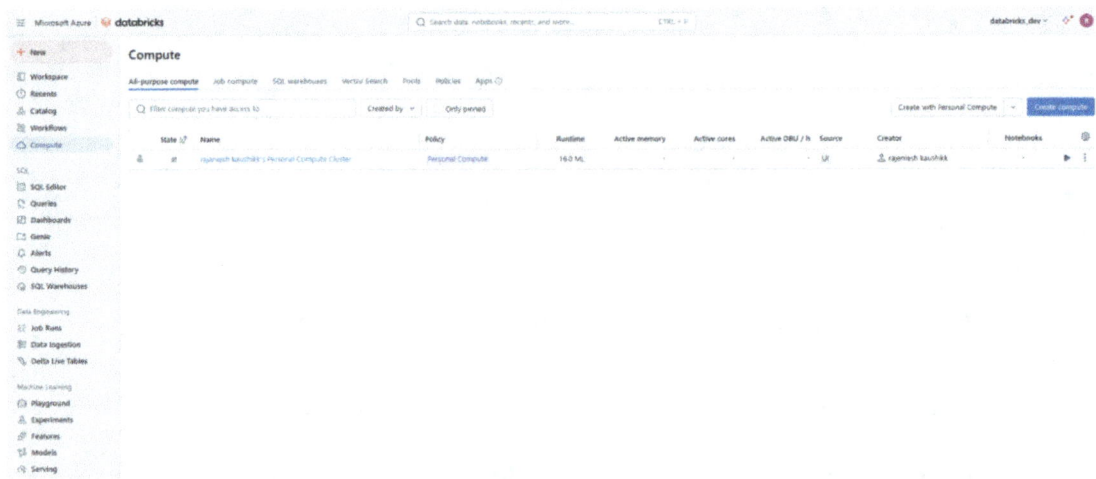

Figure 1-3. Compute tab in Databricks

4. **Job Scheduler**

    - Set up and monitor jobs via the Jobs tab, where you can view logs, execution history, and task performance metrics. Refer to the Job tab in Figure 1-4.

CHAPTER 1 GETTING STARTED WITH DATABRICKS

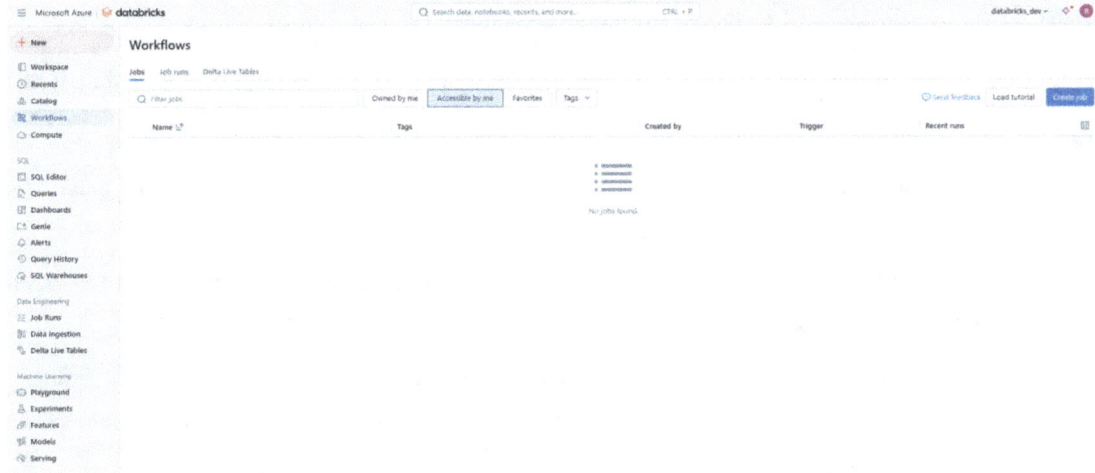

Figure 1-4. Job tab in Databricks

Creating the Databricks Account

Creating a Databricks account is the first step in unlocking the platform's robust data engineering, analytics, and machine learning capabilities. Whether you're an individual exploring Databricks for the first time or an enterprise setting up a collaborative workspace, the process is designed to be straightforward and scalable, meeting your needs. This section walks you through the entire process, from selecting the right cloud provider to accessing your workspace.

Step 1: Choosing the Cloud Provider: Finding the Right Fit for Your Databricks Environment

Selecting the right cloud provider for your Databricks environment is a crucial decision that can significantly impact your data strategy. Each cloud platform—**Azure**, **AWS**, and **Google Cloud**—offers unique capabilities and integrations, making some providers better suited for specific use cases or organizational requirements. Table 1-2 explores the strengths of each cloud provider to help you make an informed decision.

33

CHAPTER 1   GETTING STARTED WITH DATABRICKS

Table 1-2. *Strengths of Each Cloud Provider*

Feature	Azure Databricks	AWS Databricks	Google Cloud Databricks
Best For	Organizations using Microsoft tools and services	Enterprises needing high scalability and flexibility	Teams focused on advanced analytics and AI/ML workflows
Key Integrations	— Azure Active Directory (AAD) for SSO and security — Power BI for direct data visualization	— Amazon S3 for scalable storage — AWS Glue and Lambda for data workflows	— BigQuery for large-scale analytics — AI Platform for building/deploying ML models
Unique Capabilities	— Seamless integration with Azure Data Lake Storage — Optimized for Azure-native services like Synapse Analytics, Azure Data Factory	— Native support for high-performance analytics with Amazon Redshift — Machine learning with SageMaker alongside Databricks	— Real-time data processing with Pub/Sub — Handling unstructured data with Google Cloud Storage
Use Case Example	Financial services leveraging Power BI for real-time reporting	Ecommerce platform analyzing clickstream data	Media company training recommendation models with the AI Platform
When to Choose	— If you already use Azure tools like Power BI, Office 365 — If security and compliance features are a priority	— If you rely on AWS-native tools and require global scalability — If you use Amazon S3 or Glue for data pipelines	— If your team specializes in AI-driven workflows using Google tools — If you need strong AI/ML integration with BigQuery and AI Platform

Factors to Consider When Choosing a Cloud Provider

To make the best choice, consider the following factors:

1. **Existing Infrastructure**

   Select a provider that aligns with your current cloud environment to minimize complexity and ensure seamless integration with your existing systems.

2. **Team Expertise**

      Opt for the platform your team is most familiar with to reduce onboarding time and improve productivity.

   3. **Performance and Compliance Needs**

      Evaluate regional data residency requirements, security standards, and compliance regulations specific to your industry.

   4. **Scalability and Cost**

      Assess the provider's pricing model, scalability options, and cost-efficiency for your anticipated workloads.

   5. **Tool Compatibility**

      Consider the tools your organization relies on (e.g., business intelligence platforms, storage systems, and AI frameworks), and ensure they integrate seamlessly with the cloud provider.

Step 2: Registering Your Databricks Account

To register your Databricks account, follow these steps:

   1. **Navigate to the Databricks Portal**

      Visit the Databricks homepage or the marketplace page of your chosen cloud provider (e.g., Azure Marketplace, AWS Marketplace, or Google Cloud Console). Refer to the Databricks portal, as shown in Figure 1-5.

   2. **Click "Get Started" or "Try Databricks"**

      This option initiates the account creation process. Depending on your cloud provider, you may be directed to a registration or login page.

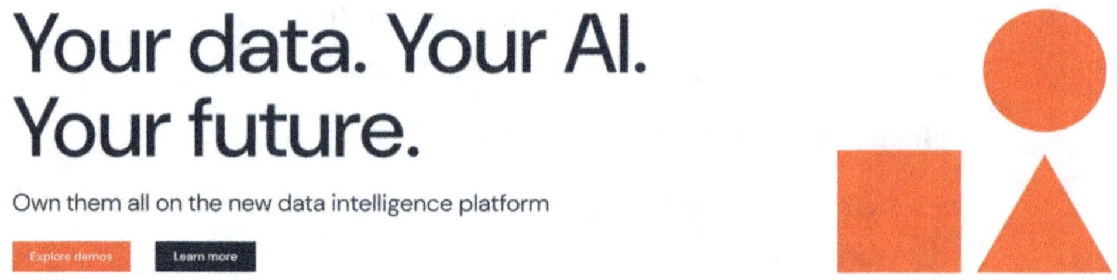

CHAPTER 1 GETTING STARTED WITH DATABRICKS

Your data. Your AI. Your future.

Own them all on the new data intelligence platform

Figure 1-5. Databricks portal

3. **Login or Create an Account**

    - **Existing Cloud Users**: Log in using your Azure, AWS, or Google Cloud credentials. See Figure 1-6.

    - **New Users**: Create an account by providing your name, organization, and email address.

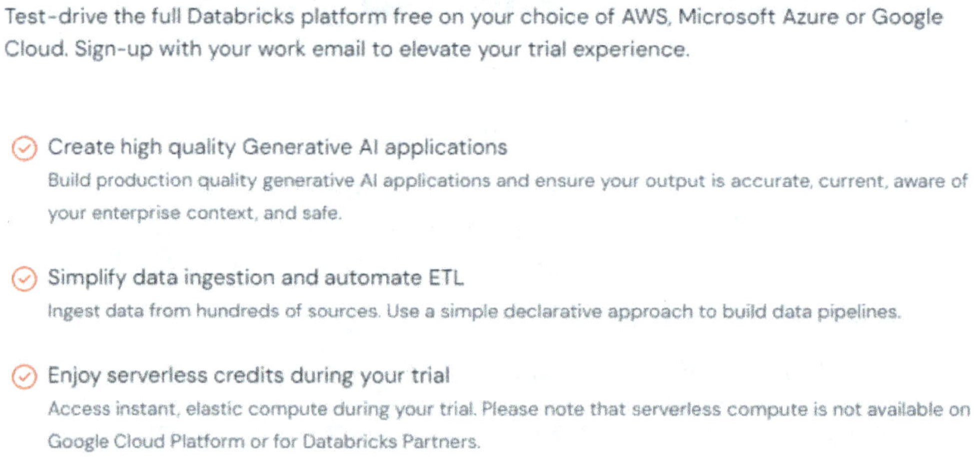

Test-drive the full Databricks platform free on your choice of AWS, Microsoft Azure or Google Cloud. Sign-up with your work email to elevate your trial experience.

⊘ Create high quality Generative AI applications
   Build production quality generative AI applications and ensure your output is accurate, current, aware of your enterprise context, and safe.

⊘ Simplify data ingestion and automate ETL
   Ingest data from hundreds of sources. Use a simple declarative approach to build data pipelines.

⊘ Enjoy serverless credits during your trial
   Access instant, elastic compute during your trial. Please note that serverless compute is not available on Google Cloud Platform or for Databricks Partners.

Figure 1-6. Try Databricks page

4. **Select Your Plan**

    Databricks offers several pricing plans tailored to different use cases:

- **Community Edition**: Free and ideal for individuals and learners, with access to basic Databricks features.

- **Standard Plan**: Designed for small to medium teams, offering robust data engineering and analytics tools.

- **Premium Plan**: Includes advanced security features, such as role-based access control (RBAC), and is suitable for larger teams.

- **Enterprise Plan**: Comprehensive support, compliance, and scalability features for large organizations with demanding workloads. Please note that the Enterprise plan is available only in GCP and AWS.

5. **Verify Your Identity**

   Some providers may require identity verification. You may need to link a credit card or provide billing details for paid plans.

Step 3: Configuring Your Workspace

Proper workspace setup ensures smooth operations and collaboration. Follow these steps:

Naming and Provisioning Your Workspace

The first step in setting up a Databricks workspace is to provision it and assign a meaningful name that aligns with your organization or project.

- **Naming Your Workspace**

  Choose a name that reflects the purpose or team using the workspace. For example, you might name it "Retail_Analytics" for a team focused on analyzing ecommerce data or "AI_Modeling" for a machine learning project.

CHAPTER 1 GETTING STARTED WITH DATABRICKS

- **Selecting a Region**

    - The region determines where your workspace and data will reside. Select a region near your team or data sources for optimal latency and high performance. Refer to the list of regions shown in Figure 1-7.

    - Compliance requirements such as GDPR or HIPAA may be considered, which may mandate specific data residency rules.

        Example: A European company selects a Databricks workspace in the European Union (EU) region to comply with GDPR.

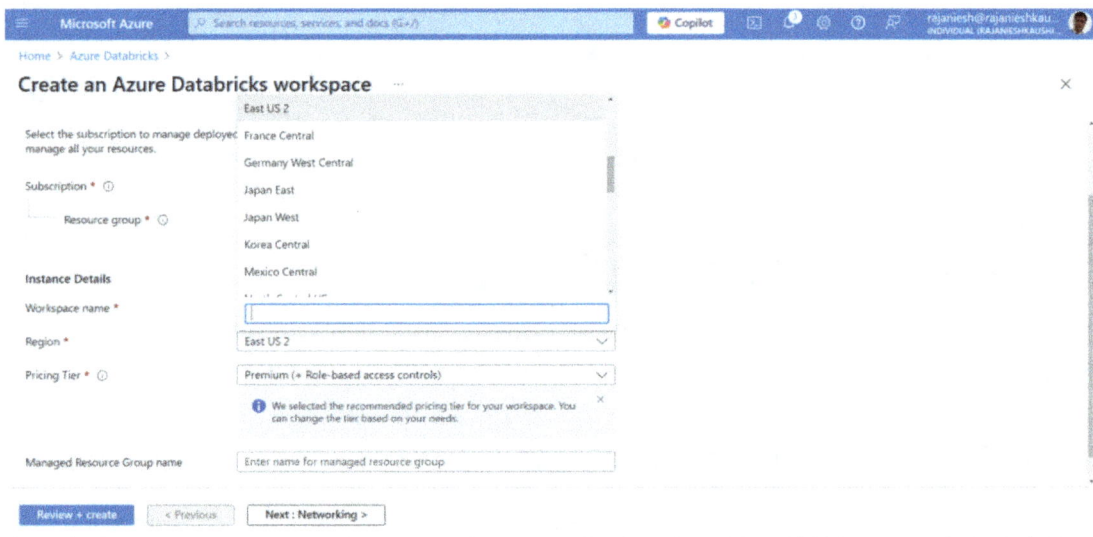

Figure 1-7. *List of available Databricks deployment regions in Azure*

Step 4: Configuring Compute Clusters

Clusters are the engines of your Databricks workspace, enabling you to process, analyze, and visualize data. Configuring clusters correctly ensures your workflows run efficiently and cost-effectively.

- **Choosing a Cluster Type**

  - **Standard Clusters**: Ideal for development, testing, and ad hoc analysis.

  - **High-Concurrency Clusters**: Optimized for collaborative environments where multiple users run concurrent workloads.

  - **Job Clusters**: Temporary clusters created for scheduled or automated tasks, such as nightly ETL jobs.

- **Setting Autoscaling**

  - Enable autoscaling to adjust the cluster size dynamically based on workload demands. This prevents over-provisioning during low activity periods and ensures sufficient resources during peak loads.

  - **Example**: An online retail platform analyzing real-time Black Friday sales uses autoscaling to handle a surge in data traffic.

- **Specifying Node Types**

  Select node types (e.g., Standard, Compute-Optimized, Memory-Optimized) based on your workload requirements. Refer to the worker type in Figure 1-8. For example:

  - Use compute-optimized nodes for analytics workloads.

  - Choose memory-optimized nodes for processing large datasets or training deep learning models.

CHAPTER 1   GETTING STARTED WITH DATABRICKS

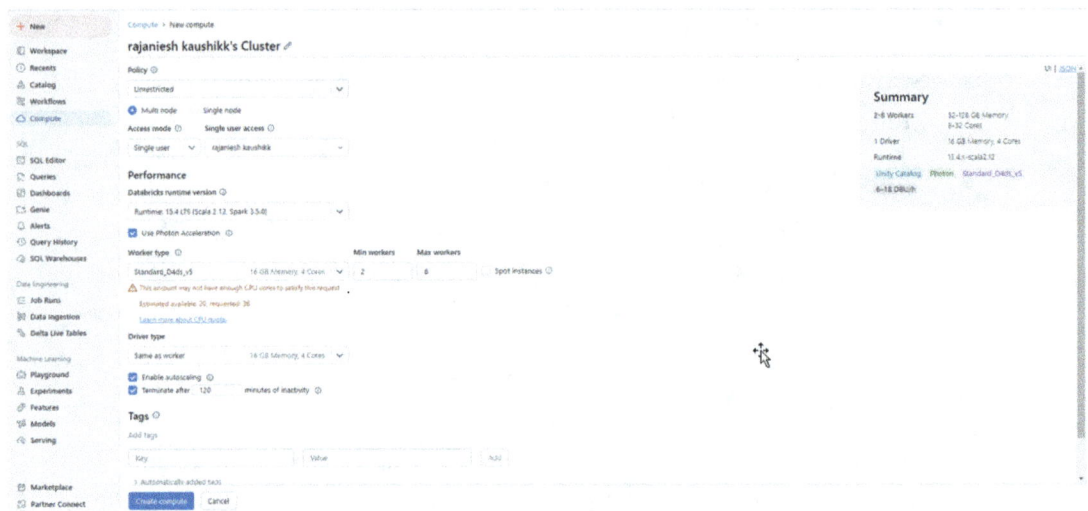

Figure 1-8. Databricks worker types

Step 5: Managing User Access and Roles

Databricks supports multiuser environments, allowing teams to collaborate securely. Configuring user access and roles ensures that sensitive data is protected while allowing appropriate access levels to different users.

- **Inviting Team Members**

    Add users to your workspace by sending email invitations. Assign them roles like Admin, Data Engineer, Data Scientist, or Analyst. See Figure 1-9 for instructions on changing the notebook for users.

CHAPTER 1   GETTING STARTED WITH DATABRICKS

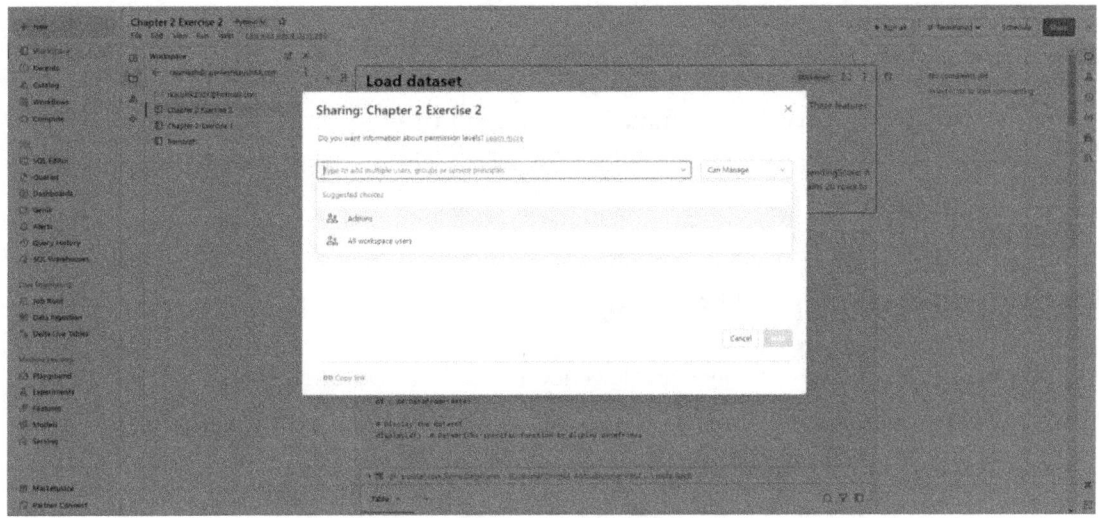

Figure 1-9. *Assigning roles to the users*

- **Role-Based Access Control (RBAC)**

    - Set granular permissions to control what users can view or modify. Refer to Figure 1-10 to view the list of permissions.

    - For example, analysts may have read-only access to reports, while engineers have full access to pipelines and clusters.

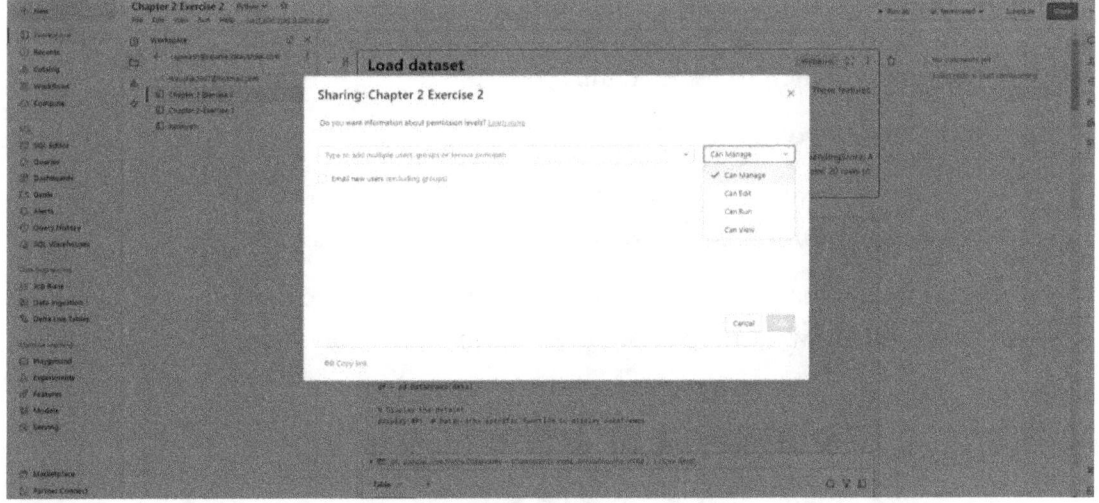

Figure 1-10. *Viewing the list of permissions*

41

- **Group Management**

    Organize users into groups based on their roles or departments, simplifying permission management. For instance, create a "Marketing Team" group with access to marketing dashboards and datasets.

Step 6: Integrating Data Sources

A functional workspace requires seamless access to data. Databricks supports a wide range of data sources, including cloud storage and real-time streaming platforms.

- **Cloud Storage Integration**

    Connect to storage solutions like Azure Data Lake Storage, Amazon S3, or Google Cloud Storage to store and retrieve data. Use secure credentials or tokens to authenticate access.

    Example: A logistics company integrates Databricks with Amazon S3 to process GPS data from delivery trucks.

- **Database Connections**

    Use JDBC or ODBC connectors to link to relational databases such as PostgreSQL, MySQL, or Snowflake.

    Example: An enterprise links Databricks to Snowflake to run SQL queries on structured sales data.

- **Real-Time Streaming**

    Configure streaming platforms, such as Kafka, Azure Event Hubs, or Google Pub/Sub, to ingest and analyze real-time data streams.

    Example: A manufacturing plant streams IoT sensor data into Databricks for real-time anomaly detection and analysis.

Workspace Deployment in Action

A healthcare startup configures Azure Databricks to analyze patient data for predictive analytics. They

1. Register for a Premium Plan to ensure HIPAA compliance.

2. Set up high-concurrency clusters for collaborative workloads.

3. Integrate Azure Data Lake for storing unstructured data and utilize Power BI for data visualization.

4. Assign roles to data scientists, engineers, and analysts, ensuring secure collaboration and effective teamwork.

5. Test the environment by running sample ETL pipelines and notebooks.

This streamlined setup enables the team to generate actionable insights while maintaining compliance and efficiency.

Tips and Best Practices for Efficient Navigation in Databricks

Navigating the Databricks interface effectively can significantly enhance your productivity and streamline your workflows. With its powerful yet intuitive design, Databricks offers tools and shortcuts to help you stay organized, minimize repetitive tasks, and maximize the platform's potential. Below are key tips and best practices to ensure a smooth and efficient experience.

Organize Your Workspace for Clarity

A cluttered workspace can hinder productivity and make collaboration challenging. By organizing your resources strategically, you can quickly locate and manage assets like notebooks, workflows, and datasets.

- **Use Folders and Naming Conventions**
    - Create folders to group related notebooks, workflows, and datasets by project or team.
    - Use consistent naming conventions (e.g., `projectname_taskname_date`) to make searching easier.

> **Example**: A marketing analytics team organizes their workspace with folders named "Campaign_2024_Q1" and "Customer_Insights."

- **Leverage Tags**

  Add tags to resources, such as clusters and jobs, for easier filtering and categorization, especially in shared environments.

Master Keyboard Shortcuts

Keyboard shortcuts can save time by reducing the need to click through menus.

- **Notebook Shortcuts**
  - Run a cell: `Shift + Enter`.
  - Add a new cell below: `Ctrl/Cmd + B`.
  - Switch between edit and command mode: `Esc` (to command) and `Enter` (to edit).

- **Navigation Shortcuts**
  - Use the search bar (`Ctrl/Cmd + K`) to locate clusters, notebooks, or jobs quickly.
  - Access recent resources via the "Recents" tab for quicker navigation.

Optimize Cluster Usage

Efficient cluster management ensures that you're balancing performance and cost while navigating compute resources.

- **Auto-Termination Settings**
  - Enable auto-termination to shut down idle clusters and reduce costs.

    Example: Set a cluster to terminate after 30 minutes of inactivity to prevent unnecessary charges.

- **Cluster Pinning**

    Pin frequently used clusters to your workspace dashboard for quick access.

- **Use Smaller Clusters for Testing**

    During development, use a small cluster to test code. Scale up only for production or resource-intensive workloads.

Leverage Search and Filtering Tools

Databricks provides powerful search and filtering tools to help you quickly locate resources.

- **Search Bar**
    - Use the universal search bar at the top of the interface to locate notebooks, jobs, clusters, or workflows by name or keyword.
    - Combine keywords with tags for precise searches.

- **Filters**

    Apply filters within tabs (e.g., Notebooks, Jobs) to narrow down results by attributes such as creation date, owner, or status.

Collaborate Effectively

Collaboration is a core feature of Databricks. Ensure that your workspace is set up for seamless teamwork.

- **Share Resources Securely**
    - Use role-based access control (RBAC) to manage permissions, ensuring users have access only to what they need.
    - Share notebooks and workflows with team members directly via the "Share" button.

- **Annotate and Document**
  - Use markdown cells in notebooks to document your process, making it easier for collaborators to understand your workflow.
- **Version Control**

  Leverage Databricks' built-in version history to track changes and revert to previous versions if needed.

Monitor Jobs and Clusters

Monitoring your jobs and clusters ensures that your workflows run smoothly and efficiently.

- **Job Monitoring Best Practices**
  - Regularly check the job dashboard to track the status of scheduled jobs and identify failures.
  - Set up alerts to receive notifications for job errors or delays.
- **Cluster Health Metrics**
  - Use the cluster dashboard to monitor performance metrics, such as CPU usage, memory utilization, and disk I/O.
  - Address performance bottlenecks by resizing clusters or optimizing tasks.

Use Workflows to Automate Repetitive Tasks

Workflows can save significant time by automating complex pipelines.

- **Define Dependencies Clearly**
  - Ensure tasks in your workflow are properly sequenced to avoid errors.

    Example: Set up a data pipeline where data ingestion runs before transformation and reporting tasks.

- **Reuse Existing Notebooks**

    Integrate existing notebooks into workflows to avoid duplicating effort.

Keep Your Environment Clean

A clean environment reduces confusion and prevents errors.

- **Archive Old Resources**

    Move outdated notebooks, workflows, and datasets into archive folders, or delete them if they are no longer needed.

- **Monitor Unused Clusters**

    Periodically review active clusters and terminate those that are no longer in use.

- **Regular Maintenance**

    Schedule periodic workspace reviews to declutter and optimize your environment.

Databricks Navigation in Action

Consider a team of data engineers working on an ETL (Extract, Transform, Load) project. They organize their workspace into folders named "Ingestion," "Transformation," and "Reporting." By using consistent naming conventions, they can quickly locate relevant notebooks. The team enables auto-termination for development clusters to save costs and shares annotated notebooks with analysts for collaboration. Using the job dashboard, they monitor scheduled workflows for daily data ingestion and processing. These best practices allow the team to navigate their Databricks workspace efficiently, reducing errors and increasing productivity.

CHAPTER 1   GETTING STARTED WITH DATABRICKS

Hands-On Lab: Setting Up and Navigating Databricks

This hands-on lab is designed to give you a practical, step-by-step experience in setting up your Databricks environment and navigating its key features. You will learn to configure your workspace, create and manage clusters, work with notebooks, automate workflows, and connect to data sources. By the end of this lab, you'll be equipped with the foundational skills to use Databricks efficiently, whether for data analysis, engineering, or machine learning.

Objectives

1. Set up and configure a Databricks workspace tailored to your organization's or project's needs.
2. Create and manage clusters to execute data workflows.
3. Develop notebooks for interactive coding and visualization.
4. Schedule tasks and automate workflows using jobs and workflows.
5. Connect to external data sources and process data effectively.

Logging into Databricks

Action Steps

1. Go to the Databricks homepage or your cloud provider's Databricks portal (Azure Marketplace, AWS Marketplace, or Google Cloud Console).
2. Log in with your cloud credentials. If you don't have an account, follow the "Creating a Databricks Account" instructions.
3. Familiarize yourself with the **main navigation pane** on the left side of the interface. This menu gives access to key components, including **Notebooks**, **Clusters**, **Jobs**, and **Data**.

Tips

- Bookmark your Databricks workspace URL for easy access.
- Use the search bar at the top of the interface to quickly find resources, such as notebooks or jobs.

Setting Up Your Workspace

Action Steps

1. **Provision Your Workspace**

   If prompted, name your workspace (e.g., "Retail_Analytics") and select a region based on compliance or performance requirements.

2. **Configure Workspace Settings**

   - Go to the **Admin Console** and adjust settings like permissions, data retention policies, and cluster defaults.
   - Enable **Single Sign-On (SSO)** for secure team access.

3. Create folders for your projects and name them Chapter 1.

Tips

- Use the **Recents** section to quickly revisit recently used notebooks, jobs, or clusters.
- Add tags to notebooks and jobs to categorize them for better organization.

CHAPTER 1   GETTING STARTED WITH DATABRICKS

Configuring Compute Clusters

Clusters are essential for running any workload in Databricks. Setting them up correctly ensures optimal performance and cost efficiency.

Action Steps

1. **Create a Cluster**

   - Navigate to the **Clusters** tab and click "Create Cluster."

   - Provide a meaningful name (e.g., "Dev_Cluster" or "ML_Training").

2. **Choose Cluster Type**

   - **Standard Clusters**: Best for development and testing.

3. **Configure Cluster Resources**

   - Select the node type:

     - Use **Compute-Optimized** nodes for analytics and SQL-heavy workloads.

   - Enable **Autoscaling** to adjust the number of nodes based on demand dynamically.

   - Set an **auto-termination policy** (e.g., terminate after 15 minutes of inactivity) to save costs.

4. **Create a Starter Warehouse: Enter the following values (see Figure 1-11 to view the starter warehouse's configuration).**

   - Enter warehouse name: Starter warehouse.

   - Cluster size: 2x-Small.

   - Scaling Min: 1 and Max: 1.

   - Type: Pro.

   - Click the **Create** button.

CHAPTER 1   GETTING STARTED WITH DATABRICKS

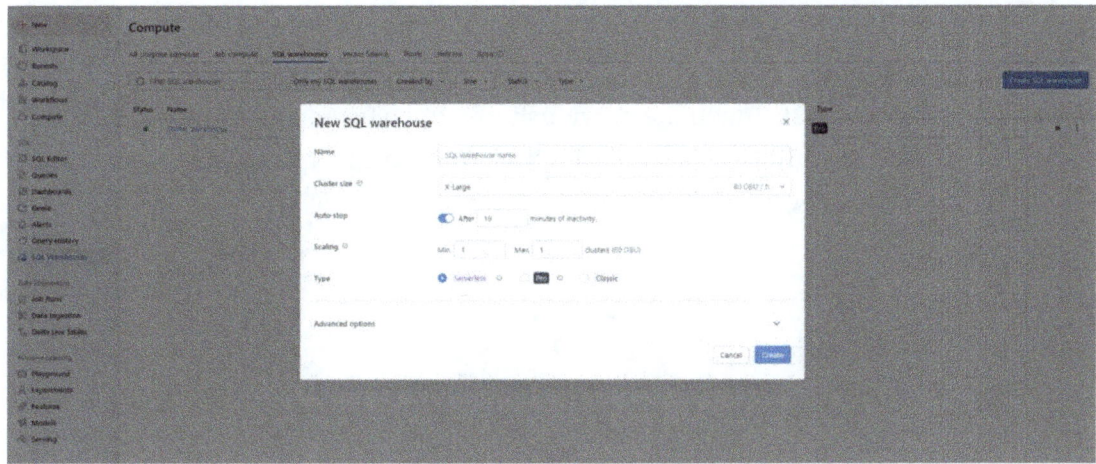

Figure 1-11. *View Starter Warehouse configuration*

Tips

- Pin frequently used clusters for quick access.
- Schedule regular reviews of idle clusters to optimize costs and resources.

Working with Notebooks

Databricks notebooks are versatile tools for writing and executing code, documenting workflows, and visualizing results.

Action Steps

1. **Create a Notebook**
   - Go to the **Workspace** tab and click "Create" ➤ "Notebook."
   - Name the notebook (e.g., "Sales_Data_Cleaning") and choose a programming language (Python).

CHAPTER 1   GETTING STARTED WITH DATABRICKS

2. **Write and Execute Code**

    - Add a simple Python command to the notebook (as shown in Figure 1-12), attach the previously created cluster, and press the Execute button or press Shift+Enter. It will display the text as visible in Figure 1-13.

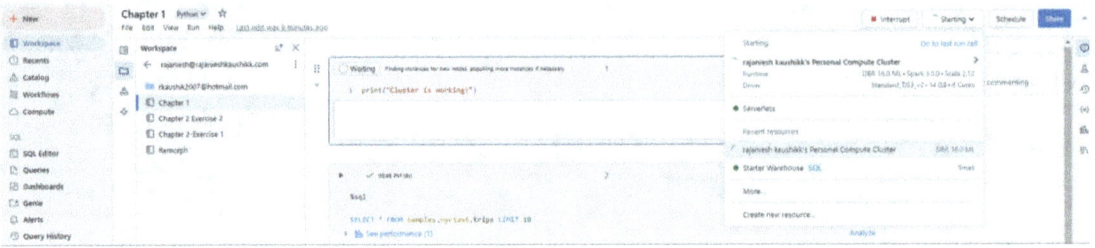

Figure 1-12. Entering a Python command in a notebook cell

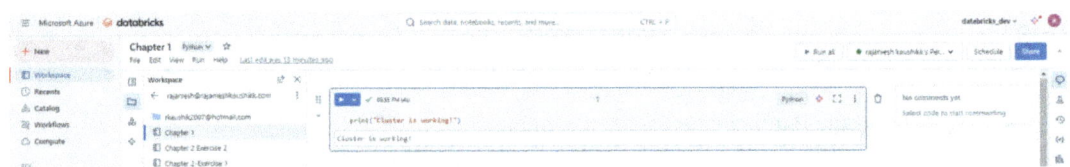

Figure 1-13. Displaying the result of the command executed in a notebook cell

```
print("Cluster is working!")
```

3. **Load a Sample Dataset**

    - Attach the notebook to the previously created SQL Warehouse, and use a built-in dataset like "nyctaxi" to perform the query (as shown in Figure 1-14):

    ```
    SELECT * FROM samples. nyctaxi.trips LIMIT 10
    ```

CHAPTER 1 GETTING STARTED WITH DATABRICKS

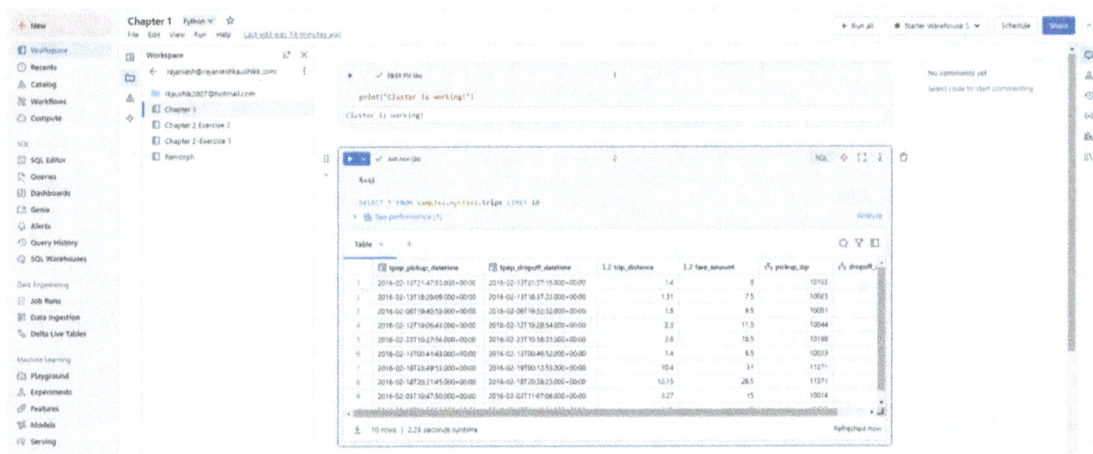

Figure 1-14. *Execute the SQL query in a notebook cell*

4. **Annotate with Markdown**

    • Add markdown cells for explanations (as shown in Figure 1-15), such as

    markdown

    ## Purpose

    This notebook analyzes sales trends by product category.

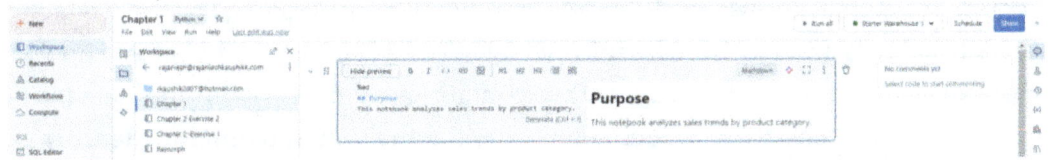

Figure 1-15. *Adding a markdown cell in the notebook*

Once you enter the text in the markdown cell, it will be visible, as shown in Figure 1-16.

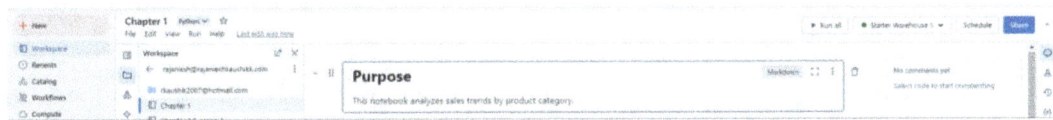

Figure 1-16. *Viewing the output of the markdown cell in the notebook*

53

CHAPTER 1   GETTING STARTED WITH DATABRICKS

Tips

- Use notebooks as a "living document" to document your thought process and results.

- Share notebooks with collaborators directly from the interface and enable version control to track changes.

Summary

This chapter explored how Databricks is a comprehensive platform for managing the data life cycle, from ingestion to analysis, while bridging the gap between data lakes and warehouses through its **Lakehouse Architecture**. We learned how Databricks empowers diverse data personas—data engineers, data scientists, and business analysts—by offering tools like Collaborative Notebooks, Managed Compute Clusters, and integrated workflows.

We also examined essential features such as governance, security, and seamless cloud integration, which make Databricks a reliable choice for modern data-driven enterprises. By walking through the process of creating a Databricks account, setting up a workspace, and managing clusters and data sources, we gained practical insights into how to start using the platform effectively.

This foundational knowledge lays the groundwork for leveraging Databricks' advanced analytics and machine learning capabilities. With a unified platform now at your disposal, the next step is to explore how Databricks can help turn your data into actionable intelligence. In the next chapter, we will transition into **machine learning**, diving into its principles and uncovering how Databricks streamlines the journey from experimentation to deployment. By understanding these concepts, you will be ready to unlock the full potential of data science and AI in real-world scenarios.

CHAPTER 2

Introduction to Machine Learning and Data Lakehouses

Machine learning (ML) is not just a trend—it's a core enabler of intelligent systems across industries. From personalized recommendations in retail to early disease prediction in healthcare, ML has become the foundation for data-driven innovation. However, building effective ML models relies on more than just algorithms—it depends heavily on robust, scalable, and unified data architectures.

This chapter introduces the essential concepts of machine learning and their intersection with modern data architectures, commonly referred to as **data lakehouses**. You will explore the different types of machine learning, understand how ML workflows operate, and **evaluate** how data lakehouses support the end-to-end ML life cycle. By the end of this chapter, you will be able to **connect** theoretical machine learning (ML) concepts with practical architectural patterns used in enterprise systems.

Learning Objectives

By the end of this chapter, you will be able to

- **Understand** the core principles and vocabulary of machine learning, including models, features, and evaluation metrics.
- **Differentiate** between supervised, unsupervised, and reinforcement learning, and **identify** the ideal scenarios for each.
- **Explain** the concept and evolution of data lakehouses and how they address the shortcomings of traditional data lakes and warehouses.
- **Analyze** how data lakehouses enable scalable and flexible machine learning (ML) workflows through unified storage and governance.

- **Apply** foundational machine learning (ML) techniques in hands-on exercises that reinforce theoretical concepts using practical examples.

- **Evaluate** real-world use cases that illustrate how organizations leverage machine learning in combination with lakehouse architectures.

This chapter lays the groundwork for building intelligent data systems by linking machine learning fundamentals with modern data infrastructure. Whether you're a data engineer, business analyst, or aspiring machine learning developer, this chapter will help you gain a broader perspective and **prepare** you for more advanced topics in data preparation, modeling, and deployment, which are covered in the upcoming chapters.

Overview of Machine Learning

Imagine teaching a child to recognize animals in pictures. You show them images of cats, dogs, and birds while pointing out which image belongs to whom. Over time, the child learns to identify these animals independently, even in pictures they've never seen. Learning from examples and applying that knowledge to new situations is how machine learning (ML) works. The key difference? Instead of teaching a child, we teach computers to learn from data.

Machine learning has become a revolutionary tool in modern technology, enabling systems to make predictions, solve problems, and adapt to new challenges based on experience. Unlike traditional programming, where we explicitly write rules for computers to follow, machine learning allows computers to discover patterns, relationships, and insights independently, improving their accuracy and usefulness over time. Let's explore how this works and why it matters.

Why Machine Learning Matters

Machine learning is everywhere, often in ways we don't even realize. ML recommends the next film based on your preferences when you stream a movie. When you shop online, ML algorithms suggest products you might like. When your email filters out spam, that's machine learning in action. These systems continually improve by analyzing massive amounts of data, learning patterns, and adapting to provide better results.

ML is more than just a tool for convenience; it's a driving force behind innovation across industries. From healthcare and finance to transportation and entertainment, machine learning enables the solution of complex problems faster and more accurately than ever.

Here are a few examples of its impact:

- **Healthcare**: Predicting patient outcomes and diagnosing diseases early
- **Finance**: Detecting fraudulent transactions in real-time
- **Transportation**: Optimizing delivery routes and powering autonomous vehicles
- **Retail**: Personalizing shopping experiences for customers

With its ability to analyze vast amounts of data, find patterns, and make decisions, machine learning is transforming how we approach challenges in both business and everyday life.

Key Concepts in Machine Learning

Machine learning might seem like magic, but it's built on a foundation of logical and essential building blocks. Let's break down these concepts to see how they fit together to create robust models that can solve complex problems.

Data: The Fuel for Learning

Data is at the heart of every machine learning system. It's the raw material that models learn from; without it, no learning can occur. Think of data as the driving lessons for a learner driver. If the learner never gets behind the wheel or experiences real-world scenarios, they'll never develop the skills to drive independently.

In machine learning, data comes in various forms:

- **Structured Data**: Organized in rows and columns, like a spreadsheet. Examples include sales records, customer details, and product inventories.
- **Unstructured Data**: Data that doesn't fit neatly into a table, such as images, videos, audio, and free text.

Good-quality data is crucial. If your data is incomplete, biased, or irrelevant, the model's predictions will suffer, no matter how advanced the algorithm. That is why the saying **"garbage in, garbage out"** is so often repeated in machine learning.

Features: The Building Blocks of Predictions

Features are the pieces of information that machine learning models use to make sense of the data. If the data is the raw material, features are the refined inputs that help the model understand the problem.

For example:

- In predicting house prices, features might include the house's size, location, number of bedrooms, and age.

- In classifying emails as spam or not, features could include the presence of specific keywords, the sender's reputation, or the length of the subject line.

Feature engineering is the process of selecting, transforming, and creating the right features—it is a critical step in machine learning. Well-engineered features can drastically improve the model's accuracy and efficiency.

Good features are those that

- Are highly correlated with the target variable, making them predictive of the outcome

- Are independent of one another, reducing redundancy and multicollinearity

- Are easy to interpret, ensuring that their impact on the model is understandable

Investing time in thoughtful feature engineering ensures your model has the best possible foundation for success.

Model: The Brain of the Operation

The model is the core of any machine learning system. It's the mathematical structure that learns patterns in data and uses those patterns to make predictions or decisions. Think of it as the brain behind the operation.

Different types of models are suited to different tasks:

- A **Linear Regression model** might predict the price of a car based on its mileage and age.
- A **neural network model** might recognize objects in images or understand spoken language.

Training the model involves feeding it data and adjusting its parameters until it can accurately capture the relationships in the data. Once trained, the model can make predictions about new, unseen data.

Training and Testing: The Learning Process

Training and testing are like the study-and-exam phases of a student's journey:

- **Training**: The model studies the data, looking for patterns and relationships. This phase involves adjusting the model's parameters to minimize prediction errors. For example, a student practices math problems repeatedly to understand the concepts.
- **Testing**: Once the model is trained, it's tested on new, unseen data (called the test set) to evaluate its performance. This ensures the model hasn't simply memorized the training data but has genuinely learned the underlying patterns. For example, the student takes a test with questions they haven't seen before to see how well they've learned.

Evaluation Metrics: The Report Card

How do you know if a machine learning model works well? This is where evaluation metrics come in. Metrics provide a way to quantify the model's performance.

Common metrics include

- **Accuracy**: The percentage of predictions the model got right.
- **Precision**: How many of the model's positive predictions were correct?
- **Recall**: How well did the model identify all the actual positives?
- **F1-Score**: A balanced measure of precision and recall.

These metrics help identify where the model is succeeding and where it needs improvement. For example, a model with high accuracy but low recall may perform poorly on imbalanced datasets, such as those used in fraud detection.

Overfitting and Underfitting: Finding the Balance

A common challenge in machine learning is finding the right balance between overfitting and underfitting.

- **Overfitting**: Imagine a student who memorizes every question from past exams but fails when faced with a slightly different test. That's overfitting. The model performs exceptionally well on the training data but struggles with new data because it has memorized specifics instead of learning general patterns.

- **Underfitting**: Now, imagine a student who barely studies and doesn't grasp the material. This is underfitting. The model is too simplistic and fails to capture the relationships in the data, resulting in poor performance on both training and test data.

Achieving a good fit requires careful tuning of the model's complexity, training duration, and other parameters. Techniques such as regularization (adding penalties for complexity) can help prevent overfitting.

Types of Machine Learning

Now that we've explored what machine learning is and its foundational concepts, let's dive into the three main categories of ML. Each type is tailored to address different problems and data, offering a unique approach for machines to learn and adapt.

Supervised Learning: Learning with a Teacher

Imagine you're learning math with the help of a teacher. The teacher gives you a set of problems and their solutions. Over time, by studying these examples, you begin to understand the patterns and rules that govern the solution of similar problems. This approach mirrors **supervised learning** in machine learning.

- **How Does It Work?**

  In supervised learning, the model is trained on **labeled data**, meaning corresponding outputs accompany the input data. The model learns to map inputs to outputs by identifying patterns in the data. Once trained, it can predict the output for new, unseen inputs. Here are some examples of supervised learning:

  - **Predicting Housing Prices**: Given data about house size, location, and features (input), the model predicts the price (output).

  - **Spam Detection**: The model classifies emails as spam or not based on labeled examples of previous emails.

- **Key Algorithms Used in Supervised Learning:** Supervised learning encompasses a wide range of algorithms, each tailored for specific tasks, for example:

  - **Linear Regression**: Predicting continuous values like house prices or sales

  - **Decision Trees**: Classifying data, such as spam detection

  - **Neural Networks**: Handling complex tasks like image recognition and natural language processing (NLP)

Supervised learning is widely used in industries where labeled data is readily available, such as finance, healthcare, and marketing.

Unsupervised Learning: Finding Hidden Patterns

Imagine your teacher hands you a box of jigsaw puzzle pieces but doesn't provide the completed picture. You start grouping similar-looking pieces, trying to make sense of the patterns independently. This is analogous to **unsupervised learning**.

- **How does it work?** The model works with unlabeled data in unsupervised learning, meaning there's no predefined output. The goal is to identify hidden patterns, groupings, or structures within the data. This is particularly useful when you don't know what to look for in your data but want the machine to explore it on its own. Here are some examples of unsupervised learning:

- **Customer Segmentation**: Grouping customers based on purchasing behavior to create targeted marketing campaigns
  - **Fraud Detection**: Identifying unusual patterns in credit card transactions that could indicate fraud
- **Key Algorithms Used in Unsupervised Learning:** Some standard algorithms used in unsupervised learning include
  - **K-Means Clustering**: Groups data into clusters based on similarity. For instance, segmenting customers into high-value and low-value groups.
  - **Principal Component Analysis (PCA)**: Reduces the dimensionality of data while retaining its most significant patterns, making it a popular tool in image processing and data visualization.

Unsupervised learning is powerful in exploratory data analysis, where the goal is to uncover insights or patterns that aren't immediately apparent.

Reinforcement Learning: Learning Through Rewards

Picture yourself playing a video game for the first time. At first, you try random moves, but as you learn which actions earn points and which lead to failure, you improve your strategy. This process mirrors **reinforcement learning**.

- **How does it work?** In reinforcement learning, an **agent** (the learner) interacts with an **environment** (the system in which it operates) by performing actions. Each action results in feedback in the form of **rewards** (positive reinforcement) or **penalties** (negative reinforcement). Over time, the agent learns the optimal strategy to maximize rewards. Here are some examples of **reinforcement learning:**
  - **Robotics**: Training robots to navigate a maze or assemble components on a production line
  - **Games**: AI systems, such as AlphaGo, which have mastered the game of Go and beaten human world champions

CHAPTER 2   INTRODUCTION TO MACHINE LEARNING AND DATA LAKEHOUSES

- **Key Concepts**

    - **Agent**: The entity making decisions (e.g., a robot or AI program)

    - **Environment**: The setting in which the agent operates (e.g., a maze or game)

    - **Reward**: Feedback based on the agent's actions, used to guide its learning

Reinforcement learning is often applied when the system evolves or involves sequential decision-making, such as self-driving cars, resource optimization, and personalized recommendations.

Comparing the Three Types of Machine Learning

Machine learning can be broadly categorized into three types: supervised, unsupervised, and reinforcement. Each type is designed to address specific problems, and choosing the right approach depends on the nature of the data and the task's objective. Table 2-1 provides a quick comparison.

Table 2-1. Types of Machine learning

Type	Labeled Data?	Goal	Example Applications
Supervised Learning	Yes	Predict or classify known outputs	Predicting housing prices, spam detection
Unsupervised Learning	No	Identify hidden patterns or groupings	Customer segmentation, fraud detection
Reinforcement Learning	No	Maximize cumulative rewards over time	Training robots, AI for games

Key Insights

- Supervised learning requires labeled data and is ideal for tasks where historical data is available to guide predictions.

- Unsupervised learning explores and discovers hidden structures within unlabeled data, making it invaluable for tasks like segmentation or anomaly detection.

- Reinforcement learning is well-suited for dynamic environments where decisions must adapt over time to maximize rewards, such as in gaming or robotics.

By understanding the distinctions and strengths of these types, you can better align your choice of algorithm with your project's objectives.

Real-World Examples and Use Cases

The intersection of machine learning and data lakehouses has already transformed industries. Here are some compelling real-world examples:

1. **Retail: Personalized Recommendations**

   - **Challenge**: Retailers aim to deliver personalized shopping experiences but struggle with siloed data across their various systems.

   - **Solution**: A data lakehouse integrates customer transaction history, browsing behavior, and demographic data, enabling real-time recommendation engines powered by machine learning (ML) models.

   - **Impact**: Increased customer engagement and higher conversion rates.

2. **Healthcare: Predictive Patient Care**

   - **Challenge**: Healthcare providers must predict patient outcomes to improve care and reduce costs.

   - **Solution**: Using a data lakehouse, patient records, imaging data, and genetic information are unified into a single system. Machine learning (ML) models are trained to predict disease progression or recommend personalized treatment plans.

- **Impact:** Improved patient outcomes and operational efficiency.

3. **Financial Services: Fraud Detection**
    - **Challenge:** Detecting fraudulent transactions in real time requires analyzing vast transactional data.
    - **Solution:** A data lakehouse stores and processes transactional data, customer profiles, and historical fraud patterns—ML models trained on this data flag anomalies for further review.
    - **Impact:** Reduced fraud losses and enhanced customer trust.

4. **Manufacturing: Predictive Maintenance**
    - **Challenge:** Equipment failures lead to costly downtime and reduced efficiency.
    - **Solution:** A data lakehouse ingests sensor data from IoT devices and historical maintenance logs. Machine learning models predict equipment failures before they occur, enabling timely maintenance.
    - **Impact:** Lower maintenance costs and improved uptime.

5. **Media and Entertainment: Content Recommendations**
    - **Challenge:** Streaming platforms must recommend content to millions of users while analyzing diverse data formats (videos, metadata, user preferences).
    - **Solution:** A data lakehouse unifies viewing history, content metadata, and user behavior. Machine learning models enable the delivery of personalized content recommendations in real time.
    - **Impact:** Increased viewer retention and satisfaction.

Hands-On Lab: Practical Exercises on Basic ML Concepts

Exercise 1: Supervised Learning—Predicting Housing Prices

Objective

This exercise demonstrates how to build a supervised machine learning model using Linear Regression to predict housing prices based on features like the number of rooms, lot size, and location score. You'll learn to process data, train a model, evaluate its performance, and visualize results in a Databricks environment.

In this hands-on lab, you'll get your first taste of implementing machine learning concepts. These exercises are designed to solidify your understanding of supervised and unsupervised learning by working through practical examples in Python. You'll build, train, and evaluate simple models using popular libraries like **scikit-learn** and **pandas**.

By the end of this lab, you will

- Implement basic machine learning models for supervised and unsupervised learning.
- Explore essential concepts like data preprocessing, model training, and evaluation.
- Visualize results to gain insights into model performance.

Scenario

Imagine working with a real estate agency that aims to predict housing prices using historical data. By training a machine learning model with labeled data (known prices), you can automate predictions for new properties, helping the agency make data-driven decisions quickly.

Step-by-Step Guide

Load the Dataset

- **What We're Doing**

    Create a small dataset representing features like the number of rooms, lot size, location score, and the corresponding price. In a real-world scenario, this data would typically come from a CSV file or database, but for simplicity, we're creating it directly in Python.

    ```python
    import pandas as pd

    # Create a dataset
    data = {

        #The Rooms column represents the number of bedrooms in the house.
        'Rooms': [2, 3, 4, 5, 6, 7, 8, 9, 10, 11],

        #LotSize represents the area of the property in square feet.
        'LotSize': [850, 960, 1200, 1000, 1500, 2000, 1250, 1450, 950, 1600],

        #LocationScore is a numerical representation of how desirable the
        location is.
        'LocationScore': [3, 4, 5, 4, 5, 6, 4, 5, 3, 6],

        #Price is the target variable we want to predict.
        'Price': [200000, 300000, 420000, 560000, 720000, 900000, 1100000,
        1320000, 1560000, 1820000]

    }

    # Convert to a DataFrame
    df = pd.DataFrame(data)

    # Display the dataset
    display(df)  # Databricks-specific function for displaying tables
    ```

- **Explanation**

    - The Rooms column represents the number of bedrooms in the house.

    - LotSize represents the area of the property in square feet.

    - Location Score is a numerical representation of how desirable a location is.

    - Price is the target variable we want to predict.

Split Data into Features and Target

- **What We're Doing**

  Separate the independent variables (features) from the dependent variable (target). This step ensures the model knows what data to use for making predictions and what data to predict.

  ```
  # Independent variables (features). X contains the columns 'Rooms',
  'LotSize', and 'LocationScore', which the model will use to
  make predictions.

  X = df[['Rooms', 'LotSize', 'LocationScore']]

  # Dependent variable (target) . y contains the Price column,
  the value the model needs to predict.
  y = df['Price']
  ```

- **Explanation**

  - X contains the columns `'Rooms'`, `'LotSize'`, and `'LocationScore'`, which the model will use to make predictions.

  - y contains the `Price` column, which is the value the model needs to predict.

Split the Data into Training and Testing Sets

- **What We're Doing**

  Divide the dataset into two subsets:

  - **Training Set**: Used to train the model

  - **Testing Set**: Used to evaluate the model's performance on unseen data

  ```
  from sklearn.model_selection import train_test_split

  #train_test_split splits the data so 80% is used for training
  and 20% for testing.
  #random_state=42 ensures reproducibility of results
  X_train, X_test, y_train, y_test = train_test_split(X, y,
  test_size=0.2, random_state=42)
  ```

- **Explanation**

  - `train_test_split` splits the data, so 80% is used for training and 20% for testing.

  - `random_state=42` ensures the reproducibility of results.

Build and Train the Model

- **What We're Doing**

  Use a **Linear Regression** model to learn the relationship between features and the target variable. The model will analyze patterns in the training data to predict house prices.

Why Was Linear Regression Chosen?

1. **Simplicity and Interpretability**

   - Linear Regression is one of the simplest machine learning algorithms.

   - It models the relationship between independent variables (features) and the dependent variable (target) as a straight line.

   - The coefficients in Linear Regression (slopes and intercept) are easy to interpret, providing insight into how each feature affects the target.

2. **Assumption of Linearity**

   - In this example, the relationship between features like the number of rooms, lot size, and location score and the target (housing prices) is assumed to be approximately linear. For example, doubling the lot size or significantly improving the location score is expected to proportionally increase the housing price, which aligns with the assumptions of Linear Regression.

3. **Quick Baseline Model**

    - Linear Regression is a great starting point for establishing a baseline model. It enables us to determine if the data exhibits any linear trends before exploring more complex algorithms.

    - We can compare our performance to that of more advanced models later if the current performance is inadequate.

4. **Low Computational Cost**

    - Linear Regression is computationally efficient, even with relatively large datasets.

    - Since the dataset in the exercise is small, the simplicity of Linear Regression makes it an ideal choice for this task.

    ```
    from sklearn.linear_model import LinearRegression

    #The model learns coefficients (weights) for each
    feature that describe their influence on the price.
    model = LinearRegression()
    #The fit method trains the model by finding the
    best-fit line that minimizes errors in predictions.
    model.fit(X_train, y_train)
    ```

- **Explanation**

    - The fit method trains the model by finding the best-fit line that minimizes prediction errors.

    - The model learns coefficients (weights) for each feature that describe their influence on the price.

Evaluate the Model

- **What We're Doing**

    Evaluate the trained model on the testing dataset to assess its ability to generalize to new data. Calculate the **Mean Squared Error (MSE)**, a metric that measures the average squared difference between predicted and actual values.

    ```
    from sklearn.metrics import mean_squared_error
    # y_pred contains the predicted prices for the test set.
    y_pred = model.predict(X_test)
    #A lower MSE indicates better model performance.
    mse = mean_squared_error(y_test, y_pred)
    print(f"Mean Squared Error: {mse}")
    ```

- **Explanation**
    - y_pred contains the predicted prices for the test set.
    - A lower MSE indicates better model performance.
    - We can also compute the R^2 score using sklearn.

        ```
        from sklearn.metrics import r2_score

        # Compute R² Score
        if len(y_test) == len(y_pred): r2 = r2_score(y_test, y_pred)
        print(f"R² Score: {r2}")
        ```

- Here Inputs:
    - **y_test**: The actual values of the target variable from the test set
    - **y_pred**: The predicted values of the target variable from the model

What Does the R^2 Score Mean?

The R^2 score represents the proportion of the variance in the target variable that the model explains:

- **$R^2 = 1.0$**: Perfect fit; the model explains 100% of the variance in the target variable.

- **$R^2 = 0.0$**: The model explains none of the variance; it's no better than a simple mean of the target values.

- **Negative R^2**: The model performs worse than a horizontal line (the mean of the target values).

How to Interpret R^2

- **High R^2 (Close to 1)**

    - It indicates that the model captures most of the variability in the data. Your model is brilliant—it effectively explains most of the reasons why prices fluctuate.

    - **Example**: If $R^2 = 0.90$, the model explains 90% of the variance in housing prices. Only 10% of the price variability is due to factors not captured by the model.

- **Low R^2 (Close to 0)**

    - It suggests that the model fails to capture the underlying patterns in the data. Your model is not helpful—it doesn't understand the patterns in the data.

    - **Example**: If $R^2 = 0.45 R^2 = 0$. The model explains only 45% of the variance, suggesting it underfits the data or that the relationship is not linear.

- **$R^2 = 0.0$**

    - It suggests that it predicts all houses are worth the same (e.g., just the average price). It explains 0% of the price differences.

- **Comparison of R^2 with MSE**

    - **MSE** provides an **absolute measure** of prediction error. Which means:

- How far are the predicted values from the actual values?
- Lower MSE indicates better performance.
- **R^2 score provides a relative measure:**
  - How well does the model perform compared to a simple mean baseline?
  - It helps in understanding how much of the variability in the data is explained by the model.
- **Use Both Metrics**
  - Use **MSE** to understand the average error magnitude.
  - Use **the R^2 score to understand** the model's goodness of fit relative to the variance in the data.

Visualize Results

- **What We're Doing**

    Plot the actual vs. predicted prices to assess the model's accuracy visually. Ideally, the points should lie close to a diagonal line, indicating perfect predictions.

    ```
    import pandas as pd

    import matplotlib.pyplot as plt
    from sklearn.linear_model import LinearRegression

    # Dataset
    data = {
        'Rooms': [2, 3, 4, 5, 6, 7, 8, 9, 10, 11],

        'Price': [200000, 300000, 420000, 560000, 720000, 900000,
        1100000, 1320000, 1560000, 1820000]  # Quadratic pattern

    }
    # Create DataFrame
    df = pd.DataFrame(data)

    # Feature and target
    X = df[['Rooms']]  # Feature
    y = df['Price']  # Target
    ```

```python
# Linear Regression model
linear_model = LinearRegression()
linear_model.fit(X, y)

# Predictions
y_linear_pred = linear_model.predict(X)

# Calculate residuals (prediction errors)
residuals = y - y_linear_pred

# Plot actual vs predicted prices with residuals
plt.figure(figsize=(10, 6))

# Scatter actual prices
plt.scatter(df['Rooms'], df['Price'], color='blue', label='Actual Prices', s=50)

# Plot predicted prices
plt.plot(df['Rooms'], y_linear_pred, color='red', label='Predicted Prices (Linear Regression)', linewidth=2)

# Add residual lines (visualizing prediction errors in dark purple)
for i in range(len(df['Rooms'])):
    plt.plot(
        [df['Rooms'][i], df['Rooms'][i]],  # x-coordinates for vertical line
        [y[i], y_linear_pred[i]],          # y-coordinates from actual to predicted
        color='darkviolet', linestyle='dotted', linewidth=1.5, label='Residuals' if i == 0
        else ""   # Label only first line
    )

# Customize the plot
plt.xlabel("Number of Rooms")
plt.ylabel("House Prices")
plt.title("Actual vs Predicted Prices with Residuals (Linear Regression)")
plt.legend()
plt.grid(True)
plt.show()

# Print residuals for reference
print("Prediction Errors (Residuals):")
print(residuals)
```

This code creates a chart, as shown in Figure 2-1, to illustrate the predicted price with residuals.

CHAPTER 2　INTRODUCTION TO MACHINE LEARNING AND DATA LAKEHOUSES

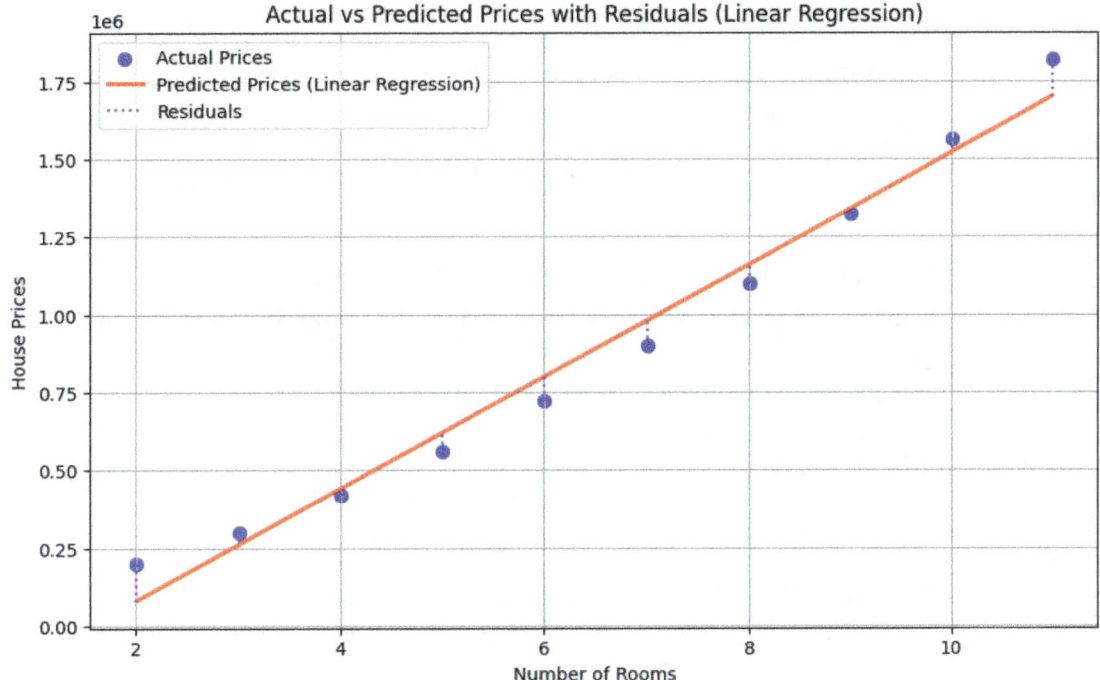

Figure 2-1. *Predicted price with residual*

Interpreting the Chart

Understanding the Axes

- **X Axis (Number of Rooms)**: This represents the independent feature that predicts house prices.

- **Y Axis (House Prices)**: This represents both the actual house prices (blue points) and the predicted house prices (red line).

Observations

1. General Trends

    - The red line represents the predicted prices using Linear Regression.

    - The blue dots represent the actual house prices.

    - The magenta (dark purple) dotted lines represent the residuals, showing the error or difference between actual prices and predicted prices.

    - Most points are close to the regression line, indicating a relatively good fit for the linear model.

2. Residuals (Prediction Errors)

    - The **dotted magenta lines** connect the actual prices to their corresponding predictions on the regression line.
    - Larger residuals (longer magenta lines) indicate a greater prediction error.
    - For this dataset, the residuals appear larger for higher-priced houses, suggesting the model struggles slightly with higher price predictions.

3. Performance Consistency

    - The model performs reasonably well across all price ranges but demonstrates **underfitting** for higher house prices.
    - The residuals for lower-priced houses (e.g., rooms 2–5) are smaller, indicating better prediction accuracy.
    - The residuals increase for higher-priced houses (e.g., rooms 9–11), indicating that the model struggles to capture the variability in higher price ranges.

Interpretation of Model Performance

1. Good Predictions for Mid-Range Prices

    - The model fits the data well for the mid-range prices, as evident by smaller residuals in this range.

2. Challenges with Higher Prices

    - For houses with more rooms and higher prices, the residuals indicate a consistent **underestimation** of prices.
    - It suggests a potential bias in the linear model's simplicity, which may not fully capture the nonlinear relationship between the number of rooms and house prices.

3. Evaluation Metrics

    - **Mean Squared Error (MSE):** A quantitative measure of the average squared differences between actual and predicted prices, providing insight into overall model error

    - **R² Score:** Indicates the proportion of variability in house prices explained by the model, with higher values signifying a better fit

4. Recommendations for Improvement

    Now we have found the issue in the model that it is unable to predict the higher cost houses well, so here are the recommendations for improvement:

    - Consider **polynomial regression** or **Random Forest regression** to capture nonlinear relationships.

    - Include additional features (e.g., location score, lot size) to improve model accuracy and address underfitting.

Comparing Polynomial Regression and Linear Regression

We will perform the same steps with polynomial regression and compare their results:

```
import numpy as np
import pandas as pd
import matplotlib.pyplot as plt
from sklearn.linear_model import LinearRegression
from sklearn.preprocessing import PolynomialFeatures
from sklearn.metrics import mean_squared_error

# Create dataset
data = {
    'Rooms': [2, 3, 4, 5, 6],
    'Price': [200000, 250000, 310000, 450000, 620000]  # Non-linear
    progression
}

df = pd.DataFrame(data)
```

```python
# Features and Target
X = df[['Rooms']]   # Feature
y = df['Price']  # Target

# Linear Regression Model
linear_model = LinearRegression()
linear_model.fit(X, y)

# Polynomial Regression Model (degree=3)
poly = PolynomialFeatures(degree=3)
X_poly = poly.fit_transform(X)
poly_model = LinearRegression()
poly_model.fit(X_poly, y)

# Prediction range
X_range = np.linspace(X['Rooms'].min(), X['Rooms'].max(), 100).reshape(-1, 1)

# Predictions for Linear and Polynomial Regression
y_linear_pred = linear_model.predict(X_range)
X_range_poly = poly.transform(X_range)
y_poly_pred = poly_model.predict(X_range_poly)

# Residuals
y_linear_residuals = y - linear_model.predict(X)
y_poly_residuals = y - poly_model.predict(poly.transform(X))

# Plot the results
plt.figure(figsize=(10, 12))

# Subplot 1: Regression Lines
plt.subplot(2, 1, 1)
plt.scatter(X, y, color='blue', label="Actual Prices", s=50)
plt.plot(X_range, y_linear_pred, color='red', label="Linear Regression Line")
plt.plot(X_range, y_poly_pred, color='green', linestyle='--', label="Polynomial Regression Line (degree=3)")
plt.legend()
plt.xlabel("Number of Rooms")
```

```
plt.ylabel("House Prices")
plt.title("Regression Analysis: Linear vs Polynomial")

# Subplot 2: Residuals
plt.subplot(2, 1, 2)
plt.scatter(X, y_linear_residuals, color='red', label="Residuals (Linear 
Regression)", s=50)
plt.scatter(X, y_poly_residuals, color='green', label="Residuals 
(Polynomial Regression)", s=50)
plt.axhline(y=0, color='black', linestyle='--', linewidth=1)
plt.legend()
plt.xlabel("Number of Rooms")
plt.ylabel("Residuals")
plt.title("Residuals Comparison")

plt.tight_layout()
plt.show()
```

This code produces the chart shown in Figure 2-2, which illustrates the differences between Linear Regression and polynomial regression, as well as their residuals.

CHAPTER 2 INTRODUCTION TO MACHINE LEARNING AND DATA LAKEHOUSES

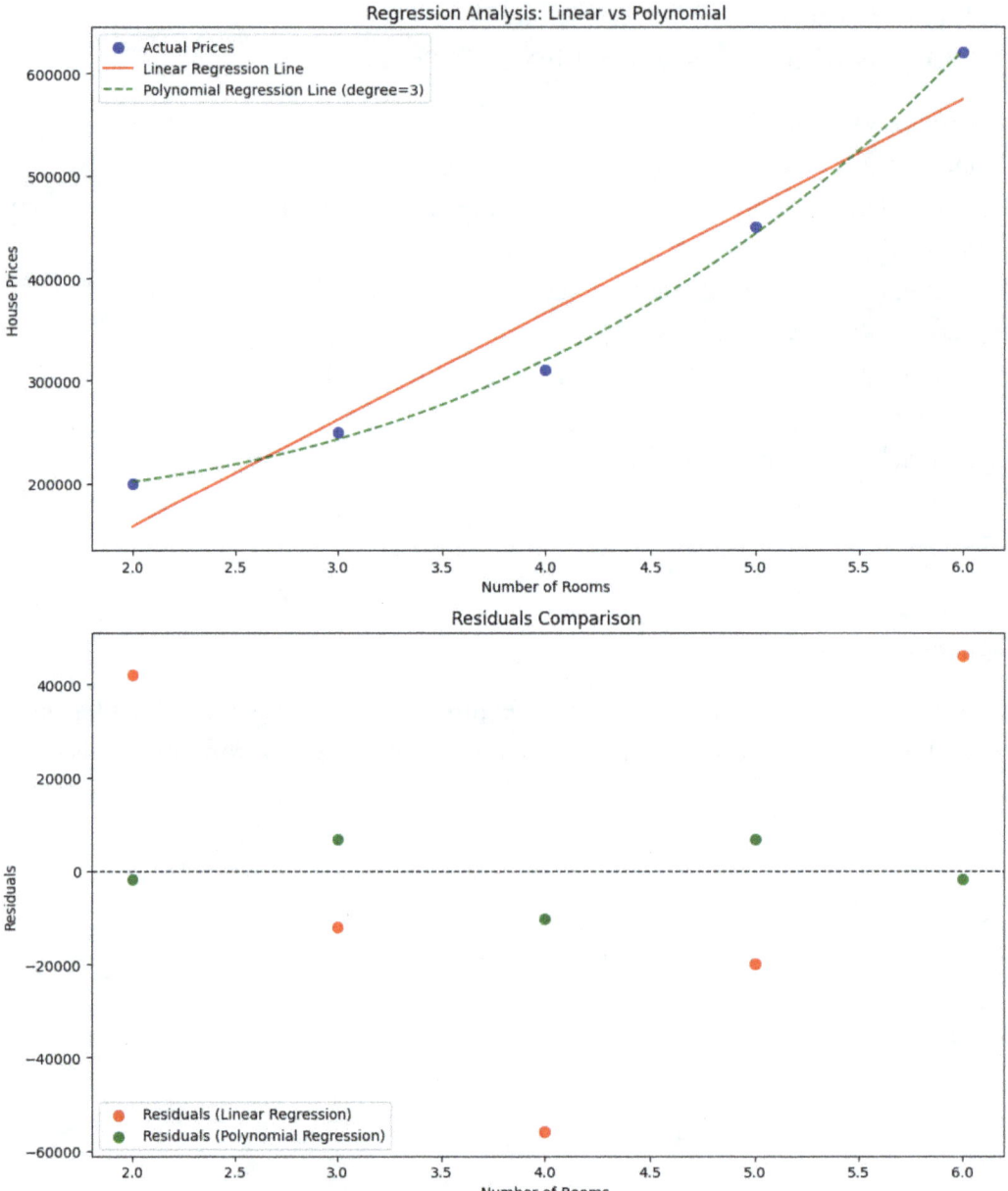

Figure 2-2. *Linear Regression vs. polynomial regression*

Interpretation

- For Linear Regression, residuals are more prominent and follow a pattern, indicating underfitting.
- Polynomial regression shows smaller, more evenly distributed residuals, suggesting a better fit.

Comparing Linear vs. Polynomial vs. Random Forest Regression

Now, we will perform the same steps with Random Forest regression and compare the results from all three regression types:

```
import numpy as np
import pandas as pd
import matplotlib.pyplot as plt
from sklearn.linear_model import LinearRegression
from sklearn.preprocessing import PolynomialFeatures
from sklearn.ensemble import RandomForestRegressor
from sklearn.metrics import mean_squared_error, r2_score

# Create a dataset with non-linear patterns
data = {
    'Rooms': [2, 3, 4, 5, 6, 7, 8, 9, 10, 11],
    'Price': [200000, 300000, 420000, 560000, 720000, 900000, 1100000,
    1320000, 1560000, 1820000]  # Quadratic pattern
}

# Convert to DataFrame
df = pd.DataFrame(data)

# Features and Target
X = df[['Rooms']]  # Feature
y = df['Price']  # Target

# Linear Regression
linear_model = LinearRegression()
linear_model.fit(X, y)

# Polynomial Regression (degree=3)
poly = PolynomialFeatures(degree=3)
```

CHAPTER 2 INTRODUCTION TO MACHINE LEARNING AND DATA LAKEHOUSES

```python
X_poly = poly.fit_transform(X)
poly_model = LinearRegression()
poly_model.fit(X_poly, y)

# Random Forest Regression
random_forest_model = RandomForestRegressor(n_estimators=100, random_
state=42)
random_forest_model.fit(X, y)

# Prediction range
X_range = np.linspace(X['Rooms'].min(), X['Rooms'].max(), 100).
reshape(-1, 1)

# Predictions
y_linear_pred = linear_model.predict(X_range)
y_poly_pred = poly_model.predict(poly.transform(X_range))
y_rf_pred = random_forest_model.predict(X_range)

# Residuals
y_linear_residuals = y - linear_model.predict(X)
y_poly_residuals = y - poly_model.predict(poly.transform(X))
y_rf_residuals = y - random_forest_model.predict(X)

# Plot the results
plt.figure(figsize=(12, 10))

# Subplot 1: Regression Lines
plt.subplot(2, 1, 1)
plt.scatter(X, y, color='blue', label="Actual Prices", s=50)
plt.plot(X_range, y_linear_pred, color='red', label="Linear
Regression Line")
plt.plot(X_range, y_poly_pred, color='green', linestyle='--',
label="Polynomial Regression Line (degree=3)")
plt.plot(X_range, y_rf_pred, color='purple', linestyle=':', label="Random
Forest Regression Line")
plt.legend()
plt.xlabel("Number of Rooms")
plt.ylabel("House Prices")
plt.title("Regression Analysis: Linear vs Polynomial vs Random Forest")
```

```python
# Subplot 2: Residuals
plt.subplot(2, 1, 2)
plt.scatter(X, y_linear_residuals, color='red', label="Residuals (Linear Regression)", s=50)
plt.scatter(X, y_poly_residuals, color='green', label="Residuals (Polynomial Regression)", s=50)
plt.scatter(X, y_rf_residuals, color='purple', label="Residuals (Random Forest Regression)", s=50)
plt.axhline(y=0, color='black', linestyle='--', linewidth=1)
plt.legend()
plt.xlabel("Number of Rooms")
plt.ylabel("Residuals")
plt.title("Residuals Comparison")

plt.tight_layout()
plt.show()

# Print Metrics for Each Model
print("Linear Regression:")
print(f"Mean Squared Error: {mean_squared_error(y, linear_model.predict(X))}")
print(f"R² Score: {r2_score(y, linear_model.predict(X))}\n")

print("Polynomial Regression (degree=3):")
print(f"Mean Squared Error: {mean_squared_error(y, poly_model.predict(X_poly))}")
print(f"R² Score: {r2_score(y, poly_model.predict(X_poly))}\n")

print("Random Forest Regression:")
print(f"Mean Squared Error: {mean_squared_error(y, random_forest_model.predict(X))}")
print(f"R² Score: {r2_score(y, random_forest_model.predict(X))}")
```

This code produces the chart to analyze the regression analysis, as shown in Figure 2-3.

CHAPTER 2 INTRODUCTION TO MACHINE LEARNING AND DATA LAKEHOUSES

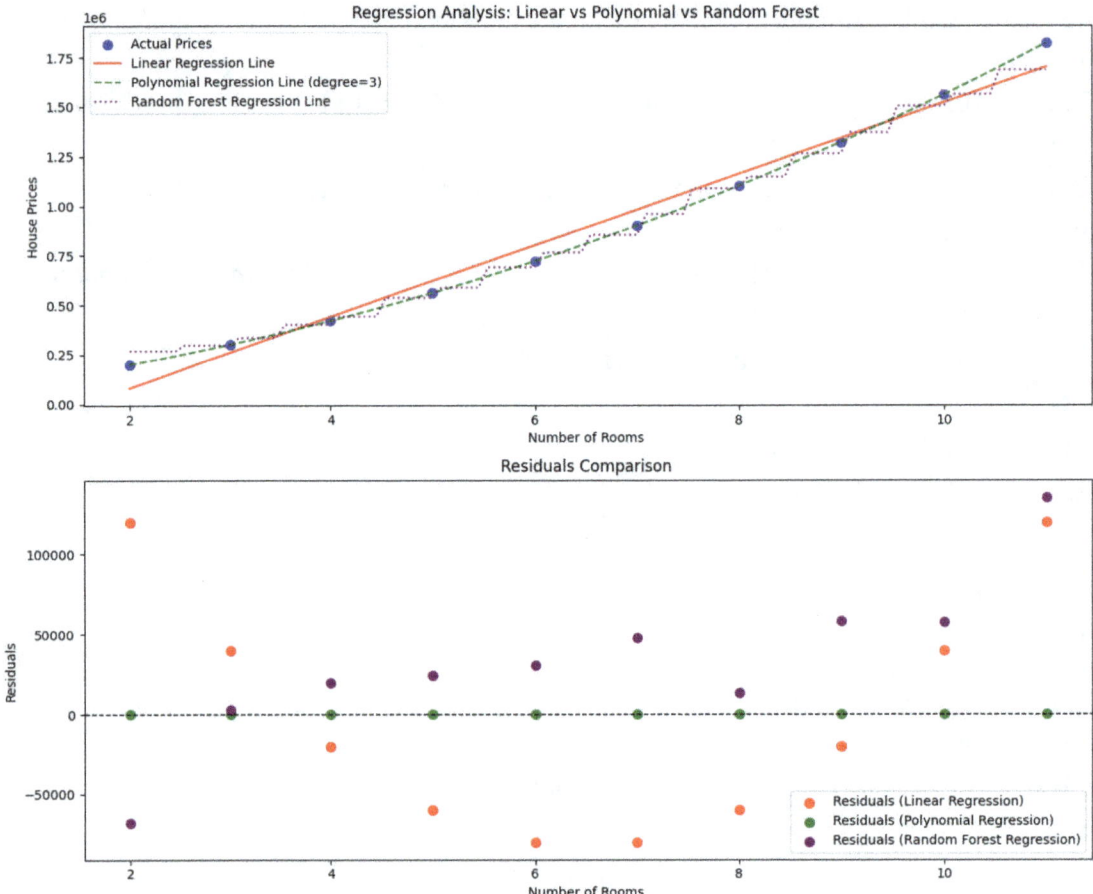

Figure 2-3. Chat showing regression analysis

Interpretation

- Polynomial regression provides the best balance between capturing the overall trend and minimizing residuals.

- Random Forest regression offers flexibility but may overfit in some scenarios.

- Linear Regression struggles with nonlinear data, leading to larger errors.

Key Insights and Takeaways

1. **Why Linear Regression?**
   - Linear Regression is easy to interpret and effective for problems where relationships between variables are linear.

2. **Impact of Features**
   - Each feature contributes differently to the final prediction. For instance, the location might substantially impact the price more than the number of rooms.

3. **Limitations of the Model**
   - Linear Regression assumes a linear relationship between features and the target. Real-world data might require more complex models (e.g., Random Forests or gradient boosting).

Exercise 2: Unsupervised Learning—Customer Segmentation

Objective

In this lab, we'll use a larger dataset to group customers based on their annual income and spending score using the **K-Means Clustering** algorithm. This unsupervised learning exercise demonstrates how to uncover hidden patterns in customer data, which can then guide personalized marketing strategies.

Scenario

Businesses often struggle to understand their diverse customer bases. Grouping customers based on their behavior or attributes enables companies to design tailored strategies, such as personalized marketing campaigns, targeted special offers, or new product launches.

For example:

- **In Retail**: Identify luxury shoppers, budget-conscious buyers, and occasional customers.
- **In Finance**: Distinguish between risk-prone borrowers and high-value investors.
- **In Healthcare**: Segment patients into those who need frequent care vs. those who require preventive measures.

CHAPTER 2   INTRODUCTION TO MACHINE LEARNING AND DATA LAKEHOUSES

Machine learning offers an efficient approach to uncovering hidden patterns in customer data through unsupervised learning techniques, such as **K-Means Clustering**. By grouping customers into clusters based on annual income and spending scores, you can extract actionable insights and enhance business decision-making.

Steps for Implementation

Load the Dataset

We'll create a dataset containing the following columns:

- CustomerID: Unique identifier for each customer
- AnnualIncome: Yearly income in dollars
- SpendingScore: A numerical representation of customer spending behavior (e.g., frequency or amount spent)

```python
import pandas as pd

# Create a larger dataset with 20 customers
data = {
    'CustomerID': [i for i in range(1, 21)],
    'AnnualIncome': [15000, 40000, 75000, 60000, 25000, 80000, 120000,
                    45000, 90000, 30000, 100000, 35000, 110000, 20000,
                    70000, 50000, 105000, 55000, 65000, 85000],
    'SpendingScore': [20, 50, 90, 70, 30, 95, 85, 40, 75, 35,
                     80, 45, 95, 25, 65, 55, 88, 60, 72, 77]
}

# Convert to a DataFrame
df = pd.DataFrame(data)

# Display the dataset
display(df)  # Databricks-specific function to display dataframes
```

Explanation

- Annual Income and Spending Score are the features we'll use for clustering.
- The display(df) function in Databricks shows the dataset in an easy-to-read tabular format.

Prepare Data for Clustering

Extract the relevant columns (Annual Income and Spending Score) to create a feature set for the clustering algorithm.

```
# Select features for clustering: AnnualIncome and SpendingScore
X = df[['AnnualIncome', 'SpendingScore']]  # Independent variables used for
                                             clustering
```

Explanation

- Clustering algorithms like K-Means require only the features as input. Here, X is the input dataset without CustomerID, which isn't relevant for clustering.

Plot the Data to Understand It

Let's plot it to understand it more:

```
import matplotlib.pyplot as plt

# Scatter plot of data
plt.figure(figsize=(8, 6))
plt.scatter(df['AnnualIncome'], df['SpendingScore'], color='blue', s=50,
alpha=0.7, edgecolor='k')
plt.title("Scatter Plot: Annual Income vs Spending Score")
plt.xlabel("Annual Income")
plt.ylabel("Spending Score")
plt.grid()
plt.show()
```

This code will produce the chart shown in Figure 2-4 to help you understand the data.

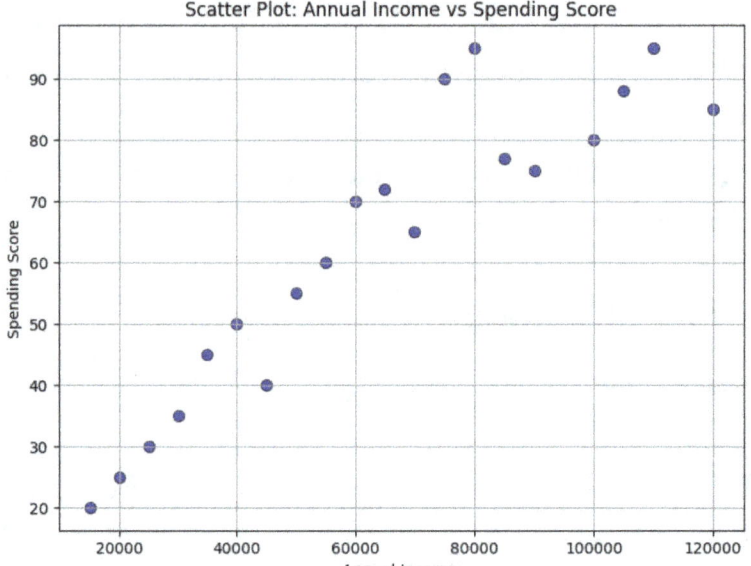

Figure 2-4. *Chart to understand the dataset*

Interpretation of the Chart and Identification of the Clustering Algorithm

Visual Analysis of the Data

The scatterplot shows distinct patterns of points distributed across the graph. Suppose the points are grouped into roughly spherical or circular clusters. In that case, K-Means Clustering is likely a good fit because it works best for isotropic clusters (similar in all directions).

Potential Groupings

In this plot, you can observe that the data points naturally group into clusters based on similarities in Annual Income and Spending Score. For example, low-income, low-spending individuals might form one cluster, and high-income, high-spending individuals might form another.

Limitations of K-Means

If the clusters are elongated, irregularly shaped, or have varying densities, alternative clustering techniques such as DBSCAN or Hierarchical Clustering might be more suitable. In this graph, however, the relatively linear progression and the potential for roughly circular clusters suggest that K-Means is appropriate.

When to Consider Alternatives to K-Means Clustering

1. **DBSCAN (Density-Based Spatial Clustering of Applications with Noise)**

   DBSCAN is ideal for datasets with **nonspherical clusters**, **varying densities**, or **noise and outliers**. It works by grouping closely packed points and marking outliers as noise. Unlike K-Means, DBSCAN does not assume that clusters are spherical or evenly sized.

   Use DBSCAN When:

   - The data contains clusters of **arbitrary shapes** (e.g., crescents, elongated shapes).
   - There are **outliers or noise** in the dataset.
   - The number of clusters is **unknown beforehand**.

Let's understand it with the help of an example: Imagine analyzing **wildlife sightings** in a national park:

- Sightings cluster around irregularly shaped watering holes.
- DBSCAN identifies these clusters and excludes sparse outliers (e.g., solitary sightings far from any watering hole).

2. **Hierarchical Clustering**

   Hierarchical Clustering builds a **treelike structure (dendrogram)** to represent how data points group at different levels. It does not require specifying the number of clusters in advance and provides flexibility to experiment with varying grouping levels.

   Use Hierarchical Clustering When:

   - The dataset is **small to medium-sized** (it can be computationally expensive for large datasets).
   - You want to visualize relationships between clusters using a **dendrogram**.
   - The number of clusters is **unknown**, and you want to experiment with different cuts in the dendrogram.

Let's understand it with the help of an example: Suppose you are analyzing **customer demographics**:

- Group customers based on income, spending habits, and age.
- Hierarchical Clustering reveals relationships, e.g., high-income customers are further split into high spenders and savers.

Key Differences with Examples

Let's summarize the key differences between these three clustering methods:

Clustering Method	Example Scenario	Why Use It?
K-Means	Segmenting customers into income-based clusters	Works well for spherical clusters (e.g., high, medium, low income) when you know the number of groups in advance
DBSCAN	Identifying wildlife clusters around irregular watering holes	Handles irregular, nonspherical clusters and removes noise (e.g., outliers far from clusters)
Hierarchical	Exploring relationships in customer demographics (e.g., age and spending)	Useful when you don't know the number of clusters and want a treelike visualization of group relationships

Visualizing the Data Before Deciding

Before deciding which clustering algorithm to use, **plot the data**:

- Use a **scatterplot** to identify cluster shapes.
- Look for
  - **Spherical Clusters:** K-Means is likely appropriate.
  - **Irregular or Crescent-Shaped Clusters:** Consider DBSCAN.
  - **Hierarchical Relationships:** Explore with dendrograms.

Apply K-Means Clustering

We'll use the K-Means Clustering algorithm to group customers into three distinct clusters. The algorithm minimizes the variance within each cluster while maximizing the distance between clusters.

Explanation

Here, n_clusters=3 specifies the number of clusters to create (this value is adjustable). random_state=42 ensures reproducibility of the results. The Cluster column contains the assigned cluster for each customer, indicating their group based on their Annual Income and Spending Score.

```
from sklearn.cluster import KMeans

# Initialize the K-Means model
kmeans = KMeans(n_clusters=3, random_state=42)  # 3 clusters for
                                                  segmentation

# Fit the model to the data
kmeans.fit(X)

# Assign cluster labels to the dataset
df['Cluster'] = kmeans.labels_   # Add a new column with cluster labels

# Display the updated dataset
display(df)
```

Explanation

- n_clusters=3: Specifies that we want three customer groups (this can be adjusted)
- kmeans.labels_: Assigns a cluster number (e.g., 0, 1, 2) to each customer based on their income and spending score

Visualize the Clusters

Visualization helps us understand the clusters by plotting the customers on a 2D graph where:

- **X Axis**: Annual Income.
- **Y Axis**: Spending Score.
- **Colors**: Represent different clusters.

CHAPTER 2 INTRODUCTION TO MACHINE LEARNING AND DATA LAKEHOUSES

Code:

```
import matplotlib.pyplot as plt

# Scatter plot of customers segmented into clusters
plt.figure(figsize=(8, 6))
plt.scatter(X['AnnualIncome'], X['SpendingScore'], c=df['Cluster'],
cmap='viridis', s=100)
plt.xlabel("Annual Income (USD)")
plt.ylabel("Spending Score")
plt.title("Customer Segmentation")
plt.colorbar(label='Cluster')  # Add color bar for cluster labels
plt.show()
```

This code will produce the customer segmentation chart shown in Figure 2-5.

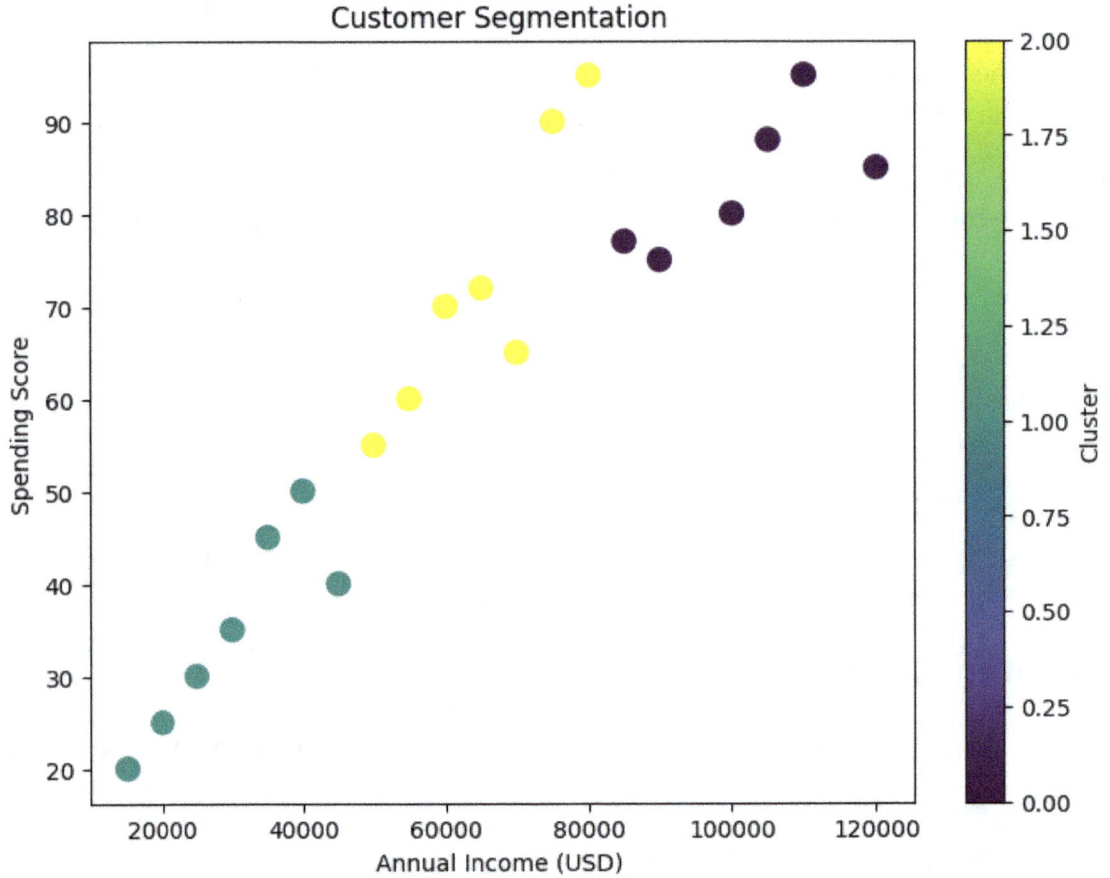

Figure 2-5. *Customer segmentation chart*

CHAPTER 2 INTRODUCTION TO MACHINE LEARNING AND DATA LAKEHOUSES

Explanation

- Each point represents a customer.
- Points with the same color belong to the same cluster.
- The visualization allows us to interpret the behavior of different customer groups (e.g., high-spenders and low-income shoppers).

Interpret the Clusters

We'll analyze the clusters to understand customer behavior from the chart presented in Figure 2-6. For example:

- **Cluster 0**: Low-income, low-spending customers (budget-conscious shoppers)
- **Cluster 1**: High-income, high-spending customers (premium shoppers)
- **Cluster 2**: Moderate-income, moderate-spending customers

CHAPTER 2   INTRODUCTION TO MACHINE LEARNING AND DATA LAKEHOUSES

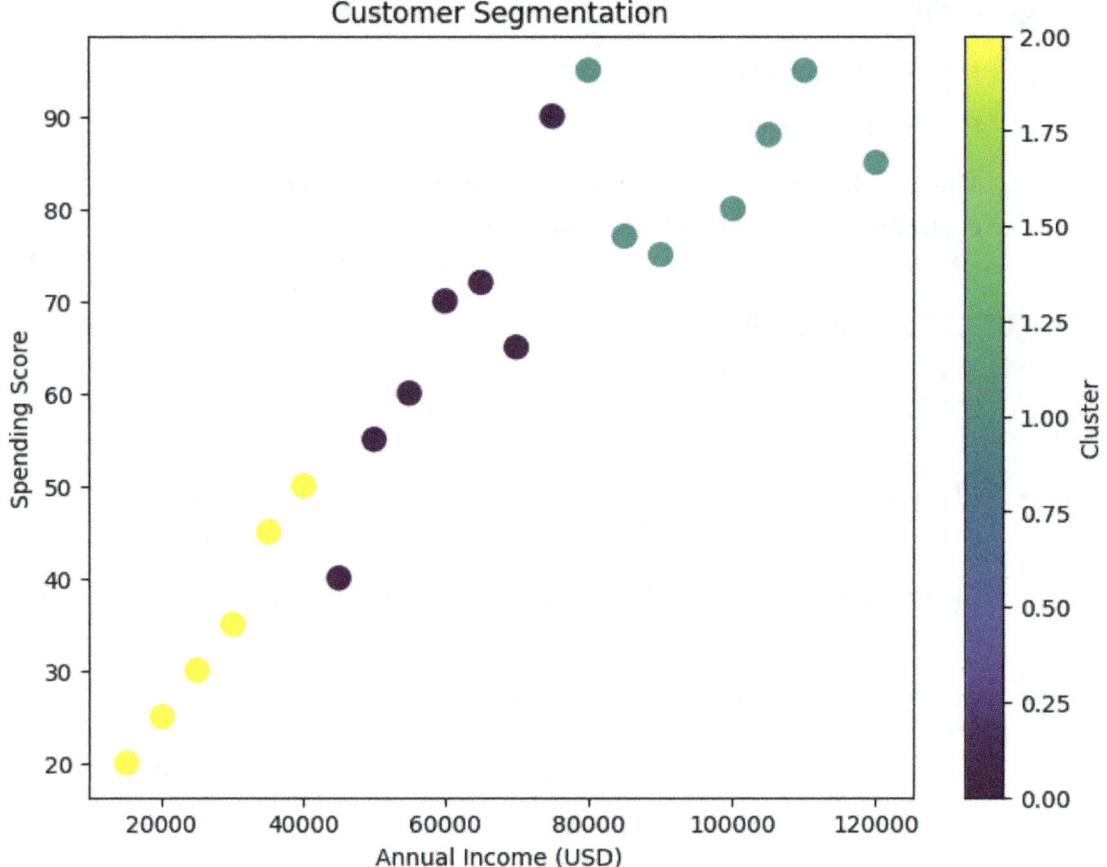

Figure 2-6. *A chart showing the customer behavior*

Why Is the Optimal Number of Clusters Important in Clustering?

Choosing the optimal number of clusters is crucial in clustering analysis because it ensures that

Clusters Represent Real Patterns:

- Too few clusters may oversimplify the data and hide meaningful distinctions between groups.

- Too many clusters may split meaningful groups into smaller, less significant ones, leading to overfitting.

Improved Interpretability

- With the right number of clusters, businesses can more easily interpret customer segments and create actionable strategies tailored to these groups.

Better Cluster Quality

- The optimal number minimizes intra-cluster distances (making clusters compact) and maximizes inter-cluster distances (making clusters distinct).

Avoids Overfitting or Underfitting

- **Overfitting**: Clusters are too granular, capturing noise instead of patterns.
- **Underfitting**: Clusters are too broad, failing to represent the data's variability.

Importance of Customer Segmentation

In the Customer Segmentation exercise, the optimal number of clusters ensures that

- **Meaningful customer groups** are identified (e.g., high-income spenders and low-income budget-conscious shoppers).
- **Actions tailored to these groups** are relevant and actionable.
- **Overlapping or irrelevant segments** are avoided, making insights practical for business decisions.

Example of Multiple Clusters

Imagine a retail dataset with **Annual Income** and **Spending Score,** and we decide to segment the customers into these clusters:

Two Clusters

- One group has a low income and spending, and another has a high income and spending.
- This grouping may oversimplify the data and miss mid-tier spenders.

Ten Clusters

- Creates overly granular groups, some of which may represent noise instead of actual patterns.
- Too many clusters can confuse decision-makers.

Three Clusters (Optimal)

- Identifies three meaningful segments (e.g., low spenders, moderate spenders, high spenders)
- Balances granularity with interpretability

How to Determine the Optimal Number of Clusters

You may wonder how we determine the optimal number of clusters. So there are these methods to determine the optimal number of clusters:

Elbow Method

- Plots the sum of squared distances (inertia) for different numbers of clusters.
- The optimal number is at the "elbow" point, where inertia decreases significantly before plateauing.

Silhouette Score

- Measures the quality of clusters. Higher scores indicate better-defined clusters.

Business Context

- Align clustering with business needs. Too few or too many clusters may not be practical.

Determine the Optimal Number of Clusters: Elbow Method

The **Elbow Method** helps to identify the optimal number of clusters for K-Means Clustering by plotting the **within-cluster sum of squares (WCSS)** against the number of clusters.

Steps

1. Start with a small number of clusters (e.g., k = 1) and increase it gradually.
2. For each value of k, calculate the WCSS, which measures the compactness of the clusters.

CHAPTER 2   INTRODUCTION TO MACHINE LEARNING AND DATA LAKEHOUSES

3. Plot WCSS against the number of clusters.

4. Look for the "elbow" point in the graph, where the WCSS reduction diminishes significantly. This point indicates the optimal number of clusters.

```
# Calculate WCSS for different cluster counts

from sklearn.cluster import KMeans
import matplotlib.pyplot as plt

# Example dataset
X = df[['AnnualIncome', 'SpendingScore']]  # Select features

# Calculate WCSS for different cluster counts
wcss = []
for k in range(1, 11):   # Test k values from 1 to 10
    kmeans = KMeans(n_clusters=k, init='k-means++', max_iter=300,
    n_init=10, random_state=42)
    kmeans.fit(X)
    wcss.append(kmeans.inertia_)

# Plot the Elbow Method
plt.figure(figsize=(8, 6))
plt.plot(range(1, 11), wcss, marker='o', linestyle='-',
color='blue')
plt.title('Elbow Method to Determine Optimal k')
plt.xlabel('Number of Clusters (k)')
plt.ylabel('WCSS')
plt.grid(True)
plt.show()
```

This code will produce the elbow chart provided in Figure 2-7.

CHAPTER 2   INTRODUCTION TO MACHINE LEARNING AND DATA LAKEHOUSES

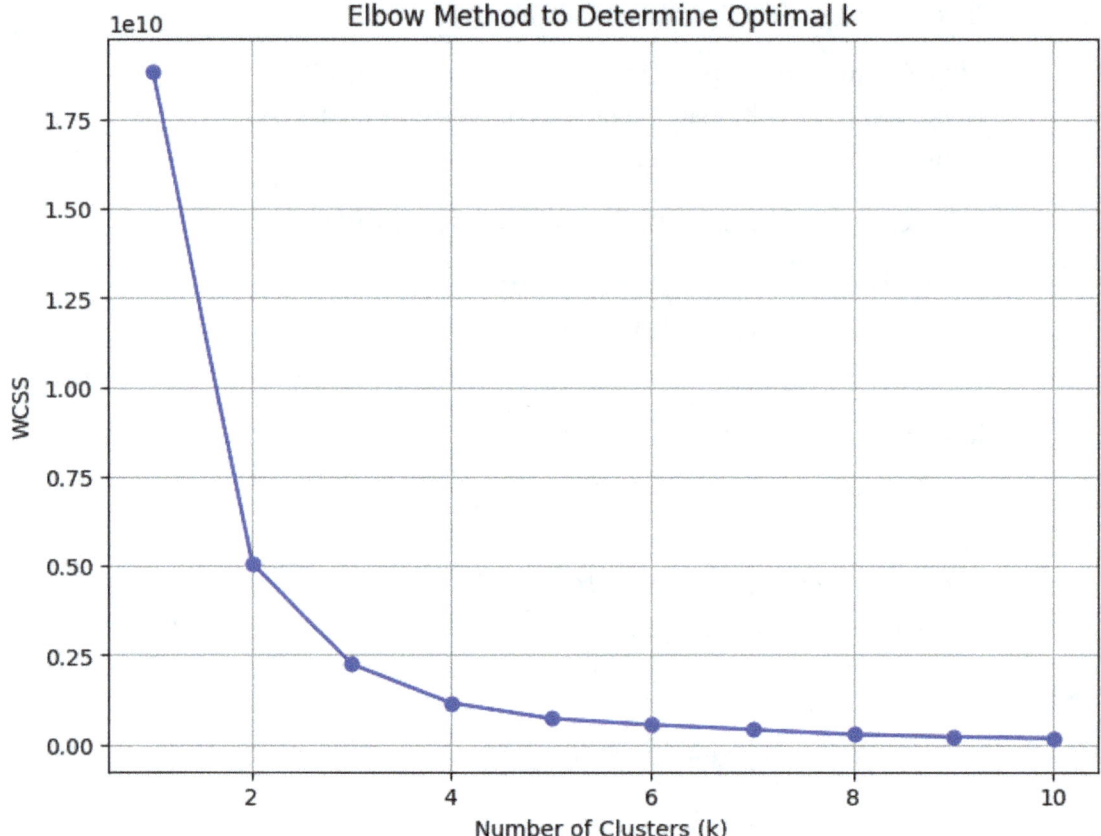

Figure 2-7.   Elbow chart

Interpretation of the Elbow Method Chart

The **Elbow Method** determines the optimal number of clusters (k) for K-Means Clustering. Here's the interpretation of the above chart:

- **X Axis (Number of Clusters, k):** Represents the number of clusters being tested.

- **Y Axis (WCSS—Within-Cluster Sum of Squares):** Measures the variance within each cluster. Lower WCSS indicates that data points are closer to the centroid of their respective clusters.

- **Elbow Point:** The "elbow" is the point where the WCSS decreases sharply and then starts to level off.

In this chart, the elbow is observed at **k = 3**, as the reduction in WCSS after this point is minimal.

1. **Optimal Number of Clusters**

    - The elbow point (**k = 3**) represents the optimal number of clusters. At this point:

        - Clusters are well-formed.

        - Increasing the number of clusters beyond this point yields minimal improvement in WCSS, indicating that additional clusters may overfit the data or represent noise.

Practical Implication

Using **k = 3 clusters would balance compactness (low WCSS) and simplicity (fewer clusters), making it a practical choice for effectively segmenting the dataset** without overfitting.

Adding Age As the Third Parameter in the Clustering and How to Interpret the Clustering

Suppose we add an extra parameter called **age** and want to understand its impact on the segmentation. When adding an extra feature like **age** to the dataset, visualizing it in 3D becomes essential because:

1. **Enhanced Understanding of Clusters**

    - A 2D plot only shows the relationship between two features, such as Annual Income and Spending Score.

    - Including a third dimension (e.g., age) reveals how clusters are distributed across all three features, offering more profound insights.

2. **Revealing Hidden Patterns**

    - Some clusters that overlap in 2D may become distinguishable in 3D, as the third axis provides an additional perspective.

    - For instance, younger customers may behave differently from older ones, and this pattern could be hidden in 2D.

3. **Better Decision-Making**
   - With all three features visible, decision-makers can create more precise strategies targeting specific customer segments (e.g., young, high-spending, low-income customers).

4. **Outlier Detection**
   - Points that deviate significantly along the Age axis may indicate outliers that require further analysis.

5. **Visual Validation**
   - A 3D plot helps validate the clustering results by showing how well-separated the clusters are across all features.

Adding the Parameter **Age** to Customer Segmentation

Imagine we have the following dataset with three features:

- **Annual Income**
- **Spending Score**
- **Age**

Clusters may represent

1. Young, low-income, high-spenders (e.g., students)
2. Middle-aged, moderate-income, moderate spenders
3. Older, high-income, high spenders

Now let's draw the dataset with the 3D plot:

```
from mpl_toolkits.mplot3d import Axes3D
import matplotlib.pyplot as plt
from sklearn.cluster import KMeans
import pandas as pd

# Example dataset with age added
data = {
    'AnnualIncome': [15000, 40000, 75000, 60000, 25000, 80000, 120000,
    45000, 90000, 30000],
    'SpendingScore': [20, 50, 90, 70, 30, 95, 85, 40, 75, 35],
```

```python
    'Age': [25, 35, 45, 30, 22, 41, 50, 29, 48, 27]
}
df = pd.DataFrame(data)

# Perform K-Means Clustering
X = df[['AnnualIncome', 'SpendingScore', 'Age']]
kmeans = KMeans(n_clusters=3, random_state=42)
df['Cluster'] = kmeans.fit_predict(X)

# 3D Scatter Plot
fig = plt.figure(figsize=(10, 8))
ax = fig.add_subplot(111, projection='3d')

# Scatter plot for each Cluster
colors = ['red', 'blue', 'green']
for cluster in range(3):
    clustered_data = df[df['Cluster'] == cluster]
    ax.scatter(clustered_data['AnnualIncome'], clustered_
    data['SpendingScore'], clustered_data['Age'],
              label=f'Cluster {cluster + 1}', s=100, alpha=0.8,
              color=colors[cluster])
ax.set_title('3D Visualization of Clusters')
ax.set_xlabel('Annual Income')
ax.set_ylabel('Spending Score')
ax.set_zlabel('Age')
ax.legend()
plt.show()
```

This code will produce the chart provided in Figure 2-8.

CHAPTER 2 INTRODUCTION TO MACHINE LEARNING AND DATA LAKEHOUSES

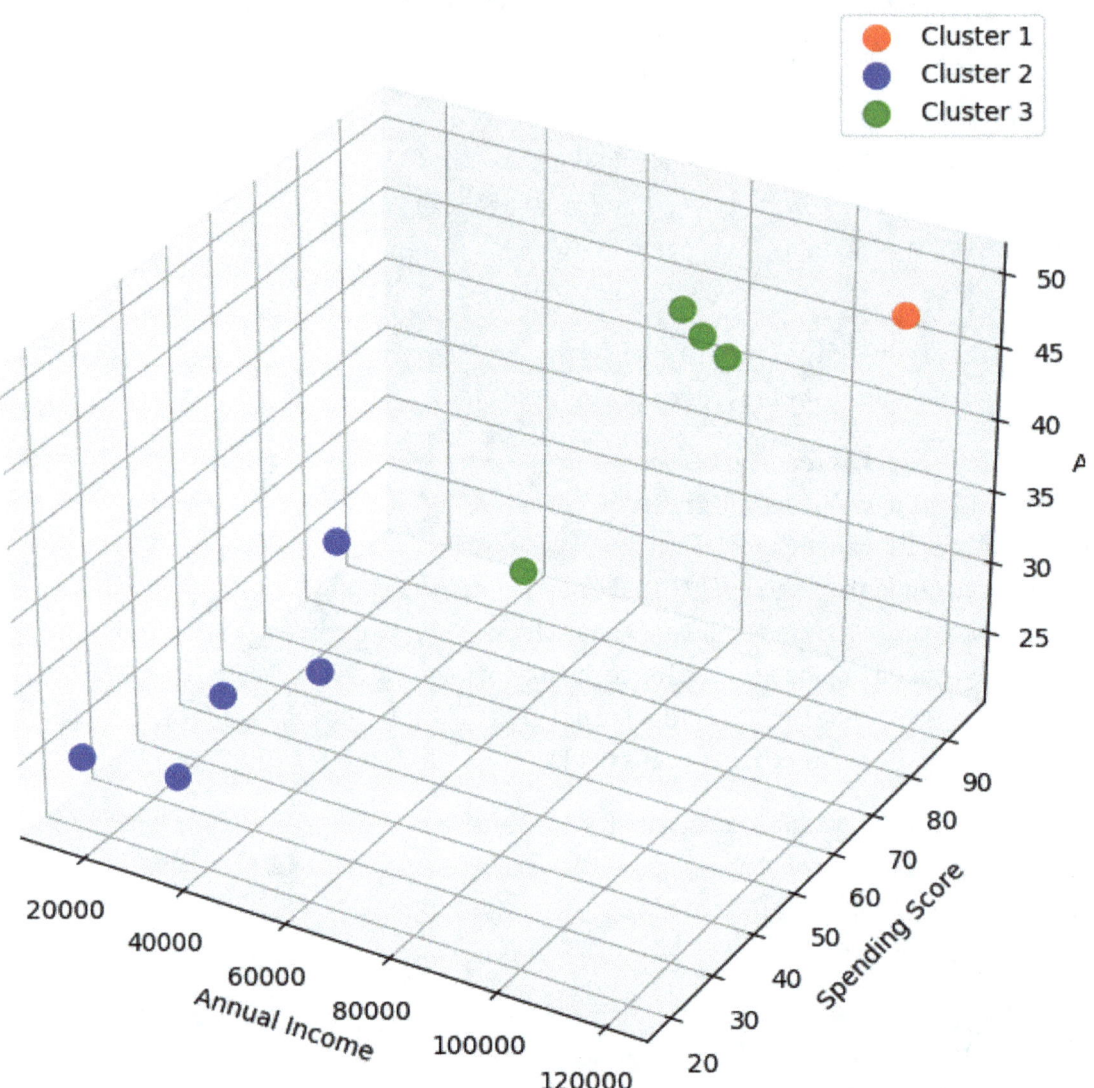

Figure 2-8. *3D visualization of a cluster*

This chart provides a more accurate representation of age, along with other relevant parameters.

What is Silhouette Score, and how do you use it to evaluate the quality of clustering?

Use the Silhouette Score to Evaluate the Quality of Clustering

The **Silhouette Score** is a metric used to assess the quality of clustering. It measures how similar a data point is to its cluster (cohesion) compared to other clusters (separation).

Why Is Silhouette Score Important?

1. **Cluster Quality Evaluation**
   - A high score indicates well-separated and cohesive clusters.
   - A low or negative score suggests poor clustering or overlapping clusters.

2. **Model Validation**
   - It helps validate the number of clusters chosen for algorithms like K-Means.

3. **Comparing Clustering Methods**
   - It provides a way to compare the effectiveness of different clustering algorithms (e.g., K-Means vs. DBSCAN).

How to Interpret Silhouette Scores

- **Score Close to 1**
  - Clusters are well-separated and compact.
  - Indicates high clustering quality.

- **Score Close to 0**
  - Clusters are overlapping or poorly defined.
  - May indicate too few or too many clusters.

- **Negative Score**
  - Data points are assigned to incorrect clusters.
  - Indicates poor clustering or incorrect assumptions.

Let's calculate the score:

```python
from sklearn.cluster import KMeans
from sklearn.metrics import silhouette_score
import pandas as pd

# Example dataset
data = {
    'AnnualIncome': [15000, 40000, 75000, 60000, 25000, 80000, 120000,
    45000, 90000, 30000],
    'SpendingScore': [20, 50, 90, 70, 30, 95, 85, 40, 75, 35]
}
df = pd.DataFrame(data)

# Select features for clustering
X = df[['AnnualIncome', 'SpendingScore']]

# Apply K-Means clustering
kmeans = KMeans(n_clusters=3, random_state=42)
df['Cluster'] = kmeans.fit_predict(X)

# Calculate silhouette score
sil_score = silhouette_score(X, df['Cluster'])
print(f"Silhouette Score: {sil_score:.2f}")
```

Interpretation of Silhouette Score

The **Silhouette Score** of **0.53** indicates that the clustering is **moderately good**. Here's what it tells us:

Key Insights

1. **Cluster Cohesion**

    - The clusters are reasonably compact, meaning that most data points are close to the center of their assigned clusters.
    - It suggests that the clustering algorithm captured some meaningful groupings in the data.

2. **Cluster Separation**

    - The clusters are somewhat well-separated but not perfectly distinct.

    - There might be a slight overlap or proximity between some clusters, which could affect their interpretability.

3. **Room for Improvement**

    - While the clustering is decent, there is room to improve cluster separation.

    - Exploring other numbers of clusters or alternative clustering algorithms (e.g., **DBSCAN** or **Hierarchical Clustering**) might yield better results.

Practical Interpretation

- **Good Enough for Analysis**: A score above 0.5 generally indicates that the clustering captures some meaningful patterns in the data.

- **Not Perfect**: The score suggests that the clusters are reasonably formed but may not fully separate the data points into distinct groups.

Business Context in Customer Segmentation Task

- **What It Means:** The clusters likely represent **low-income budget-conscious shoppers, mid-income regular spenders,** and **high-income premium shoppers.**

- **Next Steps**

    - Verify if the clusters align with business objectives.

    - Consider adding more features (e.g., age or product preference) to improve cluster quality.

    - Re-evaluate the number of clusters using the **Elbow Method** or other validation techniques. And we already performed that in the earlier step.

In this example, a Silhouette Score of 0.53 indicates moderate clustering performance. While the results are interpretable and actionable, further refinement of the data or the model may improve cluster quality and provide deeper insights. However, this is sufficient to understand the regression.

Summary

This chapter explored the fascinating intersection of machine learning and data lakehouses, providing a solid foundation for understanding and applying these technologies. You gained insight into the core components of machine learning, including data, features, models, and evaluation metrics. You explored the three main types of learning—supervised, unsupervised, and reinforcement—alongside their real-world applications. The chapter also introduces practical implementations of supervised learning models for tasks such as housing price prediction using linear, polynomial, and Random Forest regression. Additionally, you explored unsupervised learning for customer segmentation, applying K-Means Clustering and evaluating its quality using methods such as the Elbow Method and Silhouette Score. Hands-on exercises reinforced these concepts, enabling you to visualize data, refine models, and derive actionable insights effectively.

Looking ahead, Chapter 3: **Data Preparation and Management** will focus on the essential steps required to ensure your data is ready for machine learning and analytics. You'll learn to manage data effectively using tools like Unity Catalog, from ingestion and cleaning to transformation and governance. This next chapter will empower you to create robust, high-quality datasets, laying the groundwork for scalable and reliable machine learning workflows.

CHAPTER 3

Data Preparation and Management

Imagine trying to build a house without a solid foundation—the structure would be unstable, and your efforts might collapse. Data preparation and management are the foundation of any successful data-driven project. Even the most sophisticated analyses or machine learning models can falter without them.

Today's data originates from various sources, including social media, Internet of Things (IoT) devices, financial transactions, and other digital platforms. This raw data is often messy, incomplete, and unstructured, making it unsuitable for direct analysis. As data professionals, it's our responsibility to clean, transform, and organize this data so it can deliver meaningful insights.

In this chapter, you will learn how to ingest data efficiently, clean it, and transform it to ensure quality and manage it effectively. We will also explore best practices for organizing and governing data with Unity Catalog, setting you up for success in your analytics and AI projects.

Let's embark on this journey to lay the groundwork for preparing your data analysis.

Learning Objectives

By the end of this chapter, you will

- Understand various data ingestion techniques, including batch and streaming approaches.
- Learn the processes and importance of data cleaning and transformation.
- Explore key tools and libraries for effective data transformation.
- Manage data effectively using Unity Catalog.
- Implement best practices for data organization and governance to ensure effective data management and control.

CHAPTER 3   DATA PREPARATION AND MANAGEMENT

Introduction to Data Ingestion

Data ingestion is the process of importing data from various sources into a centralized system for analysis and storage. It acts as the starting point of any data pipeline, enabling organizations to harness the value of their raw data. Whether your data comes from sensors, applications, or user interactions, ensuring it's captured accurately and efficiently is critical.

There are two primary methods for data ingestion: batch and streaming, each suited to different use cases. Batch ingestion involves processing large amounts of data at scheduled intervals, whereas streaming ingestion enables the capture and processing of data in real time.

The following sections will explore these methods in depth, starting with batch ingestion.

Batch Ingestion

Batch ingestion is collecting and processing data in chunks or batches at specified intervals. This method is particularly effective for scenarios where immediate data availability is not critical, but efficiently processing large volumes of data is essential. With batch ingestion, data is grouped into discrete sets, which are then loaded into a storage system or data warehouse for processing. Examples include transaction logs, daily sales records, or sensor readings aggregated over time.

Batch ingestion is particularly effective in addressing specific data challenges. Let's understand it with a couple of scenarios:

- **Analyzing Historical Data**: A retailer needs to identify seasonal sales trends from the past five years. Attempting to process the entire dataset simultaneously can overwhelm systems and delay results. Batch ingestion enables the processing of historical data in yearly or monthly chunks, allowing retailers to efficiently uncover patterns and adjust inventory or promotions to capitalize on those trends.

- **Generating Periodic Reports**: A bank's finance team publishes a monthly income statement. Real-time updates during the reporting period could lead to inaccuracies due to incomplete transactions. Using batch ingestion, the finance team processes all finalized transactions at the close of the month, ensuring their reports are comprehensive, accurate, and ready for stakeholders.

- **Optimizing System Resources**: An ecommerce platform experiences peak traffic during business hours, making it challenging to process analytical data in real time without impacting user experience. The platform ensures that dashboards and analytics are updated without straining the system during critical hours by scheduling batch ingestion for non-peak times, such as late at night.

- **Combining Data from Multiple Sources**: A multinational corporation needs to aggregate quarterly sales data from regional offices worldwide. Real-time integration may introduce errors due to variations in data formats. Batch ingestion consolidates data from each region into a unified dataset, ensuring consistency and providing a reliable basis for global performance analysis.

- **Creating Archives or Backups**: To comply with regulatory requirements, healthcare providers must store patient records on a daily basis. Without a structured system, data might be incomplete or lost. Batch ingestion ensures that all daily records are systematically archived, meeting compliance standards and providing secure backups for future audits or emergencies.

Batch ingestion offers a dependable and structured approach to addressing these challenges, enabling organizations to manage data effectively and make informed decisions.

How to Implement Batch Ingestion

Implementing batch ingestion involves a structured set of steps and can be best understood through a real-life example. Consider a retail company consolidating daily sales data from multiple stores into a centralized system for analysis and reporting.

1. **Identify Data Sources**: The retail company collects sales data from various stores in relational databases and CSV files. For instance, Store A uses a MySQL database, while Store B exports daily sales as CSV files. Identifying these sources is the first step to setting up the ingestion pipeline.

2. **Set Ingestion Frequency**: The company decides to ingest sales data daily after stores close to ensure all transactions are included. This daily schedule allows them to prepare reports each morning with the previous day's data.

3. **Select Appropriate Tools**

    - To handle data ingestion efficiently, the company selects

        - **Azure Data Factory** orchestrates the workflow and connects to MySQL and CSV files.

        - **Apache Spark** is used for the distributed processing of ingested data, ensuring scalability as the business grows.

        - **Databricks Auto Loader** to automate the detection and incremental ingestion of new files from Store B's CSV exports.

4. **Process and Store Data**: Once ingested, the data transforms. For example, inconsistent date formats are cleaned up, and total sales are aggregated by store and product category. The processed data is then saved into a Delta Lake, a storage layer that supports high-performance analytics and ensures data reliability.

5. **Monitor and Optimize Pipelines**: The IT team sets up monitoring dashboards to track pipeline performance and identify bottlenecks. For example, if ingestion from Store A's MySQL database slows down, the team can investigate and adjust configurations or indexing for better performance.

By following these steps, the retail company ensures that all its daily sales data is consolidated, cleaned, and ready for use in morning reports and dashboards. Batch ingestion streamlines this process and provides a scalable solution for increasing data volumes as the business expands.

Now that we've covered batch ingestion with a practical example, let's explore streaming ingestion and its applications for real-time data processing.

Streaming Ingestion

Streaming ingestion enables the real-time collection and processing of data as it is generated, allowing for seamless integration with other systems. This method is particularly valuable when timeliness is critical, such as in fraud detection, real-time analytics, or event monitoring. Unlike batch ingestion, streaming ingestion processes data continuously, ensuring that the most current information is always available for analysis.

Streaming ingestion is particularly effective in addressing specific data challenges:

- **Monitoring Real-Time Events**: Consider a logistics company tracking the live location of delivery trucks. Streaming ingestion processes GPS data in real time, allowing the company to monitor deliveries and reroute trucks efficiently during traffic disruptions.

- **Detecting Fraud**: Financial institutions utilize streaming ingestion to monitor transactions in real time. For example, a bank can flag and block suspicious activities immediately after detection, such as multiple failed login attempts or unusual purchase patterns.

- **Powering Real-Time Dashboards**: A stock trading platform must display live market trends to its users in real time. Streaming ingestion ensures that stock prices, trading volumes, and market indices are continuously updated, providing traders with the insights they need to act quickly.

- **Processing IoT Data**: A smart home system collects data from sensors monitoring temperature, humidity, and energy usage. Streaming ingestion enables the system to adjust heating or cooling settings in real time based on sensor inputs, thereby optimizing energy efficiency.

How to Implement Streaming Ingestion

To better understand streaming ingestion, let's consider a ride-hailing app that tracks drivers and passengers in real time.

CHAPTER 3   DATA PREPARATION AND MANAGEMENT

1. **Identify Data Sources**: The app collects data from GPS sensors in driver and passenger devices, including location coordinates and ride statuses. This data is processed in real time to calculate metrics such as estimated arrival times (ETA), monitor the status of rides, and provide live updates to users. Challenges such as data loss due to poor network connectivity are addressed by leveraging buffering techniques in tools like Apache Kafka, ensuring no critical updates are missed. Processed data is stored temporarily in memory or a data lake for analytics and reporting.

2. **Select Appropriate Tools**: The app uses these tools to enable seamless streaming ingestion:

    - **Apache Kafka**: The app utilizes Apache Kafka to manage high-throughput data streams from thousands of devices simultaneously. Kafka buffers incoming data to handle spikes in traffic or temporary network issues, ensuring the stream remains unbroken and reliable. It is particularly effective at maintaining data order and delivering it consistently across the pipeline.

    - **Azure Event Hubs**: Azure Event Hubs acts as a scalable ingestion layer, managing data streams from multiple geographic regions. Its fault-tolerant architecture ensures the system can reliably ingest and forward data even in the event of temporary disruptions. Event Hubs integrates seamlessly with downstream tools, making it ideal for handling diverse data types.

    - **Databricks Structured Streaming**: Databricks Structured Streaming is used to process real-time data continuously. It applies transformations such as calculating estimated arrival times (ETAs), cleansing erroneous data, and standardizing input formats. It ensures the data is ready for real-time analysis and visualization, enabling fast, actionable insights for operations and user-facing dashboards.

3. **Process and Analyze Data**: Now, the app processes and analyzes the data as follows:

   - The ingested data is processed to calculate estimated arrival times (ETA), match drivers with nearby passengers, and monitor ride statuses in real time. For example, GPS data from a driver's device is analyzed to estimate the best route and arrival time, taking into account current traffic conditions. Similarly, passenger locations are matched with the closest available drivers using algorithms that take into account distance and availability. Challenges like inconsistent GPS signals or network lags are mitigated using buffering techniques and error-correction algorithms. This processed data ensures accuracy and enhances the ride-hailing platform's overall efficiency and reliability.

   - Transformation logic is applied to clean and standardize location data, addressing missing fields, inconsistent formats, and outlier values. For example, coordinates with irregular time intervals are interpolated to ensure smooth tracking, while erroneous GPS signals caused by poor connectivity are corrected using error-handling algorithms. These steps ensure the data remains consistent and reliable for downstream analytics, enabling accurate and actionable insights.

4. **Integrate with Real-Time Dashboards**: Processed data is sent to a real-time dashboard, providing operations teams and users with comprehensive, live updates. For instance, operations teams can dynamically monitor driver availability, ensuring that areas with high demand are adequately serviced. Estimated arrival times (ETAs) are continuously calculated and updated, enabling passengers to track their rides precisely. The dashboard also displays the ongoing ride statuses, helping teams quickly address issues such as delayed pickups or route deviations. This integration ensures a seamless real-time information flow, enhancing operational efficiency and user satisfaction.

5. **Monitor and Optimize:** The engineering team closely monitors stream processing performance to minimize latency and maintain operational smoothness. For instance, during peak usage hours, they might adjust Kafka partitions to distribute the load evenly across servers, ensuring seamless data flow. Additionally, they fine-tune data transformation logic to handle large bursts of incoming data, such as during a sudden surge in ride requests, effectively preventing delays and maintaining real-time accuracy.

Streaming ingestion ensures that the ride-hailing app can operate in real time, delivering a seamless experience for both drivers and passengers while optimizing operational efficiency.

By following these steps, the retail company ensures that all its daily sales data is consolidated, cleaned, and ready for use in morning reports and dashboards. Batch ingestion streamlines this process and provides a scalable solution for handling increasing data volumes as the business expands.

Now that we've covered batch ingestion with a practical example, let's explore streaming ingestion and its applications for real-time data processing.

Batch vs. Streaming Ingestion

When deciding between batch and streaming ingestion, understanding the key differences and use cases of each approach is critical. Below is an explanation of their distinctions, along with a comparison table for clarity.

Batch Ingestion

Batch ingestion involves collecting and processing data in discrete intervals or chunks. This approach is ideal for tasks where real-time processing is not required, such as generating periodic reports, analyzing historical data, or creating backups. Data is ingested and processed at scheduled times, ensuring consistency and completeness.

Streaming Ingestion

Streaming ingestion processes data continuously as it is generated. It best suits scenarios requiring real-time insights, such as monitoring live events, powering real-time dashboards, or detecting anomalies. Streaming ingestion provides immediate access to fresh data, enabling organizations to respond to events as they happen.

Table 3-1 offers a concise comparison to help determine which ingestion method best suits your requirements. Both methods can coexist in a hybrid system, addressing varying needs within a single organization.

Table 3-1. Comparison Between Batch and Streaming Ingestion

Feature	Batch Ingestion	Streaming Ingestion
Data Processing	Processes data in chunks or intervals.	Processes data continuously in real time.
Use Cases	Historical data analysis, periodic reporting.	Real-time dashboards, fraud detection.
Latency	High latency; results are available after a certain interval.	Low latency; near-instantaneous results.
System Load	Optimized for off-peak hours to reduce load.	Continuous load, requiring scalable infrastructure.
Complexity	More straightforward to implement and manage.	Requires advanced tools and monitoring.
Examples	Monthly income statements and daily sales reports.	Livestock prices, ride-hailing apps.
Tools	Apache Spark, Azure Data Factory.	Apache Kafka, Azure Event Hubs.

Standard Data Ingestion Tools and Methods

Organizations employ various tools to streamline data ingestion based on their unique requirements. Below are some of the most common tools and methods used in modern data pipelines, along with expanded details to provide a comprehensive understanding of their capabilities and applications:

> **Apache Kafka:** Apache Kafka is a powerful tool for real-time data streaming and message brokering. It excels in scenarios where high-throughput and fault tolerance are critical. Kafka organizes data into partitions, ensuring that information flows reliably and in order, even during periods of heavy traffic. For example, a ride-sharing app can use Kafka to process real-time driver locations and match them with passenger requests, ensuring efficient and seamless operations.

Additionally, Kafka's architecture makes it ideal for applications in finance, where real-time processing of transactions and fraud detection are essential.

Apache NiFi: Apache NiFi is an easy-to-use tool known for its drag-and-drop interface, which simplifies the creation of data workflows. It is particularly effective for routing and transforming data from diverse sources, such as APIs, databases, and files, without needing extensive coding expertise. For example, a smart home company might use NiFi to route temperature and humidity data from IoT sensors to a centralized dashboard, enabling real-time adjustments and monitoring.

Azure Data Factory: Azure Data Factory is a tool designed to help organizations efficiently move and transform data. It supports batch and streaming workflows, making it versatile for various use cases. For example, a retail chain can use Azure Data Factory to collect sales data from multiple stores and load it into a centralized data warehouse. Its visual interface makes setting up workflows straightforward for users without extensive technical skills. Built-in connectors for on-premises and cloud systems ensure seamless data integration, enabling automated transformations such as converting raw sales figures into detailed financial reports.

Databricks Auto Loader: This tool automatically identifies and loads new or updated files from cloud storage into your data pipeline. Thus, you don't have to manually monitor or configure file uploads. For example, a company managing daily sales data can rely on Auto Loader to detect and ingest these files as soon as they are uploaded. It works seamlessly with Delta Lake to ensure data consistency and high performance, making it ideal for scenarios that require handling growing data volumes efficiently.

AWS Glue: AWS Glue is a cloud-based tool that simplifies data movement and preparation. It benefits organizations that utilize AWS services such as S3, Redshift, or Lambda. For example, an ecommerce company could utilize AWS Glue to merge customer purchase records stored in S3 with inventory data in Redshift, thereby creating detailed sales reports. With its serverless design, Glue automatically handles infrastructure, making it easier to process data without worrying about setup or scaling. Glue also adapts quickly to changes in data format, ensuring reliable integration and cataloging for enterprise-scale data projects.

Google Cloud Dataflow: Google Cloud Dataflow is a cloud-based tool designed to simplify how organizations process data, whether in large chunks or real-time streams. It automatically adjusts resources, utilizing features like autoscaling, to ensure seamless operations even as data volumes fluctuate. For example, consider a manufacturing company utilizing Dataflow to monitor IoT sensors on its equipment. These sensors continuously send data on temperature and vibration. Dataflow processes this information in real time, identifying patterns that may indicate potential equipment failures. This enables the company to schedule maintenance before breakdowns occur, saving costs and preventing downtime.

Each tool serves specific use cases, from handling streaming data for real-time analytics to managing batch workflows for periodic reporting. The choice of tool depends on factors such as data volume, latency requirements, and integration with existing systems, ensuring that the ingestion pipeline effectively meets organizational goals. Table 3-2 shows the strengths and use cases for each tool.

Table 3-2. *Strengths and Use Cases of Each Tool*

Tool	Best For	Strengths	Example Use Case
Apache Kafka	Real-time streaming	High throughput, fault tolerance, and partitioned data handling	Processing live driver locations in ride-sharing apps
Apache NiFi	Workflow automation for diverse sources	Drag-and-drop interface supports APIs, databases, and files	Routing IoT sensor data to a central dashboard
Azure Data Factory	Hybrid data integration	Prebuilt connectors, batch, and streaming workflows	Consolidating retail store sales into a data warehouse
Databricks Auto Loader	Incremental file ingestion	Automates the detection of new files and integrates with Delta Lake	Loading daily sales files into analytics pipelines
AWS Glue	ETL in AWS environments	Serverless, dynamic schema evolution, AWS ecosystem integration	Combining purchase records with inventory data
Google Cloud Dataflow	Real-time and batch data processing	Autoscaling, real-time IoT data processing	Monitoring factory equipment for predictive maintenance

Data Cleaning and Transformation

Imagine building a house with flawed materials—cracked bricks, warped wood, or weak concrete. No matter how well-designed the structure, it is bound to fail. Similarly, messy, incomplete, or inconsistent data will lead to flawed analyses and unreliable insights. Data cleaning and transformation are the foundation for any successful data-driven project, ensuring that raw data is refined into a trustworthy asset.

This section will explore how to prepare your data effectively, focusing on techniques to clean and preprocess it. Mastering these skills can turn raw, unstructured data into high-quality, analysis-ready information.

Techniques for Data Cleaning and Preprocessing

In this section, we will discuss various data cleansing and preprocessing problems and their solution.

Handling Missing Values

- **Problem**: Missing values occur when data points are absent, leaving gaps in datasets. This issue can arise for various reasons, such as incomplete data entry, system errors, or merging datasets with inconsistent fields. Missing values can skew analyses by reducing the sample size, biasing model predictions, and weakening statistical reliability.

- **Effect**: For instance, if a dataset of customer orders has missing values in the "price" column, calculating average revenue or predicting future sales trends becomes unreliable. Models trained on incomplete data may produce biased results, which can impact decision-making processes.

- **Solution and Techniques**

    1. **Imputation**

        - Replace missing values with statistical measures, such as the mean, median, or mode.

        - Example code (Python with Pandas):

        ```
        import pandas as pd
        df = pd.DataFrame({'Price': [100, 200, None, 150]})
        df['Price'] = df['Price'].fillna(df['Price'].mean())
        print(df)
        # Output: [100, 200, 150 (mean), 150]
        ```

        This code demonstrates how to handle missing values by replacing them with the mean of the column. In this example, the "Price" column has a missing value (None), which is filled with the mean of the existing prices. This ensures that the dataset remains complete and avoids biases that can be caused by excluding incomplete rows.

Forward/Backward Fill (Time-Series Data)

Missing values in time-series data can disrupt continuity and lead to inaccurate analysis or modeling. For example, missing stock prices or weather readings can hinder trend detection and forecasting.

- **How It Works**: Forward-fill replaces missing values with the most recent valid value, while backward-fill uses the next valid value in the series. These methods are especially useful for time-dependent datasets, ensuring that trends are preserved even when data gaps exist.

```
import pandas as pd

data = {'Temperature': [30, 32, None, 35, None]}
df = pd.DataFrame(data)
df['Temperature'] = df['Temperature'].fillna(method='ffill')
print(df)
# Output:
#     Temperature
# 0         30.0
# 1         32.0
# 2         32.0 (forward-filled)
# 3         35.0
# 4         35.0 (forward-filled)
```

This code demonstrates how forward-fill fills missing values using the last recorded data point. Similarly, using `method='bfill'` applies backward-fill to use the next available value. These techniques ensure missing data doesn't break continuity, which is critical for trend analysis or visualization.

Row/Column Removal

- **Problem**: Missing values in a dataset can often constitute only a tiny percentage of the total data, yet they may disrupt analysis and model training. Excessive missing values in rows or columns can also compromise the reliability of insights derived from the dataset.

- **Effect**: Consider a survey dataset where specific questions have missing responses. Rows with many missing entries can skew averages or correlations, while columns with missing data might reduce the significance of variables in predictive modeling.

- **Solution**: Removing rows or columns with excessive missing values is practical when they do not contribute significantly to the analysis. This method ensures a cleaner dataset without introducing bias from imputations.

```
import pandas as pd

# Example dataset
data = {'Name': ['Alice', 'Bob', None], 'Age': [25, None, 30],
'Score': [85, 90, None]}
df = pd.DataFrame(data)

# Drop rows with any missing values
df_cleaned = df.dropna()
print(df_cleaned)

# Output: Only rows with complete data remain
```

By strategically removing rows or columns, you can focus on the most reliable portions of the dataset, enabling accurate and efficient analysis.

Removing Duplicates

- **Problem**: Duplicated records occur when the same data point is recorded multiple times in a dataset. This can happen due to system errors, repeated data imports, or merging datasets without proper deduplication. Duplicate records inflate the dataset size, increasing storage and processing costs, and distort analytics and decision-making by introducing redundant information.

- **Effect**: For instance, in a sales dataset, if a single transaction appears multiple times, it can overestimate revenue or sales volume, leading to flawed business strategies. Similarly, in customer data, duplicates can result in ineffective marketing campaigns that target the same individual multiple times.

CHAPTER 3 DATA PREPARATION AND MANAGEMENT

- **Solution and Techniques**

  1. **Using SQL DISTINCT**

     - Identify and remove duplicates by selecting unique rows in a dataset.

     ```
     SELECT DISTINCT *
         FROM SalesData;
     ```

  2. **Using Pandas' drop_duplicates()**

     - The drop_duplicates() method efficiently removes duplicate rows from a data frame in Python.

     ```
     import pandas as pd
     data = {'OrderID': [1, 2, 2, 3], 'Amount': [100, 200, 200, 300]}
     df = pd.DataFrame(data)
     df = df.drop_duplicates()
     print(df)
     # Output: Unique rows only
     ```

  3. **Domain-Specific Deduplication**

     - Apply logic specific to the dataset, such as comparing records based on a combination of fields (e.g., name, email, and phone number in customer data). For example, in a customer relationship management (CRM) system, duplicates might occur if the same individual is recorded multiple times due to variations in data entry. This can result in inefficient marketing campaigns targeting the same customer multiple times, wasting resources. The challenge lies in accurately identifying duplicates when slight variations exist, such as typos or variations in format. To address this, implement domain-specific deduplication rules, such as fuzzy matching techniques or leveraging unique identifiers like email addresses or phone numbers, to streamline the dataset.

     ```
     df = df.drop_duplicates(subset=['Name', 'Email'])
     ```

The code ensures that each combination of "Name" and "Email" is unique in the dataset. Only the first occurrence is retained if multiple rows share the same "Name" and "Email". Here, the drop_duplicates() function from Pandas efficiently identifies and removes duplicates based on the specified subset of columns. In customer datasets, this helps prevent double-counting individuals and sending duplicate messages in marketing campaigns.

Using these techniques, you can eliminate duplicate records, ensuring the dataset remains accurate and streamlined for analysis.

Standardizing Data Types

- **Problem:** Inconsistent data types occur when a dataset contains mixed formats for the same information. For example, a "Date" column might include a mix of text strings, such as "2023-01-01", and numerical representations, like 20230101. These inconsistencies can cause errors when performing calculations, aggregations, or visualizations.

- **Effect:** If left unaddressed, inconsistent data types can disrupt data pipelines, lead to incorrect analyses, and hinder compatibility with downstream tools or algorithms. For instance, attempting to sort dates with mixed formats may result in nonsensical orderings or outright processing failures.

- **Solution and Techniques**
    - **Data Type Conversion**
        1. Ensure that all entries in a column adhere to the intended format, such as converting text-based dates to a proper datetime object.

           ```
           import pandas as pd

           data = {'Date': ['2023-01-01', '20230102', '01/03/2023']}
           df = pd.DataFrame(data)

           df['Date'] = pd.to_datetime(df['Date'], errors='coerce')
           print(df)
           ```

```
# Output: Standardized datetime format
  Date
0 2023-01-01
1 2023-01-02
2 2023-01-03
```

- **Handling Mixed Numerical Types**

  Convert columns with mixed integers and floats to a consistent format, ensuring compatibility during calculations. Inconsistent data types within a column can cause issues during calculations, aggregations, or when feeding data into machine learning models. For example, if a column contains both integers (e.g., 100) and floats (e.g., 100.5), operations such as averaging may yield unexpected results or errors. The .astype(float) method converts all the values in the specified column to the float data type. This ensures uniformity, which is critical for numeric computations and downstream processing. For example, consider a dataset where the "Price" column has values like [100, 200.5, 300]. While most values are integers, a single float can cause operations to become inconsistent.

  ```
  df['Price'] = df['Price'].astype(float)
  ```

  After this code is executed, all values in the "Price" column will be represented as floats, e.g., [100.0, 200.5, 300.0].

- **Validating Data Types**

  Use validation techniques to detect and resolve discrepancies before analysis.

  ```
  print(df.dtypes)
  # Output: Verifies data types for all columns
  ```

  By addressing inconsistent data types, you can ensure smoother processing, accurate analytics, and greater compatibility with data tools and machine learning workflows.

Outlier Detection and Handling

- **Problem**: Outliers are extreme values in a dataset that deviate significantly from other observations. These can occur due to errors in data entry, equipment malfunctions, or rare but valid events. For example, in a dataset of house prices where most values range between $200,000 and $800,000, a $10 million entry would be an outlier. Such anomalies can distort statistical metrics, such as the mean, and negatively impact the performance of machine learning models by introducing bias.

- **Effect**: Outliers can skew summary statistics, such as increasing the mean unrealistically, leading to incorrect insights. For instance, a single unusually high transaction in sales data could lead to overestimated revenue predictions. In machine learning, these extreme values can cause models to overfit or misinterpret patterns, reducing overall accuracy.

- **Solution and Techniques**

    1. **Identifying Outliers**

        Use statistical methods such as z-scores or the interquartile range (IQR) to identify outliers.

        ```
        import pandas as pd
        import numpy as np

        data = {'Price': [200, 300, 250, 10000, 275]}
        df = pd.DataFrame(data)

        Q1 = df['Price'].quantile(0.25)
        Q3 = df['Price'].quantile(0.75)
        IQR = Q3 - Q1
        lower_bound = Q1 - 1.5 * IQR
        upper_bound = Q3 + 1.5 * IQR

        outliers = df[(df['Price'] < lower_bound) | (df['Price'] > upper_bound)]
        print(outliers)
        # Output: Rows with outliers
        ```

The first quartile (Q1) represents the 25th percentile, and the third quartile (Q3) represents the 75th percentile of the data. The interquartile range (IQR) is the difference between the third quartile (Q3) and the first quartile (Q1). Lower bound: Q1 - 1.5 * IQR → Any value below this is considered an outlier.

Upper bound: Q3 + 1.5 * IQR → Any value above this is considered an outlier. The DataFrame is filtered to include only rows where the Price is outside these bounds (either less than lower_bound or greater than upper_bound).

2. **Capping Outliers**

   This technique involves replacing extreme values (outliers) in a dataset with the nearest acceptable boundary, such as the upper or lower bound of the interquartile range (IQR). This approach ensures that outliers do not disproportionately influence statistical measures or machine learning models while retaining all rows in the dataset. For example, if a product price dataset has an upper boundary of $500 and a record shows $10,000, this value can be capped at $500 to mitigate its impact. This method is beneficial when removing rows is undesirable, such as maintaining data continuity for time-series analysis or preserving the dataset size for small datasets.

   ```
   df['Price'] = np.where(df['Price'] > upper_bound, upper_bound, df['Price'])
   ```

3. **Excluding Outliers**

   Removing rows with outlier values ensures the dataset reflects typical trends without being skewed by extreme or erroneous data points. This approach is beneficial for maintaining the integrity of statistical analyses or machine learning models, where outliers can lead to inaccurate predictions or distorted metrics. By excluding these rows, you ensure the dataset better represents the underlying patterns of the data. Example code:

   ```
   df = df[(df['Price'] >= lower_bound) & (df['Price'] <= upper_bound)]
   ```

It keeps only the rows in the DataFrame (df) where the value in the "Price" column falls within a specified range, defined by the lower_bound and upper_bound. The logical conditions (df['Price'] >= lower_bound) and (df['Price'] <= upper_bound) ensure that only rows meeting these conditions are retained. It removes rows with outlier values that lie outside the interquartile range (IQR), helping to clean the dataset by excluding extreme or anomalous values.

4. **Transforming Data**

    - Apply transformations, such as logarithmic scaling, to reduce the influence of outliers.

    ```
    df['LogPrice'] = np.log(df['Price'])
        print(df)
    ```

By addressing outliers through these methods, you can maintain the integrity of your dataset, ensuring accurate analysis and reliable model predictions.

Data Normalization and Scaling

Problem: Datasets often contain features with varying scales. For instance, a "Salary" column may range from $30,000 to $150,000, while the "Years of Experience" column spans only one to ten years. Machine learning algorithms that rely on distance metrics, such as k-nearest neighbors or support vector machines, can disproportionately weigh features with larger ranges. This imbalance can lead to inaccurate predictions and suboptimal model performance.

Effect: In a dataset that predicts employee performance, features such as "Age" and "Salary" may be unequally weighted if not appropriately scaled. A higher range in "Salary" could dominate the analysis, diminishing the influence of equally essential features, such as "Age." As a result, the model may misinterpret relationships in the data, leading to skewed outcomes.

CHAPTER 3   DATA PREPARATION AND MANAGEMENT

Solution and Techniques

1. **Min-Max Scaling**

   Min-Max scaling normalizes features by scaling values to a fixed range, typically $[0,1][0, 1][0,1]$. It eliminates the dominance of larger-scale features, making them comparable to smaller-scale features. It benefits algorithms sensitive to feature magnitudes, such as k-nearest neighbors. Additionally, it supports gradient-based optimization by improving convergence speed and stability.

   ```
   from sklearn.preprocessing import MinMaxScaler
   import pandas as pd

   data = {'Salary': [30000, 50000, 150000], 'Experience': [1, 5, 10]}
   df = pd.DataFrame(data)

   scaler = MinMaxScaler()
   scaled_data = scaler.fit_transform(df)
   print(pd.DataFrame(scaled_data, columns=['Salary', 'Experience']))
   # Output: Scaled values between 0 and 1
   ```

2. **Standardization**

   Standardization transforms features with a mean of 0 and a standard deviation of 1. Unlike Min-Max scaling, it does not bind values to a specific range but ensures that all features have comparable distributions. This technique is especially effective when features follow a Gaussian distribution or when outliers are present, reducing their impact without capping them.

   ```
   from sklearn.preprocessing import StandardScaler
   import pandas as pd

   data = {'Salary': [30000, 50000, 150000], 'Experience': [1, 5, 10]}
   df = pd.DataFrame(data)
   ```

```
scaler = StandardScaler()
standardized_data = scaler.fit_transform(df)
print(pd.DataFrame(standardized_data, columns=['Salary',
'Experience']))
# Output: Standardized values
#    Salary     Experience
# 0 -1.069045  -1.069045
# 1 -0.507093   0.267261
# 2  1.576138   0.801784
```

3. **Log Transformation**

    - Log transformation is a technique used to compress the range of a dataset by applying a logarithmic scale. It helps reduce the impact of large outliers while preserving the relative differences between data points. It is beneficial for datasets with high variance, such as income, sales, or prices, where extreme values could distort analysis and model predictions.

    Why Use Log Transformation?

    - **Reduce Skewness**: Large outliers often create skewed data distributions. Log transformation compresses high values and normalizes the data.

    - **Improve Model Performance**: Log transformation ensures that machine learning algorithms work more effectively by making data more uniform.

    - **Preserve Relationships**: Unlike capping or removing outliers, log transformation maintains the order and relative distances between data points.

    ```
    import numpy as np
    import pandas as pd

    # Example dataset with large variance in 'Salary'
    data = {'Salary': [30000, 50000, 150000]}
    df = pd.DataFrame(data)
    ```

```
# Apply logarithmic transformation
df['LogSalary'] = df['Salary'].apply(lambda x: np.log(x))

print(df)
     Salary   LogSalary
0     30000   10.308953
1     50000   10.819778
2    150000   11.918391
```

By normalizing and scaling data, you can ensure that all features contribute equally to the analysis, enhancing the accuracy and fairness of your machine-learning models.

Summary of Data Cleaning and Transformation Techniques

Table 3-3 shows the summary of data cleaning and transformation techniques.

CHAPTER 3   DATA PREPARATION AND MANAGEMENT

Table 3-3. Summary of Data Cleaning and Transformation Techniques

Technique	Problem	Effect	Solution	Code Snippet Example
Handling Missing Values	Data gaps that skew analysis and reduce model accuracy.	Biased results, reduced sample size.	Imputation, forward/backward fill, or removal of rows/columns with excessive missing values.	`df['column'] = df['column'].fillna(df['column'].mean())`
Removing Duplicates	Repeated records that inflate data size and distort analysis.	Inaccurate metrics, inflated values.	Use SQL DISTINCT, `drop_duplicates()` in Pandas, or logic for domain-specific deduplication.	`df = df.drop_duplicates()`
Standardizing Data Types	Mixed data formats (e.g., text, numeric) causing processing errors.	Errors in calculations, sorting, and aggregations.	Convert columns to consistent types (e.g., `pd.to_datetime`, `astype(float)`).	`df['column'] = pd.to_datetime(df['column'])`
Outlier Detection	Extreme values distorting statistical measures and model performance.	Skewed mean, overfitting, or incorrect predictions.	Identify outliers using the IQR/z-scores; cap, exclude, or transform values as needed.	`df = df[(df['value'] >= lower_bound) & (df['value'] <= upper_bound)]`
Normalization and Scaling	Features with varying ranges affecting ML model performance.	Overemphasis on large-scale features, biased results.	Apply Min-Max scaling, standardization, or log transformation.	`df['scaled'] = scaler.fit_transform(df[['column']])`

CHAPTER 3   DATA PREPARATION AND MANAGEMENT

Tools and Libraries for Data Transformation

Data transformation is a crucial step in the data preparation process, involving the cleaning, structuring, and enriching of raw data into a usable format for analytics, machine learning (ML), and artificial intelligence (AI) applications. This section explores the most widely used tools and libraries for data transformation, categorized by their functionality and integration with data workflows.

Open Source Libraries

Open source libraries are highly adaptable and widely adopted in data transformation pipelines. Below are some key libraries:

- **Pandas**: A Python library offering powerful data manipulation and analysis capabilities. It is widely used for cleaning, aggregating, and reshaping data.

- **Apache Spark (PySpark)**: A distributed computing framework designed for large-scale data transformation and processing. PySpark is its Python API, which is ideal for handling big data transformations in a distributed environment.

- **Dask**: A library for parallel computing in Python, used for transforming large datasets that don't fit into memory.

- **NumPy**: Used for handling numerical data transformations, including mathematical and statistical operations.

Data Integration Platforms

Platforms that integrate and transform data from various sources are critical for modern workflows:

- **Databricks**: An all-in-one platform built on Apache Spark, offering robust tools for data ingestion, cleaning, and transformation within a lakehouse architecture

- **Talend**: An integration platform with a suite of data cleansing and enrichment tools, suitable for batch and real-time data transformation

- **Informatica**: A well-known tool for data integration, providing extensive data quality and transformation features

Cloud-Native Solutions

Cloud-based solutions are increasingly popular for their scalability and ease of integration:

- **Azure Data Factory**: A managed data integration service that allows for creating workflows to transform data at scale using data flows and mapping tools

- **Google Cloud Dataflow**: A serverless tool for batch and stream data transformation, leveraging the Apache Beam model

- **AWS Glue**: A serverless data integration service that simplifies discovering, preparing, and transforming data for analytics

Specialized Transformation Tools

Certain tools focus exclusively on advanced data transformation needs:

- **dbt (Data Build Tool)**: Enables data engineers to write transformations as SQL scripts, offering version control and dependency management for data transformation workflows.

- **Kettle (Pentaho Data Integration)**: A versatile data transformation and integration tool that supports various data sources.

- **Alteryx** is a user-friendly data preparation, blending, and advanced analytics platform.

Machine Learning-Driven Transformation Tools

Modern ML tools incorporate automated data transformation capabilities, significantly streamlining workflows for machine learning projects:

- **MLflow**, integrated with Databricks, automates key aspects of data preparation, including feature engineering, experiment tracking, and data preprocessing.

- **Databricks AutoML**: A powerful feature within the Databricks platform, Databricks AutoML streamlines the preparation of data for machine learning. It supports automated data transformation and feature engineering while providing transparency into the steps performed, allowing data scientists to customize and refine their pipelines.

- **Google AutoML** and **Azure AutoML**: Both tools offer automated workflows, including data transformation, to expedite model development.

Governance and Catalog Integration

For ensuring data consistency, lineage tracking, and compliance, governance tools are essential components of data workflows. They play a vital role in organizing and managing metadata, as well as ensuring regulatory compliance.

- **Unity Catalog**: A Databricks-native tool for centralized metadata and governance that streamlines data discovery and transformation across the organization.

- **Apache Atlas**: Provides metadata management and lineage tracking to help govern transformed data.

- **Microsoft Purview**: An Azure-native data governance tool that offers end-to-end data lineage tracking, metadata management, and automated discovery, ensuring compliance with data policies and regulations.

- **Collibra**: A robust enterprise-grade governance platform that manages data catalogs, ensures data quality, and facilitates regulatory compliance through workflows and automation.

- **Alation**: A data catalog solution with strong search capabilities and collaboration features that help organizations manage their data assets effectively while maintaining compliance.

- **Informatica Axon**: Part of Informatica's suite, this tool focuses on data governance by integrating metadata management, collaboration, and compliance capabilities into a unified platform.

Best Practices for Data Transformation

- Utilize scalable tools like Apache Spark to efficiently handle big data transformations.

- Leverage cloud-native solutions for distributed and automated transformation workflows.

- Incorporate governance and catalog tools like Unity Catalog, Purview, or Collibra to ensure data quality, lineage tracking, and compliance.

- Enable transparency and collaboration by integrating governance platforms into your data workflows.

By leveraging these tools and adhering to best practices, organizations can achieve robust, scalable, and compliant data transformation pipelines, laying the foundation for advanced analytics and machine learning applications.

Managing Data with Unity Catalog

Imagine a financial services company struggling with data governance across multiple teams and geographies. Each team maintains its own datasets, leading to inconsistent access controls and duplicated efforts to clean and prepare data for analysis. As a result, sensitive customer data is exposed to potential security risks, and regulatory compliance audits become daunting.

Unity Catalog addresses this challenge by centralizing governance and providing a unified solution for managing data assets. With its role-based access control (RBAC), the company can enforce fine-grained permissions at the table, row, or column level, ensuring that sensitive data is accessible only to authorized users. Moreover, Unity Catalog's data lineage feature helps track the flow of customer data from ingestion to reporting, providing transparency and simplifying compliance. By consolidating metadata and standardizing policies, Unity Catalog eliminates silos, reduces redundancies, and secures the organization's data landscape, enabling teams to collaborate efficiently and focus on delivering business insights.

Key Problems Unity Catalog Solves

1. **Data Silos**: Consider a retail organization using Databricks workspaces across different departments. For instance, the marketing team manages customer engagement data while the finance team handles transaction records in separate Databricks environments. This fragmented approach leads to data silos as teams struggle to share and access data efficiently. Unity Catalog resolves this by integrating these workspaces into a unified governance framework. It provides a centralized metadata layer, allowing all teams to access the same datasets with consistent policies. Enabling fine-grained access controls ensures that sensitive financial data is only accessible to authorized personnel, while marketing can leverage aggregated insights. This approach not only eliminates silos but also fosters collaboration and drives better business decisions.

2. **Inconsistent Data Governance**: Imagine a healthcare organization managing patient records and research data across different teams. Without a unified governance framework, one department might allow open access to all staff for research datasets, while another restricts even authorized users from accessing patient records unless manually approved. This inconsistency leads to confusion, delays, and potential breaches of HIPAA regulations. Unity Catalog resolves this by enforcing consistent access controls and governance policies. For example,

it allows the organization to define and apply row-level and column-level permissions, ensuring that patient identifiers are visible only to authorized clinicians. At the same time, anonymized data is accessible to researchers. This consistent policy enforcement secures data, streamlines compliance efforts, and fosters stakeholder trust.

3. **Data Discoverability**: Consider a data science team in a manufacturing company trying to analyze production efficiency. Without a centralized system, team members waste hours searching for datasets scattered across different projects and cloud workspaces. Often, they end up duplicating datasets due to a lack of visibility into existing resources. Unity Catalog solves this by providing a centralized metadata layer, making searching for and discovering datasets easy. For example, a data scientist can quickly locate historical production logs and real-time sensor data using a keyword-based search in Unity Catalog. It reduces duplication, saves time, and enhances team productivity.

4. **Complex Permission Management**: Imagine a global ecommerce company with analysts and data scientists accessing customer purchase data. Without a streamlined permissions system, every team might request access to the entire dataset, risking exposure to sensitive customer details such as credit card numbers. For example, the marketing team only needs aggregated purchase trends, while the fraud detection team requires row-level access to flagged transactions. Unity Catalog simplifies this complexity by enabling role-based access control (RBAC). It allows administrators to assign fine-grained access permissions—granting the marketing team access to only aggregated data and the fraud team access to specific flagged rows. It ensures data security, meets compliance requirements, and prevents unauthorized access.

CHAPTER 3   DATA PREPARATION AND MANAGEMENT

How Unity Catalog Works

Unity Catalog is a central governance layer that integrates with the Databricks Lakehouse architecture. It allows organizations to

- **Define policies for access control, auditing, and compliance at scale**. Consider a pharmaceutical company managing clinical trial data. Without clear policies, sensitive patient information may be accessible to all employees, risking a breach of privacy regulations such as GDPR. Unity Catalog allows administrators to define specific policies, such as granting access to trial data only to authorized researchers while maintaining strict auditing to monitor who accesses the data and when. It ensures compliance, protects sensitive information, and builds trust with stakeholders.

- **Use a shared metadata model to ensure that all data users access the same information**. A shared metadata model is a centralized framework that enables all data users in an organization to access the same underlying metadata about datasets. This model ensures that different teams working on the same data have consistent definitions and attributes, reducing discrepancies and inefficiencies.

  For example, the operations team might need shipment status data from a logistics company, while the finance team may require shipping cost details. Without a shared metadata model, both teams may independently maintain records for the same shipments, resulting in duplicate efforts and potential inconsistencies in the data.

  Both teams access a unified data view with Unity Catalog's shared metadata model. Metadata, such as shipment ID, status, and costs, are centrally managed, ensuring that all teams reference the exact source of truth. It eliminates duplication, improves collaboration, and provides data consistency across departments.

  Utilize role-based access control (RBAC) and attribute-based access control (ABAC) to customize permissions based on user roles and attributes.

- **Support data lineage tracking, which helps understand data flows and dependencies**. For example, consider a banking institution managing loan applications. Data lineage tracking allows the bank to trace an applicant's data flow—from the initial collection in an online application form through credit scoring algorithms and finally into the approval system. If discrepancies arise, such as incorrect credit scores, the bank can quickly identify the source of the issue, whether it originated during data ingestion, transformation, or processing. This transparency simplifies troubleshooting and ensures regulatory compliance by providing clear documentation of data handling processes.

- **Provide native integrations with external tools and systems to streamline data governance workflows**. For example, consider an organization using Databricks for data processing and Collibra for metadata management. Unity Catalog integrates seamlessly with Collibra, enabling synchronized governance policies and consistent metadata access across platforms. It ensures that data engineers in Databricks and compliance teams using Collibra are aligned on the same data definitions and governance standards. Such integration reduces redundancy, improves collaboration, and ensures data governance workflows are streamlined and effective.

Best Practices for Data Organization and Governance

1. **Centralize Metadata Management**

    - Use Unity Catalog to centralize metadata and eliminate data silos.

    - Ensure that all metadata is up-to-date and accessible to relevant stakeholders.

2. **Adopt a Clear Data Classification Framework**

    - Classify data into public, internal, and confidential categories to align with compliance and organizational needs.

- Implement policies for handling sensitive data to ensure data security.

3. **Implement Fine-Grained Access Controls**

    - Use Unity Catalog's row-level and column-level security to restrict access based on user roles and data sensitivity.

    - Regularly review and audit access permissions to minimize risks.

4. **Enable Data Lineage Tracking**

    - Track and document the flow of data across the Lakehouse using Unity Catalog's lineage capabilities.

    - Use this information for impact analysis, compliance, and troubleshooting.

5. **Automate Governance Processes**

    - Leverage APIs and automation scripts to enforce governance policies consistently.

    - Automate routine tasks such as policy updates, access reviews, and metadata synchronization.

6. **Promote Collaboration Through Shared Data Assets**

    - Use Unity Catalog to create shared data assets accessible to cross-functional teams.

    - Encourage the use of consistent data definitions and standards across teams.

7. **Regularly Monitor and Audit Data Access**

    - Set up regular audits to track who is accessing data and how it's being used.

    - Use audit logs to detect anomalies and ensure compliance with regulatory requirements.

8. **Educate and Train Teams on Governance Tools**

    - Conduct training sessions to help teams understand Unity Catalog's features and governance capabilities.

    - Establish a culture of data stewardship to promote responsibility and accountability among data users.

By leveraging Unity Catalog effectively, organizations can ensure robust data governance, improve collaboration, and unlock the full potential of their data assets within the Databricks Lakehouse environment.

Hands-On Labs
Exercise 1: Batch Processing with Databricks

Objective

In this exercise, you will learn how to process batch data using Databricks. The goal is to simulate the data pipeline of a retail organization that manages sales data from multiple stores. Specifically, we aim to

1. **Create a directory structure in Databricks File System (DBFS)** to store data files.

2. **Generate and manage sample batch data** for two stores in different file formats: CSV for Store A and JSON for Store B.

3. **Ingest data into Spark DataFrames** and save them as Delta tables for structured querying and analytics.

4. **Combine data from multiple sources** into a consolidated table to provide a unified view of sales.

This exercise mimics real-world scenarios where data engineers work with multiple data sources, standardize the formats, and consolidate the data for downstream analytics or reporting. By the end of this exercise, you will be equipped to handle batch data pipelines using Databricks utilities, Spark, and SQL.

CHAPTER 3   DATA PREPARATION AND MANAGEMENT

Step 1: Create Directories in DBFS

In this step, we create directories in DBFS to store our batch files. These directories will house the CSV and JSON files representing data from different stores.

```python
# Define the directory path
directory_path = "dbfs:/FileStore/tables/stores"

# Check if the directory exists
if not any(file.name == "stores/" for file in dbutils.fs.ls("dbfs:/FileStore/tables/")):
    # Create the directory if it does not exist
    dbutils.fs.mkdirs(directory_path)

# Verify the directory creation
dbutils.fs.ls("dbfs:/FileStore/tables/")

storesPath="dbfs:/storesData"
# Check if the directory exists
if not any(file.name == "storesData/" for file in dbutils.fs.ls("dbfs:/")):
    # Create the directory if it does not exist
    dbutils.fs.mkdirs(storesPath)

# Verify the directory creation
dbutils.fs.ls("dbfs:/")
```

Step 2: Write Sample Data for Store A to CSV

Here, we create a sample dataset for Store A and save it as a CSV file in the previously created directory.

```python
import pandas as pd

# Define the directory path
storesPath = "dbfs:/storesData"

# Create a sample dataset for Store A in CSV format
store_a_data = {
    "ProductID": [101, 102, 103, 104],
    "ProductName": ["Widget", "Gadget", "Thingamajig", "Doohickey"],
```

CHAPTER 3　DATA PREPARATION AND MANAGEMENT

```python
    "QuantitySold": [15, 25, 35, 45],
    "SalesAmount": [150.0, 250.0, 350.0, 450.0],
    "TransactionDate": ["2023-01-01", "2023-01-02", "2023-01-03",
    "2023-01-04"]
}

# Convert the data into a Pandas DataFrame
store_a_df = pd.DataFrame(store_a_data)

# Convert DataFrame to CSV string
csv_data = store_a_df.to_csv(index=False)

# Write CSV data to DBFS
file_path = f"{storesPath}/store_a.csv"
dbutils.fs.put(file_path, csv_data, overwrite=True)

# Verify the file creation
dbutils.fs.ls(storesPath)
```

Step 3: Write Sample Data for Store B to JSON

In this step, we create a sample dataset for Store B and save it as a JSON file in the directory.

```python
import json

# Sample JSON data for Store B
store_b_data = [
    {"ProductID": 201, "ProductName": "Gizmo", "QuantitySold": 10,
    "SalesAmount": 100.0, "TransactionDate": "2023-01-01"},
    {"ProductID": 202, "ProductName": "Contraption", "QuantitySold": 20,
    "SalesAmount": 200.0, "TransactionDate": "2023-01-02"}
]

# Convert the JSON data to a string
json_data = json.dumps(store_b_data, indent=4)

# Define the file path
file_path = f"{storesPath}/store_b.json"
```

CHAPTER 3 DATA PREPARATION AND MANAGEMENT

```
# Write the JSON data to DBFS
dbutils.fs.put(file_path, json_data, overwrite=True)

# Verify the file creation
dbutils.fs.ls(storesPath)
```

Step 4: Load Data into Spark DataFrames and Save As Delta Tables

We load the CSV and JSON data into Spark DataFrames, process the data, and save them as Delta tables.

```
from pyspark.sql.functions import *
from pyspark.sql.types import *
spark.sql("CREATE catalog IF NOT EXISTS Chapter3")
# Create schema if it does not exist
spark.sql("USE catalog Chapter3"); spark.sql("CREATE SCHEMA IF NOT EXISTS exercise1")

# Load CSV data
store_a_df = (spark.read
              .format("csv")
              .option("header", "true")
              .load(storesPath+"/store_a.csv"))

display(store_a_df)
# Load JSON data
store_b_df = (spark.read
              .format("json").schema("ProductID INT, ProductName STRING,
              QuantitySold INT, SalesAmount DOUBLE, TransactionDate STRING")
              .load(storesPath+"/store_b.json"))

display(store_b_df)

# Save dataframes as tables in the specified schema
store_a_df.write.format("delta").saveAsTable("Chapter3.exercise1.sales_store_a")
store_b_df.write.format("delta").saveAsTable("Chapter3.exercise1.sales_store_b")
```

CHAPTER 3　DATA PREPARATION AND MANAGEMENT

Step 5: Query the Delta Tables

Use Spark SQL to query the Delta tables, and view the data for Store A and Store B.

```
%sql

select * from Chapter3.exercise1.sales_store_a ;
```

Step 6: Query the Delta Tables

Use Spark SQL to query the Delta tables, and view the data for Store B.

```
%sql

select * from Chapter3.exercise1.sales_store_b
```

Step 7: Consolidate Data into a New Table

Combine data from Store A and Store B into a single consolidated Delta table.

```
%sql
USE exercise1;

-- Drop the table if it already exists
DROP TABLE IF EXISTS consolidated_sales;

-- Create the consolidated_sales table
CREATE TABLE consolidated_sales AS
(SELECT *
FROM sales_store_a
UNION ALL
SELECT *
FROM sales_store_b)
```

Step 8: Verify Consolidated Data

Query the consolidated_sales table to verify that the data has been combined correctly.

```
%sql
select * from consolidated_sales
```

CHAPTER 3   DATA PREPARATION AND MANAGEMENT

Exercise 2: Streaming Data Processing in Databricks

Objective

In this exercise, you will learn how to work with streaming data in Databricks. The goal is to demonstrate Databricks' capabilities to handle real-time data ingestion, processing, and storage using Spark Structured Streaming. Specifically, you will

1. Simulate real-time data streams for sales data.
2. Process streaming data, and save it into Delta tables.
3. Perform real-time queries on the streaming data.

Scenario

You are tasked with setting up a real-time data processing pipeline for a retail organization. The organization wants to capture live sales data streams from multiple stores. Your job is to ingest the streaming data, process it in near real time, and save it into a Delta table for analysis.

Step 1: Simulate Real-Time Data Streams

In this step, we simulate a real-time data stream by generating mock sales data. Each record is written to a directory as a JSON file to mimic a live data feed.

- Define paths for streaming.
- Clean up any existing data directories, if any, and recreate new directories.

```
import json
import time
from pyspark.sql.types import StructType, StructField, StringType, IntegerType, LongType

# Step 1: Define paths for streaming
streaming_dir = "dbfs:/FileStore/tables/stream_data/"
checkpoint_path = "dbfs:/FileStore/checkpoints/streaming_query/"
delta_table_path = "dbfs:/FileStore/tables/streaming_table/"

# Step 2: Clean up any existing data
dbutils.fs.rm(streaming_dir, recurse=True)
```

CHAPTER 3   DATA PREPARATION AND MANAGEMENT

```
dbutils.fs.rm(checkpoint_path, recurse=True)
dbutils.fs.rm(delta_table_path, recurse=True)

dbutils.fs.mkdirs(streaming_dir)
dbutils.fs.mkdirs(checkpoint_path)
dbutils.fs.mkdirs(delta_table_path)
```

Step 2: Define the Schema and Load Streaming Data

Define the schema for the incoming streaming data, and load it into a Spark DataFrame. This will serve as the entry point for further processing.

```
import json
import time
from pyspark.sql.types import StructType, StructField, StringType, IntegerType, LongType

# Step 2: Generate mock streaming data
for i in range(5):
    data = {"product": f"Product-{i}", "quantity": i * 10, "timestamp": int(time.time())}
    file_path = f"{streaming_dir}stream_data_{i}.json"
    dbutils.fs.put(file_path, json.dumps(data), overwrite=True)
    time.sleep(1)

print("Mock streaming files generated.")

#   Define schema for JSON files
schema = StructType([
    StructField("product", StringType(), True),
    StructField("quantity", IntegerType(), True),
    StructField("timestamp", LongType(), True)
])
```

Step 3: Process and Save Streaming Data to a Delta Table

Save the streaming data into a Delta table for further analysis. This step ensures the data is stored in a format optimized for analytics and querying.

CHAPTER 3   DATA PREPARATION AND MANAGEMENT

- Read streaming data.
- Write the streaming data to a Delta table.

```
# Read streaming data
streaming_df = (spark.readStream
                .format("json")
                .schema(schema)
                .load(streaming_dir))

# Write the streaming data to a Delta table
query = (streaming_df.writeStream
         .outputMode("append")
         .format("delta")
         .option("checkpointLocation", checkpoint_path)
         .trigger(availableNow=True)
         .start(delta_table_path))

# Wait for the streaming to complete
query.awaitTermination()
```

Step 4: Register and Query the Streaming Delta Table

Register the Delta table in Databricks, and use SQL to perform real-time queries on the data.

```
# Step 4: Verify the Delta table content
streaming_table_df = spark.read.format("delta").load(delta_table_path)
display(streaming_table_df)
```

Exercise 3: Handling and Cleaning Batch Data in Databricks

Objective

In this exercise, you will clean and transform batch data in Databricks to prepare it for analytics. The goal is to simulate a data pipeline that resolves missing values, duplicates, and inconsistencies.

CHAPTER 3   DATA PREPARATION AND MANAGEMENT

Scenario

You are a data engineer for a retail organization that consolidates sales data from various sources. Your task is to

1. Load raw sales data with missing and duplicate records.

2. Handle missing values and standardize the data.

3. Save the cleaned data into a Delta table for analytics.

4. Validate the data pipeline.

Step 1: Create a Directory to Host the Demo Files

Create the directory in DBFS to store the consolidated sales data if it does not exist.

```
%python
output_directory_path = "dbfs:/FileStore/tables/consolidated_sales_table"

# Check if the directory exists
try:
    dbutils.fs.ls(output_directory_path)
    # If the directory exists, delete it
    dbutils.fs.rm(output_directory_path, recurse=True)
except Exception as e:
    # If the directory does not exist, do nothing
    print(f"Directory does not exist: {e}")
    dbutils.fs.mkdirs(output_directory_path)
```

Step 2: Prepare Output Directory

Set up the directory in DBFS to store the consolidated sales data. If the directory exists, delete it first.

```
%python
import pandas as pd

# Define output path
output_file_path = output_directory_path+"/consolidated_sales.csv"
print(output_file_path)
```

Step 3: Generate Sample Data

Create a sample dataset with missing values and duplicates, and save it as a CSV file in the prepared directory.

```python
# Create sample data
data = {
    "ProductID": [101, 102, 103, 104, 105, 106, 101],  # Duplicate ProductID (101)
    "ProductName": ["Widget", "Gadget", "Thingamajig", "Doohickey", None, "Gizmo", "Widget"],  # Missing ProductName
    "QuantitySold": [15, None, 35, 45, 50, None, 15],  # Missing QuantitySold
    "SalesAmount": [150.0, 250.0, 350.0, 450.0, 500.0, 600.0, 150.0],
    "TransactionDate": ["2023-01-01", "2023-01-02", "2023-01-03", "2023-01-04", "2023-01-05", "2023-01-06", "2023-01-01"],  # Duplicate TransactionDate
    "timestamp": [1672531200, 1672617600, 1672704000, 1672790400, 1672876800, None, 1672531200]  # Missing timestamp
}

# Convert to Pandas DataFrame
df = pd.DataFrame(data)

# Save DataFrame to CSV as a string
csv_data = df.to_csv(index=False)

# Write the CSV string to DBFS
dbutils.fs.put(output_file_path, csv_data, overwrite=True)
```

Step 4: Check If the File Is Saved to the Directory

Verify if the file is saved or not.

```python
# List files in the directory
files = dbutils.fs.ls(output_file_path)
display(files)
```

Step 5: Load Data into a Spark DataFrame

Load the CSV data into a Spark DataFrame, and save it as a Delta table.

```
from pyspark.sql.types import *

# Define schema explicitly
schema = StructType([
    StructField("ProductID", IntegerType(), True),
    StructField("ProductName", StringType(), True),
    StructField("QuantitySold", IntegerType(), True),
    StructField("SalesAmount", FloatType(), True),
    StructField("TransactionDate", StringType(), True),
    StructField("timestamp", LongType(), True)
])

#Load the CSV data into a Spark DataFrame
consolidated_sales_df = (spark.read
                        .format("csv")
                        .option("header", "true")
                        .schema(schema)
                        .load(output_file_path))

# Save the data to a Delta table
consolidated_sales_df.write.format("delta").mode("overwrite").saveAsTable("consolidated_sales_record")
```

Step 6: Validate Data Loading

Query the Delta table to validate the loaded data.

```
%sql
show tables;

Select * from consolidated_sales_record
```

Step 7: Handle Missing Values

Identify missing values in the dataset.

CHAPTER 3 DATA PREPARATION AND MANAGEMENT

```
# Count missing values in each column
missing_values = spark.sql("""
    SELECT
        SUM(CASE WHEN ProductName IS NULL THEN 1 ELSE 0 END) AS missing_
        ProductName,
        SUM(CASE WHEN QuantitySold IS NULL THEN 1 ELSE 0 END) AS missing_
        QuantitySold,
        SUM(CASE WHEN timestamp IS NULL THEN 1 ELSE 0 END) AS missing_
        timestamp
    FROM consolidated_sales_record
""")
missing_values.show()
```

Step 8: Verify Missing Values

Verify missing values for QuantitySold, ProductName, and timestamp.

```
%sql
SELECT * from consolidated_sales_record
```

Step 9: Calculate the Median for the Available QuantitySold Values

Calculate the median for available QuantitySold values where QuantitySold is not null, and we will use this median value for the missing value:

```
%sql
  SELECT percentile_approx(QuantitySold, 0.5) AS median
    FROM consolidated_sales_record
    WHERE QuantitySold IS NOT NULL
```

Step 10: Update Missing Values

Fill missing values for

- QuantitySold with the median of QuantitySold values
- ProductName with unknown
- timestamp with 0

CHAPTER 3 DATA PREPARATION AND MANAGEMENT

```python
default_median_quantity = 10
spark.sql(f"""
    UPDATE consolidated_sales_record
    SET QuantitySold = {default_median_quantity}
    WHERE QuantitySold IS NULL
    """)

# Fill missing QuantitySold with the median
median_quantity = spark.sql("""
   SELECT percentile_approx(QuantitySold, 0.5) AS median
    FROM consolidated_sales_record
    WHERE QuantitySold IS NOT NULL
    """).collect()[0]["median"]
print(median_quantity)

# Fill missing ProductName with 'Unknown'
spark.sql("""
    UPDATE consolidated_sales_record
    SET ProductName = 'Unknown'
    WHERE ProductName IS NULL
    """)

# Fill missing timestamp with 0
spark.sql("""
    UPDATE consolidated_sales_record
    SET timestamp = 0
    WHERE timestamp IS NULL
    """)
```

Step 11: Analyze the Cleaned Data

Perform basic analytics to validate the cleaning process.

```sql
%sql
SELECT COUNT(*) AS total_records,
       SUM(CASE WHEN QuantitySold IS NULL THEN 1 ELSE 0 END) AS
       missing_values,
       AVG(QuantitySold) AS average_quantity
FROM consolidated_sales_record;
```

Exercise 4: Managing Data with Unity Catalog in Databricks

Objective

In this exercise, you will learn how to manage and govern data using the Databricks Unity Catalog. The goal is to demonstrate the organization, security, and access to data using catalogs, schemas, and role-based permissions.

Scenario

You are a data engineer organizing and standardizing cleaned sales data in a centralized catalog. The objective is to

1. Create a catalog and schema for organizing data.

2. Save cleaned and standardized data into Delta tables.

3. Assign role-based permissions to groups for controlled access.

4. Validate data organization and permissions.

This exercise will highlight how Unity Catalog simplifies data governance and collaboration across teams.

Step 1: Load and Standardize Data

Load cleaned sales data into a DataFrame, transform timestamps into readable dates, and prepare the data for storage in Unity Catalog.

```
from pyspark.sql.functions import from_unixtime

# Example cleaned data
data = [
    (101, "Widget", 15, 150.0, 1672531200),
    (102, "Gadget", 25, 250.0, 1672617600),
    (103, "Thingamajig", 35, 350.0, 1672704000),
    (104, "Doohickey", 45, 450.0, 1672790400),
    (105, "Gizmo", 50, 550.0, 1672876800),
]
columns = ["ProductID", "ProductName", "QuantitySold", "SalesAmount", "timestamp"]
```

```python
# Create a DataFrame
cleaned_sales_df = spark.createDataFrame(data, columns)

# Convert timestamp to human-readable date
standardized_sales_df = cleaned_sales_df.withColumn(
    "TransactionDate", from_unixtime("timestamp").cast("date")
)

# Drop the raw timestamp column
standardized_sales_df = standardized_sales_df.drop("timestamp")
```

Step 2: Create a Catalog

Use SQL commands to create a catalog for organizing the data.

```
%sql
CREATE CATALOG IF NOT EXISTS retail_data_catalog;
```

Step 3: Create a Schema

Use SQL commands to create a schema inside the catalog for organizing the data.

```
%sql
CREATE SCHEMA IF NOT EXISTS retail_data_catalog.retail_data_schema;
```

Step 4: Save Data to Unity Catalog

Save the standardized sales data as a Delta table in the specified catalog and schema.

```python
# Save the table in the default schema as standardized_sales
standardized_sales_df.write.format("delta").mode("overwrite").
saveAsTable("retail_data_catalog.retail_data_schema.standardized_sales")
```

Step 5: Query the Standardized Data

Verify the data by querying the Delta table.

```
%sql
Select * from retail_data_catalog.retail_data_schema.standardized_sales
```

Step 6: Verify Table Organization

Display all tables in the schema to ensure the data is correctly organized.

```
%sql
SHOW TABLES IN retail_data_catalog.retail_data_schema;
```

Step 7: Create User Groups

Create user groups for managing permissions.

```
# List all groups
groups = spark.sql("SHOW GROUPS").collect()

# Extract the correct field (adjust based on schema)
existing_groups = [row['name'] for row in groups]  # Replace 'name' with the actual column name

# Groups to create
groups_to_create = ["analyst_group", "engineer_group"]

# Create groups if they do not exist
for group in groups_to_create:
    if group not in existing_groups:
        spark.sql(f"CREATE GROUP {group}")
        print(f"Group '{group}' created.")
    else:
        print(f"Group '{group}' already exists.")
```

Step 8: Assign Permissions

Grant SELECT permission to analysts and MODIFY permission to engineers on the Delta table.

```
%sql
-- Grant SELECT permission to analysts
GRANT SELECT ON TABLE retail_data_catalog.retail_data_schema.standardized_sales TO `analyst_group`;
```

```
-- Grant MODIFY permission to engineers
GRANT MODIFY ON TABLE retail_data_catalog.retail_data_schema.standardized_
sales TO `engineer_group`;
```

Step 9: Validate Permissions

Verify the assigned permissions on the Delta table.

```
%sql
SHOW GRANTS ON TABLE retail_data_catalog.retail_data_schema.
standardized_sales
```

Summary

Chapter 3 laid the groundwork for building reliable, insightful, and production-ready machine learning systems by focusing on one of the most critical aspects of the data science life cycle—**data preparation and management**.

We began by exploring **data ingestion techniques**, distinguishing between **batch ingestion**—ideal for periodic, high-volume imports—and **streaming ingestion**, which enables real-time analytics and responsiveness. Through real-world scenarios such as retail sales consolidation, fraud detection, and IoT sensor monitoring, you learned how to implement each ingestion method using tools like **Azure Data Factory**, **Apache Kafka**, **Databricks Auto Loader**, and **Structured Streaming**. A comparison table summarized the trade-offs between latency, complexity, and use cases for each approach.

Next, the chapter delved into **data cleaning and transformation**—the heart of making raw data usable. You learned how to handle missing values using imputation and time-series techniques, remove duplicates, standardize data types, detect and treat outliers, and apply normalization and scaling. The chapter offered both theoretical context and hands-on implementation using **Python (Pandas, NumPy, scikit-learn)** and **SQL**. These techniques ensure that downstream analytics and models are not only reliable but also fair and accurate.

We also introduced essential **tools and libraries for data transformation**, from open source packages like **Pandas**, **PySpark**, and **Dask** to cloud-native services such as **AWS Glue**, **Google Cloud Dataflow**, and **Azure Data Factory**. Special attention

CHAPTER 3   DATA PREPARATION AND MANAGEMENT

was given to governance-ready platforms like **Databricks**, **Unity Catalog**, and **dbt**, highlighting how enterprise-grade data transformation is tightly coupled with metadata management and compliance.

A major section of the chapter focused on **governing data with Unity Catalog**, showcasing how centralized metadata, RBAC/ABAC, and lineage tracking help prevent silos, maintain consistency, and support security and compliance. Use cases across industries illustrated how Unity Catalog empowers organizations to manage sensitive data and streamline operations across teams. Best practices were also outlined to guide catalog design, access control, lineage tracking, and collaborative data stewardship.

The chapter concluded with **four hands-on labs** that provided practical exposure to

- Batch and streaming data ingestion
- Data cleaning and transformation pipelines
- Unity Catalog setup for governance and secure access

Together, these labs reinforced the theoretical concepts with real-world, end-to-end examples using **Databricks Lakehouse**.

Now that you've established a clean, well-organized, and governed data foundation, you're ready to begin the exciting journey of building machine learning models. In **Chapter 4: Building Machine Learning Models**, we shift our focus to modeling workflows, covering data splitting, model training, hyperparameter tuning, and performance evaluation. You'll learn how to select appropriate algorithms, use MLflow to manage experiments, and construct scalable pipelines that turn prepared data into intelligent predictions. Let's move from wrangling data to extracting value from it through models that learn, adapt, and drive decisions.

CHAPTER 4

Building Machine Learning Models

Machine learning models are at the core of artificial intelligence and data-driven decision-making, enabling systems to learn from data and make informed predictions. However, the process of building, training, and tracking these models can be complex, requiring robust tools and frameworks to ensure efficiency and reproducibility.

One such powerful tool is MLflow, an open source platform designed to manage the entire machine learning life cycle. MLflow helps data scientists and engineers streamline experiment tracking, model management, and deployment, particularly in collaborative environments such as Databricks.

In this chapter, you will explore how to effectively use MLflow in Databricks for model training, evaluation, and experiment tracking. You will gain hands-on experience in setting up MLflow, logging model parameters, tracking metrics, and optimizing model performance. By the end of this chapter, you will have a comprehensive understanding of MLflow's capabilities and how to integrate them seamlessly into your machine learning workflow.

Learning Objectives

By the end of this chapter, you will be able to:

- Identify fundamental components of machine learning in Databricks and how they work together.

- Understand the key features and components of MLflow.

- Learn how to set up and use MLflow in Databricks.

- Choose appropriate algorithms for model training.

- Perform hyperparameter tuning and evaluate model performance.

- Track experiments using MLflow and visualize results.

CHAPTER 4   BUILDING MACHINE LEARNING MODELS

Fundamentals of Machine Learning Models

Understanding the fundamental components of machine learning workflows is crucial for effectively managing and deploying models. Several key components work together in an ML life cycle to ensure a streamlined process, enabling efficient experimentation, model tracking, and deployment. Below are the essential components of MLflow and how they function together:

1. **Model:** A machine learning model is the foundation of AI-based decision-making. It is trained on past data to identify patterns and relationships, allowing it to make predictions on new, unseen data. Models can range from simple statistical approaches, like Linear Regression, to complex deep learning architectures used in image recognition and natural language processing.

    Imagine you want to predict the price of a house based on features like location, size, and number of bedrooms. A machine learning model can analyze past house sales and learn how these factors influence prices, allowing it to estimate prices for new listings.

2. **Experiment**: An experiment is structured to test and compare different machine learning models by running multiple trials with parameter variations, datasets, or configurations. It helps data scientists analyze and identify the best-performing model based on performance metrics.

    Suppose you are training a model to predict house prices. You can run multiple experiments where you change features like location, number of bedrooms, or different regression algorithms. Tracking these runs allows you to determine which combination yields the most accurate predictions.

3. **Artifacts**: Artifacts are the recorded outputs of an experiment, including trained models, datasets, logs, visualization plots, and performance metrics. These elements help track progress, ensure reproducibility, and provide insights into model behavior over time. By storing artifacts, data scientists can revisit past experiments, compare results, and fine-tune models based on previous findings.

Suppose you are developing a model to predict customer churn for a telecom company. During training, the system generates different model versions, accuracy reports, and confusion matrices. These are all stored as artifacts, allowing you to analyze and compare model improvements over time and decide which model to deploy in production.

4. **Runs**: A run refers to a single execution of an experiment, during which a model is trained, tested, and evaluated. Each run logs essential details such as input parameters, training configurations, evaluation metrics, and output artifacts. These logs help data scientists compare different runs and refine their models efficiently.

   Suppose you are training a model to predict house prices. You conduct multiple runs by varying the learning rate and many decision tree estimators. Each run captures performance metrics, such as accuracy and error rate, helping you determine the best configuration for your final model.

5. **Model Serving**: After a model is trained and validated, it must be deployed so it can be used for making predictions. Model serving allows the model to be accessible in real-time or batch processes, ensuring that applications can use it efficiently. MLflow offers built-in capabilities for model serving, enabling seamless deployment across various cloud platforms, APIs, and edge devices.

   Suppose you have trained a machine learning model to recommend movies based on a user's watch history. Once deployed using MLflow model serving, a streaming service can send user data to the model in real time, receiving personalized recommendations instantly. This process ensures the model continuously serves predictions as new data is provided.

6. **Model Registry**: A centralized repository that facilitates model versioning, tracking, and annotation. It ensures smooth transitions from model development to production deployment, allowing teams to manage multiple model versions efficiently.

These components work cohesively to provide a structured machine learning life cycle management approach, ensuring scalability, traceability, and reproducibility throughout the entire model development and deployment process.

Introduction to MLflow

Before diving into practical implementations, it is crucial to understand MLflow, its core functionalities, and the value it brings to machine learning practitioners. MLflow is designed to simplify and enhance the ML life cycle by providing tools for tracking experiments, packaging code into reproducible projects, and deploying models efficiently. Understanding these features allows machine learning engineers and data scientists to maintain better control over their models, ensuring reproducibility, consistency, and streamlined collaboration in research and production environments.

Key Features and Components

MLflow is an open source platform that manages the entire machine learning life cycle, including experimentation, reproducibility, model versioning, and deployment. It provides a standardized approach to managing machine learning workflows, ensuring consistency, traceability, and scalability across projects. MLflow's modularity enables users to select and utilize functionalities that best suit their workflow needs, making it a flexible and powerful tool for both research and production environments. It consists of four main components.

MLflow Tracking

Tracking is essential in machine learning because models undergo multiple iterations before achieving optimal performance. By systematically recording parameters, metrics, and artifacts, tracking ensures that experiments remain reproducible, results are comparable, and insights can be derived efficiently. Without proper tracking, it would be difficult to determine which experiment settings produced the best results or how a model has evolved over time.

MLflow Tracking is a tool that simplifies this process by allowing you to log and store parameters, metrics, and artifacts from machine learning experiments. It helps data scientists monitor model performance over time, compare different versions, and make informed decisions about model improvements. By integrating with Databricks and other ML frameworks, MLflow ensures streamlined experiment tracking, making it easy to visualize and analyze results across multiple runs.

Imagine you are training a fraud detection model for a bank. You experiment with different algorithms, adjusting hyperparameters such as learning rate and tree depth. MLflow Tracking allows you to log and compare these runs, providing insights into which combination yields the best results. This structured approach ensures that past experiments can be revisited and optimized for future improvements.

MLflow Projects

Creating a well-structured project is crucial in machine learning because it ensures consistency, reproducibility, and smooth collaboration. Without a structured approach, managing different scripts, dependencies, and configurations can become confusing and lead to inefficiencies. A well-organized project makes scaling, maintaining, and sharing code with other team members or across different environments easier.

MLflow Projects provides a standardized way to package machine learning code into reusable and shareable formats. It ensures that every project has a defined structure, making it easier to replicate experiments and collaborate efficiently.

Suppose you are working on a model to predict customer churn. Instead of manually setting up different environments whenever you or a teammate wants to run the model, you can define all dependencies and execution steps in an MLflow Project file. This ensures that anyone running the project gets the same setup, leading to consistent and reproducible results across various team members and systems.

MLflow Models

Managing machine learning models can be complex due to different environments, dependencies, and configurations. MLflow Models ensure that models are stored in a structured format, making them portable, version-controlled, and reusable across various environments.

MLflow Models provide a standardized format for packaging machine learning models, allowing them to be easily deployed across various platforms, including cloud services, edge devices, and production environments.

Structure of MLflow Models

Each MLflow model consists of

- **ML Model File:** Contains metadata about the model, including its format and dependencies.

- **Artifacts Directory**: Stores the actual model files (e.g., a saved Scikit-learn model, TensorFlow graph, or PyTorch model state).

- **Code Dependencies**: Ensure the model can be executed consistently in different environments.

MLflow Registry

Managing machine learning models across different stages of development can be challenging. Without a structured registry, tracking model versions, understanding which model is currently deployed, and comparing the performance of different iterations is difficult. A model registry provides a centralized location to store, track, and manage models throughout their life cycle. This ensures consistency, reproducibility, and efficient collaboration among teams.

MLflow Registry is a centralized model management system that enables model versioning, lineage tracking, and annotations. It enables teams to manage multiple model versions efficiently, track their performance, and seamlessly transition models from experimentation to production.

Key Features of MLflow Registry

- **Model Versioning**: Keeps track of different model versions, enabling easy rollback or comparisons.

- **Stage Transitions**: Allow models to move through different life cycle stages (e.g., Staging, Production, Archived).

- **Annotations and Descriptions**: Enable teams to add metadata and comments to models for better documentation.

- **Approval and Governance**: Helps control which models are deployed and used in production.

Step-by-Step Guide to Creating an MLflow Project in Azure Databricks

MLflow is integrated within Azure Databricks, making it easy to track experiments, manage models, and deploy machine learning solutions. Follow these steps to create and use an MLflow Project effectively.

Create a New Databricks Notebook

1. Open **Azure Databricks**.
2. Navigate to the **Workspace**.
3. Click **Create ➤ Notebook**.
4. Name the Notebook (e.g., `MLFlow_Project_Setup`).
5. Please attach it to an active cluster.

Set Up MLflow Experiment Tracking

In your Notebook, set up an MLflow experiment to organize and track your machine learning runs.

```
import mlflow

# Set up MLflow experiment
mlflow.set_experiment("/Users/your_email@databricks.com/my_mlflow_experiment")
```

Load and Prepare Data

Generate and split a sample dataset.

```
from sklearn.datasets import make_classification
from sklearn.model_selection import train_test_split

# Generate sample dataset
X, y = make_classification(n_samples=1000, n_features=10, random_state=42)
X_train, X_test, y_train, y_test = train_test_split(X, y, test_size=0.2, random_state=42)
```

Train and Log a Model Using MLflow

Train a Random Forest model and log the parameters, metrics, and the model itself.

```
from sklearn.ensemble import RandomForestClassifier

# Train a model
model = RandomForestClassifier(n_estimators=100)
model.fit(X_train, y_train)

# Start MLflow tracking
with mlflow.start_run():
    mlflow.log_param("n_estimators", 100)
    mlflow.log_metric("accuracy", model.score(X_test, y_test))
    mlflow.sklearn.log_model(model, "rf_model")
```

View MLflow Experiment Tracking UI

After running the Notebook:

1. Go to **Experiments** in the Databricks UI.
2. Select **my_mlflow_experiment**.
3. View logged parameters, metrics, and models.

Register the Model in the MLflow Registry

Register the trained model in the MLflow Model Registry to track its versions.

```
# Register the model in MLflow Registry
model_uri = "runs:/<run_id>/rf_model"
mlflow.register_model(model_uri, "RandomForestModel")
```

- Replace <run_id> with the actual run ID from the MLflow experiment.

Load and Use the Registered Model for Inference

Load the registered model and make predictions.

```
import mlflow.sklearn

# Load the registered model
loaded_model = mlflow.sklearn.load_model("models:/RandomForestModel/1")

# Make predictions
predictions = loaded_model.predict(X_test)
```

Choosing the Right Algorithm for Model Training

Selecting the appropriate machine learning algorithm is crucial for building an effective model. The choice of an algorithm depends on various factors, including the type of problem, data characteristics, and computational resources.

Why Is Choosing the Right Algorithm Important?

- **Better Accuracy:** The correct algorithm ensures the model learns effectively and provides accurate predictions.

- **Faster Training and Inference:** Some algorithms train and make predictions faster than others, which is important for real-time applications.

- **Scalability:** The right algorithm ensures your model can handle growing data efficiently.

- **Deployment Efficiency:** Some models are easier to deploy in production environments than others.

Factors to Consider When Choosing an Algorithm and Why It Is Important

Choosing the right machine learning algorithm is essential because it directly impacts the model's accuracy, efficiency, and usability. The right choice ensures that your model can effectively learn from data, make accurate predictions, and be deployed efficiently. Below are key factors to consider:

Type of Problem

a) **If you need to group data into different categories, such as identifying spam emails or classifying customer types, use classification algorithms like Logistic Regression, Random Forest, or Support Vector Machines (SVM).** Logistic Regression is simple and interpretable, making it great for smaller datasets and binary classification tasks, while Random Forest is more powerful and can handle complex patterns well, especially with larger datasets. Additionally, Random Forest provides feature importance scores, which help in understanding which variables are most significant.

b) **If you want to predict a continuous value, such as house prices or sales revenue, use regression algorithms like Linear Regression, Random Forest Regressor, or Gradient Boosting.** Linear Regression is a simple and effective method that works well when the relationship between inputs and outputs is linear. Gradient Boosting and Random Forest Regressors are more powerful and can effectively handle complex, nonlinear patterns in large datasets.

c) **Clustering algorithms, such as K-Means, help group similar data points together without predefined labels.** For example, businesses can use K-Means to segment customers based on their purchasing behavior, allowing them to target specific groups with personalized marketing strategies. However, it's important to standardize data before applying K-Means to prevent features with larger ranges from dominating the results.

Size and Quality of Data

- **Small Datasets**: If you have a small amount of data, simple models like **Logistic Regression** or **Decision Trees** work well because they require fewer data points to learn patterns.

- **Large Datasets**: If you have a large dataset, more complex models like **Neural Networks** or **Gradient Boosting** can be used, as they can handle a lot of information and capture intricate patterns.

- **Messy or Incomplete Data**: If your data contains missing values or inconsistencies, tree-based models like Random Forest are a good choice because they can still perform well even without complete data.

Interpretability vs. Accuracy

- To understand how a model makes decisions, such as why a loan application is approved or rejected, consider using **Decision Trees** or **Linear Regression**. These models are easier to interpret because they show how input variables influence predictions.

- If your goal is to achieve the highest accuracy, even if the model's decisions are more difficult to explain (such as in image recognition or language translation), consider using **deep learning models** like **Convolutional Neural Networks (CNNs)**, which can capture complex patterns in large datasets.

Computational Requirements

- **If you have limited computing power**, consider using simple models such as **Logistic Regression** or **Support Vector Machines (SVM)**. These models run efficiently on bare hardware and require less processing power.

- **If you have access to powerful hardware (like GPUs or cloud-based resources)**, you can use complex models like **deep learning**. These models require more processing power but can achieve higher accuracy, especially with large datasets.

Data Type

- **Text Data**: If working with text (such as emails, reviews, or chat messages), use **Naïve Bayes** for simple classification tasks or more advanced models like **LSTMs** and **Transformer models (BERT, GPT)** for deep text understanding.

- **Image Data**: For image-related tasks (such as object detection or facial recognition), **Convolutional Neural Networks (CNNs)** are highly effective because they can identify patterns in images.

- **Tabular Data**: When working with structured data (such as spreadsheets or databases), consider using models like Decision Trees, Random Forest, or XGBoost, which excel with both numerical and categorical data.

Selecting the appropriate machine learning algorithm is crucial for developing an effective and efficient model. The correct algorithm ensures that the model learns patterns accurately, making reliable predictions while maintaining efficiency. A well-chosen algorithm optimizes training time, enhances scalability, and ensures smooth deployment in production environments. If the wrong algorithm is selected, it can lead to poor model performance, longer training times, and difficulty in interpretability. By evaluating factors such as dataset size, problem type, computational power, and the need for interpretability, data scientists can select the most suitable model for their specific use case, ultimately enhancing decision-making and business outcomes. Please refer to GitHub for the comparison table to choose the algorithms based on different parameters.

CHAPTER 4   BUILDING MACHINE LEARNING MODELS

Task	Best Algorithms and When to Use Them	Example Use Case	Advantages	Challenges	Data Type Suitability	Interpretability	Dataset Size Requirement	Missing Data Handling	Computational Requirements	Real-World Applications	Training Time	Hyperparameter Tuning Complexity	Deployment Considerations
Classification	Logistic Regression (simple and interpretable), Random Forest (handles missing data well), XGBoost (high accuracy for large datasets)	Predicting customer churn in a telecom company	Easy to interpret (Logistic Regression), high accuracy (XGBoost)	May require feature engineering (Logistic Regression), high computation for large datasets (XGBoost).	Structured, categorical data	High (Logistic Regression), medium (Random Forest), low (XGBoost)	Small (Logistic Regression), medium to large (Random Forest, XGBoost)	Handles missing data well (Random Forest, XGBoost)	Low (Logistic Regression), medium (Random Forest), high (XGBoost)	Finance, healthcare, retail	Fast (Logistic Regression), medium (Random Forest), slow (XGBoost)	Low (Logistic Regression), high (XGBoost)	Logistic Regression and Random Forest are easy to deploy; XGBoost may require optimization.
Regression	Linear Regression (basic trend analysis), Ridge Regression (reduces overfitting), Gradient Boosting (best for complex patterns)	Predicting house prices based on historical sales data	Simple and fast (Linear Regression), handles nonlinear relationships (Gradient Boosting)	Sensitive to outliers (Linear Regression), requires parameter tuning (Gradient Boosting).	Numerical and continuous data	High (Linear Regression), medium (Ridge Regression), low (Gradient Boosting)	Small (Linear Regression), medium to large (Gradient Boosting)	Requires preprocessing for missing values	Low (Linear Regression), high (Gradient Boosting)	Real estate, sales forecasting, insurance	Fast (Linear Regression), medium (Gradient Boosting)	Low (Linear Regression), high (Gradient Boosting)	Linear Regression is easy to deploy; Gradient Boosting models require tuning.
Clustering	K-Means (when clusters are well separated), DBSCAN (handles noise and varying densities), Hierarchical Clustering (useful for hierarchical relationships)	Grouping customers based on purchasing behavior	Works well with large datasets (K-Means), identifies irregular clusters (DBSCAN)	Requires choosing the right number of clusters (K-Means), computationally expensive (Hierarchical).	Structured and unstructured data	Low	Small to large (varies by algorithm)	DBSCAN handles missing values well	Medium to high	Marketing, customer segmentation, anomaly detection	Fast (K-Means), medium (DBSCAN), slow (Hierarchical)	Medium	K-Means is easy to deploy; DBSCAN may require more computational resources.

(continued)

171

CHAPTER 4 BUILDING MACHINE LEARNING MODELS

Task	Best Algorithms and When to Use Them	Example Use Case	Advantages	Challenges	Data Type Suitability	Interpretability	Dataset Size Requirement	Missing Data Handling	Computational Requirements	Real-World Applications	Training Time	Hyperparameter Tuning Complexity	Deployment Considerations
Dimensionality Reduction	PCA (preserves variance), t-SNE (best for visualization), Autoencoders (good for deep learning)	Reducing features in an image dataset before classification	Reduces computational cost, improves visualization	t-SNE does not scale well for large datasets; PCA loses interpretability.	High-dimensional numerical data	Medium (PCA), low (Autoencoders)	Medium to large	Requires handling missing data beforehand	Medium to high	Data compression, feature engineering, image processing	Medium (PCA), slow (t-SNE)	Low (PCA), high (Autoencoders)	PCA is easy to deploy; Autoencoders require specialized infrastructure.
NLP (Text Data)	Naïve Bayes (simple text classification), Transformer models (BERT/GPT for complex language tasks)	Sentiment analysis on customer reviews	Fast and efficient for small data (Naïve Bayes), state-of-the-art performance (Transformers)	Naïve Bayes assumes feature independence; Transformers need large datasets and GPUs.	Unstructured text data	High (Naïve Bayes), low (Transformers)	Small to large	Requires preprocessing of missing values	Low (Naïve Bayes), very high (Transformers)	Chatbots, sentiment analysis, document classification	Fast (Naïve Bayes), slow (Transformers)	Low (Naïve Bayes), high (Transformers)	Naïve Bayes is easy to deploy; Transformers require high computational power.
Image Processing	CNNs (standard image classification), ResNet (deep image recognition), Vision Transformers (state-of-the-art image tasks)	Detecting objects in security camera footage	Excellent accuracy in image tasks, learns spatial hierarchies	Requires large datasets, computationally expensive.	Image and video data	Low	Large	Requires data augmentation for missing values	Very high	Healthcare (medical imaging), security, autonomous vehicles	Slow	High	Deployment requires specialized hardware (GPUs, TPUs).
Time-Series Forecasting	ARIMA (good for linear trends), LSTMs (captures long-term dependencies), Prophet (best for business forecasting)	Forecasting monthly sales for a retail company	Good for trend forecasting (ARIMA), handles seasonality well (Prophet)	ARIMA assumes stationarity; LSTMs require large datasets and tuning.	Sequential and time-dependent data	Medium (ARIMA, Prophet), low (LSTMs)	Small to large	Requires handling missing timestamps	Medium to high	Finance (stock market predictions), retail sales forecasting	Medium	High (LSTMs)	ARIMA and Prophet are easy to deploy; LSTMs require tuning.

Scenario: Choosing the Right Algorithm for Customer Churn Prediction

Business Problem

A telecommunications company is experiencing a high churn rate, meaning many customers are canceling their subscriptions. To improve customer retention, the company aims to develop a machine learning model that predicts the likelihood of a customer leaving. This will allow the company to offer personalized promotions or incentives to retain them.

Identifying the Type of Problem

Since the goal is to classify customers into **"churn"** or **"no churn,"** this is a **classification problem**. For this scenario, we will consider both **Random Forest** and **XGBoost**:

- **Random Forest:** Known for interpretability and handling missing data efficiently
- **XGBoost:** Preferred for large datasets and higher predictive accuracy due to its boosting mechanism and parallel processing capabilities

Considering the Data Characteristics

- **Dataset Size:** The dataset is **large**, with numerous features, including customer demographics, service usage, and billing history. This makes **XGBoost** a strong candidate due to its ability to handle large datasets efficiently.
- **Missing Values:** Both Random Forest and XGBoost can handle missing data without requiring extensive preprocessing.
- **Data Type:** The data is structured and tabular, making both Random Forest and XGBoost suitable.

Choice: Based on the dataset's size and the need for high accuracy, we lean toward XGBoost while acknowledging the interpretability benefits of Random Forest.

Balancing Interpretability vs. Accuracy

- **Interpretability:** While Random Forest is easier to interpret, we can leverage **SHAP (SHapley Additive exPlanations)** with XGBoost to gain insights into feature importance and make the model's predictions more interpretable.

- **Accuracy:** XGBoost's boosting mechanism provides superior accuracy for large datasets, making it the preferred choice.

- **Feature Importance:** XGBoost's feature importance analysis will help the company understand key factors influencing churn, enabling targeted retention strategies.

Choice: XGBoost is selected for its balance of accuracy and interpretability through SHAP analysis.

Computational Requirements

- The telecom company is using **Azure Databricks** for scalable cloud-based computing.

- **XGBoost** is optimized for cloud environments with
  - **Parallel Processing:** Efficient handling of large datasets
  - **Resource Utilization:** Optimized for distributed computing on Databricks
  - **Scalability:** Suitable for big data scenarios

Choice: XGBoost is chosen for its ability to maximize predictive accuracy and efficiently utilize Databricks' cloud infrastructure.

Choosing the Right Algorithm Based on Data Type

- **Structured Data:** The dataset consists of structured, tabular data, making **XGBoost** a suitable choice.

- **Text Data:** If the dataset includes significant textual feedback, a Transformer-based NLP model would be considered. However, this is not the case here.

Choice: XGBoost remains the preferred model for structured tabular data.

Final Algorithm Choice

Based on all considerations:

- **XGBoost** is selected as the final algorithm for customer churn prediction due to its
  - **Superior accuracy** for large datasets
  - **Efficient use of cloud-based resources** on Azure Databricks
  - **Interpretability** through SHAP analysis to identify key churn factors

This approach enables the telecom company to accurately predict churn, prioritize high-risk customers, and implement effective retention strategies, ultimately enhancing customer satisfaction and reducing churn rates.

Model Training and Hyperparameter Tuning

This section covers an important concept in model training and hyperparameter tuning. Hyperparameter tuning is crucial because it directly impacts a model's performance, accuracy, and efficiency.

What Are Hyperparameters?

Hyperparameters are the external configurations set before training a machine learning model that influence how the model learns from data. Unlike model parameters, which are learned during training (such as the weights in a neural network), hyperparameters must be specified beforehand. Examples include the learning rate, the number of trees in a Random Forest (`n_estimators`), and the maximum depth of a tree (`max_depth`). Choosing the right hyperparameters is crucial because they control the model's complexity, training speed, and overall performance.

Example of Hyperparameters

- In a **Random Forest model**, `n_estimators` determine how many decision trees to use, and max_depth sets the maximum depth of each tree.

- In a **neural network**, hyperparameters include the number of layers, learning rate, and activation functions.

What Is Hyperparameter Tuning?

Hyperparameter tuning is the process of searching for the best set of hyperparameters to optimize model performance. This process is essential because the right combination of hyperparameters can significantly enhance model accuracy, mitigate overfitting, and expedite training. Tuning can be performed manually or through automated techniques, such as **Grid Search, Random Search**, and **Bayesian Optimization (e.g., Hyperopt)**.

Suppose you are training a spam detection model using a Random Forest classifier. You want to find the optimal number of trees (`n_estimators`) and the maximum depth of each tree (`max_depth`). Using a tool like Hyperopt, you can automate the search.

Why Is Hyperparameter Tuning Important?

Hyperparameter tuning is a critical step in building effective machine learning models. It involves finding the best combination of hyperparameters to maximize model performance, accuracy, and efficiency. Proper tuning ensures that the model generalizes well to new data, avoids overfitting, and achieves optimal results, making it an indispensable part of the machine learning workflow. Hyperparameter tuning has its advantages:

> **Enhances Model Performance**: Proper tuning finds the optimal combination of hyperparameters, improving the model's ability to make accurate predictions. Without tuning, even powerful algorithms might underperform.
>
> **Prevents Overfitting or Underfitting:** Hyperparameter tuning helps strike a balance between model complexity. For instance, setting hyperparameters such as max_depth in decision trees or learning rate in neural networks correctly ensures that the

model generalizes well to new data rather than memorizing the training data (overfitting) or failing to learn significant patterns (underfitting).

Optimizes Training Efficiency: Some hyperparameters affect the speed of training and prediction. Efficient tuning can reduce training time and computational resources, making it practical to deploy models in real-world scenarios.

Automates Model Selection: Techniques like Grid Search, Random Search, and Bayesian Optimization automate the process of exploring different hyperparameter combinations, saving data scientists time and effort.

Imagine you are building a spam detection system using a Random Forest classifier. Two key hyperparameters are

1. **n_estimators (Number of Decision Trees):** Controls model complexity. More trees usually improve accuracy but require more time to train.

2. **max_depth (Depth of Each Tree):** Determines how deep each tree grows. A larger depth can capture complex patterns but may cause overfitting.

Using Hyperopt for tuning, you can automatically find the optimal values for these parameters, ensuring the model accurately identifies spam emails without excessive computational cost. Logging these experiments in MLflow allows you to track which combinations of hyperparameters yield the best results, making it easy to reproduce successful models in the future. Here is an example of the same:

```
import mlflow
from hyperopt import fmin, tpe, hp, Trials
from sklearn.ensemble import RandomForestClassifier
from sklearn.model_selection import cross_val_score
from sklearn.datasets import make_classification

# Generate a sample dataset with 1000 examples and 10 features
X, y = make_classification(n_samples=1000, n_features=10, random_state=42)
```

```python
# Define the objective function for Hyperparameter Tuning
def objective(params):
    """
    Objective function: Defines how we evaluate model performance during
    hyperparameter tuning.
    This function is optimized by Hyperopt to find the best set of
    hyperparameters.
    """
    # Create a RandomForest model using the hyperparameters provided by
    Hyperopt
    model = RandomForestClassifier(n_estimators=int(params['n_
    estimators']), max_depth=int(params['max_depth']))

    # Perform cross-validation to evaluate the model's performance
    # Cross-validation splits the dataset into multiple subsets to ensure
    robustness in performance evaluation
    score = cross_val_score(model, X, y, cv=5, scoring="accuracy").mean()

    # Log the hyperparameters and accuracy score in MLflow for tracking
    with mlflow.start_run():
        mlflow.log_param("n_estimators", int(params['n_estimators']))
        # Number of trees in the forest
        mlflow.log_param("max_depth", int(params['max_depth']))
        # Maximum depth of the trees
        mlflow.log_metric("accuracy", score)  # Accuracy of the model

    return -score  # Hyperopt minimizes the objective function, so we
    negate the accuracy

# Define the hyperparameter search space
space = {
    "n_estimators": hp.quniform("n_estimators", 50, 200, 10),  # Number of
    trees between 50 and 200 (increments of 10)
    "max_depth": hp.quniform("max_depth", 5, 30, 1)  # Maximum depth
    between 5 and 30 (increments of 1)
}
```

```
# Explanation of Search Space:
# The search space defines the range of hyperparameters Hyperopt explores.
# - 'n_estimators' varies from 50 to 200 in steps of 10 (controls the
number of decision trees in the forest).
# - 'max_depth' varies from 5 to 30 in steps of 1 (controls how deep each
tree grows).

# Run the optimization with Hyperopt
best_params = fmin(
    fn=objective,   # The objective function to minimize
    space=space,    # The hyperparameter space to explore
    algo=tpe.suggest,   # Tree-structured Parzen Estimator algorithm for
    optimization
    max_evals=50,   # Perform 50 iterations of tuning
    trials=Trials()  # Store results of each iteration
)

# Print the best hyperparameters found
print("Best Parameters:", best_params)
```

This code demonstrates how to perform hyperparameter tuning for a Random Forest classifier using Hyperopt and log the results with MLflow. First, it creates a synthetic dataset with 1000 samples and 10 features. The objective function is defined to evaluate the model's performance based on two hyperparameters: the number of trees (n_estimators) and the maximum depth of each tree (max_depth). Inside the objective function, a Random Forest model is trained using these hyperparameters, and its accuracy is calculated through cross-validation, which helps assess how well the model performs on unseen data. The accuracy and hyperparameters are logged to MLflow for tracking. The search space defines the ranges for n_estimators (50–200) and max_depth (5–30). The code utilizes Hyperopt's Tree-structured Parzen Estimator (TPE) to efficiently explore this space, aiming to find the optimal combination of hyperparameters that maximizes accuracy. After running 50 evaluations, the best hyperparameters are printed. This approach ensures that the model is both well-tuned and its performance is reproducibly logged for comparison in future experiments.

Evaluating Model Performance

Evaluating model performance is a crucial step in the machine learning workflow because it helps determine how well a model can make predictions on new, unseen data. Performance evaluation helps identify potential issues like

- **Overfitting:** When the model learns the training data too well, including noise and irrelevant details, it performs poorly on new data.
- **Underfitting:** When the model is too simple to capture the underlying patterns in the data, leading to poor performance on both training and new data.

By evaluating performance, we can ensure that the model meets the necessary **standards of accuracy, reliability, and robustnes**s before deploying it for real-world tasks.

Key Metrics for Evaluating Model Performance

To assess a model's performance, we utilize various metrics that evaluate its predictive ability. The most common metrics are:

Accuracy: How Often the Model Is Correct

- **Definition:** Accuracy measures the proportion of correct predictions made by the model out of all predictions.
- **Formula:**

$$\text{Accuracy} = \frac{\text{Correct Predictions}}{\text{Total Predictions}} \times 100$$

- **In simple terms**, accuracy tells us the percentage of times the model was correct.

Better When:

- The dataset is **balanced**—meaning it has an equal or similar number of positive and negative cases. In such cases, accuracy can reliably indicate how well the model performs overall.

Example: High accuracy would likely indicate good model performance in a spam detection model with 50% spam emails and 50% non-spam emails.

Limitations

Misleading for Imbalanced Datasets: If one class heavily outweighs the other, accuracy can give a false sense of good performance.

- **Example:** In a rare disease detection scenario where 95% of patients are healthy:
  - A model that predicts "no disease" for everyone would have 95% accuracy but completely fail to detect the disease in the 5% who have it.

Solution: Use additional metrics, such as precision, recall, or F1-score, to assess performance in imbalanced datasets.

Precision: How Many of the Positive Predictions Were Correct

- **Definition:** Precision measures the proportion of correctly predicted positive cases out of all cases predicted as positive.
- **Formula:**

$$\text{Accuracy} = \frac{\text{Correct Predictions}}{\text{Total Predictions}} \times 100$$

- **In simple terms,** precision answers the question: "Of all the cases the model predicted as positive, how many were positive?"

Better When:

- **False Positives Are Costly:** Incorrectly predicting a positive case leads to significant consequences.

- **Example:** In **fraud detection**, predicting legitimate transactions as fraudulent can cause inconvenience and loss of customer trust.

Why This Matters: High precision ensures that when the model predicts something as positive, it is likely to be correct, reducing unnecessary actions.

Limitations

- **May Ignore Actual Positive Cases:** Focusing solely on precision might cause the model to miss many positive cases (low recall).
  - **Example:** A very precise spam filter may allow many spam emails to pass through to avoid flagging legitimate emails.

Solution: Use **recall** along with precision for a more balanced view.

Recall (Sensitivity): How Many Actual Positive Cases Were Detected

- **Definition:** Recall measures the proportion of actual positive cases that the model correctly identifies.

- **Formula:**

$$\text{Recall} = \frac{\text{True Positives}}{\text{True Positives} + \text{False Negatives}}$$

- **In Simple Terms:** Recall answers the question: "Of all the actual positive cases, how many did the model correctly identify?"

Better When:

- **Missing Positive Cases Is Costly:** When failing to identify positive cases has severe consequences.
  - **Example:** In **medical diagnosis**, missing a disease (false negative) can be life-threatening.

Why This Matters: High recall ensures that most actual positive cases are detected, minimizing the risk of missing important outcomes.

Limitations

- **May Increase False Positives:** A model that focuses only on recall may incorrectly label too many negative cases as positive.
  - **Example:** In security systems, high recall might trigger too many false alarms, causing inconvenience and desensitization.

Solution: Balance recall with precision using the **F1-score**.

F1-Score: Balancing Precision and Recall

- **Definition:** The F1-score is the **harmonic mean** of precision and recall, giving a single metric that balances both.
- **Formula:**

$$\text{F1-Score} = 2 \times \frac{\text{Precision} \times \text{Recall}}{\text{Precision} + \text{Recall}}$$

- **In Simple Terms:** F1-score helps balance the need to correctly identify positive cases (recall) with the need to avoid false positives (precision).

Better When:

- **Both False Positives and False Negatives Are Costly:**
  - **Example:** In **healthcare**, both failing to diagnose a disease (false negative) and misdiagnosing a healthy person (false positive) can have serious implications.

Limitations

- **Ignores True Negatives:** The F1-score does not account for true negatives, which may result in an incomplete reflection of the model's performance in scenarios where true negatives are crucial.

- **Example:** In spam detection, correctly identifying non-spam emails (true negatives) is also crucial.

Solution: Use the F1-score and other metrics, such as accuracy, to gain a more comprehensive picture.

Understanding Errors: False Positives vs. False Negatives

- **False Positives:** The model incorrectly predicts a positive case.
  - **Example:** Flagging a legitimate bank transaction as fraud.

Better When Lower: In cases like **fraud detection,** where false positives cause inconvenience.

- **False Negatives:** The model fails to predict a positive case.
  - **Example:** Missing a fraudulent transaction in a bank.

Better When Lower: In **medical diagnosis** or security, missing a positive case can have severe consequences.

Choosing the Right Metric

- **High Precision:** Best when false positives are costly (e.g., fraud detection).
- **High Recall:** Best when false negatives are costly (e.g., detecting diseases).
- **High F1-Score:** Best when both false positives and false negatives are important.
- **High Accuracy:** Best when the dataset is balanced.

By selecting the appropriate metric based on the problem's requirements, we can better assess and improve the model's performance.

Let's understand these complex terms with the help of a simple example: consider a **spam detection system** where the goal is to classify emails as spam or not spam:

- Out of 1000 emails, 950 are not spam, and 50 are spam.
- The model predicts 70 emails as spam, of which 40 are actual spam (True Positives) and 30 are incorrectly flagged (False Positives).
- The model also fails to detect ten actual spam emails (False Negatives).

Calculating Metrics

- **Accuracy** = (True Positives + True Negatives) / Total Samples = (40 + 920) / 1000 = **96%**
- **Precision** = True Positives / (True Positives + False Positives) = 40 / (40 + 30) = **57%**
- **Recall** = True Positives / (True Positives + False Negatives) = 40 / (40 + 10) = **80%**
- **F1-Score** = 2 * (Precision * Recall) / (Precision + Recall) = 2 * (0.57 * 0.80) / (0.57 + 0.80) = **67%**

Logging these metrics using MLflow enables systematic tracking and comparison of different model runs, allowing data scientists to refine their models iteratively and make informed decisions on model selection.

End-to-End Example: Evaluating Model Performance and Logging with MLflow

Let's consider a **real-world scenario** in which a hospital wants to develop a machine learning model to determine whether a patient has a disease based on medical test results. The goal is to predict whether a patient has the disease (Positive) or does not have the disease (Negative). The hospital wants to evaluate the model's effectiveness before deployment. Please refer to the DBC file.

Train a Classification Model

We train a **Random Forest classifier** to predict the disease status.

```
import mlflow
import mlflow.sklearn
from sklearn.ensemble import RandomForestClassifier
from sklearn.model_selection import train_test_split
from sklearn.metrics import accuracy_score, precision_score, recall_score, f1_score
from sklearn.datasets import make_classification

# Generate a synthetic dataset
X, y = make_classification(n_samples=1000, n_features=10, random_state=42)
X_train, X_test, y_train, y_test = train_test_split(X, y, test_size=0.2, random_state=42)

# Initialize and train the model
model = RandomForestClassifier(n_estimators=100, max_depth=5, random_state=42)
model.fit(X_train, y_train)
```

Make Predictions and Compute Evaluation Metrics

```
# Make predictions
y_pred = model.predict(X_test)

# Compute evaluation metrics
accuracy = accuracy_score(y_test, y_pred)
precision = precision_score(y_test, y_pred)
recall = recall_score(y_test, y_pred)
f1 = f1_score(y_test, y_pred)
```

Log Metrics with MLflow

```
# Start an MLflow run to log model parameters and metrics
with mlflow.start_run():
```

```
mlflow.log_param("n_estimators", 100)
mlflow.log_param("max_depth", 5)

mlflow.log_metric("accuracy", accuracy)
mlflow.log_metric("precision", precision)
mlflow.log_metric("recall", recall)
mlflow.log_metric("f1_score", f1)

# Log the trained model
mlflow.sklearn.log_model(model, "disease_prediction_model")
```

Interpret the Metrics

- **Accuracy:** Measures the frequency with which the model is correct. If accuracy is high, the model makes mostly correct predictions.

- **Precision:** Tells how many of the predicted positive cases were positive. A high precision means fewer false positives (incorrectly diagnosing healthy patients as sick).

- **Recall:** Measures how many actual positive cases the model correctly identified. A high recall means fewer false negatives (failing to detect sick patients).

- **F1-Score:** Balances precision and recall. If both values are important, the F1-score should be optimized.

Viewing MLflow Logs in Databricks

1. Open **Azure Databricks**, and navigate to the **MLflow Experiment UI** as shown in Figure 4-1.

2. Locate your experiment run, and click to view logged parameters and metrics.

3. Compare different runs, and improve the model by tuning hyperparameters.

CHAPTER 4   BUILDING MACHINE LEARNING MODELS

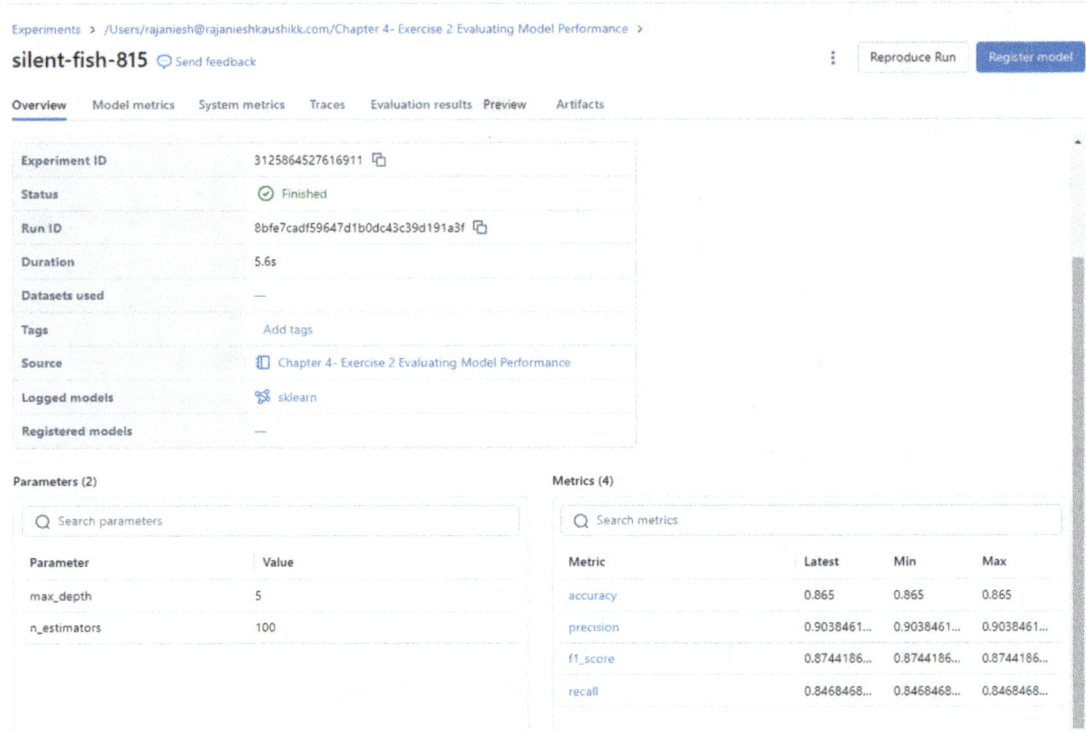

Figure 4-1. Viewing the experiments in the MLflow UI in Databricks

This structured approach ensures reproducibility and allows data scientists to systematically track and compare different models before deploying them in real-world healthcare settings.

Experiment Tracking with MLflow

In this section, we will explore the importance of experiment tracking using MLflow, a powerful tool that simplifies the process of logging, organizing, and analyzing your machine learning experiments. By the end of this section, you will have a comprehensive understanding of how to systematically record every aspect of your experiments, making it easier to reproduce, compare, and ultimately select the best-performing models.

Why Experiment Tracking Is Important

Experiment tracking is a cornerstone of the machine learning workflow, ensuring every model run is reproducible, comparable, and well-documented. By systematically recording parameters, metrics, and artifacts for each experiment, tracking enables data scientists to trace model evolution, compare performance across different versions, and efficiently identify the best configurations. Without proper experiment tracking, it becomes nearly impossible to determine which model performed best, why it did so, and how to replicate those results in future projects.

Recording and Managing Experiments

Efficient experiment tracking is vital in machine learning to ensure that every run is reproducible, comparable, and well-documented. In MLflow, you can record and manage experiments by logging parameters, metrics, and artifacts for each run. This systematic tracking enables data scientists to compare different models, understand which configurations perform best, and maintain a history of experiments for continuous improvement.

Logging Parameters and Metrics

MLflow allows you to log hyperparameters (like the number of trees in a Random Forest) and evaluation metrics (like accuracy or root mean square error) for each run. This helps in keeping track of what was tested and how it performed.

```
with mlflow.start_run():
    mlflow.log_param("num_trees", 100)   # Logs a hyperparameter
    mlflow.log_metric("rmse", 1.2)       # Logs a performance metric
```

In this example, the num_trees parameter represents the number of trees in a Random Forest, while rmse is a metric to evaluate the model's prediction error.

Tracking these details helps answer questions like

- Which set of parameters gave the best accuracy?
- How did the model perform with different configurations?

Managing Artifacts

Artifacts in MLflow include trained models, plots, and any files generated during the experiment. Storing artifacts ensures that you can revisit and reproduce past experiments.

This approach facilitates the selection of the best model for deployment by providing a comprehensive view of each experiment's performance.

```
with mlflow.start_run():
    mlflow.log_param("num_trees", 100)
    mlflow.log_metric("rmse", 1.2)
    mlflow.log_artifact("model.pkl")  # Logs a trained model as an artifact
```

Visualizing Experiment Results

Databricks provides an MLflow UI for effectively visualizing and comparing experiments. You can filter experiments based on parameters, metrics, and tags, enabling a streamlined identification of the most promising models. Figure 4-2 illustrates the model's performance, and Figure 4-3 displays the metrics across different runs.

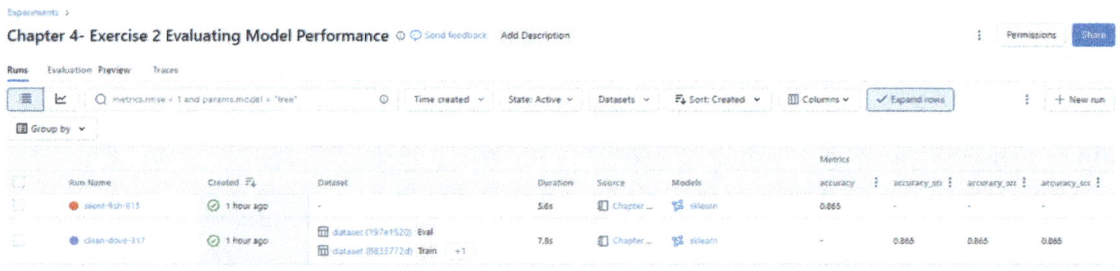

Figure 4-2. Visualizing the experiment results in MLflow

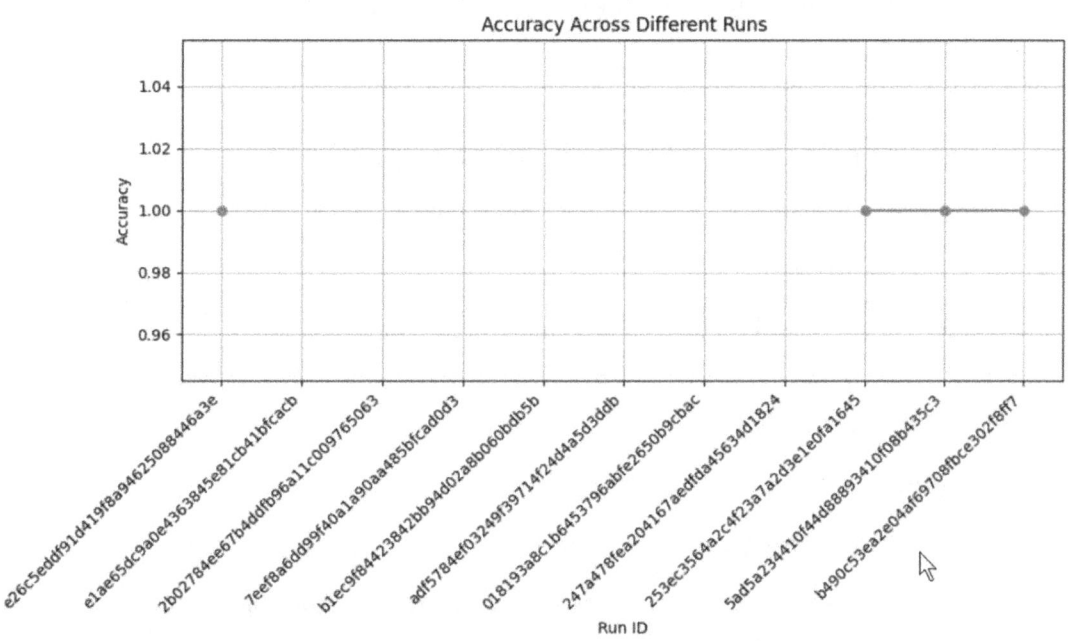

Figure 4-3. *Visualizing the metrics in the Notebook*

Hands-On Labs

Lab 1: Hyperparameter Tuning with MLflow and Hyperopt

In this lab, we will explore how to perform **hyperparameter tuning** for a **Random Forest** classifier using **MLflow** and **Hyperopt**.

Why Is Hyperparameter Tuning Important?

Hyperparameters are configurations set before training that control how the model learns from data. Tuning them helps

- **Improve model accuracy** by finding the best configurations.
- **Prevent overfitting or underfitting** by balancing model complexity.
- **Optimize training time** by reducing unnecessary computations.

Key Concepts Covered

- **Hyperparameters:** Settings like the number of trees in a forest or the max depth of trees

- **Objective Function:** A function that evaluates how well a model performs for given hyperparameters
- **Search Space:** Defines the range of hyperparameters to explore
- **MLflow Tracking:** Logs and tracks experiments for reproducibility and comparison

How the Code Works

1. **Create a Synthetic Dataset**
   - Generates data with 1000 samples and 10 features for training and testing

2. **Define an Objective Function**
   - Trains a Random Forest model with given hyperparameters
   - Uses cross-validation to evaluate performance and logs results to MLflow

3. **Set Up a Hyperparameter Search Space**
   - Specifies ranges for the number of trees (`n_estimators`) and maximum depth (`max_depth`)

4. **Run Hyperparameter Optimization with Hyperopt**
   - Uses Tree-structured Parzen Estimator (TPE) to find the best hyperparameters

5. **Log Metrics to MLflow**
   - Logs parameters and accuracy to MLflow for each experiment run

By the end of this notebook, you will

- Understand how to tune hyperparameters effectively.
- Learn how to log and track experiments using MLflow.
- Identify the best model configuration based on logged metrics.

Now, let's proceed to the code implementation.

```python
import mlflow
from hyperopt import fmin, tpe, hp, Trials
from sklearn.ensemble import RandomForestClassifier
from sklearn.model_selection import cross_val_score
from sklearn.datasets import make_classification

# Generate a sample dataset with 1000 examples and 10 features
X, y = make_classification(n_samples=1000, n_features=10, random_state=42)

# Define the objective function for Hyperparameter Tuning
def objective(params):
    """
    Objective function: Defines how we evaluate model performance during
    hyperparameter tuning.
    This function is optimized by Hyperopt to find the best set of
    hyperparameters.
    """
    # Create a RandomForest model using the hyperparameters provided by Hyperopt
    model = RandomForestClassifier(n_estimators=int(params['n_estimators']), max_depth=int(params['max_depth']))

    # Perform cross-validation to evaluate the model's performance
    # Cross-validation splits the dataset into multiple subsets to ensure robustness in performance evaluation
    score = cross_val_score(model, X, y, cv=5, scoring="accuracy").mean()

    # Log the hyperparameters and accuracy score in MLflow for tracking
    with mlflow.start_run():
        mlflow.log_param("n_estimators", int(params['n_estimators']))
        # Number of trees in the forest
        mlflow.log_param("max_depth", int(params['max_depth']))
        # Maximum depth of the trees
        mlflow.log_metric("accuracy", score)  # Accuracy of the model
```

```
    return -score  # Hyperopt minimizes the objective function, so we
                   negate the accuracy

# Define the hyperparameter search space
space = {
    "n_estimators": hp.quniform("n_estimators", 50, 200, 10),  # Number of
    trees between 50 and 200 (increments of 10)
    "max_depth": hp.quniform("max_depth", 5, 30, 1)  # Maximum depth
    between 5 and 30 (increments of 1)
}

# Explanation of Search Space:
# The search space defines the range of hyperparameters Hyperopt explores.
# - 'n_estimators' varies from 50 to 200 in steps of 10 (controls the
number of decision trees in the forest).
# - 'max_depth' varies from 5 to 30 in steps of 1 (controls how deep each
tree grows).

# Run the optimization with Hyperopt
best_params = fmin(
    fn=objective,   # The objective function to minimize
    space=space,    # The hyperparameter space to explore
    algo=tpe.suggest,  # Tree-structured Parzen Estimator algorithm for
                       optimization
    max_evals=50,   # Perform 50 iterations of tuning
    trials=Trials()  # Store results of each iteration
)

# Print the best hyperparameters found
print("Best Parameters:", best_params)
```

Lab 2: Training a Random Forest Model with MLflow

In this section, we will train a **Random Forest** classifier on a synthetic dataset and log the model's performance using **MLflow**. This approach facilitates tracking experiments and comparing different runs to identify the optimal model configuration.

CHAPTER 4 BUILDING MACHINE LEARNING MODELS

Key Objectives

1. **Generate a Synthetic Dataset:** Create a dataset with 1000 samples and 10 features for training and testing.

2. **Train a Random Forest Model:** Use a predefined number of trees (n_estimators) and depth (max_depth).

3. **Log Model and Metrics to MLflow:** Record hyperparameters, accuracy, precision, recall, and F1-score for reproducibility and comparison.

Why Use MLflow for Tracking?

- **Reproducibility:** Logs hyperparameters and metrics for every experiment, making it easy to reproduce results

- **Comparison:** Helps compare different model configurations by visualizing logged metrics

- **Version Control:** Enables tracking of model versions and their performance over time

Expected Outcome

- A trained Random Forest model with logged metrics in MLflow

- Insight into model performance through accuracy, precision, recall, and F1-score

- A structured way to compare different model configurations in Databricks

Let's proceed to the code implementation!

```
import mlflow
import mlflow.sklearn
from sklearn.ensemble import RandomForestClassifier
from sklearn.model_selection import train_test_split
from sklearn.metrics import accuracy_score, precision_score, recall_score, f1_score
from sklearn.datasets import make_classification
```

CHAPTER 4 BUILDING MACHINE LEARNING MODELS

```
# Generate a synthetic dataset
X, y = make_classification(n_samples=1000, n_features=10, random_state=42)
X_train, X_test, y_train, y_test = train_test_split(X, y, test_size=0.2, random_state=42)

# Initialize and train the model
model = RandomForestClassifier(n_estimators=100, max_depth=5, random_state=42)
model.fit(X_train, y_train)
```

Evaluating Model Performance and Computing Metrics

In this code, we will

1. **Make Predictions:** Use the trained Random Forest model to predict outcomes on the test dataset.

2. **Compute Evaluation Metrics:** Calculate key metrics such as **accuracy, precision, recall,** and **F1-score** to assess the model's performance.

3. **Understand the Importance of Each Metric:**

    - **Accuracy:** Measures how often the model's predictions are correct overall

    - **Precision:** Focuses on how many of the predicted positive cases were actually positive

    - **Recall:** Focuses on capturing as many actual positive cases as possible

    - **F1-Score:** Provides a balanced measure between precision and recall, especially useful when dealing with imbalanced datasets

Why These Metrics Matter

- **Accuracy:** Useful for balanced datasets but can be misleading if the data is skewed

- **Precision:** Important in scenarios where false positives are costly (e.g., fraud detection)

- **Recall:** Critical in cases where missing a positive case is more costly (e.g., medical diagnosis)

F1-Score: Ideal when you need to balance both precision and recall.

```
# Make predictions
y_pred = model.predict(X_test)

# Compute evaluation metrics
accuracy = accuracy_score(y_test, y_pred)
precision = precision_score(y_test, y_pred)
recall = recall_score(y_test, y_pred)
f1 = f1_score(y_test, y_pred)
print("Accuracy: {}".format(accuracy))
print("Precision: {}".format(precision))
print("Recall: {}".format(recall))
print("F1: {}".format(f1))
```

Logging Model Parameters and Metrics to MLflow

In this section, we will log the following to **MLflow**:

1. **Hyperparameters:** Key settings like `n_estimators` and `max_depth` that define the model's configuration.

2. **Performance Metrics**
   - **Accuracy:** How often the model's predictions are correct
   - **Precision:** How many of the predicted positive cases were actually positive
   - **Recall:** How well the model captures actual positive cases
   - **F1-Score:** A balanced measure of precision and recall

3. **Trained Model:** Save the Random Forest model as an artifact in MLflow.

Why Log Metrics and Parameters?

- **Reproducibility:** Helps recreate past experiments by saving the exact configuration and performance
- **Comparison:** Allows easy comparison of different model runs to choose the best-performing configuration
- **Tracking Model Evolution:** Logs how models improve over time with different configurations

Expected Outcome

- Logged parameters (n_estimators, max_depth)
- Logged metrics (accuracy, precision, recall, f1_score)
- Trained model saved in MLflow as an artifact for future reference or deployment

Let's proceed to log the metrics and parameters to MLflow!

```
# Start an MLflow run to log model parameters and metrics
with mlflow.start_run():
    mlflow.log_param("n_estimators", 100)
    mlflow.log_param("max_depth", 5)

    mlflow.log_metric("accuracy", accuracy)
    mlflow.log_metric("precision", precision)
    mlflow.log_metric("recall", recall)
    mlflow.log_metric("f1_score", f1)

    # Log the trained model
    mlflow.sklearn.log_model(model, "disease_prediction_model")
```

Lab 3: Loan Default Prediction Lab

Scenario

You are a data scientist at a financial institution tasked with building a predictive model to assess the risk associated with personal loan applications. The institution aims to automate the process of evaluating loan applications based on customer data, including income, loan amount, credit score, and repayment behavior.

In this lab, you will use **MLflow** to track the end-to-end machine learning process. This includes training a regression model that predicts loan repayment likelihood and using MLflow's experiment tracking features to log parameters, metrics, and artifacts for analysis and comparison.

Objective

- Train a regression model using a real-world loan dataset.
- Use **MLflow** to log experiment metadata including parameters, metrics, and model artifacts.

CHAPTER 4　BUILDING MACHINE LEARNING MODELS

- Visualize and compare multiple experiment runs in the MLflow UI.
- Understand how MLflow supports reproducibility and collaboration in the ML workflow.

Setup Databricks File System (DBFS)

- **Creates a directory** in DBFS to store training data
- **Defines paths** for CSV files and MLflow storage

```
# Define DBFS Paths
dbfs_directory = "dbfs:/mnt/data/loan_prediction"
dbfs_mlflow_directory = "dbfs:/mnt/data/loan_prediction/mlflow"
deltaPath = "dbfs:/mnt/data/loan_prediction/loan_data.csv"
path = "/dbfs/mnt/data/loan_prediction/loan_data.csv"

# Create directory if it does not exist
dbutils.fs.mkdirs(dbfs_directory)
print(f"☑ Directory created: {dbfs_directory}")
```

Create and Upload Loan Data

- **Creates a sample dataset** for loan applications
- The dataset includes
    - income: Customer's income (in $1000s)
    - loan_amount: Loan requested (in $1000s)
    - credit_score: 1 = Good, 0 = Bad
    - default: 1 = Default (misses payments), 0 = No Default
- Saves the dataset to **Databricks File System (DBFS)**

```
# Sample Loan Dataset
csv_content = """income,loan_amount,credit_score,default
50,10,1,0
60,15,1,0
30,7,0,1
```

CHAPTER 4 BUILDING MACHINE LEARNING MODELS

```
80,25,1,0
20,5,0,1
40,8,1,0
100,30,1,0
25,6,0,1
90,20,1,0
35,9,1,0
"""

# Save to DBFS
dbutils.fs.put(deltaPath, csv_content, overwrite=True)
print("☑ Loan data file uploaded successfully!")
```

Load and Display Data

- Loads the dataset from **DBFS** into a **Pandas DataFrame**
- Displays the dataset for verification

```
import pandas as pd
# Load the CSV file into a pandas DataFrame
pandas_df = pd.read_csv(path)
# Display the pandas DataFrame
display(pandas_df)
#In the next Cell
df = spark.read.format("csv").option("header", "true").load("dbfs:/
mnt/data/loan_prediction/loan_data.csv")
pandas_df = df.toPandas()
display(pandas_df)
```

Load Data into PySpark

- Loads the dataset as a **Spark DataFrame** for large-scale processing

```
df = spark.read.format("csv").option("header", "true").load(deltaPath)
df.display()
```

Set Up MLflow Experiment

- **MLflow** is used to track experiments in Databricks.
- We create an **MLflow experiment** to track model training.

```
import mlflow
 # Set the required configuration for model registry
experiment_path = "/Users/rajaniesh@rajanieshkaushikk.com/loan_
prediction_experiment"
dbutils.fs.mkdirs(experiment_path)

mlflow.set_tracking_uri("databricks")
mlflow.set_experiment(experiment_path)

print(f"☑ Experiment set at: {experiment_path}")
```

Train the Loan Default Prediction Model

- Trains a **RandomForestClassifier** to predict **loan default**
- Uses **income, loan amount, and credit score** as input features
- Logs model performance and parameters in **MLflow**

```
import mlflow
import mlflow.sklearn
from sklearn.model_selection import train_test_split
from sklearn.ensemble import RandomForestClassifier
from sklearn.metrics import accuracy_score

# Load dataset
df = spark.read.csv(deltaPath, header=True, inferSchema=True).
toPandas()

# Rename columns
df.columns = ["income", "loan_amount", "credit_score", "default"]

# Feature Engineering
X = df.drop("default", axis=1)  # Features
y = df["default"]   # Target
```

CHAPTER 4 BUILDING MACHINE LEARNING MODELS

```
X_train, X_test, y_train, y_test = train_test_split(X, y, test_
size=0.2, random_state=42)

# Start MLflow tracking
with mlflow.start_run():
    model = RandomForestClassifier(n_estimators=100, random_state=42)
    model.fit(X_train, y_train)

    # Make predictions
    y_pred = model.predict(X_test)
    accuracy = accuracy_score(y_test, y_pred)

    # Log Metrics
    mlflow.log_metric("accuracy", accuracy)
    mlflow.log_param("n_estimators", 100)
    mlflow.log_param("random_state", 42)

    # Log Model
    mlflow.sklearn.log_model(model, "loan_default_model")

print(f"☑ Model trained with accuracy: {accuracy:.2f}")
```

Register Model in MLflow

- Saves the trained model in **Databricks MLflow Model Registry**

```
#Put the Model URI here it starts with runs:
model_uri = "runs:/xyz/loan_default_model"
mlflow.register_model(model_uri, "LoanDefaultModel")
print("☑ Model registered successfully!")
```

Load and Make Predictions

- Loads the **MLflow model**
- Uses the trained model to make predictions on **new customer loan applications**

```
import mlflow
import mlflow.sklearn
import pandas as pd

# Load Model
model = mlflow.sklearn.load_model("models:/LoanDefaultModel/1")

# Test Data (New Loan Applications)
test_data = pd.DataFrame([
    [55, 12, 1],  # High income, good credit score → No Default (0)
    [25, 10, 0],  # Low income, bad credit score → Default (1)
], columns=["income", "loan_amount", "credit_score"])

# Make Predictions
predictions = model.predict(test_data)

# Convert to DataFrame
test_data["Default Risk"] = predictions
display(test_data)
```

Visualizing Accuracy Across Different Runs

We will visualize the accuracy of our machine learning model across multiple runs using the metrics logged in MLflow.

- **Fetches Runs:** Retrieves all runs from the specified MLflow experiment
- **Extracts Accuracy:** Pulls the accuracy metric logged for each run
- **Plots Results:** Displays a line plot to visualize how accuracy varies across runs

This plot will help us quickly identify if there are significant differences in model performance or if all runs achieved similar accuracy levels.

```
import mlflow
import pandas as pd
import matplotlib.pyplot as plt
```

CHAPTER 4 BUILDING MACHINE LEARNING MODELS

```
# Define experiment path
experiment_path = "/Users/rajaniesh@rajanieshkaushikk.com/loan_prediction_
experiment"
experiment = mlflow.get_experiment_by_name(experiment_path)

# Fetch all runs from the experiment
runs = mlflow.search_runs(experiment_ids=[experiment.experiment_id])

# Extract metrics for visualization
run_ids = runs['run_id']
accuracy_values = runs['metrics.accuracy']   # Use accuracy instead of RMSE

# Plotting Accuracy for each run
plt.figure(figsize=(10, 6))
plt.plot(run_ids, accuracy_values, marker='o', linestyle='-', color='teal')
plt.title('Accuracy Across Different Runs')
plt.xlabel('Run ID')
plt.ylabel('Accuracy')
plt.xticks(rotation=45, ha='right')
plt.grid(True)
plt.tight_layout()
plt.show()
```

Interpreting the Accuracy Plot

The plot shows the accuracy of different runs, with the X axis representing unique run IDs and the Y axis displaying the accuracy values.

Key Observations

- **Consistent Accuracy:** All runs show a consistent accuracy of **1.0**, indicating that every model version tested achieved perfect accuracy.

- **Possible Reasons for Consistency**

  - **Data Leakage:** The model might be accessing information from the target variable unintentionally.

  - **Simplified Dataset:** The data might be too straightforward, making it easy for the model to achieve perfect accuracy.

CHAPTER 4   BUILDING MACHINE LEARNING MODELS

- **Overfitting:** Such high accuracy could also suggest overfitting to the training data.

Recommended Next Steps

- **Log Additional Metrics:** Consider logging precision, recall, or F1-score for deeper analysis.

- **Plot Validation Accuracy:** To differentiate between overfitting and genuine performance.

- **Examine the Confusion Matrix:** To understand how well the model handles different classes.

By exploring these steps, we can ensure that our model's performance is both accurate and robust.

```
import mlflow
from sklearn.metrics import precision_score, recall_score, f1_score, confusion_matrix

# Use y_test as the true labels and y_pred as the predicted labels
from Cell 6
y_true = y_test  # Actual target values
y_pred = model.predict(X_test)  # Predicted values from the trained model

# Start a new MLflow run to log additional metrics
with mlflow.start_run() as run:
    # Log precision, recall, and F1-score
    precision = precision_score(y_true, y_pred, average='binary')
    recall = recall_score(y_true, y_pred, average='binary')
    f1 = f1_score(y_true, y_pred, average='binary')

    mlflow.log_metric("precision", precision)
    mlflow.log_metric("recall", recall)
    mlflow.log_metric("f1_score", f1)

    print(f"Logged metrics - Precision: {precision:.2f}, Recall: {recall:.2f}, F1-Score: {f1:.2f}")
```

Understanding the Metrics: Precision, Recall, and F1-Score

In our evaluation, we observed the following results:

- **Precision: 0.00**
- **Recall: 0.00**
- **F1-Score: 0.00**

These results might seem confusing at first, so let's break down what they mean in simple terms.

What Does Precision: 0.00 Mean?

- **Precision** tells us: **"Out of all the times the model predicted 'Positive' (1), how many times was it correct?"**
- In our case, a precision of **0.00** means the model **never correctly predicted a positive case** (class 1).
- It either predicted no positives at all or made incorrect positive predictions every time.

Example

Imagine a doctor diagnoses ten patients with a disease (positive cases), but none of them actually have it. This would give a **precision of 0.00**.

What Does Recall: 0.00 Mean?

- **Recall** tells us: **"Out of all the actual positive cases (1), how many did the model correctly predict?"**
- A recall of **0.00** means the model **missed every actual positive case** in the test data.
- In other words, whenever there was a positive case, the model predicted it as negative (0).

Example

Imagine a security scanner that fails to detect every real threat in luggage but never raises false alarms. This would result in a **recall of 0.00**.

What Does F1-Score: 0.00 Mean?

- **F1-Score** is the harmonic mean of precision and recall. It balances both metrics to give a single score.
- Since both precision and recall are **0.00**, the F1-score also becomes **0.00**.
- This suggests that the model is unable to accurately and consistently identify positive cases.

Example
If a spam filter fails to catch any spam emails, its **F1-score would be 0.00**.

Why Are All Metrics 0.00? Common Reasons

- **Class Imbalance:** If there are very few positive cases (1) compared to negative cases (0), the model might predict everything as 0.
- **Model Bias:** The model may be biased toward predicting the majority class (usually 0).
- **Incorrect Labels:** There might be an error in how labels were assigned in the test set.
- **Insufficient Data:** A small or unbalanced test set can lead to unreliable metrics.

How to Fix It: Recommendations

1. **Balance the Dataset:** Use techniques like **SMOTE (Synthetic Minority Over-sampling Technique)** to balance positive and negative cases.
2. **Change the Metric:** Consider using **AUC-ROC (Area Under the Curve-Receiver Operating Characteristic)** if precision and recall are both zero.
3. **Feature Engineering:** Improve the input features to help the model differentiate between classes.
4. **Adjust Hyperparameters:** Tweak model parameters to prevent it from being biased toward the majority class.

CHAPTER 4   BUILDING MACHINE LEARNING MODELS

By understanding these metrics, you can better diagnose why the model is performing poorly and take targeted actions to improve it!

```
import seaborn as sns
import matplotlib.pyplot as plt
import os

# Generate and plot confusion matrix
conf_matrix = confusion_matrix(y_true, y_pred)
plt.figure(figsize=(8, 6))
sns.heatmap(conf_matrix, annot=True, fmt='d', cmap='Blues', cbar=False)
plt.title('Confusion Matrix')
plt.xlabel('Predicted Labels')
plt.ylabel('True Labels')

# Save and log the confusion matrix plot
conf_matrix_path = "confusion_matrix.png"
plt.savefig(conf_matrix_path)

# Log the confusion matrix as an artifact in MLflow
with mlflow.start_run() as run:
    mlflow.log_artifact(conf_matrix_path)
    print("Logged confusion matrix as an artifact.")
```

Interpreting the Confusion Matrix

The confusion matrix helps us understand the performance of our model by comparing the **actual labels** with the **predicted labels**. Here's a simple explanation of what each cell in the matrix means:

Structure of the Confusion Matrix

	Predicted: 0 (No Default)	Predicted: 1 (Default)
Actual: 0 (No Default)	True Negatives (TN)	False Positives (FP)
Actual: 1 (Default)	False Negatives (FN)	True Positives (TP)

Explanation of Each Term

- **True Positives (TP):** Cases where the model **correctly predicted** 1 (Default) when the actual value was also 1 (Default).

  Example: Correctly identifying a loan that will default.

- **True Negatives (TN):** Cases where the model **correctly predicted** 0 (No Default) when the actual value was also 0 (No Default).

  Example: Correctly identifying a loan that will not default.

- **False Positives (FP):** (Type I Error) Cases where the model **incorrectly predicted** 1 (Default) when the actual value was 0 (No Default).

  Example: Incorrectly predicting a loan will default when it actually won't.

- **False Negatives (FN):** (Type II Error) Cases where the model **incorrectly predicted** 0 (No Default) when the actual value was 1 (Default).

  Example: Failing to predict that a loan will default when it actually will.

Key Insights from the Confusion Matrix

- **High True Positives (TP):** Indicates the model is good at predicting positive cases (Defaults).

- **High True Negatives (TN):** Indicates that the model is effective at identifying negative cases (i.e., No Default).

- **High False Positives (FP):** Could lead to unnecessary actions, like rejecting loans incorrectly.

- **High False Negatives (FN):** This could result in missing out on identifying risky loans, potentially leading to financial loss.

How to Interpret the Matrix

- **If TP and TN Are High:** The model is performing well.
- **If FP Is High:** It might be too sensitive to predicting defaults.
- **If FN Is High:** It might be underestimating the risk of default.

Next Steps to Improve Performance

1. **Tune Hyperparameters:** Adjust parameters to reduce false positives and false negatives.
2. **Feature Engineering:** Include more relevant features to help the model differentiate between classes better.
3. **Handle Class Imbalance:** Use techniques like **SMOTE** if there are more negatives than positives in the dataset.
4. **Re-evaluate Threshold:** Change the decision threshold if the balance between FP and FN is not acceptable.

By analyzing the confusion matrix, we can better understand where our model is making mistakes and how to improve its performance!

```
from sklearn.model_selection import train_test_split
from sklearn.ensemble import RandomForestClassifier
from sklearn.metrics import accuracy_score
import mlflow

# Assuming X and y are your features and labels
X_train, X_temp, y_train, y_temp = train_test_split(X, y, test_size=0.4, random_state=42)
X_val, X_test, y_val, y_test = train_test_split(X_temp, y_temp, test_size=0.5, random_state=42)

# Train the model
model = RandomForestClassifier(n_estimators=100, random_state=42)
model.fit(X_train, y_train)
```

```
# Make predictions on validation set
y_val_pred = model.predict(X_val)

# Compute validation accuracy
val_accuracy = accuracy_score(y_val, y_val_pred)

# Log validation accuracy to MLflow
with mlflow.start_run() as run:
    mlflow.log_metric("val_accuracy", val_accuracy)
```

Interpreting Validation Accuracy: 1.00

The **validation accuracy** of **1.00** means that the model correctly predicted **100% of the labels** in the **validation set**. While this might seem like an excellent result at first glance, it's essential to interpret this value cautiously.

What Does Validation Accuracy: 1.00 Mean?

- The model **did not make any mistakes** on the validation data.
- Every single prediction made by the model on the validation set was correct.
- The higher the validation accuracy, the better the model's ability to generalize—but a perfect score can sometimes indicate potential issues.

Is a Validation Accuracy of 1.00 Too Good to Be True?

In many cases, a perfect validation accuracy is a **red flag** rather than a reason to celebrate. Here are some common reasons why this might happen:

1. **Data Leakage**
   - The model might be accidentally accessing information from the target variable during training.
   - **Solution:** Double-check if features contain target information directly or indirectly.

2. **Overfitting**

    - The model might have memorized the validation data rather than learning general patterns.

    - **Solution:** Simplify the model or add regularization.

3. **Simplified Dataset**

    - The validation data might be too easy or not representative of real-world data.

    - **Solution:** Evaluate the model on a more diverse test set.

4. **Insufficient Validation Data**

    - A small or unbalanced validation set can artificially inflate accuracy.

    - **Solution:** Increase the size of the validation set for a more realistic evaluation.

How to Confirm If Validation Accuracy Is Genuine

1. **Check Test Accuracy:** Compare validation accuracy with test accuracy to see if there is a similar pattern.

2. **Log More Metrics:** Examine precision, recall, and F1-score to get a complete performance picture.

3. **Cross-Validation:** Use **k-fold cross-validation** to ensure that the high accuracy is not just due to a lucky split.

Recommended Next Steps

1. **Check for Data Leakage:** Inspect feature correlations with the target variable.

2. **Add Regularization:** Apply techniques such as L2 regularization to prevent overfitting.

3. **Expand Validation Set:** Include more samples to ensure diversity.

4. **Evaluate on Unseen Data:** Test the model on a completely separate dataset.

Achieving a validation accuracy of **1.00** can be a sign of an outstanding model or a warning signal for potential data or training issues. Careful analysis can help you distinguish between the two!

Visualizing the Experiment Result

The visualizations provided valuable insights into our model's performance:

- The **accuracy plot** indicated consistent performance across different runs, but the high accuracy raised concerns about potential **overfitting** or a simplified dataset.

- The additional metrics (**precision, recall, and F1-score**) helped us understand the model's effectiveness beyond accuracy alone.

- The **confusion matrix** highlighted how well the model distinguished between different classes.

Summary

In this chapter, you explored the complete journey of building, tuning, and evaluating machine learning models using the Databricks platform. Starting with foundational concepts in algorithm selection and hyperparameter tuning, you learned how to align model strategies with real-world problem contexts such as customer churn and loan default prediction.

You were introduced to **MLflow** as a unified platform for tracking experiments, logging models, and promoting reproducibility in collaborative environments. Through hands-on labs, you performed hyperparameter optimization using **Hyperopt**, trained a **Random Forest model**, and recorded evaluation metrics including **accuracy, precision, recall, and F1-score**.

CHAPTER 4   BUILDING MACHINE LEARNING MODELS

The chapter emphasizes the importance of metric interpretation, helping you visualize performance across model runs and understand potential concerns, such as overfitting, **when validation accuracy is too high**. You also explored how to **register models and interpret confusion matrices** to improve decision-making in production.

By completing this chapter, you are now equipped to

- Select appropriate ML algorithms based on problem type and data characteristics.
- Conduct hyperparameter tuning and understand its trade-offs.
- Leverage MLflow for reproducibility, metric tracking, and experiment management.
- Analyze key metrics and visual outputs to validate model quality.
- Build end-to-end ML workflows on Databricks for real-world use cases.

With a solid foundation in manual model development, tuning, and performance tracking using MLflow, you now have the tools to build production-grade machine learning workflows. However, as datasets scale and model complexity increases, manually selecting algorithms and hyperparameters can become time-consuming and inconsistent.

In the next chapter, **Chapter 5: AutoML and Model Optimization**, you'll explore how platforms like **Databricks AutoML** automate this process—streamlining algorithm selection, hyperparameter tuning, and model evaluation through intelligent search and optimization techniques. You'll also learn how to interpret AutoML outputs, compare model candidates, and seamlessly integrate AutoML pipelines into your enterprise workflows.

CHAPTER 5

AutoML and Model Optimization

Developing a robust machine learning model typically involves several steps, including data preprocessing, feature engineering, algorithm selection, and hyperparameter tuning. Each step requires expertise and iterative refinement, often making the process complex and time-intensive.

Automated Machine Learning (AutoML) aims to simplify this process by automating many of these tasks. By leveraging AutoML, data scientists and engineers can efficiently generate high-quality models while minimizing manual effort. This approach is particularly beneficial in accelerating model development, reducing human bias, and ensuring reproducibility in machine learning workflows.

This chapter explores **Databricks AutoML**—a powerful tool that streamlines model training, evaluation, and optimization. You'll learn to configure and run AutoML experiments, analyze the results, and apply optimization techniques to enhance model performance and refine models for real-world applications.

Learning Objectives

By the end of this chapter, you will be able to

- Understand the concept and benefits of AutoML.
- Set up and run AutoML experiments in Databricks.
- Interpret the results from AutoML experiments.
- Apply techniques for model optimization and performance tuning.

CHAPTER 5   AUTOML AND MODEL OPTIMIZATION

Introduction to AutoML

In this section, we will learn about what AutoML is, why it's widely being used, and its use cases employed in the industry.

What Is AutoML?

Automated Machine Learning (AutoML) is a technology that streamlines the complex process of building machine learning models by automating critical steps, including **data preprocessing, feature engineering, model selection, and hyperparameter tuning**. Traditionally, machine learning required data scientists to make manual decisions about which algorithms to use, how to transform data, and how to optimize model performance. AutoML eliminates much of this manual effort by systematically testing different techniques, selecting the most effective approach, and fine-tuning the model for optimal performance.

AutoML platforms enable both experienced practitioners and nonexperts to build effective machine learning models without requiring extensive data science expertise. Automating repetitive and time-consuming tasks, AutoML enables organizations to scale their machine learning efforts more efficiently. However, while AutoML provides a great starting point, understanding its outputs and fine-tuning the results is crucial for deploying high-quality models in production environments.

Why Use AutoML?

AutoML is beneficial for organizations that want to

- **Accelerate Model Development**: AutoML significantly reduces the time and expertise required to build machine learning models. Instead of manually selecting features and tuning hyperparameters, AutoML automates these tasks, allowing faster model iterations and deployment.

- **Standardize ML Workflows Across Teams**: Many organizations struggle with inconsistent machine learning practices across different teams. AutoML enforces a structured, repeatable process for model development, ensuring consistency and reliability.

- **Improve Efficiency by Automating Feature Selection and Hyperparameter Tuning**: These are two of the most challenging and time-consuming aspects of machine learning. AutoML systematically tests various configurations and selects the most effective model, thereby saving time and computational resources.

- **Reduce Human Bias in Model Selection and Evaluation**: Traditional model development relies heavily on human intuition and experience, which can introduce bias. AutoML relies on the systematic review and ranking of models, leading to more objective and data-driven decisions.

Use Cases of AutoML

AutoML is widely used across various industries to solve a range of challenges. Some everyday use cases include

- **Healthcare**: In the healthcare industry, AutoML could predict disease outcomes, diagnose conditions from medical images, and optimize hospital resource allocation.

- **Finance**: Detecting fraudulent transactions, assessing credit risk, and forecasting stock market trends.

- **Retail and Ecommerce**: Recommending products to customers, predicting sales trends, and optimizing pricing strategies.

- **Manufacturing**: Predicting equipment failures using sensor data and improving supply chain efficiency.

- **Marketing**: AutoML can assist marketing teams with customer segmentation, churn prediction, and sentiment analysis, enabling more effective campaign targeting and optimization.

CHAPTER 5   AUTOML AND MODEL OPTIMIZATION

How AutoML Improves Fraud Detection?

Consider a **fraud detection system in the banking industry**. Financial institutions process thousands of transactions per second, and detecting fraudulent activity in real time is critical. Traditionally, data scientists manually analyze transaction patterns, build machine learning models, and fine-tune them over time. However, this slow process may not be able to adapt quickly to evolving fraud techniques.

With **AutoML**, banks can automate the model training and selection process. The AutoML system

- **Ingests** real-time transaction data
- **Automatically engineers** relevant features such as transaction amount, frequency, and location
- **Trains multiple models** (e.g., Decision Trees, Random Forests, neural networks) and selects the best-performing one
- **Selects the best model** and updates it with new fraud patterns

Using **Databricks AutoML**, banks can efficiently deploy and maintain fraud detection models, reducing financial losses and improving security without requiring extensive machine learning expertise.

How AutoML Works?

AutoML platforms streamline the machine learning workflow by automating various steps involved in model development. Instead of manually handling each component, AutoML provides an end-to-end solution that makes machine learning more efficient and accessible. Below is a detailed breakdown of the typical AutoML workflow.

Data Preprocessing

Before building a machine learning model, raw data must be cleaned and transformed. AutoML handles

- **Handling Missing Values**: AutoML imputes missing data using statistical methods or removes incomplete records.
- **Feature Scaling**: Normalizes numerical data to ensure consistency and prevent one feature from dominating another.

- **Encoding Categorical Variables**: Converts categorical data into a numerical format that machine learning models can interpret.

- **Outlier Detection**: Identifies and removes anomalies that could skew model accuracy.

- **Data Splitting**: Divides the dataset into training, validation, and test sets to ensure unbiased evaluation of models.

Feature Engineering

Selecting and creating the most relevant features is crucial for model accuracy. AutoML automates

- **Feature Selection**: Identifies and keeps only the most impactful variables.

- **Feature Transformation**: Applies techniques like log transformations and polynomial features to enhance data representation.

- **Dimensionality Reduction**: Utilizes methods such as Principal Component Analysis (PCA) to eliminate redundant information and enhance efficiency.

- **Text Feature Extraction**: When working with textual data, use the Term Frequency-Inverse Document Frequency (TF-IDF) and word embeddings for text feature extraction.

Model Selection

AutoML evaluates multiple machine learning algorithms in parallel and selects the one that performs best. The process includes

- **Trains Various Models**: Evaluates Decision Trees, Support Vector Machines (SVMs), Gradient Boosting, neural networks, and other algorithms

- **Compares Model Performance**: Utilizes standardized metrics, including accuracy, precision, recall, F1-score, and RMSE

- **Uses Ensemble Learning**: Combines multiple models (e.g., bagging and boosting) to improve predictive performance
- **Eliminates Underperforming Models**: Discards models that fail to meet performance thresholds, thereby saving computational resources

Hyperparameter Tuning

To further optimize model performance, AutoML fine-tunes hyperparameters by

- **Optimizing Hyperparameters**: Utilizes Grid Search, Random Search, or Bayesian Optimization to determine the optimal settings
- **Adjusting Key Parameters**: Tweaks learning rates, neural network layers, and tree depth for optimal performance
- **Reducing Overfitting**: Applies regularization techniques to improve generalization and avoid excessive complexity

Evaluation and Ranking

Once models are trained, AutoML systematically ranks them based on their performance:

- **Uses Validation and Test Datasets**: Compares models objectively using unseen data
- **Generates Performance Reports**: Provides confusion matrices, precision-recall curves, and AUC-ROC scores
- **Provides Feature Importance Insights**: Highlights the most influential variables in model predictions
- **Offers Interpretability Tools**: Uses SHAP values to enhance transparency and trust in model decisions

Deployment

Once the best model is selected, AutoML prepares it for real-world use:

- **Manages Model Serialization and Versioning**: Saves models in a structured format to ensure reproducibility and maintain consistency across different versions.

- **Integrates It with APIs or Cloud Platforms**: Deploys models for easy accessibility and inference.

- **Continuous Model Monitoring**: Detects performance degradation over time and triggers retraining if needed.

- **Automated Retraining Pipelines**: AutoML updates models with new data to keep them relevant and accurate.

Benefits and Limitations of AutoML

As machine learning adoption grows across industries, organizations face challenges such as selecting the right models, tuning hyperparameters, and ensuring consistency in ML workflows. AutoML addresses these challenges by automating various aspects of the model development process, making machine learning more accessible, efficient, and scalable. While AutoML offers significant advantages, it also presents certain limitations that users must consider when implementing it in real-world scenarios.

Benefits of using AutoML

- **Reducing Manual Effort in Feature Engineering, Model Selection, and Hyperparameter Tuning**: Traditional machine learning workflows require extensive manual effort to identify relevant features, choose the best algorithm, and fine-tune hyperparameters for optimal performance. AutoML automates these processes, significantly reducing the time and expertise required. By systematically exploring different configurations and selecting the best-performing models, AutoML enables data scientists to focus on more strategic tasks, such as evaluating business impact, refining model outputs, and integrating machine learning into production environments.

- **Democratizing ML for Nonexperts**: Machine learning has traditionally been the domain of highly skilled data scientists and engineers. AutoML helps bridge this gap by providing user-friendly interfaces, automating model training, and offering guided workflows. It allows business analysts, healthcare practitioners, and marketing specialists to leverage machine learning insights without extensive knowledge of algorithms, coding, or statistical techniques. As a result, organizations can empower a broader group of users to derive value from AI-driven decision-making.

- **Enhancing Reproducibility in ML Experiments**: One of the key challenges in traditional machine learning is ensuring that model training and evaluation processes are reproducible across different experiments, teams, and environments. AutoML enhances reproducibility by maintaining detailed logs of data preprocessing steps, feature transformations, model configurations, and evaluation metrics. This systematic approach enables data scientists to track model changes, compare different runs, and confidently validate findings, making the deployment of consistent and reliable models in production more manageable.

Challenges and Limitations

While AutoML simplifies machine learning and accelerates model development, it is not a one-size-fits-all solution. Certain limitations, such as lack of interpretability, computational costs, and customization constraints, may impact its effectiveness in specific use cases. Organizations must carefully evaluate these factors to determine when and how to integrate AutoML into their workflows. Below are some of the key challenges and limitations of AutoML.

- **Black-Box Nature**

  AutoML models often lack interpretability, making it difficult to understand why specific predictions were made. Unlike traditional machine learning models, where data scientists manually select features and algorithms, AutoML automates much of this process, sometimes leading to results that are not easily explainable. It can be a concern in industries that require high transparency, such as finance (e.g., loan approvals) and healthcare (e.g., disease diagnosis), where understanding the reasoning behind a decision is crucial for compliance and trust.

- **Compute Costs**

    Running multiple models in AutoML can be resource-intensive, requiring significant computational power and cloud storage. AutoML solutions often train numerous algorithms in parallel and evaluate various feature sets, leading to high CPU and GPU usage. While cloud-based AutoML solutions offer scalability, they can also generate unexpected costs if not appropriately monitored. Organizations must carefully manage their computing resources and budget when deploying AutoML at scale.

- **Customization Constraints**

    Some AutoML platforms limit the ability to customize model architectures, hyperparameters, or feature engineering steps, making them less flexible for highly specialized use cases. While AutoML excels at automating standard ML workflows, it may not support advanced customizations such as domain-specific feature engineering, complex ensemble modeling, or deep neural networks with specific architectures. This limitation makes AutoML less suitable for industries requiring high model control and customization, such as scientific research or cutting-edge AI development.

- **Data Quality Dependencies**

    AutoML performance heavily depends on data preprocessing. Poor data quality, such as missing values or unstructured data, can result in suboptimal model outcomes.

By understanding both the strengths and limitations of AutoML, organizations can strategically implement it in their machine learning workflows while recognizing areas that may still require manual intervention.

Why Choose Databricks AutoML?

Databricks AutoML is designed to address machine learning challenges at scale, offering a highly efficient, cloud-native solution for enterprises. It stands out due to its deep integration with **Apache Spark**, built-in experiment tracking, and ability to efficiently handle large-scale data pipelines.

Key Advantages of Databricks AutoML

- **Scalability for Large Datasets: Databricks AutoML is natively built on Apache Spark**, making it highly scalable for massive datasets. This ensures faster data processing and model training than traditional AutoML platforms that rely on in-memory computation.

- **Seamless Data Engineering Integration**: AutoML in Databricks works within a **unified data and AI platform**, integrating directly with **Delta Lake, Databricks Notebooks, and Spark SQL**, allowing smooth transitions between data processing and model training.

- **Built-In MLflow Tracking**: Databricks AutoML **automatically logs all experiment metadata**, including model configurations, hyperparameters, and evaluation metrics, using **MLflow**. This enables better experiment tracking, reproducibility, and seamless model versioning.

- **End-to-End Machine Learning Life Cycle Support**: From **data ingestion to deployment**, Databricks AutoML allows users to preprocess data, train models, and deploy them seamlessly without needing additional infrastructure.

- **Complete Control Over Model Customization**: Unlike AutoML platforms that operate as black-box systems, **Databricks AutoML provides full access to the code behind its trained models**, enabling data scientists to refine further and optimize results based on business needs.

- **Optimized for Enterprise AI Workflows**: With its **cloud-native architecture**, Databricks AutoML dynamically scales workloads, making it an excellent choice for enterprises handling **big data pipelines, AI-driven analytics, and production ML workflows**.
- **Collaboration and Governance**: AutoML in Databricks enables teams of data scientists, engineers, and analysts to collaborate while maintaining **enterprise-grade security, access control, and governance policies**.

Databricks AutoML provides a powerful and flexible AutoML solution for organizations that leverage cloud-based big data analytics and machine learning workflows, emphasizing scalability, reproducibility, and enterprise-grade AI integration.

The next section will explore how to set up and run **Databricks AutoML experiments**, covering best practices and practical demonstrations.

Using Databricks AutoML

In this section, we will learn the steps involved in using AutoML in Databricks.

Setting Up and Running AutoML Experiments

Setting up and running an AutoML experiment in Databricks involves the following key steps.

Preparing the Dataset

Before running an AutoML experiment, the dataset must be formatted correctly to ensure smooth processing. Databricks AutoML supports structured datasets stored in formats such as **Delta Lake, Parquet, or CSV**.

For example, suppose we are working on a housing price prediction problem. In that case, we need a dataset with features such as **square footage, number of bedrooms, number of bathrooms, year built, neighborhood type, and house price, with the latter serving** as the target variable. This dataset should be stored in a location accessible to Databricks.

CHAPTER 5   AUTOML AND MODEL OPTIMIZATION

To store the dataset in **Delta Lake format**, we can use the following code:

```
from pyspark.sql import SparkSession

# Initialize Spark session
spark = SparkSession.builder.appName("AutoML Example").getOrCreate()

# Load data (example DataFrame)
df = spark.read.format("csv").option("header", "true").load("/mnt/data/housing_prices.csv")

# Save dataset in Delta Lake format
df.write.format("delta").mode("overwrite").saveAsTable("housing_price_data")
```

Ensuring the dataset is stored correctly enables Databricks AutoML to efficiently read, process, and analyze the data for model training.

Launching AutoML

Navigate to the Databricks AutoML interface and select the dataset for training.

Choosing the Machine Learning Task

When configuring an **AutoML experiment** in Databricks, you must first identify the type of machine learning problem you are solving. Databricks AutoML supports the following categories:

- **Choose Classification If Predicting Distinct Categories**
  - Used when the target variable belongs to **a set of predefined labels**. For example, predict whether a customer will churn (Yes/No), classify emails as Spam or Not, or determine if a loan application should be **Approved or Rejected**.
  - The model aims to **assign each new data point to one of the given categories**.

- **Choose Regression If Predicting Numerical Values**

  - Used when the target variable is **a continuous number** rather than a category. For example, predicting **house prices based on features** like square footage and location, estimating **sales revenue for the next quarter**, or forecasting **customer lifetime value**.

  - The model aims to **find relationships between input features and produce an exact numerical output**.

- **Choose Time-Series Forecasting If Making Future Predictions Based on Historical Data**

  - Used when the target variable is a **sequence of values changing over time**. For example, predicting **daily electricity demand**, forecasting **stock prices**, or estimating **future website traffic trends**.

  - The model learns patterns from **time-stamped data** and predicts future time points.

Configuring the Experiment

This step specifies key parameters that dictate how AutoML trains and evaluates models. These include

- **Target Variable**: The column in the dataset that AutoML should predict. For example:

  - In a **customer churn prediction task**, the target variable is `whether the customer churns` (Yes/No).

  - In a **housing price prediction task**, the target variable is `price`.

  - In a **sales forecasting task**, the target variable is `sales_volume`.

- **Training Time**: The maximum time AutoML should spend on training models. A longer training time enables AutoML to explore a greater number of models and hyperparameters, thereby improving accuracy. Users can configure time limits based on

- **Quick Exploratory Runs**: Run the model for 10–15 minutes for a fast overview of model performance.

- **Standard Model Training**: Run the model for 30 minutes to 1 hour for optimal results.

- **Extended optimization:** Run the model for multiple hours for highly accurate models in production settings.

  - **Evaluation Metric**: Determines how model performance is measured. AutoML provides various options depending on the task type:

    - **Classification**: Accuracy, F1-score, Precision-Recall (e.g., for spam detection, fraud detection)

    - **Regression**: RMSE (Root Mean Squared Error), MAE (Mean Absolute Error), R^2 (e.g., for predicting housing prices, revenue forecasting)

    - **Time-Series Forecasting**: MAPE (Mean Absolute Percentage Error) and RMSE (e.g., for predicting future sales and energy consumption trends)

By adequately configuring these parameters, users can ensure that AutoML produces models tailored to their business needs and objectives.

Executing the Experiment

Start AutoML, which will train multiple models using different algorithms and hyperparameters.

Reviewing the Experiment Results

Once the experiment is completed, AutoML provides a ranked list of models based on their performance.

AutoML in Databricks streamlines the entire process, making it accessible for experienced data scientists and business analysts without deep machine learning expertise.

Interpreting AutoML Results

Once AutoML completes the experiment, it generates multiple outputs to help users interpret the results and make data-driven decisions. Key components of AutoML results include the following.

Model Leaderboard

Once an AutoML experiment is completed, Databricks AutoML generates a **ranked list of models** based on their performance using the selected evaluation metric. The leaderboard is a comparative tool, helping users quickly identify the best model for deployment and further analysis.

- **How Models Are Ranked:** Each model is evaluated using key metrics relevant to the problem type:

    - **Regression Problems**: RMSE (Root Mean Squared Error), MAE (Mean Absolute Error), and R^2 (Coefficient of Determination) are used to assess model accuracy.

    - **Classification Problems**: Models are ranked based on metrics like Accuracy, Precision, Recall, and F1-score.

    - **Time-Series Forecasting**: Models are evaluated using MAPE (Mean Absolute Percentage Error) and RMSE.

- **Algorithm Comparison:** The leaderboard displays various machine learning algorithms, such as XGBoost, Random Forest, Logistic Regression, and Neural Networks, allowing users to compare how different techniques performed on the dataset.

- **Selecting the Best Model:** Users can easily **click on any model** in the leaderboard to view its detailed performance metrics, compare it with others, and decide whether to deploy it directly or fine-tune it further.

By reviewing the leaderboard, users can efficiently select the most accurate and reliable model for their machine learning use case, reducing the time spent on manual model evaluation.

Feature Importance Analysis

AutoML helps users understand which features (variables) have a significant impact on the model's predictions. This is important because it reveals what factors influence the outcome the most, helping scientists and business users interpret and trust the model.

Hyperparameter Tuning Summary

AutoML tests different model settings (hyperparameters) to find the best configuration. It records these settings, allowing users to fine-tune models further if needed. This helps improve accuracy and ensures the model is optimized for the dataset.

Model Explainability (SHAP Values)

SHAP (SHapley Additive exPlanations) values show how each feature contributed to a specific prediction. This makes models more transparent by explaining why a particular prediction was made, which is especially useful in regulated industries such as healthcare and finance.

Performance Metrics

AutoML evaluates models using different performance measures depending on the type of problem:

- **Regression Problems**: RMSE (Root Mean Squared Error), R^2 (the coefficient of determination, indicating how well the model fits the data), and MAE (Mean Absolute Error).
- **Classification Problems**: Accuracy, precision, recall, and F1-score measure how well the model classifies different categories.
- **Time-Series Forecasting**: MAPE (Mean Absolute Percentage Error) and RMSE to assess prediction accuracy.

Experiment Tracking with MLflow

AutoML automatically logs all models and experiments in MLflow. This feature enables users to revisit past experiments, compare model versions, and confidently deploy the most effective model.

By analyzing these results, users can determine the best model for deployment and make informed decisions about further optimizations.

Model Optimization Techniques

After running an AutoML experiment, the initial model may not always be the best-performing version. Further optimization is often required to refine the model, improve its accuracy, and enhance its overall performance. Without optimization, models might suffer from problems like overfitting, underfitting, slow inference times, or inefficient use of computational resources.

Model optimization strategies help in the following:

- **Reducing Errors**: Fine-tuning parameters and improving data quality can reduce prediction errors and increase accuracy.
- **Enhancing Model Generalization**: Prevents models from being too specific to the training data, allowing them to perform well on unseen data.
- **Increasing Efficiency**: Optimizing model complexity and resource usage leads to faster training and inference.
- **Improving Interpretability**: Selecting important features and simplifying models makes it easier to understand how predictions are made.

This section covers techniques to refine and enhance machine learning models with practical examples.

Techniques for Improving Model Accuracy

In this section, we will discuss the technique used to improve model accuracy.

Feature Engineering

Feature engineering is improving a dataset by creating new features or modifying existing ones so that a machine learning model can learn better. It involves techniques such as

- **Binning**: Grouping numerical values into categories (e.g., age groups: 0–18, 19–35, 36–60)

- **Encoding Categorical Variables**: Converting text-based categories (e.g., "Male/Female") into numbers so the model can process them

- **Feature Scaling**: Standardizing values to a standard range to prevent models from being biased toward more significant numbers

- **Creating Interaction Terms**: Combining two or more features to form a more informative variable

Feature engineering helps extract meaningful information from raw data, making it easier for the model to recognize patterns and make predictions. Well-engineered features help models learn patterns more effectively, reducing bias and improving predictive performance.

For instance, in a **customer churn prediction** model, we can create a new feature to capture customer spending behavior instead of using raw transactional data. This feature provides more meaningful insights, improving the model's ability to distinguish between high-risk and low-risk customers.

Hyperparameter Tuning

Hyperparameters are settings that control how a machine learning model learns from data. Unlike model parameters learned during training, hyperparameters must be set before training begins. They include settings like the number of trees in a random forest, the learning rate in Gradient Boosting, and the number of layers in a neural network. Choosing the correct hyperparameters enables the model to learn efficiently and make more accurate predictions.

Adjusting hyperparameters helps the model learn in a balanced way. If a model is too simple, it may not learn enough from the data (underfitting). It may memorize the training data instead of understanding general patterns (overfitting) if it is too complex. Proper hyperparameter tuning ensures the model strikes the right balance, leading to more accurate predictions.

For example, in **fraud detection using XGBoost**, adjusting hyperparameters such as max_depth (the depth of the Decision Trees) and learning_rate (the rate at which the model updates with each step) can improve accuracy. Using a method like GridSearchCV, we can try different values for these settings and select the optimal combination, thereby reducing errors and enhancing fraud detection rates.

Data Augmentation

Data augmentation is a technique for increasing the size and diversity of a dataset. It involves modifying existing data points to preserve their meaning while making them appear different to the model. Image processing can involve flipping, rotating, or changing brightness levels. In structured datasets, synthetic data points can be generated using statistical techniques to balance class distributions or fill in missing values.

When a model is trained on a small or limited dataset, it may only learn patterns specific to it and struggle to make accurate predictions on new data. Data augmentation helps by creating variations of existing data, increasing the amount of training data, and making the model more adaptable to new situations. This reduces the chances of overfitting, where a model memorizes training data instead of learning general patterns.

For instance, if the training dataset only contains neatly written characters in image classification for handwriting recognition, the model may not perform well on messy or rotated handwriting. By applying **random rotations, contrast adjustments, and stretching**, we create new variations of the original images, enabling the model to learn how to recognize handwriting in various styles and conditions, thereby improving its accuracy. In **image classification for handwriting recognition**, applying random rotations and contrast variations can improve the model's ability to recognize characters under different conditions.

Removing Outliers

Outliers are data points that are very different from most of the dataset. They may be errors, rare occurrences, or unusual values that do not follow typical patterns. These extreme values can mislead the model, making it learn incorrect patterns, which affects its accuracy and generalization ability.

Removing outliers prevents the model from being misled by extreme or incorrect data points. By eliminating these unusual values, the model can focus on recognizing meaningful patterns in the dataset, leading to more stable and accurate predictions.

For instance, in **the prediction of house prices**, if most houses in a city are priced between $200,000 and $500,000, but a few luxury mansions are listed at $10 million, these extreme prices can mislead the model. By removing such extreme values, the model can focus on learning patterns relevant to typical home prices, leading to more accurate and realistic predictions.

Ensembling Models

Ensembling is a technique that combines the strengths of multiple models to make better predictions. Instead of relying on a single model, ensembling uses multiple models with different ways of understanding the data. The overall accuracy and stability improve by averaging or voting on their predictions. The most common ensembling techniques are

- **Bagging (Bootstrap Aggregating)**: This method runs multiple versions of the same model on different data samples and averages the results (e.g., Random Forest).

- **Boosting**: This method trains models sequentially, with each model learning from the mistakes of the previous one (e.g., XGBoost, AdaBoost).

- **Stacking**: Combines the predictions of multiple models using a final meta-model that learns how to best combine them.

Ensembling helps models make better predictions by combining different learning approaches. One model might be good at identifying specific patterns, while another catches different insights. Combining multiple models reduces the risk of making mistakes and improves overall accuracy.

For example, in **credit scoring models**, instead of relying on just one model, we can use a combination of two models:

- A **Random Forest model (bagging technique)** that ensures stable and balanced predictions.

- An **XGBoost model (boosting technique)** that continuously improves by learning from past mistakes. By averaging their predictions, we get a more reliable and accurate score for evaluating credit risk.

Performance Tuning and Optimization Strategies

Performance optimization strategies are crucial in machine learning because they help improve models' efficiency, scalability, and reliability. Even if a model is highly accurate, it may not be helpful in real-world applications if it takes too long to make predictions, consumes excessive computational resources, or cannot handle large-scale data efficiently. Optimizing performance ensures that models run smoothly, process data faster, and deliver real-time insights while minimizing costs and resource usage.

Some key benefits of performance optimization include

- **Faster Model Training and Predictions**: Well-optimized models can quickly process large amounts of data, reducing the time needed for training and inference.

- **Efficient Resource Utilization**: Optimizing model complexity and infrastructure ensures that computing power is used effectively, preventing unnecessary resource consumption.

- **Better Scalability**: Performance tuning allows models to handle increasing amounts of data and users without slowing down or failing.

- **Improved Model Generalization**: Fine-tuning performance helps models maintain accuracy when deployed in production, making them more reliable in real-world scenarios.

By implementing performance optimization techniques, machine learning models become accurate but also practical and efficient for large-scale applications. Let's understand some of the performance optimization techniques.

Reducing Model Complexity

When a machine learning model is too complex, it attempts to memorize the training data rather than identify general patterns. This is known as overfitting, which leads to poor performance when making predictions on new data. Regularization techniques, such as L1 (Lasso) and L2 (Ridge) regularization, help simplify the model by reducing the impact of less important features, making the model more generalizable.

For instance, in **logistic regression for customer segmentation**, applying **L1 regularization (Lasso)** eliminates insignificant features, improving model interpretability and performance.

Optimizing Feature Selection

When a dataset has too many features, some may not provide helpful information for the model. These extra features can create noise, making it more difficult for the model to learn patterns accurately. The model focuses on only the most critical information by removing irrelevant or repetitive features, resulting in more accurate predictions and faster training. This leads to better generalization, meaning the model can make more accurate predictions on new data. It also speeds up training time and lowers computational costs.

For instance, in **sales forecasting**, suppose a dataset includes information like "day of the week," "store location," and "holiday indicator." If an analysis shows that "day of the week" does not significantly impact sales predictions, it can be removed. This helps the model learn from only the most important factors, improving accuracy and efficiency. For instance, using **SHAP values** to drop weak predictors, such as "day of the week," can improve prediction stability in sales forecasting.

Efficient Data Processing

Training a machine learning model can be time-consuming if the data is not processed efficiently. Efficient data processing techniques, such as distributed computing frameworks like Apache Spark, help accelerate the training process and mitigate memory issues. This ensures that even large datasets can be handled smoothly without slowing down computations.

When training a machine learning model, large amounts of data must be processed to find valuable patterns. If data processing is slow, the model may only utilize a small portion of the dataset, resulting in less accurate predictions. Faster data processing enables the model to analyze the entire dataset, resulting in improved learning and enhanced accuracy.

For example, hospitals collect millions of patient records in healthcare analytics, including lab results, prescriptions, and diagnoses. If we use **Apache Spark instead of Pandas**, we can process this massive dataset much faster, enabling the model to analyze all patient data rather than just a small sample. This leads to more accurate predictions for disease risk assessment and treatment recommendations.

Deploying Models with Caching

Caching is a technique for storing frequently accessed models or precomputed results so they do not have to be recalculated every time they are needed. This reduces unnecessary computation and accelerates the prediction process.

Caching allows real-time applications to deliver instant responses by reducing the time taken to generate predictions. This ensures that models can be used efficiently when fast decision-making is required, such as fraud detection or personalized recommendations.

For instance, when a user visits an ecommerce website in real-time recommendation systems, caching the **previously computed product recommendations** allows the system to instantly serve personalized suggestions instead of recalculating them from scratch for every request.

Scaling Infrastructure

Machine learning models require computing power to process data and make predictions. The training process can slow down or fail if there are not enough computing resources (CPU, RAM, or storage). Scaling infrastructure involves automatically adjusting computing resources in response to demand, ensuring smooth model training and deployment.

When a model has sufficient resources, it can train on larger datasets, perform more complex calculations, and complete training more quickly. This leads to better learning from data, improving accuracy. A model may struggle with large datasets without proper scaling, resulting in incomplete learning and inaccurate predictions.

For example, in **fraud detection for credit card transactions**, the number of transactions can spike during the holiday season. If the fraud detection model lacks sufficient computing power, it may take an excessive amount of time to analyze transactions, resulting in delays. Using **Databricks autoscaling clusters**, the system can increase computing power during peak times and scale down during low traffic, ensuring the fraud detection model runs efficiently without slowing down or missing fraudulent transactions.

CHAPTER 5 AUTOML AND MODEL OPTIMIZATION

Hands-On Lab 1: AutoML Experiment for Housing Price Prediction

Scenario

Real estate prices fluctuate based on multiple factors such as location, square footage, number of bedrooms, and market conditions. Predicting house prices accurately is crucial for buyers, sellers, and investors. Using Databricks AutoML, we can automate the training process of multiple machine learning models to determine the best-performing model for housing price prediction.

In this hands-on lab, we will

1. Generate a sample dataset containing relevant housing features.
2. Use **Databricks AutoML** to train and evaluate models.
3. Interpret the results to understand model performance and predictions.

Prerequisites

Ensure that you have a cluster created with Machine Learning runtime, as shown in Figure 5-1.

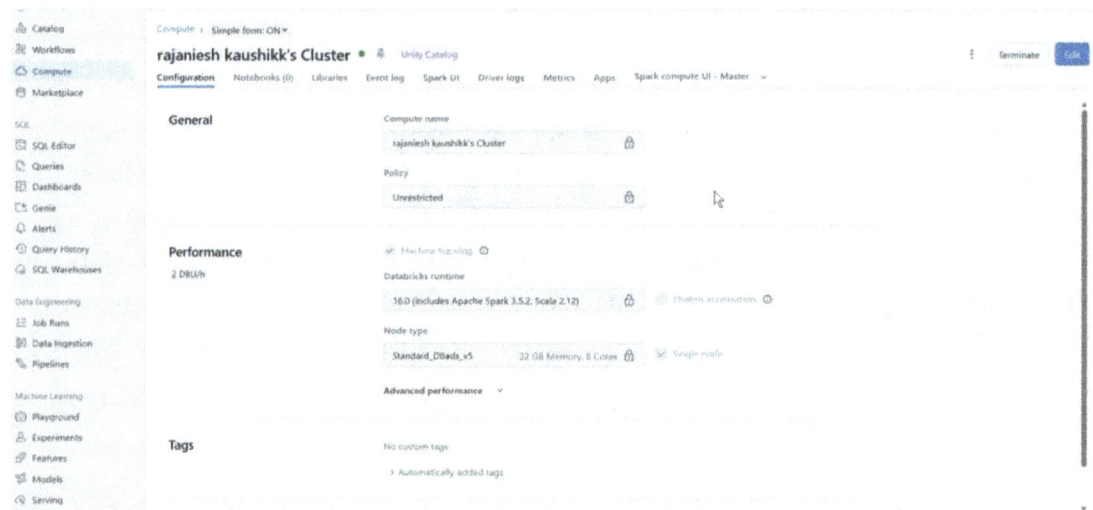

Figure 5-1. Cluster with machine learning runtime

Generating the Sample Dataset

To start our AutoML experiment, we first need a dataset. Below is the code to generate synthetic housing data, including features like square footage, number of bedrooms, and lot size. Here is the code to generate the sample data:

```
from pyspark.sql import SparkSession
from pyspark.sql.functions import rand, when
df = (spark.range(5000)
    .withColumn("square_feet", (rand()*5000 + 500).cast("double"))
    .withColumn("num_bedrooms", (rand()*5 + 1).cast("int"))
    .withColumn("num_bathrooms", (rand()*3 + 1).cast("int"))
    .withColumn("year_built", (rand()*100 + 1920).cast("int"))
    .withColumn("neighborhood", when(rand() > 0.5, "Urban").
    otherwise("Suburban"))
    .withColumn("price", (rand()*900000 + 100000).cast("double"))
)
df.write.format("delta").mode("overwrite").saveAsTable("housing_price_data")
# Display the dataset
display(spark.sql("SELECT * FROM housing_price_data LIMIT 5"))
```

This dataset represents **1000 houses**, each with randomly generated attributes. The **house price** is our target variable, which we aim to predict based on the other features.

Running AutoML in Databricks

Now that we have our dataset, we will use **Databricks AutoML** to train models and find the best-performing one.

Launch Databricks AutoML

1. Open your **Databricks Workspace**.
2. Navigate to the **Machine Learning** section.
3. Click Experiments on the left sidebar. This will be shown on the screen in Figure 5-2.

CHAPTER 5 AUTOML AND MODEL OPTIMIZATION

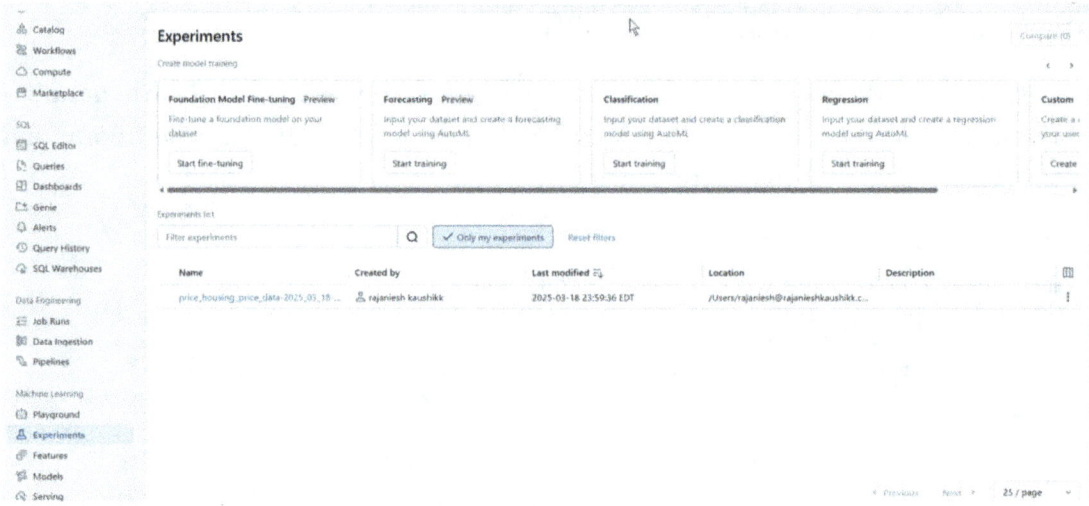

Figure 5-2. *Databricks Experiments tab*

You will select the experiment types. Click the Start Training button under the Regression tile, and you will be taken to the next screen, where you can choose the ML cluster you created earlier, as shown in Figure 5-3.

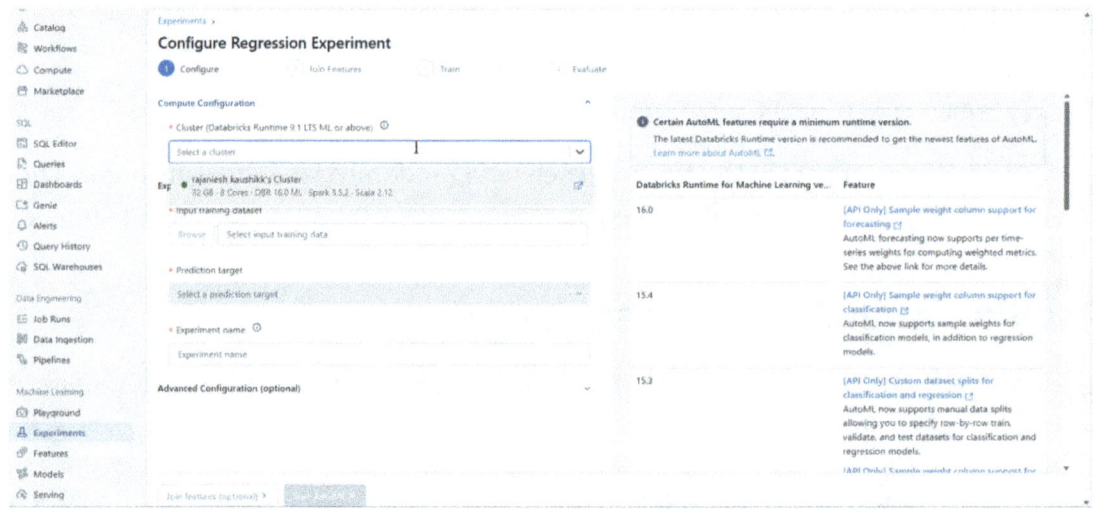

Figure 5-3. *Selecting the experiment types and other configurations*

CHAPTER 5   AUTOML AND MODEL OPTIMIZATION

Select the Dataset

1. In the input training dataset, select ***the housing_price_data*** dataset created earlier, as shown in Figure 5-4.

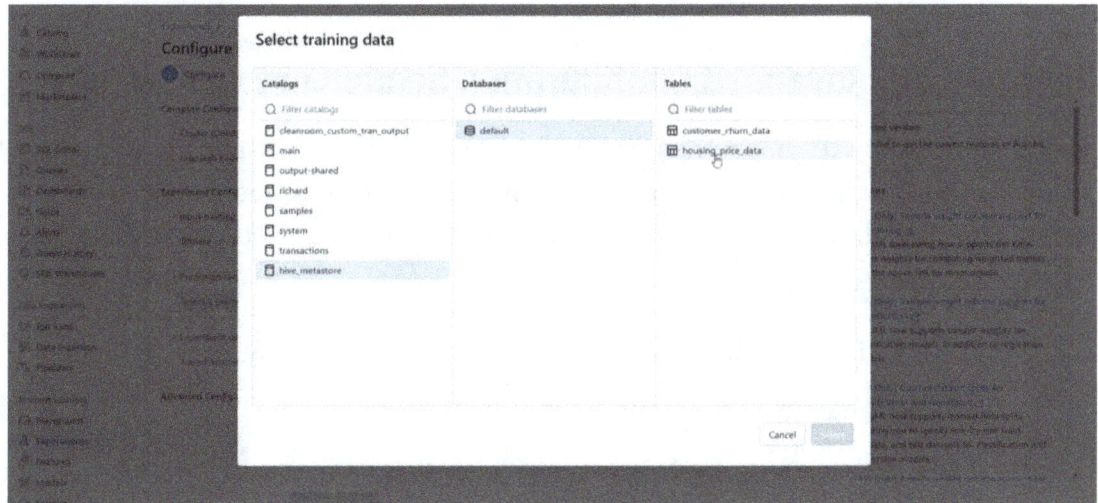

Figure 5-4. *Selecting the Datasets for the experiment*

You will now be taken to the Configure Regression Experiment screen. There, you can select the schema and prediction target, as shown in Figure 5-5.

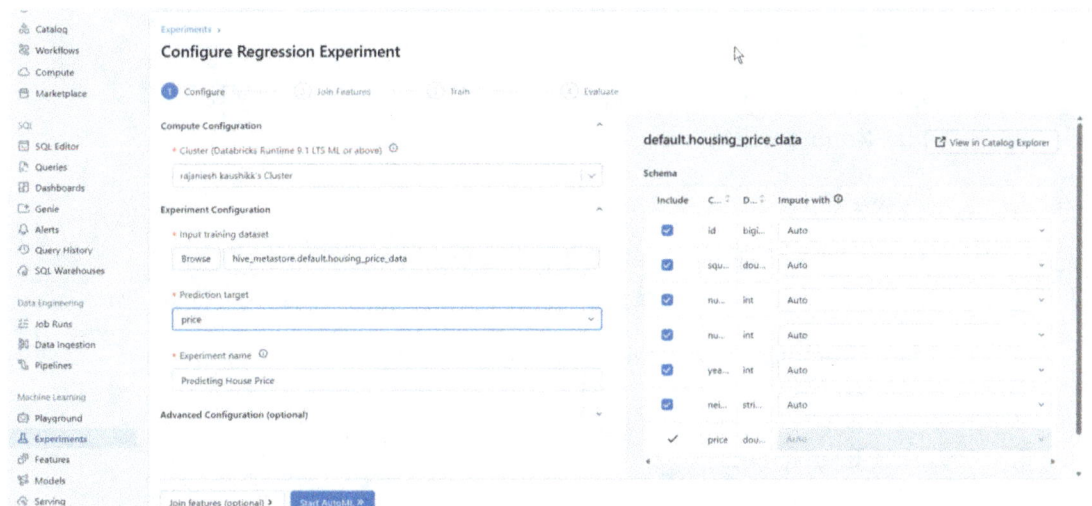

Figure 5-5. *Selecting the schema and prediction target for the experiment*

241

Choose Prediction Type

1. Select **Regression** since we predict a numerical value (**price**).

2. Set the **Target Column** price , as we aim to predict the house price based on various factors.

Configure the Advanced Configuration Section in Experiments

Expand the Advanced Configuration, and provide the values as shown in Figure 5-6. The **Advanced Configuration** section in the **AutoML experiment setup screen** enables users to fine-tune the AutoML process for improved performance and customization.

1. **Evaluation Metric**

    - This defines how the model's performance will be measured.

    - **Example**

        - R-squared: Used for **regression** models to measure how well the model explains the variance in the data

        - RMSE (Root Mean Squared Error): Measures the error in numerical predictions

        - Accuracy, F1-score: Typically used for **classification** tasks

2. **Experiment Directory**

    - Specifies the location where Databricks will store AutoML experiment artifacts.

    - **Example**

        - /Users/rajaniesh@rajanieshkaushikk.com/databricks_automl/

    - This directory will contain logs, trained models, and evaluation reports.

3. **Training Frameworks**

    - Lists the machine learning libraries AutoML will use to train models.

- **Options Available**
    - `lightgbm`: Lightweight Gradient Boosting Model (good for structured datasets)
    - `sklearn`: Scikit-learn models (e.g., Random Forest, Linear Regression)
    - `xgboost`: Extreme Gradient Boosting (performs well on tabular data)
- Multiple frameworks can be selected, allowing Databricks to compare models from different algorithms.

4. **Timeout (Minutes)**
    - The maximum duration for the AutoML experiment to run.
    - **Example**
        - `120 minutes` means AutoML will stop training models after two hours.
    - Longer time allows more models and hyperparameter tuning, but increases computational costs.

5. **Time Column for Training/Validation/Testing Split**
    - If the dataset contains a **timestamp** column, this option lets you split data into training, validation, and test sets based on time.
    - **Example**
        - In a **time-series forecasting model**, selecting a column like `transaction_date` ensures older data is used for training while newer data is used for testing.

6. **Intermediate Data Storage Location**
    - Defines where intermediate outputs (like feature engineering results) will be stored.

CHAPTER 5 AUTOML AND MODEL OPTIMIZATION

- **Options**
  - `MLflow Artifact`: Stores intermediate data in MLflow for tracking
  - `DBFS`: Stores intermediate data in **Databricks File System**

7. **Custom Data Splits**
   - Allows users to manually define how data is split for training, validation, and testing.
   - **Example**
     - If you have a `split_column` with values "train", "test", and "validate", AutoML will use these for data partitioning instead of random splits.

Figure 5-6. Selecting data partitions for training and testing

Now, you can click "Start AutoML Experiment" or click the "Join" feature. Let's understand Join Features.

Join Features

The **"Join Features"** step in the AutoML experiment setup allows users to **enhance their training dataset** by incorporating additional feature tables. This step is particularly useful when multiple data sources are involved and you want to enrich your model with more meaningful information.

1. **Feature Table Selection**

    - The drop-down labeled **"Feature Table"** allows users to select additional datasets from the **Databricks Feature Store**.

    - Feature tables contain engineered features that can improve the model's accuracy.

    - **Example Use Case**

        - If the main dataset contains housing attributes such as square feet, bedrooms, and price, an additional feature table could include economic indicators (interest rates, local job growth) to enhance prediction accuracy.

2. **Add Another Feature Table**

    - Clicking **"Add another feature table"** allows users to join multiple tables to the training dataset.

    - This is useful when features are stored in separate datasets but are linked by a common identifier (e.g., `house_id`).

3. **Schema Preview**

    - The right-side panel **displays the dataset schema**, showing

        - **Column names**

        - **Data types** (e.g., int, string, double)

        - **Imputation method** (Auto by default)

4. **Impute with (Missing Values Handling)**

    - This allows users to specify how missing values should be handled.

CHAPTER 5 AUTOML AND MODEL OPTIMIZATION

- **Options**
    - `Auto`: Let Databricks determine the best approach to handling missing values.
    - `Mean/Median`: Fill missing values with the average/median of that column.
    - `Zero/Custom Value`: Replace missing values with zero or another predefined value.
- **Example**
    - If a house has a missing number of bathrooms, AutoML can fill it using the median value from other houses.

Figure 5-7. Join Features step in the experiment

Once AutoML starts, it will automatically test different machine learning models and hyperparameters to find the best-performing model.

Interpreting AutoML Results

Once the AutoML experiment is completed, Databricks provides detailed insights about the experiment. Here is how to interpret the results:

CHAPTER 5   AUTOML AND MODEL OPTIMIZATION

Reviewing the Experiment

Navigate to the **Experiments** tab in the AutoML results, and you will find the overview section as depicted in Figure 5-8. Let's understand it:

1. **Overview**

    - **Training Dataset:** Shows the dataset used (`hive_metastore.default.housing_price_data` in this case)

    - **Target Column:** Specifies the column being predicted (`price`)

    - **Evaluation Metric:** Indicates the metric used to evaluate model performance (`val_r2_score` - R-squared)

    - **Timeout:** The total time allocated for model training (`5 minutes` in this case)

    - **AutoML Evaluation Status:** Marks completion and confirms that all runs have been recorded

2. **Best Model Information**

    - The model with the **best validation R² score** is highlighted as the top performer.

    - Users can

        - **View the Notebook for the Best Model**: This allows you to inspect the exact training code.

        - **View the Data Exploration Notebook**: Shows how the dataset was analyzed before training.

3. **Runs Table Tab**
    This section lists all **models trained during the experiment**, including

    - **Run Name:** Unique identifier for each experiment

    - **Created:** When the experiment was executed

    - **Dataset Used:** Links to the dataset used in training

    - **Duration:** Time taken for each model training run

CHAPTER 5   AUTOML AND MODEL OPTIMIZATION

- **Model Type:** Lists algorithms used (e.g., lightgbm, xgboost, sklearn)

- **Metrics (val_r2_score, RMSE, etc.):** Performance metrics for comparison

- **Source:** Links to the training notebook for deeper insights

All these settings are depicted in Figure 5-8.

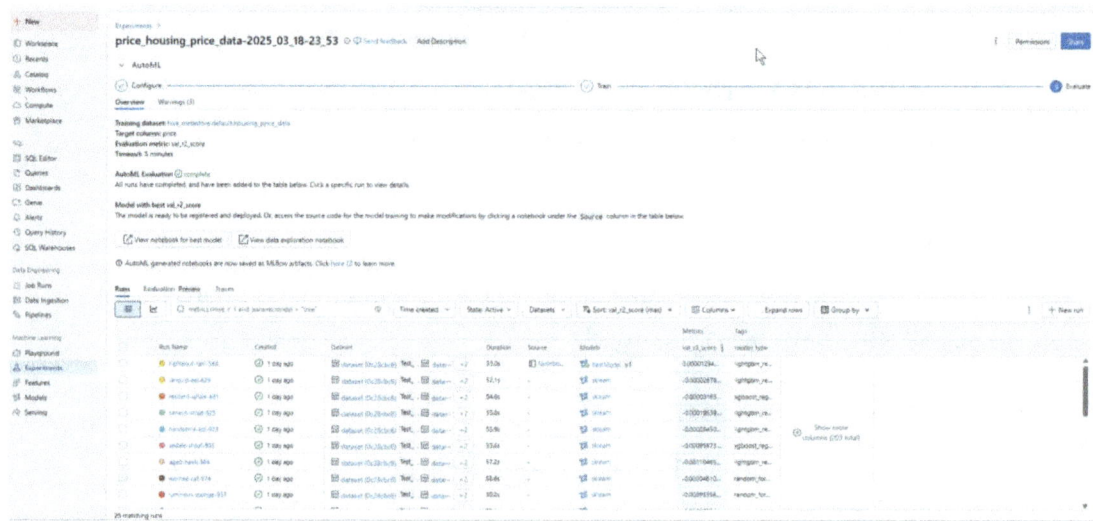

Figure 5-8. List of models trained

4. **Evaluation Tab**

    The **Evaluation** tab enables users to assess the performance of trained models using various metrics.
    Key Features in the Evaluation Tab

    - **Search Metrics Textbox:** This option allows you to add search criteria and filter the model to only those that meet these criteria.

    - *Model Comparisons:* Users can compare models based on different metrics, as depicted in Figure 5-9.

CHAPTER 5   AUTOML AND MODEL OPTIMIZATION

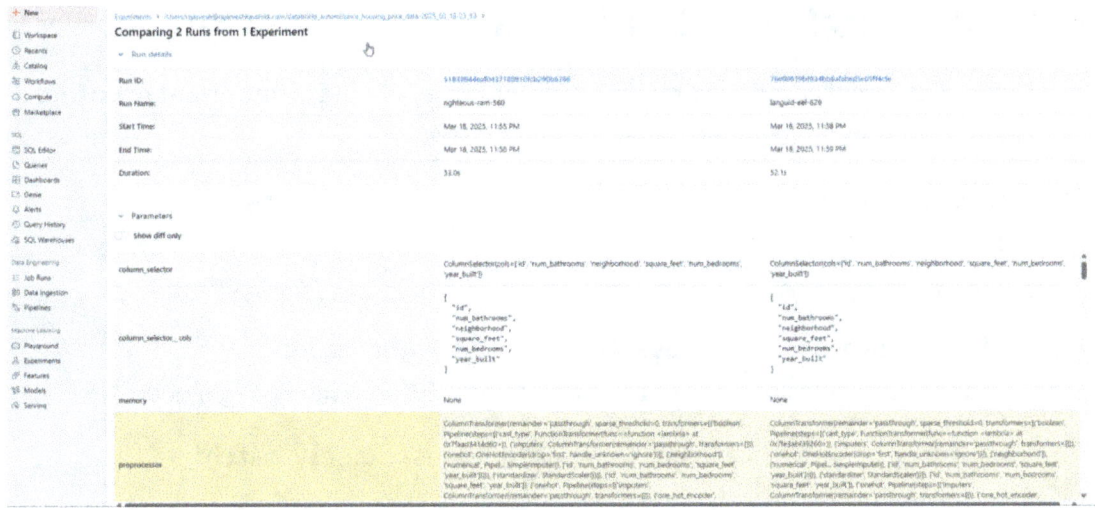

Figure 5-9. *Evaluate trained models using various metrics*

5. **Traces Tab**

    This tab displays all the traces logged for this experiment. MLflow supports automatic tracing for many popular generative AI frameworks (OpenAI, LangChain/LangGraph, LlamaIndex, DSPy, CrewAI, AutoGen, Anthropic, Bedrock, LiteLLM, Gemini, Custom), as depicted in Figure 5-10.

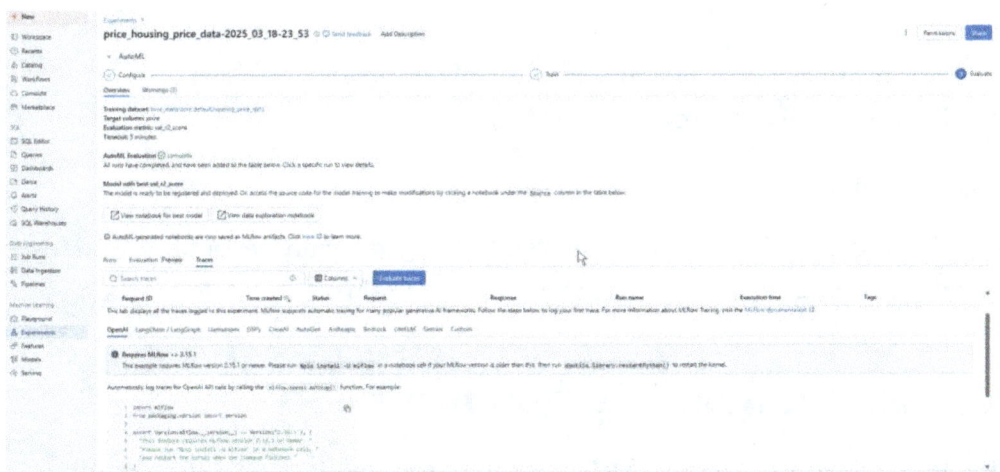

Figure 5-10. *Experiments evaluation tracing tab*

Testing the Model After Registration

Once the model is registered, testing it on a different set of data is important to ensure it generalizes well. Run the code below to test the model.

```
import mlflow.pyfunc
import pandas as pd
import numpy as np

# Load the trained model and use the run id of the model
model = mlflow.pyfunc.load_model("runs:/<Run ID of the Model>/model")

# Create a sample input dataset with data types exactly matching the
training schema
sample_data = pd.DataFrame([
    {
        "id": np.int64(1),
        "square_feet": np.float64(2500.0),   # Convert explicitly to float64
        "num_bedrooms": np.int32(3),    # Ensure int32, not int64
        "num_bathrooms": np.int32(2),   # Ensure int32
        "year_built": np.int32(2010),   # Ensure int32
        "neighborhood": "Downtown"   # String type
    }
])

# Make predictions
predictions = model.predict(sample_data)

print(predictions)
```

By following these steps, you can successfully **train, evaluate, deploy, and test a house price prediction model using Databricks AutoML.**

Databricks AutoML Python API

The **Databricks AutoML Python API** offers a programmatic approach to running AutoML experiments directly within a notebook. Instead of using the Databricks UI, users can configure and execute AutoML runs using Python, making it ideal for integration into automated workflows and reproducible experiments.

Why Use the AutoML Python API?

The Databricks AutoML Python API provides a more flexible and customizable approach compared to the UI-based AutoML experience. It allows users to dynamically configure parameters, making it easier to fine-tune model training. This API is particularly useful when integrating AutoML into automated machine learning workflows within Databricks notebooks and data pipelines. Additionally, all experiments and models are automatically logged in MLflow, providing a structured way to track, compare, and deploy models efficiently.

Running AutoML Using Python API

```
import databricks.automl

# Run AutoML for classification
summary = databricks.automl.classify(
    dataset="loan_default_data",  # Delta table containing input data
    target_col="default",  # Target column for prediction
    timeout_minutes=15,  # Experiment duration
    primary_metric="f1"  # Optimize for F1-score
)
```

Evaluating and Deploying the Best Model

After the AutoML experiment completes, we need to evaluate the best-performing model, retrieve the experiment details, and deploy the model for inference. The following steps will guide you through retrieving results and making predictions using the best-trained model.

Retrieving AutoML Results

The best model's details, including the experiment notebook and MLflow tracking information, can be accessed using the following code:

```
# Import required libraries
import mlflow
```

CHAPTER 5 AUTOML AND MODEL OPTIMIZATION

```
import databricks.automl
from pyspark.sql import SparkSession

# Retrieve the Databricks workspace URL correctly
workspace_url = spark.conf.get("spark.databricks.workspaceUrl")

# View AutoML Experiment Summary
print(f"Best model notebook: {summary.best_trial.notebook_path}")
# Best model notebook path
print(f"MLflow Experiment ID: {summary.experiment.experiment_id}")
# Retrieve the experiment ID

# Construct the MLflow Experiment URL dynamically
mlflow_url = f"https://{workspace_url}/#mlflow/experiments/
{summary.experiment.experiment_id}"

print(f"MLflow Experiment URL: {mlflow_url}")   # Display clickable MLflow URL
```

This code dynamically retrieves the Databricks workspace URL and constructs the **MLflow Experiment URL**, allowing users to analyze experiment logs, compare models, and monitor model performance.

Loading and Testing the Best Model

Once the best model has been identified, it can be loaded and used for predictions. The following code loads the model from MLflow and makes a prediction using a sample loan applicant's data:

```
import mlflow.pyfunc
import pandas as pd
import numpy as np

# Load the best trained model from MLflow
```

```
best_model = mlflow.pyfunc.load_model(f"runs:/{summary.best_trial.
mlflow_run_id}/model")

# Create a sample new applicant for prediction (Including applicant_id)
new_applicant = pd.DataFrame([{
    "applicant_id": np.int64(1),   # Placeholder value to match
    training schema
    "income": np.float64(5000),    # Monthly income
    "credit_score": np.float64(650), # Credit score
    "loan_amount": np.float64(15000),  # Loan amount requested
    "loan_term": np.int32(36),   # Loan duration in months
    "employment_status": "Employed"  # Categorical feature
}])

# Make a prediction: Will this applicant default?
prediction = best_model.predict(new_applicant)

print("Prediction:", "Default" if prediction[0] == 1 else "No Default")
```

This script loads the best model and tests it on a new sample applicant, predicting whether they are likely to default.

Hands-On Lab 2: Predicting Loan Defaults Using Databricks AutoML (Python API)

Objective

In this hands-on exercise, you will build a machine learning model using **Databricks AutoML** to predict loan defaults. This will enable financial institutions to assess loan applications more effectively and reduce credit risk. You will follow a step-by-step process, from data generation to model deployment, using Databricks AutoML via the Python API.

Chapter 5 AutoML and Model Optimization

Overview

By the end of this exercise, you will

- Generate a sample loan application dataset.
- Train a **classification model** using **Databricks AutoML**.
- Evaluate the best-performing model.
- Deploy and test the trained model using **MLflow**.

Generate Sample Loan Application Data

Create a synthetic dataset by following these steps:

1. Open a new **Databricks Notebook**.

2. Copy and paste the following code into a new **code cell** to generate a synthetic dataset of **loan applicants**:

```
# Import required libraries
from pyspark.sql import SparkSession
from pyspark.sql.functions import col, rand, when, round

# Generate synthetic dataset
loan_data = spark.range(0, 1000).withColumn("income", round(rand() * 8000 + 2000, 0)) \
    .withColumn("credit_score", round(rand() * 550 + 300, 0)) \
    .withColumn("loan_amount", round(rand() * 40000 + 5000, 0)) \
    .withColumn("loan_term", when(rand() > 0.5, 36).otherwise(60)) \
    .withColumn("employment_status", when(rand() > 0.6, "Employed").otherwise("Unemployed")) \
    .withColumn("default", when(rand() > 0.7, 1).otherwise(0))  # 30% default probability

# Save dataset as a Delta Table for AutoML
loan_data.write.format("delta").mode("overwrite").saveAsTable("loan_default_data")
```

```
# Display sample data
loan_data.show(5)
```

You should see a table with 1000 rows containing loan applicant details. The default column represents whether an applicant **defaulted on their loan** (1 = Yes, 0 = No).

Run AutoML for Loan Default Prediction

Create a new **code cell**, and run the following command to start an **AutoML experiment**:

```
# Import AutoML library
import databricks.automl

# Run AutoML for classification (loan default prediction)
summary = databricks.automl.classify(
    dataset = "loan_default_data",
    target_col = "default",  # Predicting loan default (1 or 0)
    timeout_minutes = 20,  # Set AutoML run time
    primary_metric = "f1",  # Optimize for F1-score
)
```

Databricks AutoML automatically trains multiple machine learning models and returns a summary of the best-performing model.

Evaluate AutoML Results

Create a new **code cell**, and run the following command to view the best model's details:

```
# View AutoML Experiment Summary
print(f"Best model notebook: {summary.best_trial.notebook_path}")
# Best model notebook path
print(f"MLflow Experiment ID: {summary.experiment.experiment_id}")
# Retrieve the experiment ID
```

CHAPTER 5 AUTOML AND MODEL OPTIMIZATION

```python
# Retrieve Databricks workspace URL dynamically
workspace_url = spark.conf.get("spark.databricks.workspaceUrl")

# Construct the MLflow Experiment URL dynamically
mlflow_url = f"https://{workspace_url}/#mlflow/experiments/{summary.experiment.experiment_id}"

print(f"MLflow Experiment URL: {mlflow_url}")   # Display clickable MLflow URL
```

This step provides

- A link to the **best model's notebook**
- A **clickable MLflow experiment URL** to track model training and performance

Deploy and Test the Best Model

Create a new **code cell**, and run the following command to load the best model and predict loan default for a **new applicant**:

```python
import mlflow.pyfunc
import pandas as pd
import numpy as np

# Load the best trained model from MLflow
best_model = mlflow.pyfunc.load_model(f"runs:/{summary.best_trial.mlflow_run_id}/model")

# Create a sample new applicant for prediction (Including applicant_id)
new_applicant = pd.DataFrame([{
    "applicant_id": np.int64(1),   # Placeholder value to match training schema
    "income": np.float64(5000),    # Monthly income
    "credit_score": np.float64(650),  # Credit score
```

```
        "loan_amount": np.float64(15000),  # Loan amount requested
        "loan_term": np.int32(36),  # Loan duration in months
        "employment_status": "Employed"  # Categorical feature
}])

# Make a prediction: Will this applicant default?
prediction = best_model.predict(new_applicant)

print("Prediction:", "Default" if prediction[0] == 1 else "No Default")
```

The model will return either **1 (Default)** or **0 (No Default)** based on the applicant's details.

Summary

Building a machine learning model that performs well in production traditionally requires extensive manual effort across several iterative stages, including data preprocessing, feature engineering, algorithm selection, and hyperparameter tuning. This chapter introduced **Automated Machine Learning (AutoML)** as a powerful paradigm shift that reduces complexity and accelerates development by automating many of these steps. Framed through the lens of Databricks AutoML, you gain a hands-on understanding of how modern platforms democratize access to advanced machine learning techniques, enabling practitioners to generate high-quality models with minimal intervention.

The chapter began by defining the core principles of AutoML and its widespread applicability across various industries, including healthcare, finance, manufacturing, and ecommerce. Real-world scenarios, such as fraud detection and sales forecasting, demonstrate how AutoML streamlines model development, reduces human bias, and enhances reproducibility. Readers learned how AutoML platforms handle everything from data cleansing and feature selection to model training and performance evaluation, often outperforming manual approaches through systematic optimization.

CHAPTER 5   AUTOML AND MODEL OPTIMIZATION

Using Databricks AutoML as the foundation, this chapter guides you through the complete life cycle of configuring and launching experiments, analyzing the resulting model leaderboard, and interpreting performance metrics using tools like SHAP values. The use of MLflow for automatic experiment tracking provided transparency and repeatability, which are essential for operationalizing models at scale. Beyond automation, the chapter explored advanced model optimization techniques, including feature engineering, hyperparameter tuning, ensembling, and outlier removal, emphasizing how these strategies enhance accuracy, efficiency, and model interpretability.

To reinforce these concepts, you completed two hands-on labs: one focused on housing price prediction using the Databricks AutoML UI and the other on loan default classification via the Python API. Both labs enabled readers to implement real-world solutions while building practical expertise in deploying scalable machine learning pipelines within the Databricks ecosystem.

Having now mastered the creation and refinement of models using AutoML, the next logical step is to learn how to bring these models into production environments. In **Chapter 6: Deploying Machine Learning Models**, we will explore strategies for model serving, versioning, monitoring, and life cycle management using MLflow and Databricks-native tools, ensuring that your trained models are not only accurate but also reliable, scalable, and ready for real-world impact.

CHAPTER 6

Deploying Machine Learning Models

Imagine you've just spent weeks refining a machine learning model that accurately predicts customer churn. Your Jupyter Notebook reports that the model can identify 92% of likely defectors, translating into millions of dollars in retained revenue if acted upon correctly. The team is excited. The results are compelling. The potential impact is clear.

But then comes the pivotal question:

"How do we use this model in our business?"

This question marks the transition from **data science experimentation to operational value creation**. It's the difference between a high-performing prototype and a solution that directly influences decisions in production environments.

Unfortunately, this transition—known as **model deployment**—is where many machine learning projects stall. A model that performs brilliantly in development creates **zero business value** unless deployed into a reliable, scalable system that integrates seamlessly with real-time applications or batch processes.

Model deployment is the bridge that connects the exploratory world of data science with the practical needs of business operations. Without it, even the most accurate models remain academic exercises, unused and unnoticed.

This chapter guides you through the **end-to-end process of deploying machine learning models in Databricks using MLflow**. We'll cover deployment strategies (batch, real-time, edge), environment reproducibility, dependency management, versioning, monitoring, and life cycle control—everything needed to turn your model into a production-grade service.

CHAPTER 6   DEPLOYING MACHINE LEARNING MODELS

Learning Objectives

By the end of this chapter, you will be able to

- **Evaluate deployment strategies** and select the right one for your business needs.

- **Design robust deployment architectures** that ensure scalability, security, and maintainability.

- **Implement end-to-end deployment workflows** using MLflow in Databricks.

- **Apply best practices** to reduce operational risk and increase model adoption.

- **Create monitoring systems** that track prediction quality, latency, and drift.

- **Manage model life cycles** with versioning, retraining, and rollback strategies.

Model Deployment: What It Takes to Go Live

Model deployment is often misunderstood as simply saving your trained model to a file—whether a `.pkl`, `.onnx`, or `.mlmodel`. While keeping your model is an important technical milestone, it's only the beginning of a broader journey. Real deployment makes your model available for use in a live business environment, where it can provide predictions that influence real-world outcomes.

To put it more plainly, training a model is akin to designing a prototype gadget in a laboratory. Deployment is taking that gadget, packaging it safely, distributing it to customers, and ensuring it works flawlessly in all environments—rain or shine. For a machine learning model, this means embedding it within an application, connecting it to live data sources, ensuring it responds quickly to requests, and maintaining its security and reliability.

However, deployment is not just about exposing and calling an API daily. A lot is happening behind the scenes to ensure the model performs consistently over time. It must scale gracefully when demand increases, be easy to update or roll back if

CHAPTER 6 DEPLOYING MACHINE LEARNING MODELS

something goes wrong, and provide logs and metrics so teams can monitor its behavior. It must also integrate cleanly with existing data pipelines, adhere to security policies, and be transparent enough to meet governance requirements.

For beginners, think of model deployment as setting up an automated assistant that makes predictions for your business. It should be trustworthy, fast, and smart—but also safe, compliant, and easy to maintain. In the sections ahead, we'll uncover what it takes to build such a system and why getting deployment right is just as important as building a great model in the first place.

Key Components of a Successful Deployment

To deploy a model effectively, you must address a combination of technical and operational areas that make the model production-ready. These areas are the foundational pillars upon which scalable, secure, and maintainable machine learning systems are built. Ignoring any of them can lead to brittle deployments that fail under pressure, deliver incorrect predictions, or compromise sensitive data. These domains work in unison to ensure the model's utility doesn't stop at development notebooks but thrives in live business applications. Let's explore each one in detail:

- **Model Serialization**: This is the foundational step where the trained machine learning model is saved into a portable and standardized format such as `.pkl`, `.onnx`, or `.mlmodel`. Serialization allows your model to be stored, transferred, and reused without retraining. Consider this a way to save your game progress—you'll want to return later and pick up where you left off. By serializing your model, you ensure that it can be loaded and executed in various environments, including staging, production, and mobile applications. This step is critical for reproducibility, sharing, and long-term maintenance.

- **Environment Packaging**: Machine learning models depend on specific versions of libraries and tools to function correctly. These might include Python packages such as `scikit-learn`, pandas, and numpy, or even system-level dependencies. If the environment in which you deploy your model does not match the one used during training, the model might fail or produce inconsistent results. Environment packaging captures all these dependencies so that the model can be reliably reproduced and executed anywhere—on a colleague's laptop, in a test environment, or on a production server. Tools like `requirements.txt`, `conda.yaml`, or Docker images help you establish a consistent setup. To understand it in simple terms, think of this as saving not just the dish you cooked but also the exact recipe, ingredients, and kitchen tools you used so anyone can recreate it the same way every single time.

- **Integration**: Once a machine learning model is trained and ready, it must be seamlessly integrated into the existing business systems. Integration is connecting your model to the applications and workflows that will use its predictions. This integration may involve deploying the model as a REST API that can be accessed by web or mobile applications, embedding it in a data processing pipeline for nightly batch jobs, or integrating it directly into a business intelligence dashboard where stakeholders can view predictions.

  Think of integration as adding a new smart device to your home. Whether it's a thermostat, speaker, or security camera, it must be connected to your home network and configured to work with your daily routines. Similarly, models must be accessible to the right systems and people, with well-defined inputs and outputs, so that they can produce actionable insights at the right time and place. A well-integrated model becomes part of the decision-making process, not just a separate technical artifact.

- **Security**: In any production system, especially those involving machine learning models that may process sensitive data, security must be a top priority. Security in model deployment involves several critical practices that protect both the model and the data it operates on. This security process includes enforcing access controls to ensure that only authorized users or systems can interact with the model, setting up audit trails to record who accessed what and when, and applying data protection policies that comply with industry regulations, such as GDPR or HIPAA.

  Security is like locking the doors and setting up surveillance in a building where important work is being done. You wouldn't want just anyone walking in or sensitive documents being read by the wrong eyes. Likewise, you don't want unauthorized code modifying your model or someone intercepting prediction results over the network.

Proper security practices help build trust in your ML solution and protect your organization from data breaches, misuse, or legal consequences.

- **Monitoring** involves continuously observing and analyzing the performance of a deployed model in real-world scenarios. This monitoring process includes tracking prediction accuracy, latency (the time it takes for the model to respond), throughput (the number of predictions it can handle), and changes in input data patterns, commonly referred to as data drift. A model that worked well during training may start to degrade in production due to shifts in customer behavior, seasonality, or new market conditions. These issues might go unnoticed without proper monitoring, leading to poor decisions or user dissatisfaction.

  For example, imagine a model that predicts product demand for a retail chain. Initially, it performs well, helping optimize inventory. However, customer preferences shift over time, and a new competitor enters the market. If monitoring isn't in place to flag these changes, the model may continue making outdated predictions, resulting in overstocked or understocked shelves. Effective monitoring would trigger alerts or dashboards that signal the need to retrain or recalibrate the model to maintain its value in a changing environment.

- **Life Cycle Management**: Life cycle management refers to the processes that support a machine learning model throughout its operational life, from initial deployment to eventual retirement. This life cycle process involves updating the model when new data becomes available, rolling back to a previous version if a new deployment causes issues, and maintaining a clear version history for traceability and compliance purposes.

  For example, consider a recommendation engine used by a streaming platform. Over time, user preferences evolve, and new content is added constantly. The recommendation model must be updated periodically to reflect these changes. If a new version of the model performs poorly, perhaps due to flawed training data, it should be possible to quickly revert to the previous stable version. By maintaining a versioned registry of all models and tracking changes over time, teams can manage updates with greater confidence, troubleshoot issues more effectively, and meet regulatory requirements for audit and transparency.

These components form the operational scaffold that enables a model to move beyond experimentation.

Case Study: Launching a Product to Market

Think of model deployment as similar to shipping a consumer product. It's not just about creating something useful—it's about ensuring that it reaches the user in a way that's safe, reliable, and ready for use. In the same way that companies must plan for manufacturing, packaging, transportation, delivery, and customer support for a product, machine learning teams must carefully orchestrate the steps that turn a model into a production-ready solution.

For instance, launching a new smartphone involves more than just building the device; it also requires careful planning and execution. The phone must be packaged with accessories and instructions, tested for compatibility with various networks, shipped to global markets, monitored for performance once in users' hands, and regularly updated with new software. Even a top-tier product can quickly lose its reputation if these steps are not taken.

The model deployment follows a similar multistep path:

1. **Packaging**: Your model and its dependencies (libraries, configurations, environment details) must be bundled to work together in the target environment.

2. **Compatibility**: Just as a phone must support SIM cards and power adapters in various regions, models need validation to ensure they handle inputs, outputs, and schemas as expected in production systems.

3. **Delivery**: The model must be transferred and activated at its final destination, whether it is a cloud-based endpoint, an embedded edge device, or an internal batch pipeline.

4. **Monitoring**: Once live, the model's behavior should be continuously checked to detect anomalies, prediction errors, performance degradation, or any sign of data drift.

5. **Maintenance**: As business needs evolve, models must be retrained or replaced periodically to remain relevant and accurate. This step, similar to issuing firmware updates, ensures the model remains aligned with evolving data and expectations.

Even the most accurate model, which achieves 99% accuracy during development, can fail to deliver value if these operational elements are not properly addressed. Deployment is the true test of a model's readiness, requiring careful attention to infrastructure, user integration, and long-term support.

Refer to the "Managing the Model Life Cycle and Updates" section for an in-depth breakdown of the full model life cycle, including strategies for monitoring, retraining, and model retirement.

Deployment Strategies and Considerations

Selecting the right deployment strategy is one of the most critical decisions when transitioning a machine learning model from experimentation to production. This choice influences everything from system performance and cost-efficiency to user experience and long-term maintainability.

Unlike traditional software deployment, machine learning models operate in environments where data changes rapidly, and model predictions must adapt in near real time or at scale. Therefore, your deployment strategy must be tailored to

- **Prediction frequency** refers to how often a machine learning model is expected to generate predictions. Some models may only need to run once a day, such as daily sales forecasts, while others may be called upon thousands of times per second, as in real-time personalization engines. For example, a demand forecasting model for a retail chain might run every night, whereas a clickstream-based recommendation model could make predictions every time a user views a webpage.

- **Latency tolerance** is the delay between sending an input to a model and receiving the output. Some use cases can tolerate delays of minutes or even hours, such as generating monthly reports. Others, like fraud detection, require responses in milliseconds. For instance, a ride-sharing app's routing model must produce directions instantly based on live traffic data to be useful.

- **Data volume** refers to the size and speed of the incoming data that the model must process. Models serving millions of users or analyzing sensor data from thousands of IoT devices must be designed to process high-throughput data streams. For example, a video analytics model processing footage from security cameras at a large airport must handle a massive data volume and scale accordingly.

- **Business Criticality**: Not all predictions have the same business impact. A model used to rank email newsletters may affect click-through rates modestly, whereas a model that denies or approves loans carries significant financial and regulatory implications. For instance, a model predicting ICU admission risk in healthcare must be highly accurate and stable because it directly influences critical medical decisions.

This section explores three dominant deployment paradigms—batch, real-time, and edge—outlining their strengths, limitations, and ideal use cases.

Ultimately, your deployment strategy must strike a balance between technical requirements (e.g., throughput, performance) and business objectives (e.g., cost control, system integration). This section will explore the three most common deployment paradigms—**batch**, **real-time**, and **edge**—along with their trade-offs and best-fit scenarios.

Batch Deployment

Batch deployment processes large volumes of data at scheduled intervals. Instead of reacting to individual prediction requests in real time, this approach collects data over a defined period, such as hourly, daily, or weekly, and processes it all at once. This process makes it ideal for scenarios where insights are needed in bulk rather than instantly.

For example, a telecom company executes a churn prediction model every Sunday night, evaluating millions of customer profiles. The resulting predictions are loaded into their CRM system and used to guide retention campaigns for the entire week, allowing the business to plan outreach without requiring immediate responses.

When to Use Batch Deployment
Batch deployment is best suited for scenarios where immediate results are unnecessary and the data processing workload can be scheduled. It excels in environments with large, structured datasets that arrive periodically and where cost-effective resource management is a priority.

For example, generating weekly marketing campaign lists based on customer segmentation can tolerate a delay because the insights are used for long-term planning rather than real-time decision-making. In such cases, delayed predictions do not compromise business value.

Batch deployment is also well-suited for businesses with regular operational cycles. For instance, a bank may score overnight risk on all customer portfolios after market close when system resources are more available and response time is less critical.

Finally, it enables organizations to minimize infrastructure costs by running compute-heavy models during off-peak hours. For example, a logistics company can schedule its route optimization models to execute at night, saving on peak-time compute charges and balancing load across its infrastructure.

Advantages of Batch Deployment
Batch deployment offers a range of benefits that make it a compelling choice for organizations dealing with large volumes of structured data and predictable workloads. Its strength lies in its simplicity, scalability, and cost-efficiency, particularly when immediate responses are not required. Below are some of the key advantages:

- It enables high resource efficiency by running jobs during off-peak hours when compute resources are either less expensive or underutilized. This scheduling flexibility enables organizations to optimize infrastructure utilization while minimizing the costs associated with peak-time execution. For instance, a retail analytics model might be scheduled to run at 2:00 AM, leveraging lower-cost compute clusters to generate sales forecasts across hundreds of stores simultaneously.

- It offers operational simplicity by eliminating the need for complex deployment infrastructure, such as REST APIs or high-availability endpoints. Batch jobs can often be executed with simple scheduling tools or orchestration systems, such as Apache Airflow, making them easier to manage and troubleshoot. For example, an insurance company might use a nightly job to calculate premium adjustments without worrying about uptime requirements or load balancing.

- Batch jobs scale effectively with distributed processing frameworks, such as Apache Spark or Databricks. These frameworks can break large datasets into smaller chunks and process them in parallel across a cluster. This approach ensures that even terabytes of data can be handled efficiently. For instance, a national logistics firm may utilize Spark to score millions of package delivery routes in a matter of hours, thereby optimizing its daily shipping operations.

Limitations

While batch deployment offers a streamlined and resource-efficient approach for many predictive tasks, it comes with inherent trade-offs that can affect its suitability in time-sensitive or dynamic business scenarios. Understanding these limitations is essential when determining if batch processing aligns with the goals of your machine-learning solution.

- **High Latency:** Since predictions are made on a fixed schedule rather than in response to real-time input, the insights produced may no longer accurately reflect the system's current state by the time they are consumed. This delay can undermine the model's relevance, especially in rapidly changing environments. For example, generating churn scores once per week may be too late if a customer has already disengaged days earlier.

- **Inflexible in Dynamic Environments**: Batch deployments are not ideal for use cases where immediate action is critical. They lack the responsiveness required for scenarios where data changes rapidly and decisions must be made in real time. For instance, in fraud detection, relying on batch processing could result in missed opportunities to block suspicious transactions as they occur, potentially leading to financial loss.

Real-Time Deployment

Real-time deployment, also known as online serving, enables machine learning models to deliver predictions instantly in response to live requests. Unlike batch processing, which operates on pre-collected datasets, real-time systems continuously listen for incoming data and respond without delay. This setup is ideal for use cases where immediate action is crucial and every millisecond matters.

For example, a credit card fraud detection model evaluates transactions as they happen. When a customer initiates a payment, the model quickly analyzes the transaction's characteristics and returns a decision to approve, flag, or decline it—all within milliseconds—helping to prevent fraud in real time.

When to Use Real-Time Deployment

Organizations should consider real-time deployment when the value of a prediction diminishes rapidly with time. It is best suited for use cases that require instant feedback or automated responses, particularly those that drive business-critical functions or enhance user experiences.

For example, a dynamic pricing engine on an ecommerce website adjusts product prices based on current demand and the pricing of competitors. If the model takes several minutes to respond, the opportunity to convert the customer may be lost. Similarly, in route optimization for delivery fleets, real-time traffic data must be incorporated instantly to avoid delays.

Real-time deployment is also essential when applications require low latency to maintain user engagement or compliance. In the financial sector, for instance, loan approval systems rely on immediate risk evaluation to approve or reject applications while users remain on the platform.

Advantages of Real-Time Deployment

Real-time deployment offers several distinct benefits for applications where timing, responsiveness, and data freshness play a central role:

- It enables instant decision-making by returning predictions in milliseconds, allowing businesses to act on insights as soon as data becomes available. For example, an airline might use real-time models to dynamically adjust ticket prices during a flash sale based on seat availability and user demand.

- It enhances data freshness by utilizing the most recent input data at the time of prediction. This ensures that the system reflects the latest conditions, which is critical in fast-paced industries. For instance, an investment advisory app can provide more accurate recommendations by evaluating the most current market signals.

- It enhances user experience by offering seamless and interactive systems that respond promptly to user inputs. For example, a chatbot that predicts user intent and retrieves relevant answers instantly delivers a more satisfying and efficient interaction.

Limitations of Real-Time Deployment

Despite its benefits, real-time deployment also introduces challenges that organizations must carefully manage.

- Real-time systems incur higher operational costs because they require an always-on infrastructure that can handle incoming requests at any time. It often includes provisioning for peak load conditions. For example, a travel booking site must support traffic surges during holiday sales, resulting in increased infrastructure spending.

- Managing real-time deployments increases operational complexity. Teams must configure and maintain systems for load balancing, autoscaling, monitoring, and failover to ensure high availability and reliability. For instance, a ride-hailing platform needs to maintain a resilient prediction service that scales with user demand and handles infrastructure failures without degrading response times.

- These systems are sensitive to traffic spikes and require over-provisioning or rapid autoscaling to avoid latency issues. Without careful planning, spikes in request volume can overwhelm the system, leading to slower responses or service interruptions. For example, a sports betting app that receives thousands of simultaneous queries before a major game must scale automatically to maintain performance.

Understanding these trade-offs is essential when deciding whether real-time deployment aligns with your application's requirements and business objectives.

Edge Deployment

Edge deployment brings machine learning intelligence directly to the location where data is generated—on IoT devices, smartphones, industrial sensors, or embedded systems. By performing inference locally, edge deployment eliminates the need to send data to the cloud for processing. This proximity to data sources not only reduces latency but also enhances system reliability, privacy, and responsiveness.

Think of this as placing a decision-maker on-site. Instead of relying on remote systems, devices embedded with machine learning models can act immediately based on local input. This model suits use cases where fast, autonomous decision-making is critical and where transmitting data to a centralized cloud system would create delays or expose sensitive information.

When to Use Edge Deployment

Organizations should consider edge deployment when cloud-based inference introduces bottlenecks, privacy concerns, or operational inefficiencies. It is particularly advantageous when decisions must happen instantly or when data transmission is costly or impractical.

For example, autonomous vehicles must make split-second navigation decisions. Relying on cloud connectivity for inference would introduce dangerous latency. By deploying models directly on the vehicle's onboard systems, the car can process sensor data and respond in real time.

Another relevant case involves manufacturing facilities using predictive maintenance. By installing models on local sensor hubs, the facility can analyze thermal and vibration data in real time to anticipate equipment failure, without the need to upload high-frequency signals to the cloud.

Edge deployment is also ideal in remote locations where network access is intermittent. For instance, a drone conducting agricultural surveys in a rural area can analyze images on-device to detect crop health issues and return results post-flight.

Advantages of Edge Deployment

Edge deployment offers several compelling advantages for scenarios requiring low-latency decisions, offline operation, and data sovereignty:

- It delivers ultra-low latency by running inference directly on the device where the data is generated. For example, a wearable health monitor can detect anomalies, such as arrhythmias, in real time and alert users without waiting for server communication.

- It supports offline operation, allowing systems to remain functional even in environments with no or intermittent connectivity. For instance, oil rigs equipped with edge AI devices can continue to monitor and control machinery even when satellite communication is lost.

- It enhances privacy by keeping sensitive data on-device and transmitting only insights or alerts to central systems. This approach aligns well with regulatory requirements in healthcare and finance. For example, smart cameras in a retail store can flag suspicious behavior without uploading raw video footage.

- It improves bandwidth efficiency by avoiding constant data uploads to cloud servers. Instead of sending terabytes of video or sensor readings, the device can transmit lightweight summaries or alerts. It is especially valuable in applications like remote surveillance or environmental monitoring.

Limitations of Edge Deployment

Despite its strengths, edge deployment comes with its own set of challenges that organizations must address when architecting solutions:

- Devices at the edge often have limited computing and memory resources, which constrain the size and complexity of models. Developers must compress or optimize models for lightweight deployment. For example, a smart speaker may only support a small keyword recognition model due to hardware limitations.

- Updating models across many edge devices introduces logistical challenges. Coordinating and managing over-the-air (OTA) updates at scale requires secure distribution pipelines and robust versioning strategies to ensure seamless updates. For instance, updating predictive models on thousands of point-of-sale terminals spread across different retail locations demands precise scheduling and rollback mechanisms.

- Edge deployment is not well-suited for large-scale data aggregation and centralized analytics. Applications that depend on analyzing massive datasets across users, systems, or time periods must still rely on cloud or hybrid architectures. For example, training a recommendation engine based on multi-region purchase histories requires data centralization that edge environments cannot provide.

Understanding these trade-offs allows teams to identify where edge deployment adds the most value and how to integrate it effectively within a broader machine learning system architecture. Table 6-1 presents a comparison of different deployment types.

Table 6-1. *Comparison Between Batch Deployment, Real-Time Deployment, and Edge Deployment*

Criteria	Batch Deployment	Real-Time Deployment	Edge Deployment
Use Case	Scheduled, large-volume processing	Immediate, per-request prediction	Offline or latency-critical scenarios
Prediction Latency	High (minutes to hours)	Low (milliseconds to seconds)	Near-zero (milliseconds)
Scalability	High (with distributed computing frameworks)	Must scale to handle traffic spikes	Limited by device capacity
Resource Efficiency	High (runs at set times)	Variable (idle resources during low load)	High for local processing
Data Freshness	Low	High	High
Complexity	Low to moderate	Moderate to high	High (requires distribution and optimization)
Update Frequency	Infrequent (scheduled)	Frequent (retraining, hot-swapping)	Infrequent (requires OTA updates)
Ideal For	Customer churn, batch reporting	Fraud detection, personalization	IoT sensors, autonomous systems

There is no one-size-fits-all approach to model deployment. **Batch, real-time, and edge strategies** each serve different needs, depending on how quickly predictions are required, the nature of the data, and the constraints of the deployment environment, as depicted in Figure 6-1.

CHAPTER 6 DEPLOYING MACHINE LEARNING MODELS

A robust machine learning system often uses a **hybrid of deployment strategies**, adapting to the needs of different users, business processes, and infrastructure constraints.

In the following sections, we'll explore how to assess and plan for deployment environments, integration patterns, and governance needs—all crucial components in building production-grade machine learning (ML) systems.

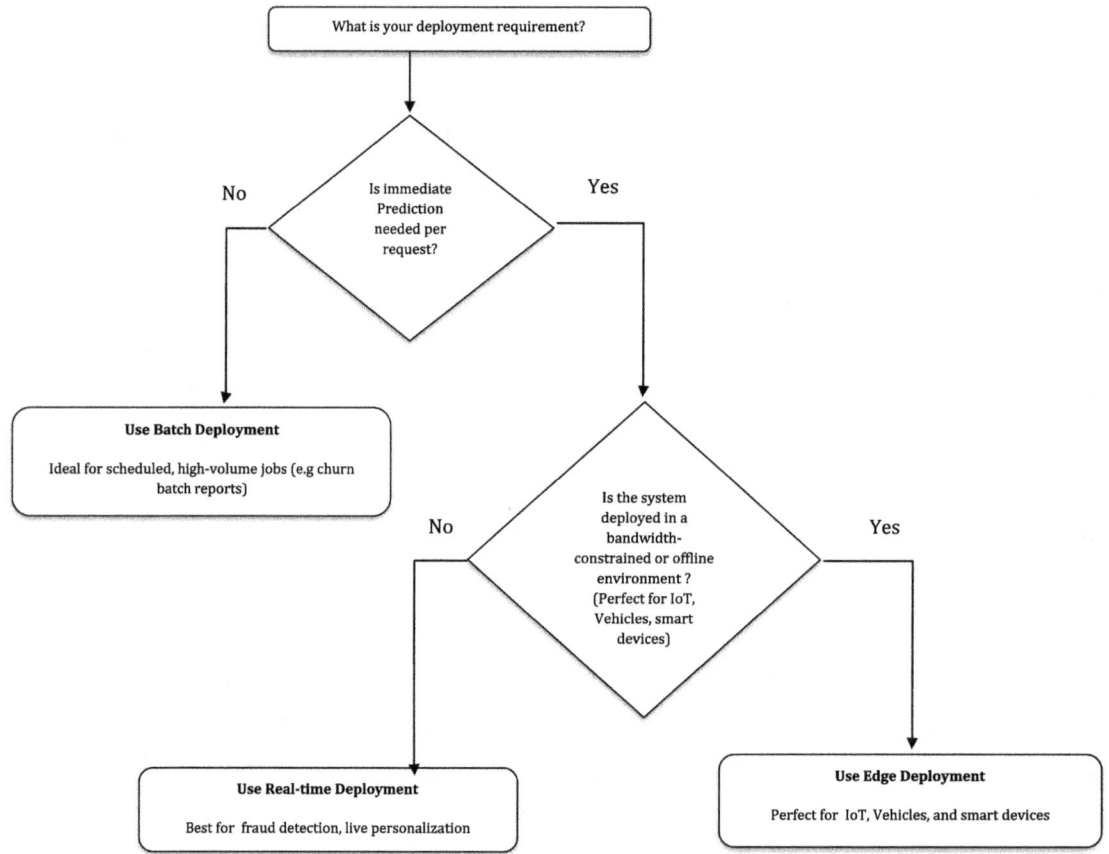

Figure 6-1. Choosing a deployment model

Deployment Considerations

Selecting a deployment strategy—batch, real-time, or edge—is only the beginning of operationalizing a machine learning model. Beyond choosing where and how to deploy, practitioners must also consider a set of cross-cutting concerns that impact the

CHAPTER 6 DEPLOYING MACHINE LEARNING MODELS

model's functionality, scalability, and long-term maintainability. These deployment considerations apply universally, regardless of the deployment mode, and play a critical role in building production-grade systems.

Addressing these considerations early helps ensure that models perform reliably in diverse environments, remain traceable and secure, and can be updated or rolled back when needed. This section introduces two foundational aspects: model serialization and computational resource planning.

Model Serialization

Model serialization is the process of converting a trained machine learning model into a standardized format that allows it to be saved, transferred, and reloaded consistently across different environments. Without proper serialization, even a high-performing model in development may fail during production deployment due to mismatches in format, dependencies, or environment settings.

Think of serialization like packaging a delicate scientific instrument for international shipment. You must protect all the components, maintain their exact configuration, and include setup instructions to reassemble and calibrate the equipment correctly upon arrival. Similarly, serialization ensures your model preserves its integrity from development to staging and production environments.

Figure 6-2 illustrates a typical MLflow model artifact structure that captures metadata, environment information, and multiple deployment "flavors."

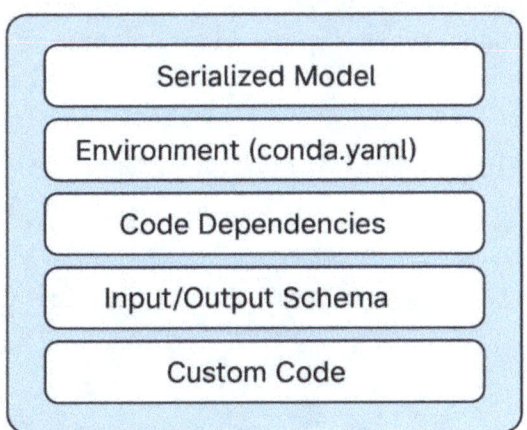

Figure 6-2. MLflow model artifact structure

Common Serialization Formats

Table 6-2 summarizes the most widely used serialization formats, each suited to different scenarios depending on interoperability, performance, and security needs.

Table 6-2. Model Serialization Format Summary

Format	Description	Best Used For
Pickle	Native Python format: simple but insecure and non-portable	Prototypes or single-language pipelines
ONNX	Open Neural Network Exchange; supports cross-platform model conversion	Interoperable, hardware-agnostic deployments
PMML	XML-based standard includes both models and data preprocessing steps	Enterprise and legacy ML systems
MLflow Format	Framework-agnostic format with metadata, environment, and multiple flavors	Production pipelines and Databricks-native use

How to Perform MLflow Serialization

The example below demonstrates how to serialize a scikit-learn model into ONNX format using the sklearn library. This is particularly useful for hardware-agnostic deployments across platforms like Azure, AWS, or edge devices:

```
# Example of ONNX conversion for a scikit-learn model
from skl2onnx import convert_sklearn
from skl2onnx.common.data_types import import FloatTensorType
import onnx
# Define input type
  initial_type = [('float_input', FloatTensorType([None, 4]))]

# Convert scikit-learn model to ONNX
  onnx_model = convert_sklearn(sklearn_model, initial_types=initial_type)

# Save the model
with open("model.onnx", "wb") as f:
    f.write(onnx_model.SerializeToString())
```

Serialization is not a minor implementation detail—it is foundational for model reproducibility, cross-platform compatibility, and robust deployment workflows. It enables teams to version models, roll them back, and consistently audit performance across the entire ML life cycle.

Computational Resources

Just as a high-performance engine must be matched with the right fuel and transmission system, deployed machine learning models require infrastructure that supports their computational profile and operational demands.

Key Factors Influencing Resource Requirements

Before deploying a model, it is essential to evaluate the infrastructure resources required to support the model's architecture and workload. The following factors influence those requirements and should guide your selection of deployment hardware, environment, and scaling strategy:

- **Model Complexity**: Deep neural networks, such as BERT or GPT, require extensive computation and often rely on GPUs, whereas simpler models, like Logistic Regression, can run on CPU-only environments.

- **Input Data Size**: High-resolution images, long text sequences, or multi-sensor inputs require more memory and storage bandwidth.

- **Throughput**: The expected prediction volume (e.g., queries per second) determines whether serverless, autoscaling, or dedicated clusters are the most suitable options.

- **Latency Requirements**: Applications such as fraud detection or conversational AI may require sub-second responses, underscoring the need for high-speed inference engines and low-latency computing environments.

Cloud vs. Edge Considerations

When evaluating whether to deploy models in cloud or edge environments, it's essential first to understand the differing infrastructure requirements, performance trade-offs, and deployment constraints that each option presents. The following guidelines help inform that decision and ensure your model runs efficiently within its intended context.

Cloud Deployment Guidelines

Cloud deployment offers scalable and flexible infrastructure options for hosting machine learning models in centralized environments. Teams can leverage a wide range of compute configurations, storage options, and networking services to meet the specific needs of their applications. Below are some practical guidelines to help align model requirements with appropriate cloud resources:

- Use GPU-accelerated instances for neural networks and vision models.

- Select memory-optimized instances for workloads with high-dimensional feature sets.

- Configure autoscaling to adapt to traffic bursts.

- Use serverless architecture for infrequent or bursty workloads.

Edge Deployment Guidelines

Edge deployment introduces a unique set of requirements compared to cloud-based deployments. Given the limited processing power, memory, and battery life of edge devices, teams must take deliberate steps to optimize their models and minimize resource consumption. The following recommendations outline how to adapt machine learning workloads for edge environments:

- Optimize models using techniques like quantization, pruning, or distillation to run on constrained devices.

- Utilize resource-aware strategies to optimize battery life and minimize thermal output.

- Prioritize embedded accelerators (e.g., TPUs, NPUs) for efficient inference.

CHAPTER 6   DEPLOYING MACHINE LEARNING MODELS

Deployment Tip   Always test your model under realistic operating conditions before rolling it out in production. Simulate average and peak usage to benchmark response time, stability, and scalability. It helps avoid surprises and ensures the infrastructure supports routine operations and traffic spikes.

Integration Requirements

A machine learning model cannot operate in isolation. To deliver real business value, it must integrate seamlessly into the broader enterprise architecture. Effective integration is more than just a technical achievement—it also requires alignment across teams, tools, and processes to ensure smooth collaboration and operational success.

Integration must account for a variety of enterprise constraints, including data ingestion, security, and monitoring. If any of these components are misaligned, the entire system can become fragile or fail to meet performance expectations.

Key Integration Areas

Below are the primary areas where integration plays a vital role in making ML models production-ready:

- **Data Ingestion**: The model must receive timely, clean input from systems like APIs, message queues (e.g., Kafka, Kinesis), databases, or files. Any mismatch in data format or latency can lead to incorrect inferences or model failure. For example, a real-time pricing engine relying on delayed data feeds can lead to pricing errors that impact revenue.

- **Authentication and Authorization**: Secure access to model endpoints is essential. Integrating with enterprise authentication protocols, such as OAuth2, SAML, or Active Directory, ensures that only authorized users or systems can invoke the model. For instance, a loan approval system must authenticate user sessions before issuing predictions.

- **Monitoring and Logging**: Models must expose performance metrics and logs to observability platforms such as Prometheus, CloudWatch, or Splunk. This process allows teams to detect drifts, performance bottlenecks, and failures early. For example, an ecommerce platform can use these tools to monitor prediction latency and error rates across regions.

- **Application Interfaces**: Determine how applications consume predictions via REST APIs, streaming endpoints, or embedded calls. The response format, latency, and error-handling strategy must align with the expectations of the downstream system. For instance, a customer service chatbot must receive predictions in a format compatible with its dialogue engine, with minimal delay.

Collaboration and Documentation

Effective integration also requires collaboration between data scientists, who understand the logic and assumptions of the model, and production engineers, who manage its scalability, availability, and maintainability.

To enable this collaboration, both groups should agree on

- Expected input/output schemas
- Data encoding conventions (e.g., time zone handling, categorical encoding)
- API contracts, including required parameters and response structure
- Error-handling protocols (e.g., fallback values, retries, HTTP status codes)

Warning Semantic mismatches—such as inconsistent decimal precision or differing category mappings—can create silent data bugs that are difficult to detect. It is essential to define and thoroughly validate shared conventions before deployment.

Compliance and Governance

As machine learning systems become embedded in critical workflows, organizations must comply with legal, ethical, and internal governance standards. Governance isn't just a risk-mitigation strategy—it's a pillar for building scalable, defensible, and trustworthy AI systems.

Organizations that neglect governance open themselves to reputational harm, regulatory fines, and legal challenges. Conversely, well-governed models can pass audits, satisfy stakeholders, and evolve in a responsible manner.

Key Governance Areas

Several governance requirements span industries and should be addressed for all production ML systems:

- **Regulatory Compliance**: Models must adhere to domain-specific regulations such as
  - HIPAA for healthcare data privacy
  - GDPR for user data protection in the EU
  - FCRA and GLBA in financial services for decision transparency and data handling
- **Model Explainability**: Stakeholders may require insight into why a model made a certain prediction. Tools like SHAP (SHapley Additive exPlanations) and LIME (Local Interpretable Model-Agnostic Explanations) allow users to interpret and trust model decisions. For example, financial regulators might mandate a clear explanation for why a credit score changed.
- **Audit Trails**: It's critical to log all model activities. These logs should include prediction timestamps, input data, model version, user IDs (if applicable), and confidence scores. It supports root-cause analysis, regulatory compliance, and quality assurance.
- **Approval Workflows**: Before models move into production, teams should implement structured review and approval processes. It includes documented testing, sign-offs by responsible teams, and a clear record of change management.

CHAPTER 6   DEPLOYING MACHINE LEARNING MODELS

Implementing Model Governance

Organizations must adopt specific components and operational procedures to translate governance principles into practice. These elements form the backbone of a well-governed ML life cycle by offering transparency, traceability, and control. Whether you are working in a regulated industry or want to enforce quality standards across teams, these building blocks provide the structure needed to ensure your models remain accountable, safe, and trustworthy. Table 6-3 highlights key components commonly used in governance frameworks:

Table 6-3. Key Components Used in Governance Frameworks

Component	Description
Model Registry	Tracks version history, deployment status, and ownership metadata
Documentation Standards	Enforces consistent descriptions of model objectives, datasets, and limitations
Review Procedures	Incorporates peer and stakeholder feedback pre- and post-deployment
Access Controls	Uses role-based permissions to manage model access and update privileges

Good governance is not a bureaucratic overhead—it is a competitive advantage. Governed models are easier to monitor, audit, retrain, and replace. They can scale confidently across teams and geographies, serving as a foundation for building AI systems that stakeholders can trust.

A successful model deployment pipeline involves far more than selecting an inference strategy. Teams must also consider serialization standards, infrastructure readiness, system integration, and responsible governance. By addressing these factors early and comprehensively, organizations can deploy machine learning systems that are robust, scalable, and aligned with enterprise values and regulations.

Deployment success depends on more than choosing a serving strategy. It requires thoughtful attention to **serialization**, **resource planning**, **system integration**, and **governance**. Treating these elements as first-class citizens in your deployment pipeline ensures that models deliver value reliably and responsibly at scale, aligning with enterprise goals.

Cloud-Based Deployment

Cloud-based deployment hosts machine learning models on AWS, Azure, Google Cloud, or Databricks platforms. It has become the default choice for modern machine learning operations because of its scalability, global reach, flexible pricing, and integrated support for MLOps workflows.

Deploying models in the cloud provides access to managed infrastructure, elastic computing, and high availability, thereby reducing operational complexity and accelerating time-to-value.

Key Deployment Approaches in the Cloud

Cloud platforms offer various deployment methods, each tailored to support specific use cases, performance requirements, and operational needs. By providing diverse deployment models—from highly abstracted managed services to granular, containerized, and serverless options—cloud providers empower teams to align their deployment strategies with project goals, resource availability, and governance requirements. This flexibility allows organizations to optimize deployments based on scalability, control, portability, or cost-efficiency:

1. **Managed ML Services**

   Managed services, such as Databricks Model Serving, enable teams to deploy, scale, and manage machine learning models with minimal operational overhead. These platforms abstract the complexities of infrastructure provisioning, security management, and deployment orchestration, allowing data science teams to focus on model development and iteration. They integrate seamlessly with MLOps pipelines and often include built-in tools for tracking model versions, promoting artifacts through different stages, and monitoring performance. These platforms typically offer

   - Autoscaling to adjust compute based on demand
   - Simple endpoint provisioning through UI or CLI
   - Built-in model registries for tracking and versioning
   - Life cycle management features for staging and promotion

This option suits teams prioritizing speed, ease of use, and integration with MLOps pipelines.

2. **Container-Based Deployment**

   Packaging models such as Docker containers enable organizations to encapsulate the model, its dependencies, and the runtime environment into a single, portable unit. This flexibility allows teams to consistently deploy and operate models across various platforms, including public and private clouds. Organizations gain precise control over compute resources, scaling behavior, and service availability by leveraging container orchestration tools such as Kubernetes or Azure Kubernetes Service (AKS). This method facilitates efficient versioning, repeatable deployments, and environment isolation, making it ideal for complex enterprise ML workflows. Containers support

   - Isolation of dependencies and runtime environments
   - Consistent deployment across development, staging, and production
   - Multi-cloud or hybrid deployment strategies

   This approach is well-suited for enterprise environments where control, customization, and portability are essential.

3. **Serverless Inference**

   Serverless platforms, such as AWS Lambda, Azure Functions, and Google Cloud Functions, provide a lightweight, event-driven execution model that enables machine learning models to run without the need for pre-provisioned infrastructure. These platforms manage resource allocation dynamically, invoking compute power only when an event or request occurs. As a result, teams can deploy models quickly with minimal setup while enjoying a high degree of scalability and operational simplicity. This approach is particularly useful for integrating ML inference into workflows like webhooks, mobile app interactions, or real-time alerts, where invocation patterns are unpredictable or infrequent. Benefits include

- No infrastructure provisioning or server management
- Automatic horizontal scaling
- Cost efficiency for low-throughput or event-driven workloads

Serverless inference is ideal for use cases such as fraud scoring, anomaly detection, or user-triggered recommendations, where inference is required sporadically or in bursts.

Benefits of Cloud-Based Deployment

Cloud environments provide a comprehensive and adaptable foundation for deploying machine learning models at scale. Their ability to dynamically adjust resources, integrate with popular MLOps tools, and offer built-in services for monitoring and security has made them the preferred choice for both startups and enterprises. The combination of flexibility, performance, and ease of access allows teams to accelerate experimentation, simplify operations, and scale production workloads with confidence. Below are some of the most impactful advantages of deploying in the cloud:

- **Scalability**: Resources scale automatically in response to workload, ensuring consistent performance despite varying demands.
- **Reduced Operational Overhead**: Providers manage security patches, operating system updates, load balancing, and hardware recovery.
- **Consumption-Based Pricing**: Costs align with actual usage, enabling efficient budgeting and avoiding over-provisioning.
- **Global Availability**: With data centers located across various regions, cloud platforms minimize latency and facilitate compliance with regional data residency laws.

Considerations and Challenges

While the cloud offers numerous advantages, it also introduces operational and architectural trade-offs that teams must carefully evaluate. These trade-offs often stem from the abstraction and scale that cloud environments provide, which can inadvertently introduce challenges around cost visibility, dependency management, and regulatory compliance. Understanding these trade-offs upfront allows teams to make informed decisions and design cloud deployments that are robust, scalable, and cost-effective:

- **Vendor Lock-In**: Relying on proprietary services may hinder future migrations. Containerization and open standards can help mitigate this risk.

- **Cost Management**: Without quotas and monitoring tools, teams can inadvertently incur high costs, especially during experimentation or unexpected usage spikes.

- **Data Privacy and Sovereignty**: Sensitive data may need to reside in specific regions due to legal or regulatory constraints (e.g., GDPR, HIPAA). Although cloud providers support regional hosting and compliance certifications, the deploying organization is responsible for ensuring legal alignment.

When to Choose Cloud-Based Deployment

Cloud deployment is well-suited for organizations and projects that prioritize agility, global scale, and operational efficiency. It is especially effective when the use case demands rapid scaling, access to managed services, or streamlined collaboration across geographically dispersed teams. Consider adopting cloud-based deployment in the following scenarios:

- Applications with fluctuating or unpredictable demand
- Teams that want to minimize infrastructure maintenance
- Organizations operating across multiple geographies
- Machine learning workflows that benefit from elastic computing, rapid prototyping, and seamless integration with cloud-native tools

In the following section, we will explore other deployment environments, including on-premises, hybrid, and edge deployments, and help you evaluate the trade-offs between them.

On-Premises Deployment

While cloud platforms have become the dominant choice for machine learning operations, on-premises deployment remains a vital strategy for organizations with unique infrastructure, compliance, or security requirements. Hosting models within an organization's data centers or private networks provides complete environmental control, making it an attractive option for regulated industries and performance-critical applications.

On-premises deployment allows teams to fine-tune compute resources, enforce strict access policies, and manage sensitive data without relying on third-party infrastructure. Although it introduces more operational responsibilities, it provides stability, consistency, and governance benefits that cloud platforms may not match in specific contexts.

Types of On-Premises Environments

On-premises deployment is not a one-size-fits-all approach. It encompasses a range of infrastructure options tailored to meet diverse technical and organizational needs:

- **Private Cloud Infrastructure**: Platforms such as OpenStack, VMware, and Red Hat OpenShift enable enterprises to create internal cloud environments that replicate the flexibility of public cloud services while maintaining infrastructure ownership. These setups are ideal for large organizations seeking to modernize without a full migration to the cloud.

- **Bare Metal Servers**: Deploying models directly on physical servers provides maximum performance and control. This configuration is well-suited for compute-intensive tasks such as GPU-based deep learning inference or real-time processing that requires low-latency hardware access.

- **Edge Servers**: These systems reside close to the data source—in factories, retail stores, hospitals, or remote offices. They support real-time decision-making and eliminate the need for constant connectivity to central servers. Edge servers are particularly valuable in industrial IoT or mission-critical use cases where uptime and latency are paramount.

Advantages of On-Premises Deployment

Organizations deploying on-premises can realize several strategic benefits: beyond meeting regulatory obligations, they gain enhanced control, consistent performance, and long-term cost efficiency for certain workload profiles.

- **Full Infrastructure Control**: Teams can customize hardware configurations, enforce network security protocols, and optimize performance based on workload characteristics. It is essential for companies with niche requirements or custom hardware accelerators.

- **Data Privacy and Compliance**: On-premises systems support regulatory adherence by ensuring sensitive data stays within organizational or national borders. This is particularly important in sectors governed by regulations, such as HIPAA, GDPR, PCI-DSS, or financial regulations.

- **Predictable Performance**: Dedicated infrastructure eliminates the unpredictability associated with shared cloud resources, ensuring consistent and reliable performance. Applications benefit from consistent response times and reliable throughput.

- **Cost Predictability for High Utilization**: Although upfront capital costs are high, long-term operational expenses may be lower than cloud-based deployments for workloads that run continuously or at a large scale.

Challenges of On-Premises Deployment

Despite the control it offers, on-premises deployment introduces several logistical and financial challenges. These challenges can impact deployment timelines and long-term sustainability if not properly planned and managed.

- **High Upfront Costs**: Organizations must invest in servers, storage, networking gear, data center space, and software licenses. This can slow time-to-value and create budgetary constraints for smaller teams.

- **Maintenance Responsibility**: All aspects of the infrastructure, including hardware failures, firmware updates, operating system patches, and scalability, must be managed in-house. This requires a skilled operations team and well-defined incident management procedures.

- **Geographic Limitations**: On-premises systems have limited reach, unlike global cloud providers. Expanding to international locations or enabling regional redundancy demands significant logistical planning and infrastructure duplication.

When to Choose On-Premises Deployment

On-premises deployment is most appropriate when the use case or organization demands absolute control over infrastructure and data. It is particularly well suited for

- Enterprises with strict security policies or data localization mandates
- Applications that require deterministic, low-latency performance (e.g., healthcare diagnostics, trading systems)
- Consistent high-throughput workloads that justify long-term hardware investment
- Deployment in regions or facilities with limited cloud connectivity or unstable networks

In the next section, we'll explore hybrid deployment models that combine the benefits of on-premises systems with the elasticity of cloud platforms.

Hybrid Deployment

Most organizations do not operate exclusively in the cloud or fully on-premises. Instead, they adopt hybrid deployment strategies that offer the best of both worlds. Hybrid deployments allow teams to allocate workloads based on specific business, regulatory, or technical requirements, simultaneously optimizing for security, cost, and performance.

This flexible approach enables enterprises to keep sensitive data or mission-critical systems within their local infrastructure while leveraging cloud platforms for scalability, innovation, and rapid development. As a result, hybrid deployment strategies are increasingly becoming the norm in organizations navigating digital transformation while maintaining operational continuity.

Common Hybrid Deployment Patterns

Hybrid architectures support multiple deployment patterns designed to maximize flexibility and control. These patterns enable organizations to tailor deployment strategies that align with their technical capabilities, compliance requirements, and business objectives. As data volumes grow and regulatory requirements evolve, hybrid models provide a scalable and adaptable path forward:

- **Train in the Cloud, Deploy On-Premises**: Use the cloud's elastic compute resources for training models on large datasets, then deploy them on-premises for inference where data privacy or latency requirements are critical. For example, a hospital might train predictive models in the cloud using anonymized datasets but perform real-time inference locally for patient monitoring.

- **Sensitive Models On-Premises, Others in the Cloud**: Organizations often segment workloads based on risk. Sensitive or regulated applications remain on-premises, while low-risk services, such as recommendation engines or user segmentation, run in the cloud. This approach supports scalability without compromising compliance.

- **Development in the Cloud, Production On-Premises**: Teams use cloud environments for experimentation, model development, and rapid iteration. Once validated, they deploy production versions of the models on local infrastructure to meet compliance, stability, or latency goals.

Advantages of Hybrid Deployment

Hybrid strategies offer significant operational flexibility, serving as a bridge between traditional infrastructure and cloud-native operations. They allow organizations to preserve the value of existing systems while experimenting with new cloud-based capabilities. This balance supports smoother transitions and reduces the risk of disruption during digital modernization.

- **Flexibility of Placement**: Organizations can strategically choose the best execution environment for each workload, balancing latency, cost, security, and compliance needs.

- **Gradual Cloud Adoption**: Teams can modernize incrementally, introducing cloud services alongside legacy systems without committing to a full-scale migration.

- **Balance Between Control and Convenience**: Hybrid deployments provide governance over critical data and infrastructure while leveraging the scalability and innovation of managed cloud services.

- **Business Continuity**: If either cloud or on-prem systems experience downtime, hybrid architectures can reroute workloads to maintain operations. This redundancy improves system resilience.

Challenges of Hybrid Deployment

Despite their flexibility, hybrid environments introduce operational complexity that must be managed effectively. These challenges stem from maintaining consistency, security, and availability across distinct infrastructures. Without proper planning, hybrid architectures can become fragmented and difficult to scale.

- **Increased Architectural Complexity**: Managing resources across disparate platforms involves orchestrating challenges related to identity, networking, security, and system configuration.

- **Consistency Enforcement**: Teams must ensure model parity across cloud and on-prem deployments. It requires rigorous version control, consistent runtime environments, and end-to-end testing.

- **Integration Overhead**: Bridging cloud and local environments often necessitates the use of middleware or APIs that synchronize data and model artifacts, adding an engineering and operational burden.

- **Resource Fragmentation**: Distributing workloads across multiple environments may result in suboptimal resource utilization if not carefully monitored and balanced.

When to Choose Hybrid Deployment

Hybrid deployment is ideal for organizations with mixed operational needs, particularly when workloads differ significantly in terms of security, latency, and compliance requirements. It provides the flexibility to optimize infrastructure choices for each component of the machine learning (ML) pipeline. It is especially effective in the following scenarios:

1. Enterprises that are migrating to the cloud but must retain control over highly sensitive workloads

2. Organizations subject to compliance or data residency laws that vary by region or department

3. ML pipelines with divergent resource needs—for example, cloud-based training and on-premises inference

4. Use cases that benefit from the elasticity of the cloud while maintaining the security and predictability of on-prem infrastructure

Deploying Models in Databricks

Modern machine learning workflows don't end at model development. One of the most critical stages—**deployment**—often presents the most unexpected challenges. This section examines how MLflow, deeply integrated into Databricks, facilitates the overcoming of these hurdles to enable **scalable, reproducible, and production-ready deployments**.

Using MLflow for Model Deployment and the Deployment Challenge

Before we explore how MLflow enables streamlined deployment within Databricks, it's essential to understand why deployment is particularly challenging in machine learning workflows, especially for those new to operationalizing models.

You've probably heard the phrase from developers: "But it works on my machine!" This familiar frustration becomes even more complex in machine learning. In traditional software development, you primarily move application code from development to production. But with machine learning, you must transfer not only the code but also a tightly coupled set of components, including

- Preprocessing logic (e.g., how raw data is cleaned or transformed)
- Feature engineering steps (e.g., how input variables are created)
- Model binaries (the trained model file itself)
- Environment dependencies (software libraries and runtime versions)
- Versioned libraries (like specific versions of `pandas` or `scikit-learn`)
- Input/output schema assumptions (how data is structured when the model runs)

If any of these components differ between your development and production environments—even slightly—your model might produce incorrect predictions or fail silently in difficult-to-detect and debug ways. These issues can be especially frustrating for ML practitioners, as they may appear even when everything works locally.

A Real-World Example: Churn Prediction Gone Wrong

Imagine you are building a model to predict customer churn using Databricks. During development, your model is trained using a specific environment setup:

- `pandas==1.3.4`
- `scikit-learn==1.0.2`
- A custom function that cleans the data by removing missing values and encoding categorical variables

Everything works well during training, and your results look promising. However, when you deploy the model to a production cluster, you unknowingly use slightly newer versions of some libraries. This change introduces subtle differences in behavior that compromise the model's reliability:

- The updated `scikit-learn==1.1.0` processes missing values differently when performing one-hot encoding.

- Your custom data-cleaning script wasn't packaged or version-controlled and was left out of the deployment.

- The production environment silently omits a key transformation step in your notebook.

As a result, the model starts misclassifying loyal customers as likely to churn. These incorrect predictions trigger unnecessary retention offers or churn alerts, leading to wasted resources and damage to business credibility. This example illustrates why treating model deployment as a disciplined engineering task, not just a final step, is essential.

MLflow: A Unified Solution for Deployment Challenges

MLflow is an open source platform that manages the entire machine learning life cycle—from experimentation and tracking to packaging and deployment. In the deployment context, MLflow provides a consistent, structured, and repeatable process that enables teams to move models from development to production without losing key configurations or encountering unexpected failures.

Consider MLflow as a specialized moving company to make this more relatable. Just as a good moving company not only transports your belongings but also ensures your new home is set up exactly the way you left it, MLflow preserves every essential detail:

- It doesn't just transport your model (like furniture).

- It replicates your production "home" to match the development environment—same layout, same settings, and same tools in the right place.

This level of fidelity is crucial because even minor mismatches in software versions or configurations can significantly impact model performance in production. MLflow automates much of this alignment and reduces manual error.

CHAPTER 6   DEPLOYING MACHINE LEARNING MODELS

With just a single command, MLflow can

- Package your model and its dependencies into a self-contained, portable artifact for deployment.

- Record and preserve the exact input and output schema used during model training to validate future predictions.

- Generate an environment specification file (e.g., `conda.yaml` or `requirements.txt`) that captures every library and version used.

- Register the model in a centralized Model Registry, making it discoverable, versioned, and governed.

- Enable seamless deployment to various targets, such as REST APIs for real-time inference, batch jobs for scheduled scoring, or edge devices for offline operation.

Figure 6-3 visualizes the typical life cycle for deploying a model using MLflow in Databricks. This diagram highlights the end-to-end flow, from training and logging to deployment across different environments and integration endpoints. Understanding this flow helps clarify how each MLflow component contributes to a robust deployment pipeline.

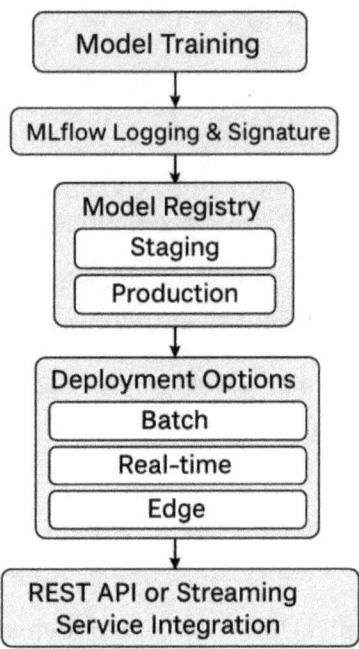

Figure 6-3. *Model deployment life cycle*

Because MLflow is deeply integrated into Databricks, these capabilities are accessible and optimized for large-scale enterprise environments. This integration makes Databricks one of the most production-ready platforms available for model deployment, simplifying a process that is often highly error-prone and resource-intensive.

Understanding MLflow's Approach to Deployment

One of MLflow's greatest strengths is its ability to simplify and standardize the process of deploying machine learning models. This phase often introduces the most risk and complexity in real-world scenarios, especially when inconsistencies exist between development and production environments. MLflow addresses these issues through a philosophy grounded in three key principles: model packaging, environment reproducibility, and infrastructure-agnostic portability.

CHAPTER 6   DEPLOYING MACHINE LEARNING MODELS

How Does MLflow Package a Model As a Complete Artifact?

When you save a model using MLflow, you are not merely serializing a Python object; you are also capturing the model's metadata. MLflow constructs a self-contained, portable artifact with everything necessary for consistent inference. This design eliminates the need to manually track dependencies or perform additional configuration steps downstream.

To make this easier to understand, let's break down what MLflow includes and why each part is important for deployment, even if you're new to MLOps. Think of this process as packaging your model into a carry-on bag that contains everything it needs to function reliably in any environment.

MLflow automatically includes the following components:

- **Serialized Model**: This is the machine learning model you trained, saved in a format that computers can reload and use later. Formats such as Pickle, ONNX, or TorchScript enable you to transfer the model between different tools or systems.

- **Dependencies**: These are the libraries (such as scikit-learn or pandas) that the model relies on to function correctly. Including them ensures that the model has all the necessary tools when someone else runs it.

  Environment Specification: This is similar to a recipe file (`conda.yaml` or requirements.txt) that lists the exact versions of all required software. It helps recreate the same setup where the model was originally trained, reducing errors.

- **Schema Signatures**: These are optional descriptions that define the type of input data the model expects and the type of output it will produce. It serves as a contract to ensure that data aligns with the model's requirements.

- **Custom Code**: This includes any additional logic (like special data cleaning steps) written by the developer. Packaging it with the model ensures all custom behavior is included in the deployment.

Think of this as packing your model in a suitcase—filled with its tools, instructions, and environment—all zipped and ready for reliable use on any compatible platform.

How to Log a Model with MLflow?

Below is a concise example demonstrating how to log a model reproducibly using MLflow. This process captures the model and its associated parameters, environment, and metadata. This way, anyone can reload and serve the model in another environment without needing to reconfigure or retrain it manually.

```
import mlflow
from sklearn.ensemble import RandomForestClassifier

# Assume X_train and y_train are defined
model = RandomForestClassifier(n_estimators=100)
model.fit(X_train, y_train)

with mlflow.start_run(run_name="Simple RF Model") as run:
    mlflow.log_param("n_estimators", 100)
    mlflow.sklearn.log_model(
        model,
        "random_forest_model",
        input_example=X_train.iloc[:5],
        registered_model_name="churn_predictor"
    )
    print(f"Model saved with run ID: {run.info.run_id}")
```

This produces a model artifact that can be reloaded into another script, containerized into a Docker image, registered into the Model Registry, or deployed as a REST API—all without modifying the code or rebuilding the environment.

How Does MLflow Ensure Environment Reproducibility?

Machine learning models often perform well during development but fail to behave consistently once deployed. This is typically caused by mismatches in the software environment, such as different versions of Python or libraries, or missing custom code. This issue is called the "it worked on my machine" problem.

MLflow addresses this challenge by automatically capturing the environment in which the model was trained. When you log or save a model with MLflow, it generates a file named conda.yaml. This file acts as a blueprint for recreating the same setup elsewhere.

The generated file captures

- The exact version of Python used for training
- All pip and conda packages required to run the model
- Any custom libraries or modules that were part of the training script

This detailed snapshot ensures that whether the model runs in staging, production, or on a colleague's system, it behaves exactly as it did during development. This consistency is crucial for reliability, debugging, auditing, and scaling models across different environments.

Sample conda.yaml File

```
name: mlflow-env
channels:
  - conda-forge
dependencies:
  - python=3.8.12
  - pip=21.3.1
  - pip:
    - mlflow==1.23.1
    - scikit-learn==1.0.2
    - pandas==1.3.4
    - numpy==1.21.4
    - cloudpickle==2.0.0
```

🔧 **Pro Tip** You can manually customize conda_env files to fine-tune your environment or accommodate hardware-specific dependencies like CUDA versions for GPU inference.

CHAPTER 6   DEPLOYING MACHINE LEARNING MODELS

The MLflow Deployment Philosophy

MLflow treats deployment not as a one-time event but as a continuous, reliable, and standardized process. This approach ensures that machine learning models remain stable, reproducible, and maintainable across various production environments. Rather than manually handling configurations or dependencies, MLflow enables teams to focus on delivering insights while it manages the operational overhead of deployment.

This philosophy is grounded in three key principles:

- **Packaging Models As Portable Artifacts with Reproducible Logic**: MLflow packages not just the model but also the necessary code, environment files, and metadata required to run it elsewhere, ensuring the logic behind predictions remains consistent.

- **Capturing Training Environments for Consistent Runtime Execution**: MLflow records the full environment configuration (Python version, library versions, and custom code) used during training, allowing deployments to reproduce the exact conditions.

- **Supporting Deployment Across REST APIs, Batch Jobs, Edge Devices, and Embedded Systems**: MLflow supports a variety of deployment targets, making it easy to serve models wherever they are needed—whether in real-time applications, periodic batch jobs, or resource-constrained devices at the edge.

By removing much of the manual work and reducing the room for error, MLflow provides data scientists and MLOps engineers with a robust toolset to confidently and consistently deploy models, whether to the cloud, an internal microservice, or an edge computing device.

Common Deployment Patterns Supported by MLflow

MLflow supports a range of deployment patterns, each designed to accommodate different production use cases and operational goals. The optimal deployment approach should be chosen based on several key factors:

- **Latency Requirements**: Determine whether your application needs real-time responsiveness (e.g., fraud detection) or can operate with scheduled processing (e.g., nightly reports).

- **Infrastructure Constraints**: Consider where the model will run—on the cloud, on-premises, or at the edge—and the availability of compute resources.

- **Integration Needs**: Assess how tightly the model needs to integrate with other components, such as APIs, enterprise applications, or IoT devices.

Understanding these parameters helps in selecting the most suitable MLflow deployment strategy—whether it's batch processing, REST API serving, edge deployment, or embedding models into applications.

Batch Inference

Batch inference is a method where predictions are made for large groups of data simultaneously, rather than one at a time. Think of it like running a report every night, rather than constantly checking data throughout the day. For example, a company might run a model every evening to find out which customers are most likely to cancel their service soon. This type of setup is efficient because it uses computer resources only at scheduled times. It also works well with existing systems that already move and process data in batches, like ETL (Extract, Transform, Load) pipelines that prepare data overnight.

Real-Time API Serving

Real-time serving means your machine learning model is available to make predictions instantly whenever needed. This is achieved by setting up the model behind a REST API—an interface that enables other software to send data and receive predictions quickly in return.

This type of deployment is essential when decisions must be made in seconds or less. For example:

- When someone makes a payment online, the system can immediately check if it's a potential fraud.

- While applying for a loan online, the applicant's details can be evaluated instantly to generate a credit score.

- In apps like Netflix or Amazon, your recent activity can be analyzed in real time to recommend movies or products you're likely to enjoy.

CHAPTER 6   DEPLOYING MACHINE LEARNING MODELS

Real-time APIs enable the direct integration of intelligence into user-facing applications, thereby enhancing speed and personalization.

Edge Deployment

Edge deployment refers to the process of installing and running machine learning models directly on local devices rather than sending data back and forth to the cloud or a central server. This approach is useful when you don't have a strong or consistent internet connection or when you need results extremely quickly, without delay.

In edge deployment, the model is packaged in a way that allows it to run independently on devices such as sensors, mobile phones, or small computers. This reduces the time it takes to get predictions and keeps data processing local, which can also improve privacy.

Examples include

- A factory machine equipped with a small computer that monitors its health and predicts maintenance needs without needing to send data to a central system
- A fitness tracker that recognizes your activity (like walking or running) right on your wrist without needing internet access
- A mobile app used in remote areas that uses a model to make predictions offline, such as diagnosing crop diseases in farming applications

Edge deployment is all about bringing intelligence closer to where the data is generated.

Embedded Deployment

Some enterprise applications require the machine learning model to be integrated directly into the software itself rather than running separately as a service. This is known as embedded deployment. It enables the application and the model to work together as a single unit, eliminating the need for external calls to obtain predictions.

MLflow makes this possible by letting you export models in a flexible and portable format, such as `mlflow.pyfunc`. This format can be used in various programming environments, enabling developers to integrate the model directly into their codebase.

This method is particularly helpful in scenarios where tight integration and rapid response are required. For example:

- A shopping app might use a recommendation engine embedded directly within the app to suggest products instantly while the user browses.

- A logistics software system may include a pricing model that updates shipping costs in real time without relying on a separate prediction service.

Embedded deployment enhances the user experience by ensuring that predictions occur quickly and reliably within the core application.

MLflow Model Registry: Your Model's Home in Production

Once a model has been trained and its performance has been verified, the next step is to manage it responsibly as it moves through different stages of use. MLflow Model Registry helps with this by providing a central place where models are stored, versioned, and tracked over time.

Think of the Model Registry as a well-organized digital library made just for machine learning models:

- **Version Control**: Every time a model is updated—maybe it's retrained with better data or improved in some way—a new version is automatically recorded. This helps teams understand what changed, compare model performance over time, and even roll back to an older version if needed.

- **Life Cycle Staging**: The registry enables you to assign labels to each version of the model based on its stage in the journey. For example, you might mark a new model as "Staging" while it's being tested, then move it to "Production" once it's live, and eventually mark it as "Archived" when it's no longer in use. This helps teams avoid confusion about which version is being used.

- **Collaboration**: Important details, such as who created the model, when it was last updated, what changes were made, and the reasons behind them, can be stored alongside the model. This transparency enables teams to work together more effectively and ensures accountability.

By using MLflow's Model Registry, organizations can manage models in a professional, secure, and traceable way, reducing errors and making model deployment more reliable.

MLflow Deployment Quick Checklist

Use the following checklist to ensure your model is production-ready with MLflow. Table 6-4 shows the checklist.

Table 6-4. MLflow Quick Deployment Checklist

☑ Task	Description
Model Serialization	Save the model using an appropriate MLflow flavor (e.g., `mlflow.sklearn`, `mlflow.pyfunc`) to ensure compatibility with MLflow tools and APIs.
Environment Capture	Use the automatically generated `conda.yaml` file to reproduce the training environment, including the Python version and all dependencies.
Registry Versioning	Register your model in the MLflow Model Registry. Assign life cycle stages, such as Staging or Production, to track deployment readiness and ensure optimal deployment.
Deployment Target Selection	Choose the most appropriate serving pattern: — **Batch inference** for offline bulk processing — **Real-time serving** for immediate APIs — **Edge deployment** for on-device prediction — **Embedded deployment** for tight integration into applications
Validation in Isolated Environment	Always test the model in a clean, isolated environment or container before pushing to production to catch dependency or configuration errors early.

> ✻ **Pro Tip** Consider integrating this checklist into your CI/CD pipeline to automate environment validation and staging promotion steps.

Best Practices for Deployment in Production

Deploying a machine learning model for the first time may seem straightforward, but ensuring it operates consistently, reliably, and efficiently over time in a real production environment is far more complex. Production environments often involve live data, high usage, integration with external systems, and strict requirements around stability and reproducibility.

This section outlines the best practices for ensuring your machine learning models are production-ready using MLflow and its supporting tools.

Environment Reproducibility and the Dependency Challenge

ML models rely on many third-party libraries (like `pandas`, `scikit-learn`, or `numpy`), each with specific version requirements. A small version difference can lead to unexpected behavior—e.g., a model trained using `scikit-learn 1.0.0` may give slightly different results if deployed using `1.1.0`. These issues are often hard to detect but can cause serious performance drops.

MLflow helps manage this challenge by automatically logging your training environment. When you log a model with MLflow using `mlflow.<flavor>.log_model(...)`, it captures the entire environment setup in a `conda.yaml` file, including

- Python version
- Library versions
- Framework-specific requirements (e.g., `xgboost`, `sklearn`)

This ensures that your model behaves the same in production as it did during training.

Example of `conda.yaml`:

```
name: mlflow-env
channels:
  - defaults
dependencies:
```

```
  - python=3.9.7
  - scikit-learn=1.0.2
  - pandas=1.3.5
  - pip:
    - cloudpickle==2.0.0
```

Validating Environments Before Deployment

Even though MLflow automatically records the environment used during model training, it's crucial to manually test and validate that environment before deploying the model to production. This involves setting up a clean, isolated staging environment that closely mirrors your actual production setup, using the same operating system, Python version, libraries, and other system configurations. Doing this ensures that your model won't break due to missing dependencies, version mismatches, or platform-specific issues. Think of it as a dress rehearsal: if everything works smoothly in staging, it's much more likely to work in production, too.

Additional Best Practices for Dependency Management

Managing dependencies effectively is essential for stable model deployment. Here are some practices that can help avoid common pitfalls and ensure smooth transitions from development to production:

- **Use Isolated Virtual Environments**: Tools like `conda`, `venv`, or `virtualenv` allow you to create a dedicated environment for each project. This ensures that your model doesn't run into unexpected issues caused by conflicting dependencies from other projects.

- **Pin Package Versions**: Rather than allowing flexible versioning, such as scikit-learn >= `1.0.0`, it's best to pin exact versions of critical packages. This prevents accidental upgrades that could change functionality and affect your model's performance.

- **Test in Clean Environments**: Before deploying to production, always test your model in a clean environment that closely replicates the production stack. This step helps you catch missing packages or system-specific bugs early.

- **Use Containers When Needed**: For more complex systems with many dependencies or cross-platform requirements, consider using Docker. Containers package your model and its environment into a consistent, portable unit that runs reliably anywhere, whether on a cloud server or local machine. MLflow supports exporting models as Docker containers for this purpose.

These practices help ensure that your model not only runs reliably but also does so reproducibly across different systems.

Troubleshooting Model Deployment Issues

Even when you follow all the recommended best practices, deploying machine learning models into real-world production environments can still be challenging. These challenges may arise from several sources: the environment in which the model runs might be slightly different from the one used during development; the model might rely on outdated or incompatible libraries; or there could be issues in how the model interacts with real-time data, external systems, or scaling infrastructure. Problems like schema mismatches, missing dependencies, or even network outages can all disrupt a successful deployment.

Because of this complexity, it's important not to treat deployment as a "one-and-done" task. Instead, model deployment should be approached as a continuous and iterative process that needs constant monitoring, validation, and improvement. This mindset enables teams to respond quickly to issues, optimize performance over time, and maintain the model's reliability in evolving production conditions.

Dependency Management Errors

Common Symptoms

Before diving into how to resolve dependency management issues, it's essential to understand how these problems typically manifest. These errors often occur when your model is moved from the development environment, such as your laptop or a training server, to the production environment, where some packages may have different versions or be missing entirely.

Common indicators of dependency mismatches include

- `ImportError: cannot import name 'F1Score' from 'sklearn.metrics'`
- `ModuleNotFoundError`
- Subtle behavioral changes (e.g., inconsistent predictions)

Solutions

To fix and prevent dependency-related issues in production, it's important to take a structured approach that ensures consistency between your development and deployment environments. Below are several practical strategies that help achieve that consistency:

- **Log and Validate Environments Using `conda.yaml` or `requirements.txt`**: Always record your project's environment setup during model training. This ensures that the same configuration can be used later during deployment, reducing the risk of version mismatches or missing libraries.

- **Pin Versions for Every Critical Dependency (e.g., `scikit-learn=1.0.2`)**: Avoid using vague version ranges. Pinning exact versions helps guarantee that no unexpected changes in software behavior will be introduced when dependencies are reinstalled.

- **Use Clean Test Environments**: Before deploying, test your model in a fresh environment that mimics production. This practice helps uncover issues such as missing packages, OS-specific bugs, or conflicting libraries that are often overlooked during the development process.

- **Use Containers**: Docker containers can package your model and its full environment—including OS, Python version, and dependencies—into a single, reproducible unit. This approach provides a consistent deployment experience across all platforms, from local servers to cloud-based infrastructure.

Data Schema Mismatches

Schema issues arise when the format, structure, or content of the input data at inference time differs from what the machine learning model was originally trained on. This can occur if column names differ, required fields are missing, or the order or type of data has been altered. Even subtle changes, such as passing a string where a number is expected, can cause the model to fail or behave unpredictably.

Examples include

- Missing features (`ValueError: feature 'customer_tenure' not found`)

- Wrong data types (`TypeError: Cannot cast array from dtype('O') to dtype('float64')`)

Solutions: In the sections below, we will discuss solutions to overcome the Data schema mismatch:

- **Use MLflow Model Signatures**

    MLflow lets you capture and enforce the structure of input and output data using model signatures. A model signature is a recorded definition of the expected format, such as column names and data types, based on the data used during training. By logging this signature along with the model, MLflow ensures that any future input data is automatically checked for compatibility, preventing schema mismatch errors before they happen. This feature helps maintain consistency between training and inference environments, improving model reliability during production deployment.

    ```
    from mlflow.models.signature import infer_signature
    signature = infer_signature(X_train.iloc[:5], y_pred[:5])
    mlflow.sklearn.log_model(model, "model", signature=signature)
    ```

    When the model is served, the API automatically checks if incoming data matches the expected schema.

CHAPTER 6   DEPLOYING MACHINE LEARNING MODELS

Add Preprocessing Logic to Enforce Input Schema

To make your deployment more resilient and error-proof, it is essential to implement explicit preprocessing logic that checks and, if necessary, corrects the input schema before handing it off to the model. This step acts as a safety net to catch mismatches early and protect your pipeline from failing silently or unpredictably. The goal is to ensure that the incoming data always conforms to what the model expects in terms of structure, order, and types. This includes

- Checking for missing or unexpected columns
- Ensuring columns are in the correct order
- Validating and casting data types as needed

Below is a reusable Python function that performs schema enforcement by validating and transforming incoming data to match the expected structure:

```python
def preprocess_inference_data(input_data, expected_columns):
    """Validate and transform input data to match expected format"""

    # Check for missing columns
    missing_cols = set(expected_columns) - set(input_data.columns)
    if missing_cols:
        raise ValueError(f"Missing required columns: {missing_cols}")

    # Select only the expected columns and enforce ordering
    return input_data[expected_columns]
```

Using this function before inference can prevent schema-related crashes and ensure reliable predictions across inconsistent data sources.

Document Expected Input Formats Clearly

Beyond code, good documentation is critical in avoiding schema mismatch errors. When multiple teams interact with a model—or when a model is reused in new contexts—clear technical documentation ensures everyone understands what data the model expects.

As part of your deployment workflow:

- Include example payloads that show correct column names, data types, and formats.
- Log metadata with the model artifact, including required fields, valid ranges, and categorical value options.
- Provide reusable schema validation utilities or templates to downstream developers.

When schema validation logic, metadata, and documentation are bundled together, your model becomes easier to consume and more resilient to failure.

Combining schema validation tools, such as MLflow model signatures, with explicit data validation logic and supporting them with comprehensive documentation can significantly reduce the risk of schema-related failures. This ensures your model receives the data it expects safely and reliably, leading to more robust and predictable deployments.

Resource Constraints

Deploying a machine learning model to production often reveals constraints that weren't apparent during development. Local development environments tend to offer more generous computing resources or at least predictable usage patterns. However, once a model is live, serving real-time requests, handling unpredictable data volumes, or running on shared cloud infrastructure, it can face significant resource bottlenecks.

These constraints can manifest in various ways, including

- **Timeout errors** during inference as the model fails to return predictions within an acceptable timeframe
- **Out-of-memory errors** due to large batch sizes or memory-intensive preprocessing pipelines
- **High latency**, even under normal loads, compared to what was observed during local testing

Such issues can disrupt user experience, cause application instability, and, in extreme cases, lead to complete service outages.

CHAPTER 6   DEPLOYING MACHINE LEARNING MODELS

Diagnosing and Right-Sizing Resources

The model's resource usage must be profiled before deployment to mitigate these challenges. This involves measuring the amount of memory and computing resources the model consumes under realistic workloads and then provisioning resources accordingly.

The following Python function offers a simple way to **simulate and monitor resource usage** for a deployed model over repeated inference cycles:

```python
import time
import psutil
import os

def profile_model_resources(model, sample_input, iterations=100):
    """Profile model resource usage during inference"""
    memory_usages = []
    latencies = []
    
    # Get baseline memory usage
    process = psutil.Process(os.getpid())
    baseline_memory = process.memory_info().rss / (1024 * 1024)  # MB
    
    for _ in range(iterations):
        # Measure memory before inference
        start_memory = process.memory_info().rss / (1024 * 1024)
        start_time = time.time()
        
        # Run inference
        _ = model.predict(sample_input)
        
        # Measure inference latency
        latencies.append((time.time() - start_time) * 1000)  # ms
        
        # Measure memory after inference
        end_memory = process.memory_info().rss / (1024 * 1024)
        memory_usages.append(end_memory - start_memory)
```

```
    return {
        "avg_latency_ms": sum(latencies) / len(latencies),
        "p95_latency_ms": sorted(latencies)[int(0.95 * iterations)],
        "avg_memory_mb": sum(memory_usages) / len(memory_usages),
        "max_memory_mb": max(memory_usages),
        "baseline_memory_mb": baseline_memory
    }
```

This profiling function can help you answer key deployment questions:

- What is the average and 95th percentile latency?
- How much additional memory does each inference consume?
- What is the baseline memory footprint of the model process?

Armed with this data, you can fine-tune resource allocations on your production infrastructure—adjusting autoscaling policies, upgrading instance types, or refactoring your model to reduce memory overhead.

Networking and Connectivity Issues

In production environments, machine learning models typically operate in conjunction with other systems. They often need to communicate with external services such as data APIs, authentication providers, storage layers, or orchestration systems. As a result, networking and connectivity issues are among the most common and frustrating problems encountered during model deployment.

Common Symptoms

When a deployed model or service is unable to reach its required endpoints, you may encounter errors such as

```
ConnectionError: Failed to establish a connection to endpoint
```

or

```
TimeoutError: Request timed out after 30 seconds
```

These issues can be intermittent or persistent and may be caused by DNS resolution problems, firewall rules, latency spikes, or unstable upstream services.

CHAPTER 6   DEPLOYING MACHINE LEARNING MODELS

Recommended Solutions

Implement robust error handling, connection management, and diagnostic capabilities to make your model deployment more resilient to these issues.

- **Implement Automatic Retries**

    Using retry mechanisms allows your application to recover from transient network failures. Python's requests library, when combined with urllib3's retry strategy, provides a flexible way to add automatic retries with exponential backoff:

    ```
    import requests
    from requests.adapters import HTTPAdapter
    from requests.packages.urllib3.util.retry import Retry

    def create_session_with_retries(retries=3, backoff_factor=0.3):
        """Create a requests session with automatic retries"""
        session = requests.Session()
        retry = Retry(
            total=retries,
            read=retries,
            connect=retries,
            backoff_factor=backoff_factor,
            status_forcelist=[502, 503, 504]
        )
        adapter = HTTPAdapter(max_retries=retry)
        session.mount('http://', adapter)
        session.mount('https://', adapter)
        return session

    # Use the session for network calls
    session = create_session_with_retries()
    response = session.post(endpoint_url, json=payload, timeout=10)
    ```

This code snippet ensures that failed requests due to temporary server errors or unstable networks are automatically retried, reducing the likelihood of user-visible errors.

- **Enable Connection Pooling**

  For high-volume applications, avoid creating a new HTTP connection for each request. Using a persistent session object with connection pooling improves performance and reduces overhead:

  - Maintain a single requests.Session() object per thread or process.
  - Reuse connections when making multiple calls to the same host to improve performance.

- **Set Appropriate Timeouts**

  Always configure **both connection and read timeouts** for any network operation. This prevents your service from hanging indefinitely while waiting for a slow or unresponsive endpoint:

  ```
  response = requests.post(
      url,
      json=data,
      timeout=(3.05, 27)  # (connect_timeout, read_timeout)
  )
  ```

  - The **connect timeout** limits how long the client waits to establish a connection.
  - The **read timeout** limits how long the client waits for a response after connection.

  Omitting timeouts can block threads or resources under load, especially in microservices or inference pipelines.

CHAPTER 6   DEPLOYING MACHINE LEARNING MODELS

- **Use Network Diagnostics**

    Implement simple network diagnostic tools to ensure connectivity between your deployment environment and external systems. These may include

    - Ping or traceroute scripts
    - Port availability checks (e.g., using `telnet` or `nc`)
    - Internal health check endpoints
    - Logging of request URLs, response times, and failure reasons

These tools help isolate whether the root cause lies within the network, the client code, or the external service.

By implementing these best practices—automatic retries, connection reuse, sensible timeouts, and diagnostics—you can significantly enhance the robustness and production readiness of your machine learning services. Network failures are inevitable, but their impact can be gracefully minimized with a well-architected approach.

Model Serving Performance Issues

Deploying a machine learning model into production is a significant milestone, but it is not the end of the journey. Over time, models may exhibit **performance degradation**, especially as data patterns evolve or traffic increases. Understanding and proactively addressing performance issues is key to maintaining a reliable user experience and scalable architecture.

Common symptoms of performance bottlenecks include

1. **Increasing Latency**: Prediction requests take longer to complete, which can potentially impact the user experience.

2. **Request Queuing**: Backlogged inference requests suggest that the serving infrastructure is under-provisioned or improperly tuned.

3. **Timeout Errors**: During peak load periods, inference calls may fail, resulting in timeouts being returned to users or upstream systems.

To address these issues, adopt a performance-first mindset. This includes **monitoring latency metrics**, **tracking request throughput**, and **profiling model behavior under load**. Databricks provides built-in tools such as **MLflow logs**, **Spark**

metrics, and **model serving dashboards** to help isolate and analyze these performance trends. Additionally, autoscaling, resource optimization, and model distillation techniques should be considered to improve responsiveness.

Troubleshooting Checklist

When things go wrong in production, a structured troubleshooting process helps resolve issues efficiently and minimizes downtime. Below is a systematic checklist to guide your debugging workflow:

1. **Verify Environment Consistency**
   Verify that the production environment accurately reflects the development environment. Inconsistencies in Python versions, library dependencies, or hardware configurations can introduce unexpected behavior.

2. **Validate Input Data**
   Ensure that the data passed to the model matches the schema and format used during training. Issues often arise when real-world inputs contain nulls, outliers, or unexpected categorical values.

3. **Check Resource Utilization**
   Monitor CPU, memory, disk I/O, and GPU (if applicable) to identify potential resource bottlenecks during inference.

4. **Review Logs**
   Dive into logs generated by both the model and the serving infrastructure. These logs may contain stack traces, warning messages, or data validation failures.

5. **Test Incrementally**
   Isolate the failure using simplified or synthetic inputs to identify the root cause. This helps determine whether the issue stems from specific input values, data volume, or model logic.

6. **Compare Environments**
   Run the same inference locally or in development to check for discrepancies. Differences in output or behavior can reveal environment-specific issues.

7. **Monitor Network Traffic**
   Verify that all components (e.g., databases, APIs, external services) are communicating properly for distributed systems. Network failures can mimic model errors.

8. **Check for Scaling Issues**
   Analyze whether the issue appears only under heavy load. This can indicate issues with autoscaling policies, insufficient resources, or connection pool exhaustion.

By applying this checklist, teams can transition from reactive firefighting to a more **proactive and diagnostic-driven approach**, ensuring models remain both **functional and performant** in production.

External Integration Patterns

While Databricks provides a powerful platform for model training and deployment, real-world applications often require integrating these models into broader **enterprise ecosystems**. Whether you're embedding predictions into dashboards, APIs, or mobile apps, choosing the right integration pattern is crucial for achieving scalability, performance, and maintainability.

REST API Integration

One of the most common approaches is to expose model predictions via **RESTful APIs**. REST APIs provide a standardized and flexible interface for other systems to invoke real-time models.

Databricks simplifies this process by **automatically provisioning REST endpoints** for models deployed through MLflow. However, you may build a custom API wrapper using frameworks like FastAPI or Flask for more control over routing, input validation, or business logic. This wrapper can act as a middle layer, abstracting and securing access to the underlying model.

REST API integration is especially suitable for:

- Web applications need real-time recommendations.
- Internal dashboards triggering on-demand predictions.
- Scheduled batch jobs making bulk inference calls.

Webhook Integration

For event-driven workflows, **webhooks** offer an asynchronous method for invoking models. Instead of polling for predictions, external systems can **trigger model inference** upon specific events (e.g., a new user sign-up, transaction, or alert).

Webhooks are useful in use cases where

- An external event initiates the prediction request.
- The response is not required immediately.
- The pipeline benefits from asynchronous handling (e.g., fraud detection, background scoring).

Message Queue Integration

Message queues such as Kafka, RabbitMQ, or Azure Event Hubs provide a scalable backbone for ML inference in high-throughput or asynchronous environments.

Instead of sending prediction requests directly, applications **enqueue messages** containing the input data. A separate model-serving component consumes these messages, performs inference, and optionally writes the results back. This pattern is ideal for

- Handling traffic spikes without overwhelming your model endpoints
- Decoupling producers (data sources) from consumers (models)
- Ensuring fault tolerance and message reprocessing capabilities

Mobile Application Integration

Mobile applications present a distinct set of challenges for machine learning (ML) integration due to limited bandwidth, varied device capabilities, and sensitivity to latency. To ensure a responsive and consistent experience, two main integration strategies are commonly used:

- **Cloud-Based API Integration**

    Most mobile apps rely on REST APIs to interact with hosted models. This approach keeps the app lightweight while allowing for centralized model updates and performance scaling in the back end.

- **Integration with Enterprise Systems**

  Mobile apps within enterprise ecosystems often need to integrate with platforms such as **CRM**, **ERP**, or **data warehouses**. These integrations require secure and robust patterns that support bidirectional data flow, often through enterprise gateways or middleware layers.

When designing mobile integrations, always consider:

- **Latency:** Optimize API response time to avoid blocking the user interface.

- **Offline support:** Cache predictions locally if applicable.

- **Data usage:** Minimize payload sizes and avoid large downloads during inference to optimize performance.

Integration Best Practices

As your machine learning models transition from development to deployment, integrating them with real-world systems becomes crucial for generating business value. This process is not just about connecting endpoints—it involves building resilient, secure, and maintainable systems that adapt to evolving business requirements and models. Below are recommended best practices to guide your integration strategy.

Secure API Access

Security should be a foundational pillar of your integration design. Always protect your APIs using industry-standard authentication mechanisms, such as **OAuth 2.0** or **API keys, to ensure secure access**. In addition, take the following precautions:

- **Implement rate limiting** to prevent abuse or denial-of-service attacks.

- **Validate incoming requests** to reject malformed or unauthorized traffic.

- **Encrypt data in transit** using TLS to protect sensitive user or business data.

Error Handling and Resilience

Real-world systems are unpredictable, and model endpoints may occasionally fail or be temporarily unavailable. Your integration strategy should gracefully handle these situations:

- Enable **graceful degradation** by reverting to the default behavior when the ML service is unavailable.
- Use **retry logic with exponential backoff** to recover from transient issues.
- Provide **clear, actionable error messages** to help developers quickly diagnose and resolve issues.

Versioning

Model evolution is inevitable, and updates can break downstream consumers without proper versioning. So, always establish a clear versioning strategy by following these versioning practices:

- **Version your APIs and endpoints** to maintain backward compatibility.
- Include **model version identifiers** in responses for debugging and audit.
- Support **canary or staged deployments** to test new model versions on a subset of users before rolling out to the full user base.

Performance Optimization

API performance has a direct impact on user experience and system costs. Optimize for speed and efficiency wherever possible with these best practices:

- **Cache frequently requested predictions** to reduce redundant computations.
- Use **connection pooling** for back-end services to minimize latency.
- **Batch multiple predictions** in a single request to improve throughput when applicable.

Monitoring Integration Points

Operational visibility is vital for maintaining service reliability. Monitor the model's performance and the interaction points with external systems. Follow these best practices to achieve operational visibility:

- Track **API latency, throughput, and error rates** over time to gain insight into performance trends.

- Instrument **dependency tracking** to detect cascading failures or service slowdowns.

- Set up **proactive alerting** for integration anomalies or system outages to ensure timely detection and resolution.

By following these best practices, organizations can build robust bridges between machine learning models and the wider application ecosystem. Whether integrating with mobile apps, web portals, or enterprise platforms, a well-architected approach ensures that ML's predictive power translates into tangible business outcomes.

Monitoring and Maintaining Deployed Models

Imagine you've spent months building a robust churn prediction model. After meticulous tuning and validation, it goes live, powering your company's customer retention efforts. A few weeks later, marketing reports that the model's predictions are no longer producing the desired outcomes. What happened?

In many cases, model drift refers to the gradual degradation of model performance resulting from changes in data patterns. This decline can go unnoticed without regular monitoring until significant damage is done, resulting in lost revenue, poor user experience, or regulatory exposure.

Model deployment is not the end of your machine learning journey. It marks the beginning of a new operational phase that requires **continuous monitoring and maintenance**. Just like a car needs regular servicing to remain roadworthy, your models need oversight and adaptation to stay valuable.

In this section, you'll learn how to

- Monitor deployed models effectively.

- Detect issues such as data drift and performance degradation.

- Implement alerting systems.
- Manage model updates and life cycle transitions.

Setting Up Monitoring and Alerting

Model monitoring systematically tracks a model's performance, health, and impact after deployment. Without it, you're flying blind—unaware if your model delivers value, fails silently, or causes harm.

For example, consider a fraud detection model at a financial institution:

- If it becomes overly aggressive, it may block legitimate transactions, hurting customer trust.
- It may allow fraud to occur if it becomes lax, resulting in financial loss.

Monitoring mitigates such risks by providing

- **Early Warning Systems**: Detect performance drops before they impact the business.
- **Performance Visibility**: Understand how the model is behaving in real-world conditions.
- **Feedback Loops**: Inform retraining and system improvement.

What to Monitor: Key Metrics

Monitoring tracks model performance, latency, and data drift to ensure reliable predictions. You need to assess different dimensions to understand the model's health.

A. **Performance Metrics**

   These metrics assess **prediction quality** depending on your model type:

   - **Classification models use these metrics**:
     - Accuracy, Precision, Recall
     - F1-score
     - AUC-ROC

- **Regression models can use these metrics**:
  - Mean Absolute Error (MAE)
  - Root Mean Squared Error (RMSE)
  - R-squared

Track these metrics over time and compare them to baseline validation metrics. Significant deviation can indicate model drift or degraded input quality.

B. **Operational Metrics**

These metrics reflect the health of the **serving infrastructure**:

- **Inference Latency**: Time taken for prediction (critical for real-time systems)
- **Throughput**: Number of requests served per second/minute
- **Error Rates**: Request failures due to timeouts, exceptions, and other issues
- **Resource Utilization**: CPU, memory, disk—monitored to detect bottlenecks or scaling needs

In Databricks, you can use platform metrics, logging systems, and Databricks SQL dashboards to track these indicators.

C. **Data Drift Metrics**

Drift occurs when the **input data changes** from what the model was trained on. Key indicators include

- **Statistical Drift**: Use metrics like KL divergence, PSI, or Jensen-Shannon distance.
- **Feature Distribution Shifts**: Monitor changes in mean, standard deviation, and quantiles.
- **Missing Values**: Increased nulls or missing rates can skew predictions.

Drift is often a precursor to performance decline—monitoring it provides a **proactive alert system.**

Creating Dashboards and Alerts

Dashboards

To build these dashboards, use Databricks SQL or integrate with BI tools like Power BI, Grafana, or Databricks AI/BI dashboard. Visual dashboards offer real-time insights into

- Prediction accuracy trends
- Distribution of inputs and outputs
- Drift detection signals

Alerts

While dashboards offer visibility, **alerts** provide a proactive defense against potential issues. In Databricks, you can configure alerts using SQL Alerts, MLflow events, or external notification services. Here are some best practices for alerts:

1. **Set thresholds** based on business impact, not just statistical significance.
2. **Use severity levels** (e.g., Critical, Warning, Info).
3. **Include context** in messages (e.g., baseline values, model version).
4. **Define response playbooks** for different alert types.
5. **Refine alerts over time** to reduce false positives and increase actionability.

The Monitoring Life Cycle

Monitoring should evolve alongside your model. Monitoring should be regularly updated as the model and its data evolve. Adjust thresholds, add new metrics, and evolve based on real-world feedback. Here is the life cycle of the monitoring alerts as depicted in Figure 6-4:

- Start with **basic accuracy tracking**.
- Add **drift detection** as patterns emerge.
- Eventually, include **business KPIs** and **economic impact metrics**.

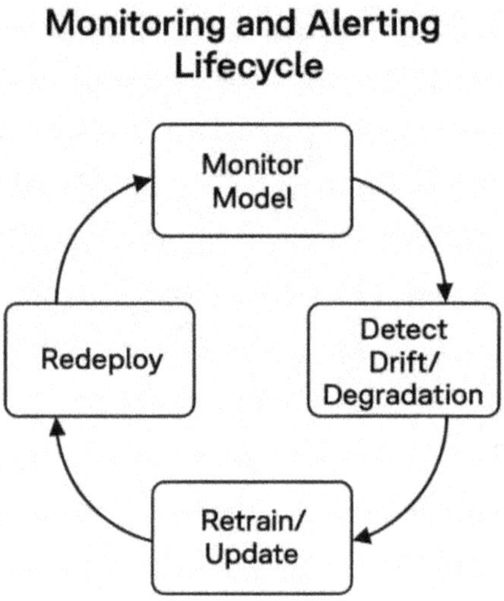

Figure 6-4. Monitoring the life cycle of the deployed model

Managing the Model Life Cycle and Updates

In this section, we will discuss the model life cycle and triggers to update models.

Understanding the Model Life Cycle

Machine learning models, like software systems, have life cycles. Table 6-5 outlines the various stages they undergo.

Table 6-5. Stages of the Model Life Cycle

Stage	Description
Development	Data prep, feature engineering, training, and testing
Validation	Rigorous performance checks and approval gating
Deployment	Integration into live systems with data pipelines or APIs
Monitoring	Continuous tracking of performance and system behavior
Maintenance	Updates, retraining, or architectural modifications
Retirement	Decommissioning outdated models or replacing them with better alternatives

Triggers for Model Updates

You'll know it's time to refresh a model when you observe these issues in your model:

- **Performance degradation** (e.g., drop in F1-score, spike in MAE)
- **Data drift** (features no longer match training distribution)
- **Concept drift** (real-world relationships between inputs and outputs evolve)
- **Business requirement changes** (new regulations or strategy shifts)
- **User feedback** (qualitative signals from customers or internal stakeholders)

Regularly scheduled retraining (e.g., monthly or quarterly) may also be appropriate, especially for high-impact models.

Hands-On Exercise: Predict Customer Churn and Serve the Model via REST API

Scenario

A telecom company operates in a highly competitive market where acquiring new customers often costs significantly more than retaining existing ones. One of the biggest challenges they face is customer churn, which occurs when users cancel or stop using the service. Losing high-value customers not only impacts revenue but also damages customer lifetime value and market share.

To address this, the company aims to build a machine learning model that can proactively identify customers at risk of leaving based on patterns in their historical usage, payment behavior, service interactions, and demographics.

With an accurate churn prediction model in place, the business can

- Target at-risk customers with personalized offers, discounts, or improved service plans.
- Optimize customer service efforts by prioritizing outreach to those most likely to leave.

CHAPTER 6 DEPLOYING MACHINE LEARNING MODELS

- Reduce overall attrition rates, saving millions in lost revenue over time.

- Boost long-term customer satisfaction and retention.

Objectives

In this hands-on lab, we will

- Train a simple churn prediction model using scikit-learn.

- Log the model with MLflow in Databricks.

- Register the model in the MLflow Model Registry.

- Transition it to the Production stage and enable model serving.

- Invoke the model using REST API for real-time predictions.

Step 0: Create Unity Catalog Schema (if it does not already exist). Replace "main" with your catalog name and "ml_models" with your desired schema name:

```
catalog_name = "main"
schema_name = "ml_models"
spark.sql(f"CREATE SCHEMA IF NOT EXISTS {catalog_name}.{schema_name}")
```

Step 1: Train a Churn Prediction Model Using scikit-learn. We'll generate a synthetic classification dataset and use a RandomForestClassifier to train a simple model.

```
from sklearn.datasets import make_classification
from sklearn.model_selection import train_test_split
from sklearn.ensemble import RandomForestClassifier
import pandas as pd

X, y = make_classification(n_samples=500, n_features=10, n_informative=5, random_state=42)
X = pd.DataFrame(X, columns=[f"feature_{i}" for i in range(10)])
y = pd.Series(y, name="churn")

X_train, X_test, y_train, y_test = train_test_split(X, y, test_size=0.2, random_state=42)
```

```
clf = RandomForestClassifier(n_estimators=100)
clf.fit(X_train, y_train)
```

Step 2: Log in and Register the Model with Unity Catalog. We'll use MLflow to log the model, input example, and a model signature for reproducibility.

```
import mlflow
import mlflow.sklearn
from mlflow.models.signature import infer_signature

mlflow.set_registry_uri("databricks-uc")

with mlflow.start_run(run_name="Churn_Model_Training") as run:
    mlflow.log_param("n_estimators", 100)
    signature = infer_signature(X_train, clf.predict(X_train))
    mlflow.sklearn.log_model(
        sk_model=clf,
        artifact_path="model",
        signature=signature,
        input_example=X_train.iloc[:5],
        registered_model_name="main.ml_models.ChurnModel"
    )
```

Step 3: Assign Alias for Production Deployment

```
from mlflow import MlflowClient
client = MlflowClient()
client.set_registered_model_alias("main.ml_models.ChurnModel", "prod", 1)
```

Step 4: Enable Model Serving. Navigate to **Models** in the Databricks UI. Select ChurnModel under the schema ml_models, click **Serve this Model**, and turn on the REST endpoint.

CHAPTER 6 DEPLOYING MACHINE LEARNING MODELS

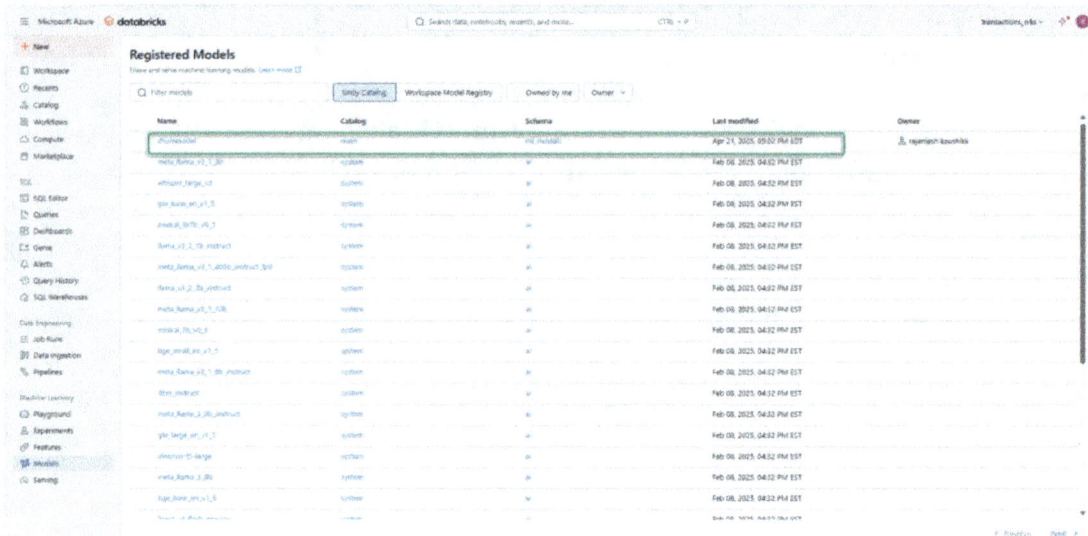

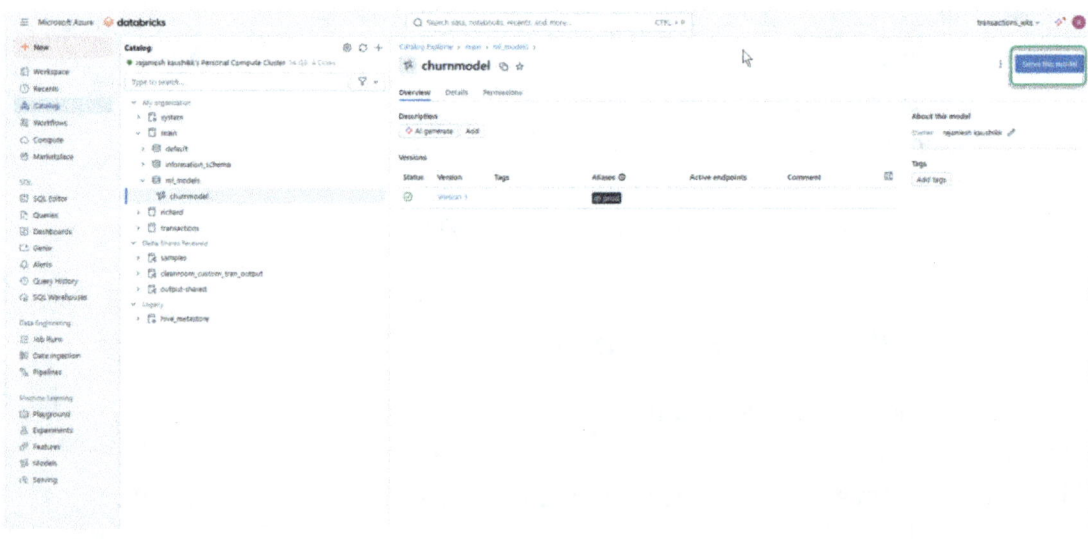

CHAPTER 6   DEPLOYING MACHINE LEARNING MODELS

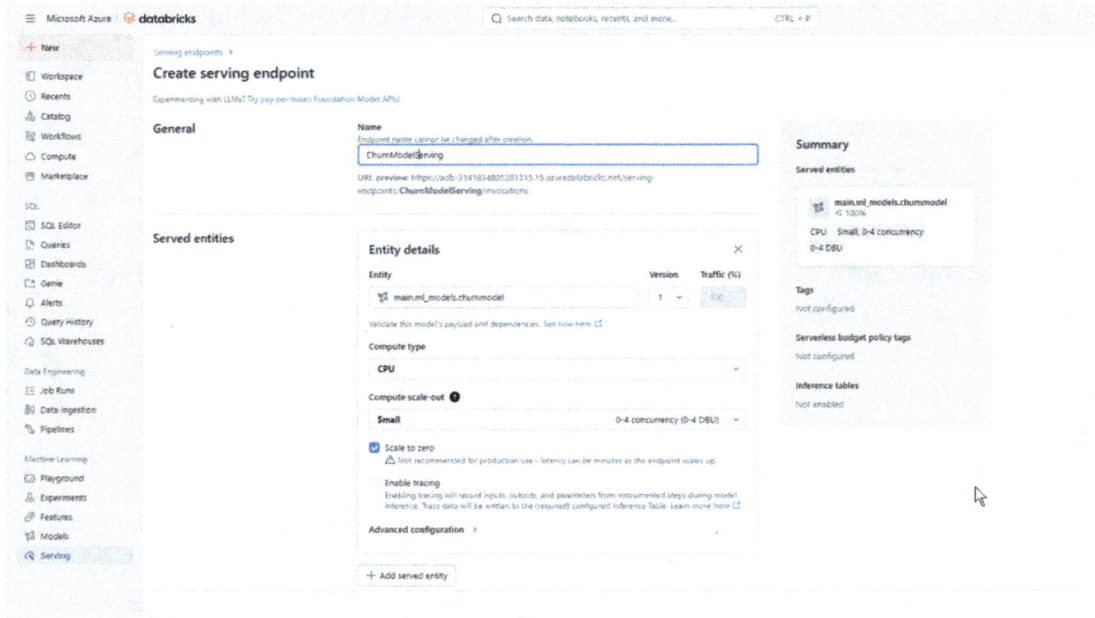

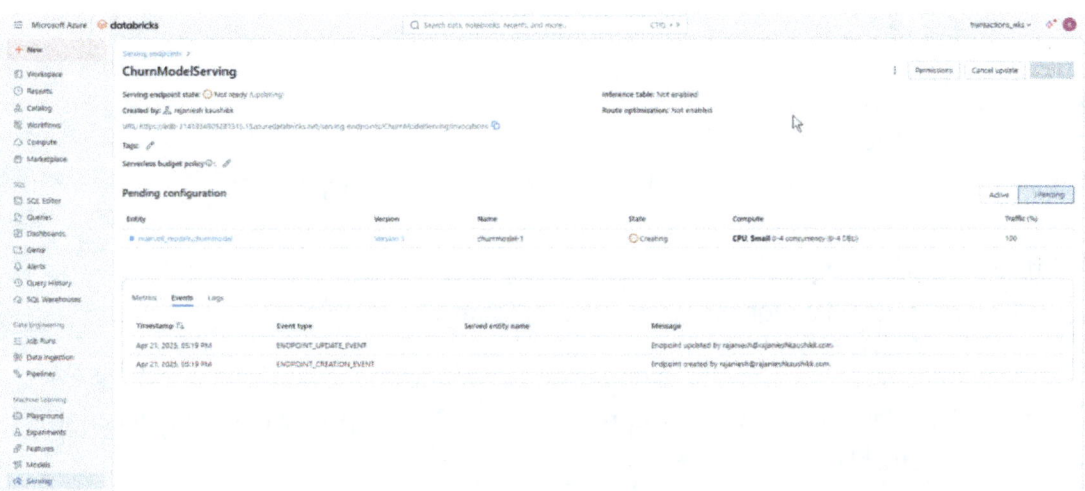

Step 5: Send a Prediction Request Using REST API

```
import requests
import json

# Replace with your actual values
```

331

CHAPTER 6   DEPLOYING MACHINE LEARNING MODELS

```python
DATABRICKS_TOKEN = "Replace it with Actual Databricks Token value"

url = "Replace the Model Serving URL"

headers = {
    "Authorization": f"Bearer {DATABRICKS_TOKEN}",
    "Content-Type": "application/json"
}

# example input: match features used in training
payload = {
    "dataframe_split": {
        "columns": [f"feature_{i}" for i in range(10)],
        "data": [
            [-0.2, 0.4, -1.1, 0.1, -0.6, 1.2, 0.3, -0.4, 0.9, 1.5]
        ]
    }
}

  Send the request
response = requests.post(url, headers=headers, json=payload)

# Output prediction
print("Prediction Response:", response.json())
```

Step 6: Understanding the Prediction Outcome. The response to your API call will return something like

`{"predictions": [1]}`

Interpretation:

- 0: Customer will **not** churn.
- 1: Customer **will** churn.

Summary

This chapter walked you through the **post-deployment journey**—the critical phase where machine learning systems either **thrive** or **fail silently**.

You learned how to

- Implement robust monitoring using performance, operational, and drift metrics.
- Build dashboards and configure alerts for early issue detection.
- Manage the life cycle of models using updates, retraining, and retirement strategies.
- Use Databricks and MLflow as your operational toolkit for monitoring and versioning.

Deployment is not a finish line—it's the start of a continuous improvement loop that keeps your models accurate, efficient, and trustworthy.

In Chapter 7: Advanced Topics in Machine Learning, we shift our focus from operational excellence to **ethical responsibility**. You'll learn how to

- Interpret model decisions using explainable AI (XAI) techniques.
- Detect and mitigate algorithmic bias.
- Embed fairness, transparency, and accountability in your ML pipelines.
- Explore the emerging landscape of responsible AI and compliance-ready data systems.

Whether you're deploying models in finance, healthcare, or public policy, understanding the **why** behind model predictions is just as crucial as deploying them effectively.

CHAPTER 7

Advanced Topics in Machine Learning

As machine learning continues to reshape enterprise workflows, the focus has expanded beyond model accuracy to broader concerns, including interpretability, fairness, and responsible AI governance. Organizations across industries—from telecom and finance to healthcare and retail—are increasingly expected to **justify**, **audit**, and **govern** the decisions made by machine learning systems. This shift marks a new phase in the maturity of AI adoption: one where trust, transparency, and accountability are no longer optional—they are essential.

Databricks, with its unified Lakehouse Architecture, is uniquely positioned to meet these evolving expectations. Built on Delta Lake and powered by Apache Spark, the Databricks platform offers native support for MLflow, Unity Catalog, and Mosaic AI—tools that enable seamless model development, deployment, observability, and governance integration. These capabilities allow data scientists and ML engineers to train performant models and ensure that those models can be **explained**, **audited**, and **aligned** with ethical and regulatory standards.

For instance, a company might deploy a churn prediction model in a telecom setting that flags high-risk customers before contract renewal. While the model performs well on traditional metrics such as precision and recall, the marketing and customer success teams cannot act on its predictions without understanding what features, such as call volume, customer support ticket frequency, or billing disputes, drive the model's outputs. A lack of explainability can stall business action and erode both internal and external trust. Worse still, if the model disproportionately targets specific regions or demographics, it may introduce regulatory risk and reputational damage.

In this chapter, we will **explore** a range of advanced machine learning topics—starting with explainable AI (XAI) techniques such as SHAP and LIME, followed by strategies to detect and mitigate bias, and finally, a forward-looking view of AI trends

CHAPTER 7 ADVANCED TOPICS IN MACHINE LEARNING

within the Databricks ecosystem. Each section emphasizes practical implementation using Databricks-native tools such as MLflow for experiment tracking, Unity Catalog for metadata and governance, and Mosaic AI for integrating generative and foundation model capabilities.

Learning Objectives

By the end of this chapter, you will be able to

- **Explain** the role of model interpretability in enterprise ML systems and how it influences decision-making and compliance.

- **Implement** explainability techniques using SHAP and LIME within Databricks notebooks and track results using MLflow.

- **Evaluate** fairness in model outcomes and apply techniques to mitigate bias using Python-based tools and Unity Catalog lineage.

- **Design** workflows that integrate ethical considerations and governance principles using Databricks-native features.

- **Anticipate** emerging trends in ML, such as LLMOps and adaptive learning, and describe how Databricks supports these evolutions.

Overview of Explainability Techniques: SHAP, LIME, and Beyond

Once a team understands that accurate predictions are insufficient, the next question is: *How do we explain what the model is doing?* Some models, such as Decision Trees or Linear Regression, are relatively easy to follow. You can trace how each input affects the outcome. However, many real-world models are significantly more complex, such as deep learning models or ensembles like random forests. These powerful models can deliver high accuracy but are often hard to understand. That's where **explainability techniques** come in.

Interpretability techniques can be categorized into two main groups: **model-specific** and **model-agnostic**. Model-specific methods are tightly linked to the structure of the model itself. For example, Decision Trees or Linear Regression models are easy to interpret directly because they expose their inner logic. A Linear Regression model that predicts prices based on brand, weight, and discount can be understood by examining the coefficients in a retail pricing scenario. You can even write the prediction as a formula. These models are great for clarity but may miss subtle patterns in complex data, such as nonlinear relationships or interactions between features. For example, a simple Decision Tree might examine income and credit utilization separately, missing the interaction between them. If both increase slightly simultaneously, a person is more likely to repay a loan, increasing the chance of approval. A complex model, like a gradient boosted tree, can capture this combination and adjust the prediction accordingly.

The second category is **model-agnostic interpretability**, often referred to as post-hoc methods because they are applied after the model has been trained. These techniques do not rely on the internal structure of the model, making them flexible enough to work with any algorithm, from decision forests to deep neural networks. Think of model-agnostic methods like a translator that explains the behavior of a complex system to a human in simple terms. For example, a claims department might utilize a machine learning model to identify potentially fraudulent claims in the insurance industry. Suppose the model identifies a claim as suspicious. In that case, the fraud investigators need to understand why—was it due to a high claim amount, inconsistencies in the reported incident, or an unusual pattern in claim history? Post-hoc methods, such as SHAP and LIME, can provide these insights, enabling investigators to prioritize cases and document their rationale. Without clear explanations, the team risks acting on unreliable signals, which could lead to delays, increased costs, or wrongful denials.

In the subsequent sections, we will explore SHAP, LIME, and partial dependence plots.

SHAP

SHAP (SHapley Additive exPlanations) utilizes concepts from game theory to demonstrate the contribution of each feature to a specific prediction. Imagine a loan approval model that uses income, age, credit score, and employment history. SHAP can tell you that a credit score increase added +0.3 to the approval probability, while age reduction decreased it by -0.1. SHAP is valuable because it provides consistent, fair explanations for individual predictions and overall feature importance.

SHAP is often employed in high-stakes situations, such as financial risk modeling or medical diagnostics, where fairness and accuracy are crucial. However, it requires more computing power and time, especially with large datasets.

CHAPTER 7   ADVANCED TOPICS IN MACHINE LEARNING

LIME

LIME (Local Interpretable Model-Agnostic Explanations) takes a different approach. It explains one prediction at a time by creating a simple, hypothetical model that behaves similarly to the real one in the vicinity of that prediction. For example, if a model predicts that a patient is at risk of hospital readmission in a healthcare setting, LIME can show that the key factors were recent emergency room visits and high blood pressure. LIME is faster and easier to use than SHAP, but it may yield different results each time and lack the same level of mathematical rigor.

Partial Dependence Plots

Partial Dependence Plots (PDPs) are a visualization technique used to understand the average effect of a single feature on a model's prediction. Unlike SHAP or LIME, which explain individual predictions, PDPs demonstrate how the model's predictions change when a single feature value is altered while keeping all other feature values constant. This helps identify whether the relationship between a feature and the outcome is linear or nonlinear or has thresholds.

For example, a PDP could be used to analyze how a customer's income level affects their loan approval probability in a retail banking scenario. As you increase the income from low to high, the PDP may reveal that the likelihood of loan approval rises steadily until a certain point and then levels off. This indicates to the bank that additional income does not increase approval chances beyond a certain income threshold. PDPs provide global insights into feature behavior, making them ideal for communicating model logic to nontechnical stakeholders.

To help you choose the right technique, Table 7-1 shows the comparison of SHAP, LIME, and Partial Dependence Plots (PDPs).

Table 7-1. Comparison Between SHAP, LIME, and PDP

Technique	Strengths	Limitations	Best Used For
SHAP	It provides consistent, fair explanations grounded in game theory. It works for both local (individual) and global (overall) insights.	Computationally expensive for large datasets. Interpreting it can be complex without visual tools.	High-stakes applications, such as finance, healthcare, or legal domains, where fairness and auditability are crucial.
LIME	Quick to implement and easier to explain in a user-facing environment. Focuses on local behavior for one prediction.	Results may vary across runs. Less stable and mathematically grounded than SHAP.	Dashboards, rapid prototyping, or debugging a single prediction's outcome.
PDPs	It helps visualize the average effect of one feature on predictions across the dataset. Visual graphs make it simple to interpret.	Assumes features are independent; does not capture interactions between features.	Exploring global feature trends in business scenarios like pricing or credit scoring.

This side-by-side comparison should help guide your decision, taking into account context, complexity, and the intended audience.

Databricks makes it easy to use both tools. You can install SHAP or LIME in your cluster, run them in a notebook, and create visualizations to explore the results. Using **MLflow**, you can log these explanations along with your models. With **Unity Catalog**, you can tag them with metadata and manage who has access to them. This enables data scientists, analysts, and business users to work together when interpreting model behavior.

In the next section, we'll walk through a hands-on approach to using SHAP in Databricks to generate local and global explanations for your model.

Ethical Considerations in Machine Learning

As machine learning systems assume greater responsibility in healthcare, finance, education, and criminal justice domains, ethical considerations have shifted from theoretical discussions to urgent design requirements. A model's accuracy is no longer the sole measure of success—fairness, transparency, accountability, and societal impact must also be considered. Without safeguards, models can replicate existing biases, make decisions that are difficult to justify, and cause real-world harm. Ethical machine learning involves designing systems that not only function technically but also align with human values and institutional responsibilities.

This section examines two crucial aspects of responsible AI: recognizing and mitigating bias, as well as ensuring transparency and accountability throughout the machine learning life cycle.

Recognizing and Addressing Bias

As machine learning models become more embedded in real-world decision-making, the risks of unintentionally amplifying bias grow significantly. Models are only as fair as the data on which they are trained, and historical data often reflects societal inequalities, structural discrimination, or biased sampling. If these biases go unrecognized, the resulting models can reinforce systemic injustice, undermining the very goals they were designed to support.

Bias in machine learning can originate from many sources. **Historical bias** arises when past decisions were unjust—for instance, if loan approvals historically favored one demographic over another, the training data will encode that unfairness. **Representation bias** occurs when the data doesn't include all groups equally, such as under-representing women in tech-related job applications. **Measurement bias** occurs when the data used in a model do not accurately reflect what is being measured. Sometimes, we use indirect data, such as a person's ZIP code, to estimate their income. However, this can be misleading because ZIP codes reflect social patterns, such as where certain racial or income groups tend to reside, rather than actual income levels. In another case, if we use someone's education level to predict their job performance, it might be unfair to people who don't have access to the same schools or opportunities, even if they possess the right skills.

Bias can also sneak in during other steps, like

1. **Labeling**: When humans provide examples to the model (such as "spam" or "not spam"), their own biases may influence their choices.

2. **Feature Selection**: If we pick the wrong inputs without checking their fairness.

3. **Model Evaluation**: If we don't test how well the model performs across different groups (such as gender or ethnicity), we might not notice its unfairness.

To address these concerns, it's important to embed fairness checks into every part of the machine learning process, using simple and structured steps:

- **Exploratory Data Analysis (EDA):** This is like checking your ingredients before cooking. We examine the data to ensure that all types of people, including men and women, as well as different age groups, are fairly represented. If not, the model might not learn to make good predictions for underrepresented groups.

- **Model Auditing:** After training, we test the model's performance for different groups. If it makes more mistakes for one group than another, it might not be very objective and needs to be fixed.

- **Fairness Constraints:** These specialized tools enable the model to treat people more fairly. They might adjust the training data or modify the model's behavior to reduce unfair outcomes.

- **Transparency and Documentation:** Writing down how the data was collected and how the model works helps others understand what might be unfair. This includes noting which features could be sensitive or biased and being honest about the model's limitations.

For instance, a credit scoring model might be trained in financial services on past lending decisions. If that history reflects discriminatory practices, such as denying loans more frequently to applicants from certain ZIP codes or socioeconomic backgrounds, the model will learn to replicate those patterns. Without auditing and intervention, this can lead to unfair outcomes, as a highly qualified applicant may be denied credit solely based on demographic correlation. By applying fairness-aware techniques and regularly evaluating the model across various demographics, including race, gender, and income brackets, teams can identify and correct these hidden risks before deployment.

Addressing bias is not just an ethical imperative—it's also a business necessity. Biased models can result in regulatory penalties, brand damage, and a loss of customer trust. Proactively recognizing and mitigating bias ensures that machine learning supports equitable decision-making, particularly in sensitive domains such as lending, hiring, healthcare, and education.

The next section will examine how transparency and accountability can be operationalized through responsible documentation and stakeholder alignment.

Ensuring Fairness and Accountability

Fairness in machine learning isn't just about avoiding bias—it's about creating trustworthy, explainable systems that align with ethical and legal standards. This means ensuring that models perform equitably across different groups and that organizations take responsibility for the outcomes those models produce. Accountability must be built into the entire machine learning (ML) life cycle, from data collection to deployment and monitoring. This section will explore fairness-aware algorithms, transparency frameworks, and governance practices that support responsible AI.

Fairness-aware algorithms are designed to improve the equity of model predictions. These can include preprocessing techniques (e.g., reweighting the training data to ensure balance), in-processing methods (e.g., incorporating fairness constraints into the learning objective), and post-processing strategies (e.g., adjusting predictions after the model is trained). For example, in a university admissions model, a fairness-aware classifier might adjust decision thresholds to ensure equal opportunity across gender or socioeconomic groups. These methods help reduce the impact of historical bias while maintaining predictive performance.

To support transparency, teams can use tools such as **model cards** and **datasheets for datasets**. A **model card** summarizes the key details about a trained model, including its intended use, performance across subgroups, ethical considerations, and known limitations. A **datasheet** documents the data's source, structure, quality, and contexts where it may or may not be appropriate. Together, these artifacts serve as living documentation that can be reviewed by technical teams, business stakeholders, and regulators alike.

Transparency checklists are also gaining popularity. These are structured forms used during development to prompt teams to reflect on the social impact of their design decisions. For instance, the Deon checklist, developed by DrivenData, includes questions such as "Did you consider the potential for this model to be used in harmful ways?" or "How will you handle incorrect predictions?" These tools encourage developers to think beyond code and consider real-world consequences.

At the organizational level, **AI governance practices** provide a framework for accountability. This includes defining roles and responsibilities, setting review checkpoints, and maintaining audit trails of decisions made throughout the development process. Establishing ethical review boards or cross-functional working groups can ensure that diverse perspectives are included when evaluating sensitive use cases.

Regulatory Implications and Compliance

As machine learning models influence increasingly sensitive decisions—from credit approvals to healthcare diagnoses—regulatory scrutiny has grown sharper. Governments and industry bodies worldwide are rolling out new policies to ensure that AI systems are transparent, fair, and accountable. Organizations must now consider technical performance and legal and ethical obligations. This section examines key regulatory frameworks and how enterprises embed compliance and responsible AI practices within their MLOps pipelines.

One of the most influential regulations in the European Union is the General Data Protection Regulation (GDPR). GDPR includes the "right to explanation," which means that individuals affected by automated decisions can ask for clear reasons behind those decisions. This affects how companies build and deploy models, particularly in high-impact areas like finance or insurance. For instance, if a model declines a loan, the organization must be able to explain why, even if the model is complex and its reasoning is not readily apparent.

Another upcoming regulation is the **EU AI Act**, which categorizes AI systems into four risk levels—minimal, limited, high, and unacceptable—and applies stricter rules to higher-risk categories. Systems used in hiring, credit scoring, or medical diagnosis often fall into the "high-risk" category and must meet rigorous requirements for transparency, accountability, and human oversight. Companies deploying such models must maintain detailed documentation, perform risk assessments, and implement clear processes for monitoring model performance and fairness.

CHAPTER 7   ADVANCED TOPICS IN MACHINE LEARNING

In the United States, regulatory efforts are evolving on a sector-by-sector basis. For example, the **Equal Credit Opportunity Act (ECOA)** and **Fair Lending laws** require financial institutions to ensure that their decision-making models do not discriminate based on race, gender, or other protected attributes. In healthcare, models must comply with **HIPAA** and FDA regulations, particularly in diagnostic tools or clinical decision support systems.

Enterprises increasingly integrate responsible AI frameworks into their MLOps pipelines to stay compliant. This includes automating bias checks, versioning models with audit trails, logging explanations through tools like SHAP and MLflow, and tagging sensitive datasets using services like Unity Catalog. Many organizations also embed human review checkpoints, maintain documentation with model cards, and align with internal ethics boards before deploying models into production.

For example, a global bank might include a fairness audit step before registering every model in the MLflow Model Registry. This step ensures that models meet ECOA and GDPR requirements and that any rejected applicants have access to a documented explanation of the decision. Similarly, a health-tech firm may tag high-risk models in the Unity Catalog and route them through additional clinical validation workflows before release.

Regulations are evolving quickly, and staying ahead requires reactive compliance and proactive governance. By embedding compliance into their AI development life cycle, organizations can ensure legal alignment and ethical responsibility, protect users, enhance trust, and reduce regulatory risk.

In the next section, we'll explore how these principles shape future trends in machine learning, from interpretable model architectures to AI legislation-aware design patterns.

For example, in a healthcare startup building a diagnostic tool, governance practices might require model documentation (via model cards), tracking approvals through MLflow and Unity Catalog, and engaging a compliance lead to review the fairness metrics. By integrating these structures, the organization ensures that fairness is not left to chance—it becomes part of standard operating procedure.

Ultimately, ensuring fairness and accountability isn't about checking boxes—it's about building models that earn trust and withstand scrutiny. In the next section, we'll examine how emerging machine learning trends impact the future of ethical and interpretable AI.

CHAPTER 7 ADVANCED TOPICS IN MACHINE LEARNING

Future Trends in Machine Learning

As machine learning matures, innovations reshape how models are built, deployed, and governed. The future of machine learning (ML) is being driven by shifts in both technology and infrastructure, from increasingly powerful foundation models to smarter, multi-agent systems capable of reasoning and collaboration. At the same time, data platforms like the Lakehouse Architecture are evolving to support these new demands, blending scalable compute with flexible, governed storage. Understanding these trends is crucial for ML practitioners seeking to stay ahead and develop systems that are performant, adaptable, ethical, and aligned with emerging regulations.

In this section, we'll explore key developments influencing the future of machine learning and examine how they integrate with the modern data and AI stack.

Emerging Technologies and Architectures

Machine learning is experiencing a wave of innovation beyond traditional predictive modeling. Among the most significant advances are **foundation models**, **multimodal learning**, and **compound AI systems, each expanding AI's capabilities and use cases**.

Foundation models, such as OpenAI's GPT, Google's PaLM, or Meta's LLaMA, are large-scale models trained on vast amounts of data. These models can be fine-tuned for specific tasks or utilized as general-purpose engines for natural language processing, code generation, summarization, and other applications. In Databricks, these models can be integrated through the Model Serving APIs or hosted within the Unity Catalog as part of an organization's governed AI workflows.

Multimodal learning refers to models that can understand and generate outputs across various data types, including text, images, audio, and structured tables. For example, a multimodal model could combine X-ray images, physician notes, and lab results in a healthcare scenario to deliver a more holistic diagnosis. This trend pushes ML architectures to be more flexible and deeply integrated across data types, requiring platforms like Databricks to support seamless access to diverse modalities within the lakehouse.

Compound AI systems take it a step further by combining multiple models or agents to collaborate on solving complex tasks. This could involve a planning agent, a reasoning module, and a generative model working together in sequence. These systems often leverage orchestration tools like LangChain or Semantic Kernel, raising new challenges in monitoring, coordination, and responsibility. With its unified governance and cross-functional data access, the lakehouse model provides a strong foundation for building and scaling these compound systems.

As these architectures evolve, so too must the underlying data platform. **Data lakehouses** are becoming AI-native by directly embedding machine learning (ML) tools, governance controls, and compute layers into the platform. Databricks is leading this evolution by integrating MLflow, Unity Catalog, AutoML, and real-time inference into the Lakehouse ecosystem. This makes it easier to support the training, tuning, serving, and auditing of sophisticated ML models—all in one place.

Together, these emerging technologies are transforming what is possible with machine learning. Organizations can build smarter, more accountable AI systems ready for tomorrow's challenges by combining powerful model architectures with flexible, governed infrastructure.

The next section will examine how to future-proof your ML practice by aligning architectural decisions with scalability, interpretability, and regulatory readiness.

Future Trends in Machine Learning

As machine learning matures, innovations reshape how models are built, deployed, and governed. The future of machine learning (ML) is being driven by shifts in both technology and infrastructure, from increasingly powerful foundation models to smarter, multi-agent systems capable of reasoning and collaboration. At the same time, data platforms like the Lakehouse Architecture are evolving to support these new demands, blending scalable computing with flexible, governed storage. Understanding these trends is crucial for ML practitioners seeking to stay ahead and develop systems that are performant, adaptable, ethical, and aligned with emerging regulations.

In this section, we'll explore key developments influencing the future of machine learning and examine how they integrate with the modern data and AI stack.

Emerging Technologies and Architectures

Machine learning is experiencing a wave of innovation beyond traditional predictive modeling. Among the most significant advances are **foundation models**, **multimodal learning**, and **compound AI systems,** each of which is expanding AI's capabilities and use cases.

CHAPTER 7   ADVANCED TOPICS IN MACHINE LEARNING

Foundation models, such as OpenAI's GPT, Google's PaLM, or Meta's LLaMA, are large-scale models trained on vast amounts of data. These models can be fine-tuned for specific tasks or utilized as general-purpose engines for natural language processing, code generation, summarization, and other applications. In Databricks, these models can be integrated through the Model Serving APIs or hosted within the Unity Catalog as part of an organization's governed AI workflows.

Multimodal learning refers to models that can understand and generate outputs across various data types, including text, images, audio, and structured tables. For example, a multimodal model could combine X-ray images, physician notes, and lab results in a healthcare scenario to deliver a more holistic diagnosis. This trend pushes ML architectures to be more flexible and deeply integrated across data types, requiring platforms like Databricks to support seamless access to diverse modalities within the lakehouse.

Compound AI systems take it a step further by combining multiple models or agents to collaborate on solving complex tasks. This could involve a planning agent, a reasoning module, and a generative model working together in sequence. These systems often leverage orchestration tools like LangChain or Semantic Kernel, raising new challenges in monitoring, coordination, and responsibility. With its unified governance and cross-functional data access, the lakehouse model provides a strong foundation for building and scaling these compound systems.

As these architectures evolve, so too must the underlying data platform. **Data lakehouses** are becoming AI-native by directly embedding machine learning (ML) tools, governance controls, and compute layers into the platform. Databricks is leading this evolution by integrating MLflow, Unity Catalog, AutoML, and real-time inference into the Lakehouse ecosystem. This makes it easier to support the training, tuning, serving, and auditing of sophisticated ML models—all in one place.

Together, these emerging technologies are transforming what is possible with machine learning. Organizations can build smarter, more accountable AI systems ready for tomorrow's challenges by combining powerful model architectures with flexible, governed infrastructure.

The next section will examine how to future-proof your ML practice by adapting systems that learn continuously from streaming data.

CHAPTER 7   ADVANCED TOPICS IN MACHINE LEARNING

Real-Time and Continual Learning

Traditional machine learning systems are often trained once on a static dataset and then deployed into production with occasional retraining cycles. While this approach works for many use cases, it struggles in environments where data changes rapidly or new patterns emerge over time. In domains such as fraud detection, stock trading, or personalized recommendations, relying on outdated models can lead to inaccurate predictions and missed opportunities. To address this, the industry is shifting toward **real-time and continual learning systems** that adapt as new data flows in.

Real-time learning refers to models that can update or retrain based on fresh data from streaming sources. Instead of waiting for batch updates, these systems can incorporate recent user behavior, transaction logs, or sensor data to refine predictions in near real time. For example, an ecommerce platform might use streaming data to adjust product recommendations instantly after a user interacts with the site. Tools like Apache Spark Structured Streaming, Delta Live Tables, and model serving APIs in Databricks support the ingestion, processing, and real-time inference needed to enable such adaptive pipelines.

Continual learning, also known as lifelong learning, extends this idea by enabling models to learn incrementally over time without forgetting previously acquired knowledge. This is especially important when deploying models in dynamic environments, such as a predictive maintenance system in manufacturing, where new equipment types are introduced. Continual learning helps avoid catastrophic forgetting by preserving learned patterns while integrating new ones, often using techniques such as elastic weight consolidation, rehearsal methods, or architectural expansion.

Integrating real-time and continual learning into the **Databricks Lakehouse** is becoming more accessible. Streaming data can be captured using Auto Loader or Kafka integration, processed with Delta Live Tables, and fed into retraining workflows via MLflow Tracking and Pipelines. These models can be versioned and served through MLflow Model Registry, while Unity Catalog ensures metadata lineage and access control. As new data arrives, models can be retrained periodically or incrementally and deployed automatically, reducing latency between insight and action.

By adopting adaptive learning systems, organizations can maintain the relevance of their models, reduce manual retraining cycles, and enhance their responsiveness to change. These patterns represent the next frontier in production ML, where models predict and evolve.

The next section will examine how large language models and generative AI techniques are integrated into the traditional machine learning workflow.

CHAPTER 7   ADVANCED TOPICS IN MACHINE LEARNING

ML in the Age of Generative AI

The rapid rise of **generative AI**, especially large language models (LLMs), is transforming the traditional boundaries of machine learning. While classical machine learning (ML) workflows have focused on structured predictions, such as classification, regression, or clustering, generative models open up new possibilities for synthesis, reasoning, and context-aware decision-making. The convergence of LLMs with traditional ML pipelines enables the creation of hybrid systems that are more adaptable, conversational, and intelligent.

Large language models, such as GPT, Claude, and LLaMA, can now be integrated into enterprise workflows through APIs or embedded natively in platforms like Databricks. These models can generate humanlike text, summarize documents, translate language, answer questions, and even write code. They enhance model interpretability, user interaction, and domain-specific knowledge retrieval when paired with traditional machine learning (ML) components.

For example, a classical ML model might predict weekly sales based on historical trends and promotions in a retail demand forecasting pipeline. When paired with an LLM, the system could also analyze vendor emails, product descriptions, or market reports to refine or explain the forecast in natural language. This creates a more holistic solution that combines statistical rigor with contextual awareness.

One powerful application is **Retrieval-Augmented Generation (RAG)**, where large language models (LLMs) dynamically query structured databases, data lakes, or vector stores to generate informed and up-to-date responses. This bridges the gap between static model knowledge and real-time enterprise data. In Databricks, this can be implemented by combining LLM APIs with Unity Catalog, Delta Tables, and Feature Store lookups, creating multilayered workflows that are both generative and grounded in reality.

Generative models also support **the automated generation of ML documentation and explanations**, making it easier for teams to write model cards, interpret outputs, and communicate decisions to stakeholders. By turning technical outputs into human-readable summaries, LLMs improve transparency and trust.

However, the adoption of LLMs also brings new challenges. These include controlling hallucinations, ensuring prompt consistency, managing token costs, and securing sensitive data. Integrating these models responsibly requires careful governance, strong data pipelines, and human oversight. Unity Catalog, for example, helps trace which data sources LLMs interacted with, while MLflow can log prompt versions and performance metrics.

CHAPTER 7   ADVANCED TOPICS IN MACHINE LEARNING

The future of ML is not about replacing classical models with LLMs but **augmenting** them to create systems that are explainable, conversational, and context-aware. As organizations embrace generative techniques, they'll unlock new capabilities across customer service, research, analytics, and decision automation—blending prediction with creativity at scale.

In the final section, we'll summarize the key takeaways from this chapter and consider how organizations can strategically prepare for these transformative shifts in machine learning.

Hands-On Lab: Explainability and Governance for Loan Default Risk Prediction

In this lab, you'll build a production-ready explainability workflow using SHAP, MLflow, and Unity Catalog on Databricks. The lab simulates a real-world scenario from financial services where explainable and governed AI is not optional—it's mandatory.

Problem Statement

A mid-sized financial institution plans to deploy a machine learning model to predict **loan default risk** for new applicants. To comply with internal governance and external regulations, the model must

- Provide clear explanations for every prediction.
- Enable traceability and documentation across model versions.
- Deliver interpretable outputs that business users can understand.
- Support comparison of model behavior across retraining cycles.

This lab guides you in building a workflow that meets all these needs using explainability and MLOps tooling on Databricks.

Objective

Your goal is to build an end-to-end explainability pipeline that integrates seamlessly with Databricks' governance and MLOps tools. You will

- Train a loan default risk model using **XGBoost** or **scikit-learn**.
- Generate **SHAP-based local and global explanations** for the model's predictions.

- Log SHAP plots and artifacts with **MLflow**.

- Register and document models using **MLflow Model Registry**.

- Enrich metadata and enforce governance using **Unity Catalog**.

- Compare interpretability across **multiple model versions** to support audits and continuous improvement.

Lab Workflow

This lab is structured to simulate a production-ready machine learning scenario. You will follow these steps:

1. **Create a structured dataset** simulating loan applications and default outcomes.

2. **Train a model** using XGBoost or scikit-learn.

3. **Generate SHAP explanations** for individual and global predictions.

4. **Log SHAP plots and artifacts** using MLflow for traceability.

5. **Register the model** in the MLflow Model Registry.

6. **Add governance metadata** using Unity Catalog (e.g., purpose, data lineage, risk level).

7. **Retrain a second model version** with modified parameters or data.

8. **Compare SHAP explanations across versions** to detect shifts in feature importance.

You'll not only build explainable models but also implement the infrastructure needed for **auditability, accountability, and compliance** in high-stakes environments.

Create a Realistic Loan Default Dataset

In this step, we will generate a synthetic dataset that simulates real-world loan applications. The dataset will include both numerical and categorical features relevant to credit risk modeling, such as

- Credit score (scaled between 300 and 850)
- Annual income

CHAPTER 7   ADVANCED TOPICS IN MACHINE LEARNING

- Loan amount and loan term
- Number of open credit accounts
- Debt-to-income ratio
- Employment status and loan purpose

We will also introduce a **target variable** called default, which represents whether a loan is likely to default (1) or not (0).

Unlike purely random data, we'll inject **domain-inspired logic** to simulate realistic business conditions:

- Low credit scores and high debt ratios increase risk.
- "Personal" loans tend to have higher default rates.
- Employment status and income levels are correlated.

The default label is not assigned randomly. Instead, we calculate a synthetic risk score based on attributes such as credit score, debt ratio, and loan purpose. An applicant is labeled as defaulting (1) if their risk score exceeds a defined threshold. This does **not** result in all records having a default value of 1.

This structure ensures that SHAP and model interpretability techniques generate **meaningful, nonrandom explanations**, making the lab exercise more authentic and aligned with real-world use cases in the financial domain.

```
# Import necessary Python libraries
import pandas as pd  # For working with tabular data (rows and columns)
import numpy as np   # For working with numbers and arrays
from sklearn.datasets import make_classification  # To generate synthetic
classification data

# Set a random seed so results are reproducible every time you run the code
np.random.seed(42)

# Generate a base dataset with numeric features for binary classification
# - 1000 rows (applicants)
# - 6 numeric features
```

```python
# - 4 of them are useful for prediction, 2 are noise
# - Class separation is increased to make patterns more distinct
X, y = make_classification(
    n_samples=1000,
    n_features=6,
    n_informative=4,
    n_redundant=0,
    class_sep=1.5,
    random_state=42
)

# Convert the generated features into a structured table (DataFrame)
# Name the columns to match features found in loan applications
df = pd.DataFrame(X, columns=[
    'credit_score', 'income', 'loan_amount', 'loan_term',
    'num_open_accounts', 'debt_to_income_ratio'
])

# Apply scaling to convert raw numbers into realistic business ranges
# Example: Scale credit score between 300 and 850
df['credit_score'] = (df['credit_score'] * 50 + 650).clip(300, 850).astype(int)

# Make income realistic (e.g., $30,000 to $150,000)
df['income'] = (np.abs(df['income']) * 25000 + 30000).astype(int)

# Scale loan amounts to fall between $5,000 and ~$50,000
df['loan_amount'] = (np.abs(df['loan_amount']) * 10000 + 5000).astype(int)

# Set loan term between 12 and ~36 months
df['loan_term'] = (np.abs(df['loan_term']) * 5 + 12).astype(int)

# Set the number of open accounts to a small integer range
df['num_open_accounts'] = (np.abs(df['num_open_accounts']) * 2 + 3).astype(int)
```

CHAPTER 7   ADVANCED TOPICS IN MACHINE LEARNING

```python
# Scale debt-to-income ratio to realistic percentages (e.g., 10% to 40%)
df['debt_to_income_ratio'] = (np.abs(df['debt_to_income_ratio']) *
15 + 10).round(2)

# Prepare to generate categorical variables and a custom 'default' label
employment_status = []  # To store employment status for each row
loan_purpose = []       # To store loan purpose for each row
adjusted_y = []         # To store whether the loan defaults (1) or not (0)

# Loop through each row in the dataset
for i in range(len(df)):
    score = df.loc[i, 'credit_score']
    income = df.loc[i, 'income']
    dti = df.loc[i, 'debt_to_income_ratio']

    # Assign employment status based on income level
    if income < 40000:
        employment_status.append('unemployed')
    elif income < 60000:
        employment_status.append('self-employed')
    else:
        employment_status.append('employed')

    # Assign a loan purpose using random selection but with specific
    probabilities
    loan_purpose.append(np.random.choice(
        ['home', 'car', 'education', 'personal'],
        p=[0.25, 0.25, 0.20, 0.30]  # More people apply for personal loans
    ))

    # Compute a custom risk score:
    # - Higher debt-to-income ratio and lower credit score = more risk
    # - Add extra risk if loan purpose is 'personal'
```

```
        risk_score = (850 - score) + dti + (loan_purpose[i] ==
        'personal') * 20

        # If risk is high, mark as default = 1; otherwise, default = 0
        default = 1 if risk_score > 130 else 0
        adjusted_y.append(default)

# Add new columns to the DataFrame
df['employment_status'] = employment_status
df['loan_purpose'] = loan_purpose
df['default'] = adjusted_y    # This is our target column for ML

# Show the first few rows of the final dataset
df.head()
```

Train a Binary Classification Model

With our dataset ready, we will now train a **machine learning model** to predict whether a loan will default. This is a binary classification problem, where the target column default takes values 0 (no default) or 1 (default).

We will use **XGBoost**, a widely adopted gradient boosting library known for its performance and interpretability. The model will be trained on the structured features we created earlier.

Later in the lab, this model will serve as the foundation for generating SHAP explanations and governance artifacts.

```
# Import necessary modules for training and evaluating the model
from sklearn.model_selection import train_test_split      # Used to split
data into training and test sets
from sklearn.preprocessing import LabelEncoder            # Used to
convert categorical values into numbers
from xgboost import XGBClassifier                         # XGBoost
algorithm for classification
from sklearn.metrics import accuracy_score                # Used to
calculate how accurate the model is
```

CHAPTER 7   ADVANCED TOPICS IN MACHINE LEARNING

```python
# Make a copy of the dataset so we don't change the original
data = df.copy()

# Convert categorical values to numeric values using label encoding
# ML models like XGBoost need numbers, not strings
le_emp = LabelEncoder()
# Encoder for 'employment_status'
le_purpose = LabelEncoder()
# Encoder for 'loan_purpose'
data['employment_status'] = le_emp.fit_transform(data['employment_status'])   # e.g., 'employed' → 0, 'self-employed' → 1
data['loan_purpose'] = le_purpose.fit_transform(data['loan_purpose'])         # e.g., 'car' → 0, 'home' → 1, etc.

# Separate the input features (X) from the target column (y)
X = data.drop(columns='default')   # Features used to predict (all columns except 'default')
y = data['default']                # Target column (what we want to predict)

# Split the data into training and testing sets
# 75% used for training, 25% for testing
# 'stratify=y' ensures the same proportion of defaults (1s) in both sets
X_train, X_test, y_train, y_test = train_test_split(
    X, y, test_size=0.25, random_state=42, stratify=y
)

# Create and train an XGBoost classifier
# 'use_label_encoder=False' prevents a warning message
# 'eval_metric=logloss' sets the evaluation metric for training
model = XGBClassifier(use_label_encoder=False, eval_metric='logloss')
model.fit(X_train, y_train)  # Train the model using training data

# Predict the outcomes for the test set
preds = model.predict(X_test)
```

```
# Calculate and print the model's accuracy
# Accuracy = % of predictions the model got right
acc = accuracy_score(y_test, preds)
print(f"Test Accuracy: {acc:.2%}")   # Example output: Test Accuracy: 86.40%
```

Generate SHAP Explanations

Now that the model is trained, we'll use **SHAP (SHapley Additive exPlanations)** to understand how each feature contributes to predictions.

SHAP assigns an importance value to each feature for a given prediction. We'll use it to produce

- **Local Explanations**: Why did the model make a specific prediction for one applicant?
- **Global Explanations**: Which features influence the model most across all predictions?

This step is crucial for transparency and regulatory alignment, particularly in the financial services sector, where institutions must clearly explain individual credit decisions.

```
import shap

# Initialize TreeExplainer
explainer = shap.Explainer(model, X_train)

# Compute SHAP values for the test set
shap_values = explainer(X_test)

# Display one local explanation
shap.plots.waterfall(shap_values[0])
```

The output of the SHAP plot is displayed in Figure 7-1.

CHAPTER 7   ADVANCED TOPICS IN MACHINE LEARNING

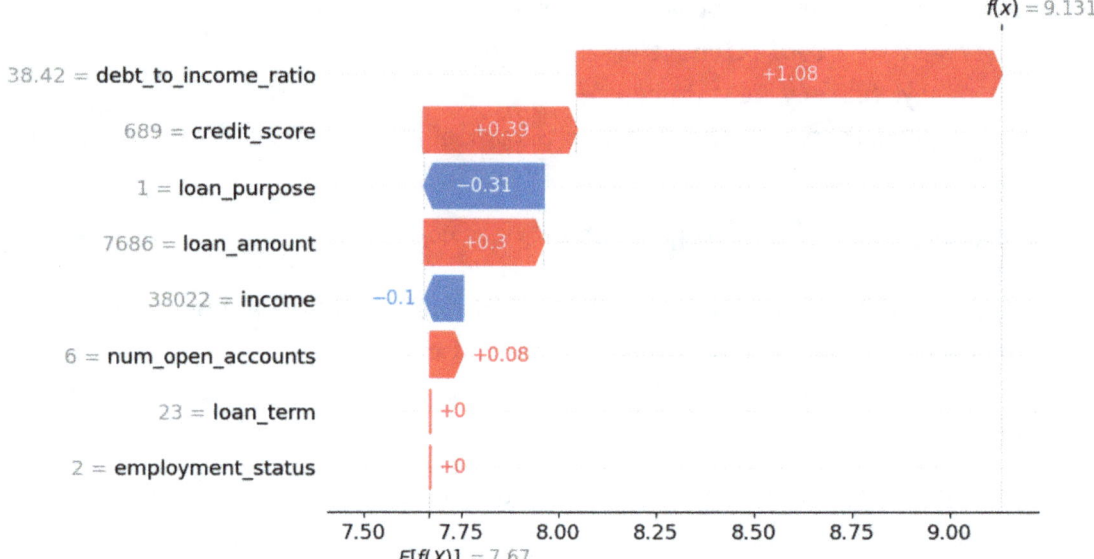

Figure 7-1. SHAP plot

Understanding the SHAP Waterfall Plot

A **SHAP waterfall plot** visualizes how individual features contributed to a single model prediction. It breaks down the difference between the model's **baseline prediction** (the average output across all samples) and the final prediction for a specific data point (e.g., a particular loan applicant).

What the Waterfall Plot Represents

- **E[f(X)] (Base Value):** This is the model's average prediction across the training set. It's the starting point on the horizontal axis.
- **f(x):** The model's output for a specific individual, after accounting for the impact of that individual's features.
- **SHAP Values:** These represent how much each feature increased or decreased the prediction, relative to the base value:
    - **Red bars** push the prediction **higher** (toward default in a risk model).
    - **Blue bars** push the prediction **lower** (toward non-default).
    - The **length** of each bar reflects the magnitude of its impact.

Interpreting This Specific Plot

- **Prediction Value:** The model output (f(x)) is approximately **9.13**, which is **higher than the average** (base ≈ 7.67). This indicates that the model predicts a **high default risk** for this applicant.

- **Debt-to-income ratio (DTI)** had the **strongest impact**, adding **+1.08** to the prediction. A high DTI is a major risk factor.

- **The credit score was added by +0.39, suggesting that a below-average score also contributed to the** risk.

- **The loan amount** added **+0.30** to risk, likely due to a higher-than-average requested amount.

- **Loan purpose** decreased the risk slightly (**-0.31**), possibly because the loan was not for a high-risk purpose.

- **Income** and **number of open accounts** had minimal influence, while **loan term** and **employment status** contributed nothing measurable in this case.

This plot helps explain the **"why"** behind the model's decision for one applicant. It provides stakeholders, such as business users, risk officers, or regulators, with a clear and **traceable narrative** behind each prediction.

What the Waterfall Plot Does Behind the Scenes

Let's say your model predicts this:

- The **average prediction** the model makes for all applicants is **7.67**.
- For **this specific applicant**, the model predicts **9.13**.

So, the key question becomes:

What prompted the prediction to increase from 7.67 to 9.13?

That difference of **+1.46** is explained **feature by feature**, like a story. Each SHAP value represents a feature's influence on shifting the prediction higher or lower.

CHAPTER 7   ADVANCED TOPICS IN MACHINE LEARNING

Visual Breakdown of SHAP Contributions

Feature	Value	SHAP Contribution	Direction and Impact
debt_to_income_ratio	38.42	**+1.08**	Increased risk significantly (big red bar)
credit_score	689	**+0.39**	Lower score = more risk
loan_purpose	"personal"	**-0.31**	Safer purpose = reduced risk
loan_amount income	7686	**+0.30**	Larger loan amount added slight risk

Visualize Global Feature Importance

In addition to local explanations, SHAP can help us understand the overall behavior of the model by summarizing which features most influence predictions across the dataset.

The **Beeswarm plot** visualizes the distribution of SHAP values for each feature:

- Each point is a prediction.
- The color shows the feature value (e.g., low to high credit score).
- The position on the x axis shows the impact on the model's output.

This view helps identify **which features matter most** and how they typically affect the outcome.

```
# Generate a beeswarm plot to visualize global feature impact
shap.plots.beeswarm(shap_values)
```

The Beeswarm plot is displayed in Figure 7-2.

CHAPTER 7   ADVANCED TOPICS IN MACHINE LEARNING

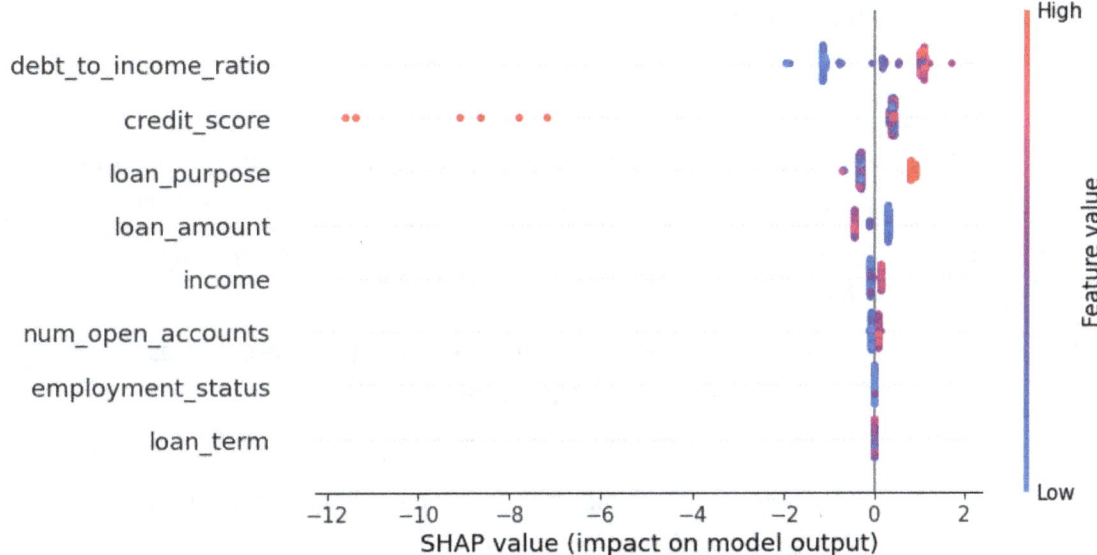

Figure 7-2. Beeswarm plot

Understanding the SHAP Beeswarm Plot

The SHAP Beeswarm plot shows how individual features impact the model's predictions across the entire dataset. Each dot represents one applicant. This plot helps us understand **which features are most influential** and whether they **increase or decrease the predicted risk**.

How to Read the Plot

- **Y Axis (Features):** Lists the top features ranked by importance

- **X Axis (SHAP Value):** Measures how much each feature pushed a prediction:

    - Values > **0** pushed the model to predict higher risk (more likely to default).

    - Values < **0** pushed the model to predict lower risk (less likely to default).

- **Color of Dots**

    - **Red = High value** for that feature (e.g., high DTI, high credit score)

    - **Blue = Low value** for that feature (e.g., low income, low credit score)

Insights from This Plot

Feature	Insight
debt_to_income_ratio	Surprisingly, higher DTI (red dots) resulted in lower predictions in many cases. This may indicate an unexpected data pattern or inverse correlation.
credit_score	A high credit score (red) shifted predictions downward, aligning with business expectations.
loan_purpose	Some loan purposes increased predictions, while others decreased them. Possibly, "personal" loans are riskier.
loan_amount	Larger loans tended to increase risk slightly.
income	Higher income had **a minimal effect on predictions, possibly due to being overshadowed by the DTI**.
loan_term, employment_status	Had **very little influence**, suggesting they don't meaningfully affect the model's predictions in this dataset.

This plot reveals how the model uses input features to make decisions. It helps analysts, auditors, and business teams understand the **"why" behind the predictions**. If a new model version changes the pattern, this plot can help detect **shifts in logic or feature influence**.

Log SHAP Artifacts with MLflow

To enable auditability and version control, we'll log our SHAP outputs using **MLflow**. This includes

- The trained model
- SHAP visualizations (as image files)
- The SHAP value matrix (as a NumPy array)

Logging these artifacts allows teams to revisit past explanations, compare interpretability across model versions, and satisfy compliance documentation requirements.

Let's start by creating a local file for the SHAP Beeswarm plot and log it as an MLflow artifact.

```
import mlflow
import matplotlib.pyplot as plt
import os
import numpy as np

# Start an MLflow experiment
mlflow.set_experiment("/loan-risk-shap-lab")

with mlflow.start_run() as run:
    # Log the trained model
    mlflow.sklearn.log_model(model, "xgboost_model")

    # Save and log SHAP beeswarm plot
    plt.figure()
    shap.plots.beeswarm(shap_values, show=False)
    plt.title("SHAP Beeswarm Plot")
    plt.tight_layout()
    plot_path = "shap_beeswarm.png"
    plt.savefig(plot_path, dpi=300)
    mlflow.log_artifact(plot_path)

    # Save and log SHAP values as NumPy array
    np.save("shap_values.npy", shap_values.values)
    mlflow.log_artifact("shap_values.npy")
```

Figure 7-3 displays the SHAP and Beeswarm plot, which will be logged in MLflow.

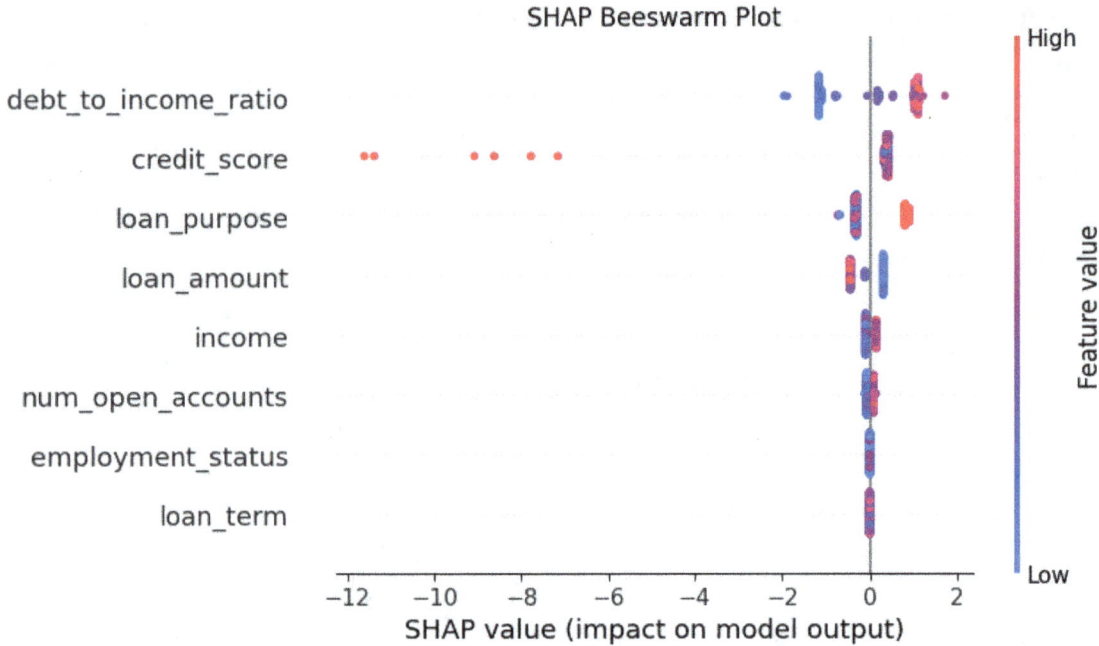

Figure 7-3. SHAP and Beeswarm plot

Register the Model and Enrich with Unity Catalog Metadata

After training and logging the model, we will now **register it in MLflow Model Registry**. This allows us to version our models, promote them to different stages (e.g., Staging, Production), and track lineage.

We'll also **enrich the model with governance metadata** using **Unity Catalog**, such as

- The model's intended use
- Data lineage (which table or dataset it was trained on)
- Compliance tags or risk levels

These metadata annotations enhance model transparency, facilitate regulatory audits, and enable teams to make informed decisions about deployment.

```
from mlflow.tracking import MlflowClient

client = MlflowClient()
run_id = run.info.run_id

# Register the model
model_name = "loan_default_risk_model"
model_uri = f"runs:/{run_id}/xgboost_model"

registered_model = mlflow.register_model(model_uri=model_uri,
name=model_name)

# (Optional) Add tags or metadata using Unity Catalog APIs or MLflow.
set_tags
mlflow.set_tag("model_type", "XGBoost")
mlflow.set_tag("domain", "Financial Services")
mlflow.set_tag("risk_level", "High")
mlflow.set_tag("intended_use", "Loan default risk assessment")
```

After we register the model in MLflow, it will be listed as shown in Figure 7-4.

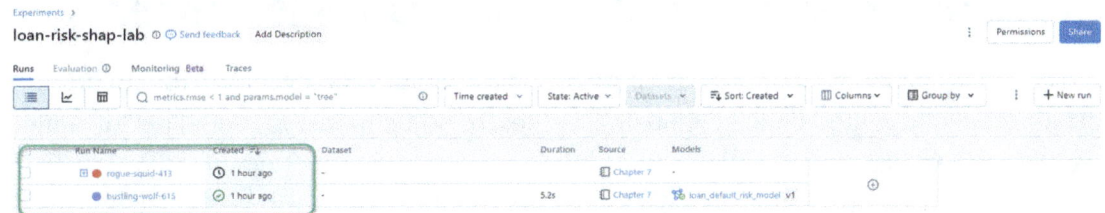

Figure 7-4. *A view of registered ML models*

When you click the model, it will display the tags applied during registration, as shown in Figure 7-5.

CHAPTER 7   ADVANCED TOPICS IN MACHINE LEARNING

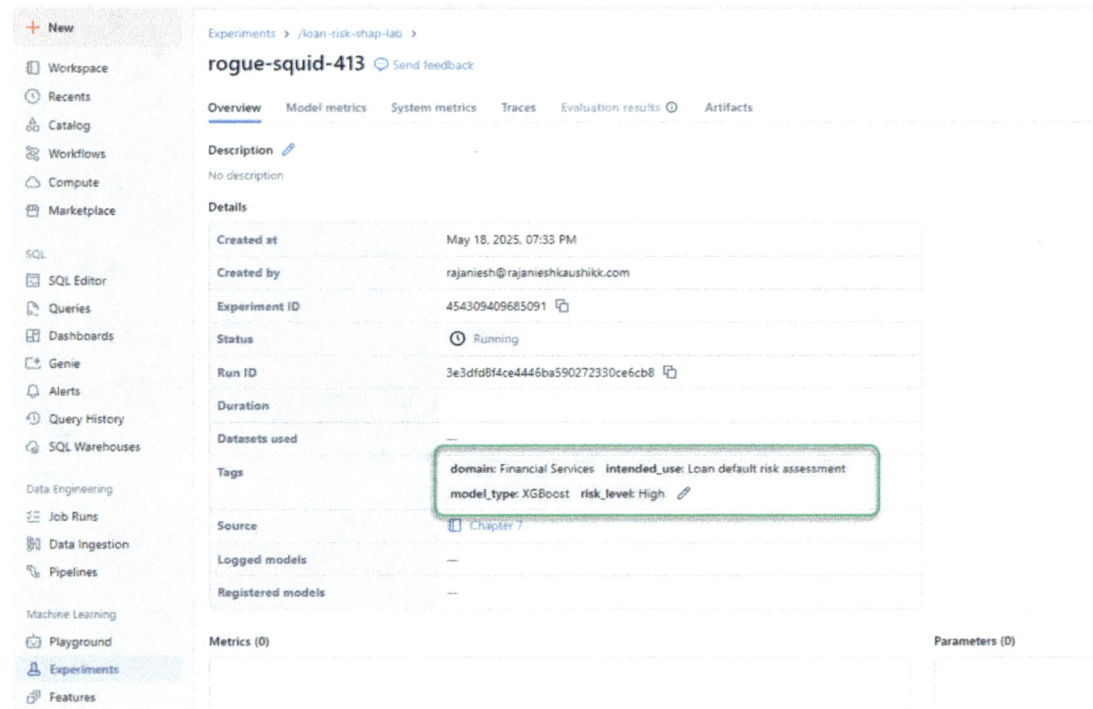

Figure 7-5. Model detail view

Train a New Model Version and Compare Interpretability

In real-world scenarios, machine learning models are retrained over time due to the introduction of updated data, new business rules, or adjustments to model performance. In this step, we will

- Train a **second version** of the model with slightly different parameters.
- Generate SHAP values again.
- Log artifacts under a **new MLflow run**.
- Compare feature attributions across versions to detect changes in model behavior.

This comparison is crucial for model governance, particularly in regulated environments where models evolve. It allows teams to verify whether the explanations remain consistent or if new features begin driving decisions.

```python
# Slightly tweak the model (e.g., change max_depth or learning_rate)
model_v2 = XGBClassifier(
    use_label_encoder=False,
    eval_metric='logloss',
    max_depth=6,
    learning_rate=0.1
)

model_v2.fit(X_train, y_train)
preds_v2 = model_v2.predict(X_test)

print(f"Model v2 Accuracy: {accuracy_score(y_test, preds_v2):.2%}")

# Start a new run for version 2
with mlflow.start_run(nested=True) as run2:
    # Log updated model
    mlflow.sklearn.log_model(model_v2, "xgboost_model_v2")

    # Recalculate SHAP
    explainer_v2 = shap.Explainer(model_v2, X_train)
    shap_values_v2 = explainer_v2(X_test)

    # Save and log global explanation
    plt.figure()
    shap.plots.beeswarm(shap_values_v2, show=False)
    plt.title("Model v2 - SHAP Beeswarm")
    plt.tight_layout()
    plot_path_v2 = "shap_beeswarm_v2.png"
    plt.savefig(plot_path_v2)
    mlflow.log_artifact(plot_path_v2)

    # Save SHAP values as an array
    np.save("shap_values_v2.npy", shap_values_v2.values)
    mlflow.log_artifact("shap_values_v2.npy")
```

CHAPTER 7   ADVANCED TOPICS IN MACHINE LEARNING

This will display the SHAP Beeswarm chart for the newly trained model, as depicted in Figure 7-6.

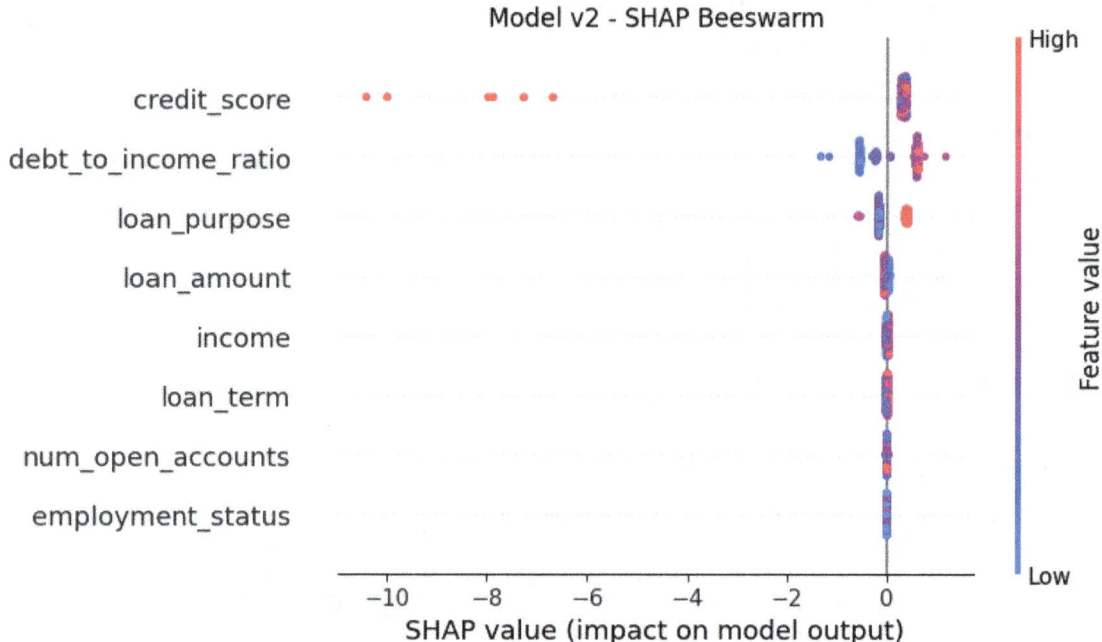

Figure 7-6. *SHAP Beeswarm chart*

Compare SHAP Explanations Across Model Versions

Now that we have logged two different versions of the model, we will compare their **SHAP-based global explanations**.

By plotting Beeswarm summaries side by side, we can inspect whether:

- The **same features remain important** across versions.

- The **influence of any feature** has shifted dramatically.

- Any **unexpected changes** indicate potential model drift or retraining risk.

This interpretability audit step is crucial in regulated industries, where changes to decision logic must be tracked, reviewed, and clearly **explained**.

```
import matplotlib.pyplot as plt

# Create side-by-side SHAP beeswarm plots
fig, axs = plt.subplots(1, 2, figsize=(16, 6))
```

CHAPTER 7   ADVANCED TOPICS IN MACHINE LEARNING

```
plt.sca(axs[0])
shap.plots.beeswarm(shap_values, show=False)
plt.title("Model v1 - SHAP Beeswarm")

plt.sca(axs[1])
shap.plots.beeswarm(shap_values_v2, show=False)
plt.title("Model v2 - SHAP Beeswarm")

plt.tight_layout()
plt.show()
```

This code will compare two versions of the model side by side, comparing the features depicted in Figure 7-7.

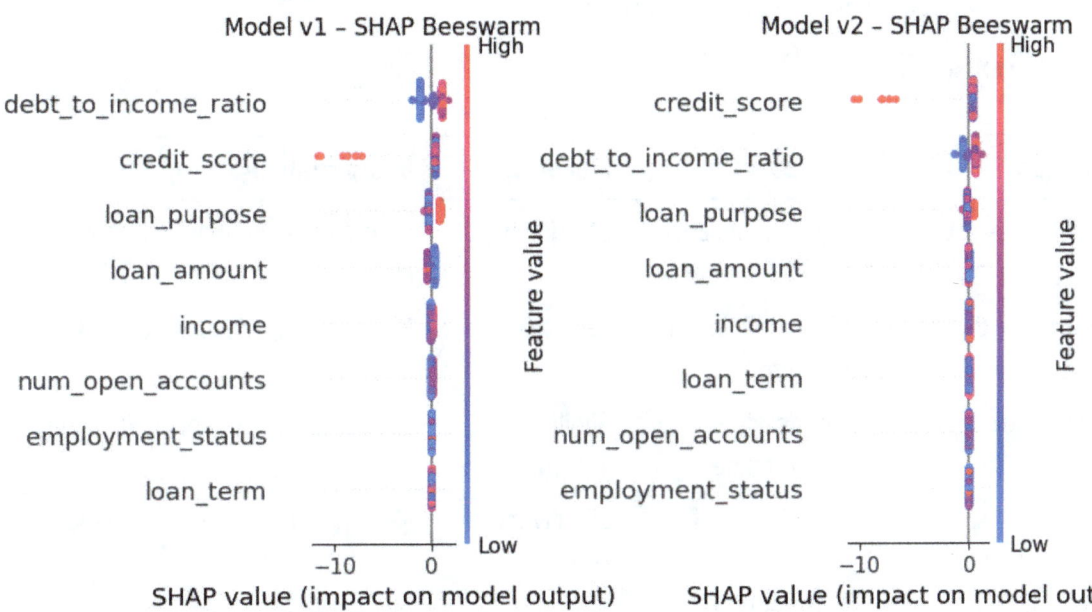

Figure 7-7. *Side-by-side comparison of two models with their SHAP Beeswarm chart*

Comparing SHAP Beeswarm Plots Across Model Versions

This side-by-side visualization compares the SHAP Beeswarm plots for **Model v1** and **Model v2**. Each plot shows how individual features contributed to predictions across the dataset.

- **Y Axis:** Top features used by the model, ranked by importance
- **X Axis:** SHAP values indicating the direction and strength of impact:
    - Values > 0 = Feature increased the risk prediction.
    - Values < 0 = Feature decreased the risk prediction.
- **Color:** Reflects the actual feature value for each applicant
    - High value (e.g., high credit score)
    - Low value (e.g., low income)

Key Observations

Feature	Model v1	Model v2	Interpretation
credit_score	Strong influence	Still dominant	Consistently the most important feature
debt_to_income_ratio	Most influential feature	Less prominent	Model v2 depends **less on DTI**
loan_purpose	Moderate importance	Similar influence	Feature behavior remained stable
loan_term	Negligible effect	Slightly more visible	New model may be learning more from loan term
income, employment_status	Minimal impact	Same	Still not strong predictors

☑ Why This Matters
This comparison helps validate

- Whether the **model logic changed** between versions
- If any **unexpected shifts** occurred (e.g., critical features lost influence)
- Whether changes align with **domain knowledge and compliance expectations**

Such explainability tracking is vital in production environments where ML models are continuously retrained and audited.

Summary

This chapter examines the critical advancements and considerations that will shape the next generation of machine learning systems. From explainability to ethics, architecture to accountability, the field is evolving beyond performance metrics to embrace principles of transparency, fairness, and adaptability.

We began by examining the importance of **explainable AI**, highlighting techniques such as SHAP, LIME, and Partial Dependence Plots (PDPs). These tools help demystify model behavior, offering local and global insights that enhance stakeholder trust.

The chapter then addressed **ethical considerations**, focusing on recognizing bias, ensuring fairness, and aligning with regulatory requirements. We discussed practical methods for bias auditing and introduced documentation practices, such as model cards and datasheets. We also reviewed regulations such as GDPR and the AI Act, showing how organizations embed responsible AI within their MLOps pipelines.

Looking ahead, we explored **emerging trends** including foundation models, multimodal architectures, compound AI systems, and real-time/continual learning. These innovations are transforming how models are trained and interact with enterprise data. The section on **generative AI** highlighted the role of LLMs in augmenting traditional machine learning (ML) workflows, enabling context-aware systems that can explain, summarize, and generate insights on demand.

CHAPTER 7 ADVANCED TOPICS IN MACHINE LEARNING

Together, these topics highlight the transition from static, isolated machine learning (ML) models to dynamic, explainable, and ethically governed AI ecosystems. By leveraging the full capabilities of the Databricks Lakehouse—MLflow, Unity Catalog, AutoML, and real-time infrastructure, practitioners can build future-ready systems that are both powerful and responsible.

In the next chapter, we will explore the evolution of Lakehouse AI and dive into DBRX, Databricks' powerful open source foundation model. We'll examine how this architecture supports Retrieval-Augmented Generation (RAG), scalable model serving, and unified governance, enabling organizations to securely and at scale operationalize generative AI.

CHAPTER 8

Lakehouse AI and Retrieval-Augmented Generation (RAG)

Artificial intelligence (AI) is no longer an experimental edge technology—it has become central to enterprise strategy. Today's organizations are seeking to embed AI into the fabric of their operations, from customer service and fraud detection to compliance and personalization. This demand has shifted expectations: modern platforms must support not only data analytics but also native AI and ML capabilities that operate directly where data resides.

Lakehouse AI answers this need by integrating machine learning and generative AI development within the Databricks Lakehouse architecture. It eliminates traditional silos between data and AI, providing a unified experience that enables governed, scalable, and efficient model development and deployment. This built-in approach significantly reduces the operational complexity of moving data across systems or managing fragmented ML infrastructure.

One particularly transformative design pattern enabled by Lakehouse AI is **Retrieval-Augmented Generation (RAG)**. RAG augments large language model (LLM) outputs with context retrieved from real-time, enterprise-specific data. This method significantly enhances the relevance, factuality, and trustworthiness of generated responses—especially in high-stakes environments such as finance, healthcare, or legal services. Rather than relying solely on a model's pretraining, RAG allows LLMs to reason over your actual business knowledge.

CHAPTER 8   LAKEHOUSE AI AND RETRIEVAL-AUGMENTED GENERATION (RAG)

In this chapter, you will examine how Lakehouse AI and RAG work together to enable intelligent, secure, and context-aware applications. You will also see how Databricks-native capabilities such as Vector Search, Unity Catalog, and MLflow support the full life cycle of enterprise-grade generative AI solutions.

Learning Objectives

By the end of this chapter, you will be able to

- **Understand** the role of Lakehouse AI in modern data architectures and its support for scalable AI/ML workloads.

- **Explore** the RAG pattern, its architecture, and its advantages for enterprise applications.

- **Build** RAG-based workflows using Lakehouse-native tools, such as Vector Search and Unity Catalog.

- **Analyze** real-world use cases where RAG enables AI-driven insights across various industries, including finance, healthcare, and retail.

Let's begin by understanding what Lakehouse AI is and why embedding ML and generative AI tooling directly into the data platform offers a powerful advantage.

Introduction to Lakehouse AI

Lakehouse AI is Databricks' built-in framework for machine learning, deep learning, and large language model (LLM) development—all natively embedded in the Lakehouse Platform. Instead of requiring organizations to use external ML platforms or deploy complex data pipelines, Lakehouse AI empowers users to build and deploy intelligent applications directly where their data resides. This co-location reduces latency, improves security, and accelerates development.

By integrating key components—such as AutoML, model tracking, real-time serving, Vector Search, and LLM support—Lakehouse AI offers a unified experience for data scientists, ML engineers, and business analysts alike. These features are all governed by the Unity Catalog, which provides centralized access control and data lineage tracking for enhanced compliance and auditability.

Imagine a telecom company storing customer support tickets in Delta tables. With Lakehouse AI, users can classify tickets by urgency, deploy the model in real time, and generate executive summaries using a hosted large language model (LLM) like GPT-4 or

LLaMA 3—all from within the same workspace. In a healthcare context, Lakehouse AI can support triage classification, patient risk flagging, and clinical note summarization while maintaining compliance with HIPAA or regional data protection laws.

This native integration streamlines workflows by eliminating the need to transfer data across systems or juggle third-party AI services. As a result, teams can focus more on innovation and less on infrastructure while maintaining a secure and governed environment for model life cycle management.

Key Features and Capabilities

Lakehouse AI is composed of tightly integrated components that span the entire machine learning and AI development life cycle. These tools are optimized for scalability, governance, and collaboration, enabling teams to develop, monitor, and manage AI solutions from experimentation to production in a unified environment.

MLflow Integration

MLflow is a critical component of Lakehouse AI, enabling transparent and reproducible machine learning experimentation. MLflow is fully integrated within the Databricks environment, allowing users to track each model training run, including hyperparameters, performance metrics, input datasets, and resulting artifacts such as models and plots. It is especially valuable in collaborative environments where multiple data scientists iterate on the same problem or need to compare models over time.

For example, a team building a credit risk model can log each experiment variation using MLflow, compare ROC curves for different classifiers, and select the best-performing candidate with full visibility into the decision-making process. The system stores each model version in a centralized model registry, where users can annotate it, promote it to production, or roll it back if needed. In regulated environments, this level of traceability helps satisfy auditing and compliance requirements with ease.

Model Serving

Databricks Lakehouse AI offers built-in model serving, enabling organizations to deploy trained models as REST endpoints for real-time or batch inference. Lakehouse AI eliminates the need for external model hosting infrastructure, allowing models to be deployed directly from the MLflow model registry with a single command or user interface (UI) action. The serving infrastructure automatically scales to meet traffic demands, which is especially beneficial for high-throughput applications.

Consider a retail company that trains a personalized recommendation model during nightly batch processing. Using Lakehouse AI's model serving, they can expose this model to the ecommerce front end, allowing it to return real-time product suggestions when a user logs in. If traffic spikes during a seasonal sale, the serving cluster scales up automatically, ensuring a low latency and uninterrupted user experience.

Feature Store

The Databricks Feature Store provides a centralized, governed repository for storing, managing, and reusing machine learning features across projects and teams. It ensures that the same logic used to engineer features during training is consistently applied during inference, thereby reducing the risk of data leakage and model drift. Each feature, along with its metadata, is stored, including its computation logic, owners, and version history.

For instance, a fraud detection team may calculate the "average transaction amount over the last 24 hours" as a feature during training. By registering this feature in the Feature Store, other teams working on customer analytics or credit scoring can reuse the same feature, ensuring alignment and saving engineering time. The Feature Store supports point-in-time lookups and real-time feature serving, making it a crucial tool for production-grade machine learning systems.

Vector Search

Vector Search in Databricks enables efficient storage and retrieval of dense vector embeddings—a foundational requirement for semantic search and Retrieval-Augmented Generation (RAG) use cases. It allows organizations to index documents, images, or any other unstructured data as vector embeddings and then perform similarity searches using queries encoded in the same vector space.

For example, a legal team could embed thousands of compliance documents into a vector index. When a user asks a question like "What clauses address GDPR data retention?" the query is converted into a vector and matched against the index to retrieve top-ranked passages. These retrieved results can then be passed to a model, such as GPT-4 or LLaMA 3, to generate accurate, grounded responses tailored to the enterprise context.

Unity Catalog Governance

Unity Catalog serves as the governance backbone of Lakehouse AI, providing a unified security and lineage layer across all AI assets, including models, data, notebooks, features, and vector indexes. It enforces role-based access control, allows fine-grained permissions on resources, and maintains full audit trails for compliance and operational transparency.

In a healthcare setting, Unity Catalog can ensure that only authorized personnel can access models trained on protected health data. It is also governed by Unity Catalog, which enforces secure access and traceability, as expanded in the "Implementing Governance on RAG Pipelines" section. It enables complete traceability, which is essential for meeting regulatory requirements in industries such as finance, government, or pharmaceuticals.

Benefits of Lakehouse AI

Lakehouse AI delivers more than a set of tools—it brings strategic alignment, operational efficiency, and scalable intelligence into the core of enterprise data platforms. The following benefits illustrate how organizations gain long-term value by adopting a Lakehouse-native AI architecture.

End-to-End Workflow Integration
One of the standout advantages of Lakehouse AI is the ability to execute the entire ML life cycle—from data ingestion to model deployment—within a single unified platform. This workflow integration eliminates the friction associated with context switching between data engineering, modeling, and deployment tools. For example, a data engineer can transform and clean data in Delta Lake, and an ML practitioner can immediately use that output in a model training notebook—all within the same workspace. The model can then be deployed and served without leaving the environment. This continuity improves team collaboration, accelerates development timelines, and reduces the risk of losing context or introducing inconsistencies during handoffs between tools. In production environments, this kind of workflow efficiency can significantly shorten the time from data to decision.

Reduced Data Movement and Latency
In traditional architectures, ML workflows often require exporting data to external platforms for training or serving, which introduces unnecessary latency, security risks, and operational overhead. Lakehouse AI eliminates these steps by keeping AI workloads co-located with the data stored in Delta Lake. Since training, inference, and monitoring all occur natively within the Databricks environment, there is minimal need to duplicate or transport data. This architecture significantly reduces I/O bottlenecks, making real-time and near-real-time inference more feasible. For instance, in an online fraud detection system, keeping inference close to the transactional data enables immediate

responses to suspicious activity. This tight data-model proximity also enhances consistency between training and production environments, thereby reducing drift and debugging complexity.

Enterprise-Grade Governance and Compliance
With Unity Catalog at its core, Lakehouse AI provides a governance-first architecture that simplifies compliance across every layer of the ML life cycle. Organizations define and enforce granular access controls over datasets, models, features, and even vector indexes, ensuring that only authorized users access sensitive data. The system logs every interaction, and full lineage tracking enables users to trace predictions back to the data and feature pipelines that generated them. Such traceability is particularly important in regulated industries, such as healthcare, banking, and government, where models must pass rigorous audits or justify decisions for legal or ethical reasons. For example, a financial institution could track how a credit scoring model concluded and provide regulators with a complete lineage trail—from raw data to final score—ensuring transparency and compliance.

Operational Efficiency Through Automation
Lakehouse AI reduces manual effort by automating many of the repetitive or error-prone steps in model development and deployment. With tools like AutoML, teams can automatically train and evaluate multiple models without writing extensive code, while MLflow logs every experiment and model version behind the scenes. Once a model is selected, native model serving enables one-click deployment to real-time inference endpoints. These automation layers dramatically reduce the time and skill required to operationalize models. For example, a marketing analyst with limited ML experience can use AutoML to generate a lead-scoring model and then deploy it to production with minimal support from the data science team. Organizations use automation to enhance repeatability and scalability, and they establish standardized pipelines that they replicate across various use cases and departments.

Cross-Functional Collaboration
Lakehouse AI facilitates seamless collaboration among traditionally siloed roles, including data engineers, ML practitioners, and business analysts. The platform offers both code-first and low-code options, so technical users can build sophisticated pipelines in notebooks, while business users can interact through graphical interfaces or SQL endpoints. Shared assets, such as features, models, and dashboards, are governed under the Unity Catalog, ensuring that everyone works with the same trusted resources.

This consistency improves communication across teams and makes AI projects more transparent and maintainable. For example, a product manager can explore predictions through a dashboard, a data scientist can refine the model in Python, and an engineer can deploy it—all within a shared, secure workspace. This democratization of AI fosters innovation and accelerates adoption across the organization.

Foundation for Generative AI

Lakehouse AI supports modern generative AI use cases by providing built-in integration with embedding models, Vector Search, and large language models such as GPT-4 or LLaMA 3. These capabilities enable enterprises to implement Retrieval-Augmented Generation (RAG) pipelines easily, build semantic search tools, and develop internal chatbots powered by their organizational knowledge. Because these tools are governed by the Unity Catalog and executed within the Lakehouse environment, companies can deploy generative AI solutions without compromising data security or operational control. For instance, a legal department could use Vector Search to index thousands of internal contracts and pair it with an LLM to answer compliance questions, dramatically reducing manual review time. This readiness enables organizations to quickly explore and adopt cutting-edge AI capabilities while maintaining the scalability, governance, and traceability required for enterprise success.

Lakehouse AI empowers organizations to scale AI development with agility, transparency, and security—eliminating silos while preserving governance. Its integration of ML tooling, data access, and model serving into a single governed platform makes it a foundational pillar for operationalizing both predictive and generative AI workloads across industries.

In the next section, we'll introduce Retrieval-Augmented Generation (RAG). This key design pattern integrates enterprise data into large language model (LLM) workflows to produce grounded, reliable, and context-aware AI applications.

Retrieval-Augmented Generation (RAG): A Foundation for Enterprise LLMs

Generative AI systems powered by large language models (LLMs) show impressive fluency, but they often lack factual accuracy, contextual grounding, and access to real-time enterprise data. These limitations are particularly problematic in domains where the consequences of misinformation or outdated responses are severe. As organizations adopt LLMs for production workloads, they increasingly need architectures that bridge these gaps without retraining massive models or sacrificing control.

Retrieval-Augmented Generation (RAG) addresses this need by combining enterprise retrieval techniques with large language model (LLM)-based generation. Instead of relying solely on what the model already knows, RAG enables systems to fetch relevant, up-to-date content at inference time—improving trust, transparency, and usefulness across a range of business-critical use cases.

In the following sections, you'll examine the mechanics of the RAG pattern, explore its modular architecture, and discover the tooling options that make it viable within a Lakehouse AI environment.

What Is RAG and Why Does It Matter?

Retrieval-Augmented Generation (RAG) is a powerful design pattern that helps large language models (LLMs) produce more accurate, reliable, and context-aware responses. Traditional LLMs, while capable of generating humanlike text, often suffer from a lack of real-time knowledge and may produce outdated or incorrect answers—a phenomenon known as hallucination. RAG solves this by integrating live access to external knowledge sources directly into the inference process.

Without RAG, LLMs rely solely on the information encoded during pretraining, which may be months or even years out of date, and lack visibility into proprietary enterprise data. As a result, they may generate vague, unverifiable, or even misleading answers—a significant issue in sensitive industries such as healthcare, finance, and law. For example, a legal assistant LLM asked about current compliance regulations may provide a general explanation based on outdated data, potentially leading to costly decisions. With RAG, that same assistant can retrieve and reference the most recent regulation text before formulating its response.

Traditional LLMs function like a black box—they generate responses based on their training data but can't validate or cite real-time internal information. RAG bridges this gap. By combining semantic search across your Delta Lake data with the LLM's natural language generation, you build AI applications that are context-aware, and responses are grounded in your actual business data.

- **Traceable**: You can point users to the source used to generate an answer.

- **Flexible**: Works across structured and unstructured content, like emails, policies, or knowledge bases.

For instance, in a legal setting, a RAG-powered assistant can reference contracts, case law, or compliance rules to answer questions like: "What clause outlines early termination rights in the Smith vs. Greenfield contract?"

RAG also improves transparency. Because the system retrieves context from identifiable sources, it can display to users which documents contributed to each response, allowing them to verify or challenge the LLM's output. The ability to trace the model's reasoning is critical in sectors such as finance, law, and compliance, where explainability is essential for AI-generated answers.

Finally, RAG enables organizations to maintain lightweight and secure LLM systems. Rather than fine-tuning large models on sensitive internal data, they can keep the models frozen and manage the retrieval layer. This separation of concerns improves agility, reduces infrastructure costs, and minimizes risk exposure.

RAG Architecture and Components

The architecture of a typical RAG pipeline consists of four main components: a retriever, a vector index or knowledge store, an embedding model, and a generator, such as a large language model (LLM). These components work together in a pipeline that helps answer user questions accurately and in a way that's easy to understand, using trusted information stored within an organization.

The process begins with the **embedding model**. When a person types in a question, such as "How do I reset my account password?"—the system needs to understand not only the words used but also the meaning behind them. To achieve this, the embedding model converts the question into a numerical format known as a "vector." This process is important because computers do not understand language the way humans do; they require all information in numerical form.

The vector captures the overall meaning and intent behind the question, making it easier to compare it to other pieces of text, even if those texts use different words. For instance, someone else might ask the same question using different wording: "How can

I change my login credentials?" Even though this sentence doesn't use the same words, it means almost the same thing. Because both sentences have similar meanings, their vector representations will be close to each other in what is called an "embedding space."

This ability to recognize different wordings of the same idea is crucial. It ensures that the system isn't limited to exact matches but can respond accurately even when people phrase their questions in different ways. This scenario is especially helpful in customer support systems, chatbots, or internal knowledge tools, where users often express similar issues in unique ways.

After the system converts the question into a vector, it searches for matching information. At this stage, the vector index or knowledge store plays a key role. This specialized database holds vectors that represent company documents, FAQs, support tickets, and other text-based content. The system has already converted and stored these documents as vectors in advance. It then compares the user's question vector to the stored vectors to identify the most relevant documents—much like finding the coordinate closest to a query point. For example, if the question concerns resetting passwords, the system may retrieve help articles and policy snippets related to password recovery procedures.

Next comes the **retriever**, which is responsible for selecting and pulling out the most relevant content. From the list of matches in the vector index, the retriever typically selects the top-k documents—these are the ones most closely related to the user's question. It bundles them into a "context block," which is essentially a carefully chosen set of information that the language model will use as reference material. For example, in a telecom company, if a customer asks about international roaming charges, the retriever might grab relevant pages from the latest pricing handbook.

Finally, the **generator** takes over. It is usually a large language model, such as GPT-4 or LLaMA 3. It receives two things: the user's original question and the retrieved content. Instead of guessing an answer from scratch, it uses the retrieved content to produce a clear, well-formed answer that is grounded in factual information. In the earlier example, the model might respond with, "To reset your password, go to the account settings page and click on 'Reset Password.' You will receive a confirmation link via your registered email." Figure 8-1 illustrates the entire flow.

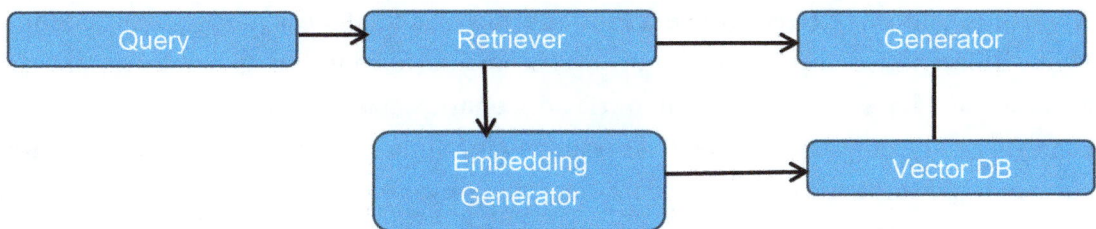

Figure 8-1. *RAG architecture and its components*

This separation of duties—embedding, indexing, retrieving, and generating—makes the RAG pipeline modular and adaptable. Each part can be updated or improved independently of the others. Organizations can utilize more effective embedding models, update documents in the knowledge store, or fine-tune retrieval logic without needing to retrain the entire large language model (LLM). This flexibility makes RAG an ideal choice for deploying AI in real-world environments where both accuracy and maintainability are crucial.

Model and Tooling Options

Implementing RAG on the Databricks Lakehouse platform involves selecting the right tools across both the retrieval and generation layers. Fortunately, Lakehouse AI offers robust support for open source and enterprise-grade tooling, enabling flexible and secure RAG development.

For **language generation**, organizations can use models such as **OpenAI's GPT-4** or deploy open source alternatives like **LLaMA 3**, **Mistral**, or **Mixtral**. You can access these models via Databricks Model Serving or integrate them through APIs. Using open source models provides greater control over cost, deployment, and privacy, ideal for organizations that need on-premise or air-gapped solutions.

For **retrieval and embedding**, Databricks offers an integrated solution through **Databricks Vector Search**, a managed service designed to perform fast and secure similarity searches on vectorized data. Vector Search allows users to store dense vector embeddings of documents and retrieve the most relevant entries based on similarity to a given query. It is essential in Retrieval-Augmented Generation (RAG), where the relevance and speed of retrieval directly impact the accuracy of the generated response.

Embeddings are numerical representations of text that capture its meaning, generated using specialized models. Databricks supports a range of high-performance embedding models, including **BGE (BAAI General Embedding)**, **E5 (Embedding from**

Everything), and **GTE (General Text Embeddings)**. Each of these models is suited for slightly different use cases. BGE is known for strong performance in general-purpose retrieval tasks. E5 excels in zero-shot retrieval scenarios, making it ideal for queries where no prior examples exist. GTE is optimized for multilingual environments, enabling teams to build semantic search systems that function across various languages.

You'll be able to select the appropriate embedding model based on your specific requirements. For example, if you are building a customer support assistant who must understand queries in multiple languages, GTE is a strong candidate. If you need a general search tool that can handle a wide range of enterprise documents, BGE might be more suitable. For niche domains where labeled data is scarce, E5's zero-shot capability is particularly valuable.

Once generated, embeddings are stored in Delta tables on Databricks and indexed using Vector Search. This setup allows fast retrieval of relevant content at scale while ensuring governance, security, and version control through native integration with Unity Catalog and MLflow.

To orchestrate the RAG pipeline efficiently, frameworks like **LangChain** and **Prompt Flow** provide modular building blocks and workflow automation. These tools help manage the process of retrieving relevant documents, formatting the retrieved content into prompts, and generating final answers with language models.

LangChain is a popular open source framework designed to simplify the development of applications that use LLMs alongside external data sources. It allows developers to chain multiple steps, such as calling an embedding model, querying a vector database, and formatting a prompt into a single reusable pipeline. LangChain integrates seamlessly with Databricks, enabling users to log key artifacts, including prompt inputs, retrieved documents, and generated responses, into **MLflow**. This integration adds observability and governance to every stage of the AI pipeline, which is essential in regulated industries or production-grade systems.

Prompt flow, a Microsoft offering, provides a visual and code-first environment for building, debugging, and managing large language model (LLM) workflows. It supports versioning, parameter tuning, and prompt testing, which helps teams iterate and deploy faster. Prompt flow is particularly useful when working with predefined prompt templates and structured data flows, providing teams with a more guided experience.

Together, these frameworks help streamline complex tasks, reduce boilerplate code, and promote reuse. By combining LangChain's flexible chaining logic with Prompt Flow's visual orchestration and MLflow's experiment tracking, teams can build robust RAG applications that are transparent, traceable, and easy to maintain.

Unity Catalog plays a key role in RAG governance by restricting access to underlying data sources and controlling visibility into vector indexes. It ensures that only authorized users or services can retrieve sensitive content for use in prompts. For instance, a financial RAG system can enforce policies so that analysts querying client investment records only receive documents they're entitled to view.

Together, these tools enable enterprises to create RAG workflows that are accurate, secure, and maintainable, providing a robust foundation for LLM-powered applications across various domains, including support automation, policy search, risk analysis, and beyond.

In the next section, you'll **build on this foundation** by learning how to **implement RAG workflows using Databricks-native tools**, including Delta tables, Vector Search, and Unity Catalog.

Building RAG Pipelines with Lakehouse AI

In the previous section, you explored the key components and architecture that make Retrieval-Augmented Generation (RAG) effective for enterprise use. You learned how embedding models, vector indexes, retrievers, and generators work together to enable LLMs to produce responses that are both accurate and grounded in organizational data. While understanding the conceptual model is essential, implementing these concepts effectively requires a solid implementation strategy.

That's where the Databricks Lakehouse platform excels. It provides an integrated, scalable foundation for building production-grade RAG pipelines, eliminating the need to manage complex third-party stacks. From ingestion and vectorization to indexing and generation, Databricks provides first-class support for every stage of the RAG workflow.

In this section, you'll dive into hands-on implementation using Delta tables for document storage, Vector Search for similarity retrieval, Unity Catalog for governance, and MLflow for experiment tracking. You'll not only see how each tool fits into the pipeline but also understand how to operationalize these steps to deliver real-time, context-aware AI applications within your enterprise.

CHAPTER 8   LAKEHOUSE AI AND RETRIEVAL-AUGMENTED GENERATION (RAG)

Implementing RAG with Delta Tables and Vector Search

The first step in an RAG pipeline is to collect, organize, and store the source documents that the system will later use to retrieve relevant context. These documents can include everything from internal memos and customer support tickets to product manuals, compliance documents, or domain-specific knowledge bases. This diversity in content makes it critical to store them in a format that supports both flexibility and reliability.

In Databricks, **Delta tables** handle this foundational step. Delta tables enhance traditional data lake storage by offering version control, schema enforcement, and ACID-compliant transactions, thereby improving data management and reliability. It means your data remains consistent and trustworthy—even if the system is interrupted mid-process or the table is accessed concurrently by multiple users. Think of Delta tables as intelligent spreadsheets that not only store content but also track how and when it changes.

To begin, you'll ingest various types of source documents, such as emails, PDFs, FAQs, and support transcripts, into your Databricks environment. Since they come in multiple formats, you'll use notebooks to parse and normalize the content. For instance, OCR tools or PyPDF can convert PDFs to plain text while the system extracts metadata, such as document type, author, and timestamp, into structured columns. The cleaned and annotated data is then stored in a Delta table, effectively creating a searchable and queryable document repository.

But making the content retrievable by keyword alone isn't enough. Users may not phrase their questions in the same way as documents. That's where **embedding models** come in—models like BGE, E5, or GTE convert sentences and paragraphs into numerical vectors that represent their semantic meaning. For example, the sentences "How can I return a product?" and "What's the refund procedure?" may look different on the surface but mean the same thing. Embedding models translate both into similar vectors, allowing for effective similarity search.

You apply these models using Spark UDFs or Hugging Face integrations in Databricks. The output vectors are stored in another Delta table, indexed alongside the original text. This setup enables your system to connect raw language queries with meaningful, high-accuracy document matches—even when keywords don't overlap.

Next, you use **Databricks Vector Search** to create an index over this embedding table. Vector Search uses specialized algorithms to quickly compare the user's query vector with all stored document vectors and return the closest matches. It's like a highly intelligent recommendation engine that doesn't just match terms—it matches ideas. For

CHAPTER 8   LAKEHOUSE AI AND RETRIEVAL-AUGMENTED GENERATION (RAG)

instance, if someone types "how to handle defective merchandise," the system might return a guideline that uses completely different words, such as "damaged goods returns policy."

Finally, the system passes the most relevant document snippets retrieved through Vector Search into the LLM (introduced in the "Key Features and Capabilities" section) to generate a grounded, context-aware response. This output is far more reliable than a generic LLM response because it draws directly from actual enterprise knowledge.

This full pipeline—from data ingestion to embedding, indexing, retrieval, and response generation—can be scheduled and maintained using Databricks Jobs, orchestrated via Workflows, and enhanced with frameworks like LangChain. The result is a fast, secure, and intelligent system that helps users find high-quality answers using real organizational data. Let's understand the end-to-end flow of building the RAG pipeline in detail:

Building the RAG Pipeline

A Retrieval-Augmented Generation (RAG) pipeline in Databricks using DBRX typically follows a structured, multistep workflow that transforms enterprise data into intelligent, contextual responses. The goal is to create a closed-loop system that automatically answers user questions using relevant data retrieved and processed in real time. This architecture enables enterprises to convert their existing data assets—stored in formats such as Delta tables or document archives—into interactive, question-answering systems that are accurate, grounded, and efficient.

1. **Data Preparation**: Begin by organizing your content. Upload structured datasets (like SQL tables) or unstructured content (PDFs, policy documents, or emails) into **Delta tables** in your Lakehouse. These Delta tables serve as the central repository for enterprise knowledge.

2. **Embedding**: After preparing your content, the next step is to convert it into a format that the computer can understand and search efficiently. This technique is called embedding. An embedding is a mathematical representation of text, specifically, a vector of numbers, that captures the meaning of words, sentences, or whole documents.

Imagine summarizing each document into a unique numerical fingerprint. This fingerprint enables the system to compare pieces of text based on their meaning rather than just exact word matches. DBRX or compatible models, such as BGE (BAAI General Embedding) or E5 (Embeddings from Sentence Transformers), are used to create these embeddings.

To gain a deeper understanding, consider how humans associate ideas. When someone mentions "employee perks," you might automatically think of "benefits" or "compensation." Embeddings capture this relationship mathematically, helping the system understand that "staff perks" and "employee benefits" likely refer to the same concept. This semantic similarity enables AI-driven search to be accurate even when users phrase things differently. Without embeddings, a search engine would rely only on exact keyword matches, missing the deeper connections between related terms.

3. **Indexing**: After generating embeddings, the next step is to store and organize them to facilitate quick search. This process is called indexing. Imagine having thousands of documents, each converted into a mathematical fingerprint. Without proper indexing, finding a match would be akin to searching for a needle in a haystack.

   Databricks Vector Search addresses this problem by creating a specialized type of catalog—a vector index—that enables the system to compare and retrieve similar vectors efficiently. Instead of comparing entire documents, it compares their embeddings using distance metrics, such as cosine similarity. The closer the vectors are, the more similar the meanings.

   This semantic indexing enables RAG systems to return relevant answers even when users ask questions in different ways. For example, whether someone types "termination clause" or "contract end conditions," the system can match both to the same passage in the database because their embeddings are closely related. Vector Search enables this matching process to be fast, scalable, and reliable.

4. **Query:** Once a user enters a question, whether through a chatbot, web portal, or search box, the system first processes the question using the same embedding technique described earlier. It means the question is transformed into a vector, capturing its meaning in mathematical form.

   That vector is then compared to all the vectors stored in the system's vector index. Using similarity metrics (like cosine similarity), the system measures how close the question's meaning is to the meanings of previously indexed content. The system then selects the top-k most relevant content pieces with the closest semantic match.

   This process makes RAG so powerful. Instead of simply retrieving documents that match a few keywords, it retrieves content that aligns with the actual intent behind the user's question. For example, if a user asks, "Who approves large purchases in our finance policy?" The system might pull a paragraph that doesn't even contain the words "approve" or "large purchase" but still answers the question based on meaning because the embeddings are similar.

   This step is the core of "retrieval" in Retrieval-Augmented Generation, enabling the LLM to access and reason over your enterprise knowledge dynamically and contextually.

5. **Generation**: After the system identifies the most relevant information during the query step, it passes the content chunks to the LLM model. But instead of simply dumping the content into the model, a carefully crafted prompt guides the LLM's behavior. Think of a prompt as clear instructions or a framework for the task you want the model to perform.

   For example, the prompt might read: *"Using the following excerpts from our legal contracts, answer the user's question in plain English..."* This prompt tells the LLM model exactly what to do—use the retrieved context to generate a grounded, focused answer.

This step is critical because it ensures that the model's response is linguistically fluent and directly tied to the retrieved evidence. Without this controlled prompt, LLM might stray off-topic or make assumptions. However, with the right framing and context, it acts like a trained assistant, referencing the correct documentation to deliver precise and trustworthy results.

This process can be automated using orchestration frameworks like **LangChain** or **Semantic Kernel**, which help chain together data ingestion, retrieval, and generation workflows. The result is an intelligent assistant who understands your business language and answers questions with the precision of a domain expert.

Case Study: Legal Document AI Assistant

Let's use a realistic example to illustrate how RAG and DBRX can work together in the legal domain.

Imagine a mid-sized law firm that stores thousands of client contracts, non-disclosure agreements (NDAs), and service agreements in its Lakehouse. Traditionally, if an attorney needed to find a specific clause, such as indemnity terms, they would manually sift through folders, browse SharePoint documents, or search using the Ctrl+F function. This process is time-consuming, prone to oversight, and requires deep familiarity with the document structure.

Now, with a RAG-powered DBRX solution, the firm builds a smart legal assistant. When a lawyer types:

"Show me the indemnity clause in our vendor agreement with Acme Corp."

Here's what happens:

1. The assistant converts the question into a semantic vector.

2. It uses Databricks Vector Search to find the most relevant contract snippets in Delta format.

3. LLM receives the retrieved text snippets along with the prompt:
   "Using the following text, explain the indemnity clause clearly."

4. LLM generates a precise, human-readable summary and a clickable citation to the original clause.

This setup saves legal professionals hours of manual review, ensures legal accuracy, and democratizes access to complex documents, even for junior attorneys or legal aides with limited experience.

This case study highlights the transformational value of combining enterprise data with intelligent AI workflows. In the following sections, we'll explore how tools such as Databricks Vector Search and Unity Catalog further support scalable and secure RAG systems.

In the next section, you'll explore how to use Unity Catalog to add governance, track data lineage, and enforce secure access to documents and generated responses.

Implementing Governance on RAG Pipelines

While the technical mechanics of building an RAG pipeline are critical, ensuring that it operates securely, transparently, and in compliance with organizational policies is equally vital. The **Unity Catalog** plays a central role in this process. Unity Catalog is Databricks' unified governance solution, providing a consistent layer of control across data, machine learning (ML) models, features, and even prompts and outputs used in AI workflows. It simplifies access management, helps ensure compliance, and enhances auditability.

In an enterprise setting, not every employee should have access to all data. For example, financial analysts may need to access product pricing data, while HR personnel should only be able to view employee evaluations. **Unity Catalog** applies fine-grained access controls at various levels, including entire datasets, specific tables, individual rows, or columns. Imagine a situation where a customer support assistant queries documents for a refund policy—the assistant should access product manuals but not internal HR memos. Unity Catalog enforces those boundaries without requiring additional code.

Let's consider a healthcare use case: A hospital wants to use an RAG system to summarize clinical notes and patient interactions. Physicians require full access to patient data, whereas medical researchers should only view anonymized datasets. Unity Catalog enables the creation and enforcement of these rules from a central location. The system integrates compliance directly into the workflow, allowing developers to avoid creating separate data copies and maintaining multiple pipelines.

Another critical feature is **data lineage tracking**. Unity Catalog automatically logs how data moves through the system—from ingestion and embedding to retrieval and final LLM output. It means that if a user receives an unexpected answer from an AI application, you can trace it back to the source document, view the transformations and embeddings applied, and validate or correct the process. This visibility is essential not only for debugging but also for meeting audit and regulatory requirements, particularly in industries such as finance and healthcare.

Unity Catalog also works closely with **MLflow**, Databricks' experiment tracking framework. Through this integration, you can log and monitor all prompt inputs, outputs, model versions, and even LLM parameters used in your RAG applications. Suppose a customer-facing chatbot begins giving inconsistent or incorrect responses. MLflow enables you to examine recent prompt sessions, track model version updates, and roll back or fine-tune as needed. This setup creates a feedback loop where governance and experimentation work in tandem.

By integrating Unity Catalog and MLflow into your RAG pipeline, you're not just securing data—you're building trust, traceability, and accountability into your AI systems. These controls enable teams to innovate more quickly while ensuring the system remains aligned with corporate policies and regulatory standards.

In the next section, you'll learn how to fine-tune LLM behavior using prompt engineering and add safety and quality controls through guardrails and observability tools.

Prompt Engineering and Guardrails

Once your RAG pipeline is in place and integrated with tools like Vector Search and Unity Catalog, the next critical component is prompt engineering. This section focuses on designing effective prompts for DBRX and implementing safeguards—called guardrails—to ensure the generated outputs remain relevant, safe, and aligned with business requirements.

What Is Prompt Engineering?

Prompt engineering is crafting inputs (prompts) to guide a language model's behavior. Even the most powerful LLMs, including DBRX, require well-structured prompts to produce accurate and helpful responses. A prompt acts like a set of instructions—it frames the user's intent, specifies the format of the desired output, and can even provide context or examples.

A **prompt template** is a reusable structure that contains placeholders for context-specific variables. It ensures consistency and efficiency when crafting prompts across multiple use cases.

For example:

"You are a [role]. Given the following [document type or context], [task instruction]. Ensure your output follows [format or style guidance]."

Generated Prompt

"You are a helpful HR assistant. Given the following excerpt from the company's HR policy document, summarize the onboarding process into three clear and concise bullet points. Make sure each point starts with an action verb and reflects the correct sequence."

Context: ["All new employees must attend orientation within the first week, complete required compliance training modules, and schedule a meeting with their assigned team lead to discuss project expectations."]

Effective prompts are clear, specific, and include context. These components significantly influence the quality of answers, especially when combined with RAG workflows that require the meaningful processing of retrieved content.

What Are Guardrails?

Guardrails are predefined rules, filters, or constraints designed to shape and restrict the behavior of a language model, ensuring it produces outputs that are safe, relevant, and aligned with business or regulatory standards. In enterprise applications, particularly those in regulated industries such as healthcare, finance, or legal, guardrails help mitigate risks by preventing unintended or inappropriate model responses.

The importance of guardrails lies in their ability to reduce hallucinations (plausible-sounding but incorrect answers), enforce content policies, and promote consistency across AI-generated content. Even with well-crafted prompts, a model like DBRX might produce off-topic, noncompliant, or harmful outputs without guardrails.

Guardrails can take various forms depending on your use case, organizational policies, and the level of control needed. They serve as preventative and corrective measures that influence a model's behavior during inference. Whether you're trying to avoid sensitive data leakage or enforce specific formatting, selecting the right guardrail mechanisms is critical for responsible AI deployment.

- **Content Filtering:** This type of guardrail prevents the model from generating specific types of content that could be harmful, offensive, or confidential. For instance, you might block the model from outputting profanity, disclosing sensitive personal information such as social security numbers, or providing unverified health advice. It helps ensure compliance with privacy laws and ethical guidelines.

- **Response Formatting Constraints:** These constraints ensure that the model follows a specific structure in its replies. For example, if you're building an AI assistant that generates checklists, you might require all responses to be formatted as numbered steps or bullet points. This process improves readability and usability, particularly in applications such as documentation assistants or internal knowledge bots.

- **Vocabulary or Domain Constraints:** In regulated or technical environments, it may be necessary to encourage the use of approved terminology or block certain language. For example, in healthcare, you may want to enforce the use of standardized medical terms (like "hypertension" instead of "high blood pressure") or restrict informal phrasing in legal documents. It helps maintain professionalism, accuracy, and adherence to compliance standards.

These guardrails can be implemented at multiple levels—within the prompt itself, through model configuration, or at the application layer that processes model outputs.

Tools for Prompt Management and Testing

- Developers manage and improve prompts through an iterative process, using tools like Azure Prompt Flow, Databricks notebooks, or MLflow Tracking to

    - **Experiment with Different Prompt Variations:** You can change how you phrase the instruction, adjust the tone or level of detail, or vary the output format to identify which type of prompt best guides the model.

    - **Track Which Prompts Yield the Most Useful Outputs:** Log the success and failure of prompts to analyze which ones generate accurate, compliant, or high-quality answers across use cases.

    - **Record Prompt–Response Pairs for Audit and Retraining:** Maintain a versioned log of prompts and their outputs to improve future generations, troubleshoot errors, and demonstrate accountability for business or regulatory reviews.

For example, you might log multiple prompts for summarizing compliance policies and evaluate them based on clarity, completeness, and legal alignment. Over time, this becomes a repository of prompt patterns that can be reused, versioned, and improved.

By combining prompt engineering and guardrails, teams can control DBRX's output more precisely, ensuring that even complex queries are handled responsibly, accurately, and aligned with business rules.

The next section explores how to apply these principles in real-world industries, including healthcare, finance, and retail.

Real-World Use Cases and Industry Applications

With a strong understanding of RAG architecture, prompt engineering, and guardrails in place, it's time to explore how these concepts work across different industries. This section highlights how LLMs and Lakehouse AI are already transforming business operations and decision-making across the healthcare, finance, and retail sectors.

Each use case reflects a real-world scenario where organizations leverage LLM-powered Retrieval-Augmented Generation (RAG) pipelines to solve critical challenges—such as summarizing unstructured documents, extracting insights from transactional data, or improving customer experiences through AI-generated narratives.

These examples will help you

- Visualize how to apply Lakehouse AI capabilities in your industry.

- Understand the impact of fine-tuned prompts, contextual grounding, and governance mechanisms.

- Recognize opportunities to scale AI solutions responsibly across departments and workflows.

Let's examine how healthcare providers utilize LLMs for clinical note summarization and patient documentation enhancements.

Healthcare: Clinical Note Summarization

Healthcare providers deal with large volumes of unstructured data, including physician notes, discharge summaries, and electronic health records (EHRs). This data is rich in patient context but often difficult to search, summarize, or analyze at scale.

Hospitals and clinics can automatically summarize clinical notes into standardized formats by integrating large language models (LLMs) into a Retrieval-Augmented Generation (RAG) pipeline. For instance, a prompt like: "You are a clinical documentation assistant. Given the following physician note, summarize the patient's condition, diagnosis, and treatment plan in three bullet points."

You can pair it with a retrieved note from a Delta table containing EHR text. LLMs generate a concise, structured output that medical coders or attending physicians can quickly review.

It can improve productivity, reduce transcription errors, and accelerate decision-making—all while maintaining compliance and data traceability through the Unity Catalog. For example, a hospital uses DBRX to automate the summarization of admission notes. Instead of manually reviewing each chart, physicians receive a summary of the most recent patient entries, saving time and supporting consistent documentation practices across departments.

Finance: Fraud Detection and Document Analysis

Financial institutions face a dual challenge: monitoring real-time transactional activity to detect fraud and analyzing large volumes of unstructured documents such as tax filings, credit reports, and investment disclosures. Many teams now utilize Retrieval-Augmented Generation workflows powered by large language models (LLMs) to meet these demands and enhance precision, scalability, and decision-making speed.

In a typical use case, a bank embeds regulatory reports and historical customer data into a vector index. When a compliance officer asks: "You are a financial compliance assistant. Review the following transaction summary and highlight any patterns indicative of potential fraud." LLM evaluates recent transactions against past patterns and regulatory context retrieved from enterprise data sources. The model can then generate a summary outlining risk factors, triggering alerts, or assisting with case documentation.

Additionally, LLM can analyze unstructured documents such as loan applications or investment prospectuses. For instance, when asked: "Extract the key risk disclosures from this document and summarize them in bullet points." the model returns structured summaries, allowing compliance officers to review, approve, and archive the content efficiently.

Financial institutions can streamline fraud detection, reduce manual overhead, and maintain compliance with regulatory mandates by combining contextual retrieval with prompt engineering and proper governance.

CHAPTER 8   LAKEHOUSE AI AND RETRIEVAL-AUGMENTED GENERATION (RAG)

Retail: Intelligent Product Recommendations

Retailers continually seek ways to personalize shopping experiences, increase conversion rates, and foster customer loyalty. With large volumes of product data, user reviews, inventory catalogs, and customer interactions, providing contextually relevant recommendations at scale is a significant challenge.

By leveraging large language models (LLMs) in a Lakehouse AI environment, retail businesses can build intelligent assistants that generate personalized product descriptions, summarize customer sentiment, or suggest complementary items. For example, LLM can respond to a prompt like: "You are a product recommendation engine after retrieving user browsing behavior and product metadata. Given the customer's recent activity and the product catalog, suggest three related items they will likely purchase." The model uses context from vectorized user behavior logs and product details stored in Delta tables to generate targeted recommendations in natural language.

For example, a retail website integrates LLM into its recommendation engine. When a user views a high-end camera, the AI suggests compatible lenses, tripods, and cleaning kits based on prior purchase behavior and similar customer journeys. These insights increase upselling opportunities while improving the customer experience.

With prompt engineering and guardrails, retailers can ensure the recommendations are relevant, brand-aligned, and free from bias—helping to build trust and drive repeat business.

In the next section, we'll put these ideas into practice with a hands-on lab that walks you through implementing a RAG-based AI assistant using LLM and Lakehouse AI in a Databricks environment.

Lab: Building a Vector Search-Powered HR Chatbot on Databricks

Objective
The goal of this lab is to build a **Retrieval-Augmented Generation (RAG)** chatbot that can answer HR-related questions by retrieving the most relevant documents from a **Databricks Vector Search index** and using a **foundation large language model (LLM)** to generate natural language responses.

Chapter 8 Lakehouse AI and Retrieval-Augmented Generation (RAG)

By the end of this lab, you will

- ☑ Create and index HR policy data into a Delta table.
- ☑ Generate embeddings and sync them into a **Vector Search index**.
- ☑ Use a Databricks-hosted **LLM endpoint** to answer natural language queries.
- ☑ Chain everything together using **LangChain** into a complete RAG pipeline.
- ☑ Log, version, and serve the chatbot with **MLflow**.

This hands-on lab provides a full-stack demonstration of how to combine Vector Search, LLMs, and enterprise infrastructure on Databricks to build intelligent applications grounded in trusted data.

Step 1: Install Required Libraries

To begin, install the necessary libraries that will be used throughout the lab. These include

- `databricks-vectorsearch`: Enables vector indexing and search over Delta tables
- `MLflow`: For experiment tracking and model deployment
- `pandas`: Data manipulation and transformation
- `streamlit`: Optional UI for chatbot interaction
- `databricks_langchain`: Integration between LangChain and Databricks services

Run the following command in a notebook cell:

```
%pip install databricks-vectorsearch -U MLflow pandas streamlit databricks_langchain
```

Step 2: Restart the Python Kernel

After installing the required libraries in Step 1, it's important to restart the Python kernel so that all packages are properly initialized and available in your environment.

Run the following command in a notebook cell:

%restart_python

Step 3: Create Catalog and Schema Using PySpark

To organize and manage your HR policy data, create a catalog named rag_demo and a schema named chatbot_hr.

> **Note** This ensures that all your Delta tables and related resources are logically grouped under a clean namespace.

```
# Create catalog and schema using PySpark
spark.sql("CREATE CATALOG IF NOT EXISTS rag_demo")
spark.sql("USE CATALOG rag_demo")
spark.sql("CREATE SCHEMA IF NOT EXISTS chatbot_hr")
spark.sql("USE SCHEMA chatbot_hr")
```

After running this command, you will see that the rag_demo catalog and chatbot_hr schema are visible, as depicted in Figure 8-2.

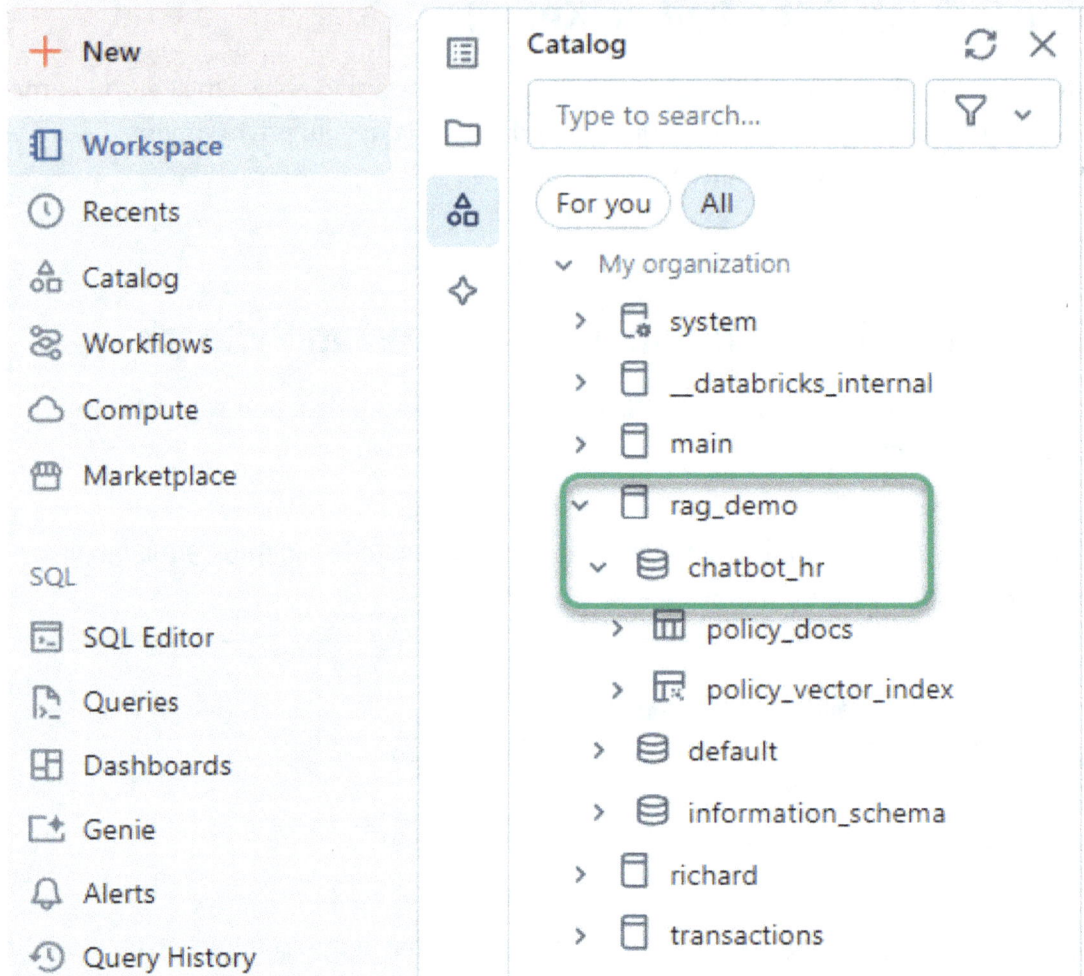

Figure 8-2. rag_demo catalog and chatbot_hr schema in Catalog view

Step 4: Load HR Policy Sample Data into a Delta Table

In this step, you'll create a sample dataset of HR policies and store it in a Delta table named `policy_docs` within the `rag_demo.chatbot_hr` schema.

This table simulates a knowledge base with the following structure:

- `doc_id`: A unique identifier for each document
- `title`: A short title describing the policy
- `content`: The full content or summary of the HR policy

CHAPTER 8 LAKEHOUSE AI AND RETRIEVAL-AUGMENTED GENERATION (RAG)

Example policies include:

- Leave policy
- Remote work guidelines
- Parental leave
- Dress code
- Working hours
- Reimbursement process
- Training budgets
- Code of conduct

This structured dataset will be indexed later using **Databricks Vector Search** to support fast and intelligent retrieval of relevant content based on user questions.

```
from pyspark.sql.types import StructType, StructField, StringType
sample_data = [
    ("001", "Leave Policy", "Employees are entitled to 20 vacation days per
    year."),
    ("002", "Remote Work", "Remote work is allowed up to 3 days per
    week."),
    ("003", "Parental Leave", "New parents can take up to 12 weeks of paid
    leave."),
    ("004", "Dress Code", "Business casual attire is recommended."),
    ("005", "Working Hours", "Standard working hours are 9 AM to 5 PM,
    Monday through Friday."),
    ("006", "Reimbursement", "Employees may claim up to $500 monthly for
    approved expenses."),
    ("007", "Training Budget", "Each employee has a yearly training budget
    of $2000."),
    ("008", "Code of Conduct", "All employees must adhere to respectful
    communication policies.")
]
schema = StructType([
    StructField("doc_id", StringType(), False),
    StructField("title", StringType(), True),
```

```
    StructField("content", StringType(), True)
])
df = spark.createDataFrame(sample_data, schema=schema)
df.write.format("delta").mode("overwrite").saveAsTable("rag_demo.chatbot_
hr.policy_docs")
```

Step 5: Verify HR Policy Data in SQL

Run the SQL command below to confirm that your HR policy data has been successfully saved into the Delta table.

This step queries the rag_demo.chatbot_hr.policy_docs table and displays the content that forms the basis of your chatbot's knowledge base.

This verification ensures the table is correctly structured and ready for embedding and vector indexing in the next steps.

```
%sql
-- The dataset for your knowledge base has been loaded for you in the init
notebook.
SELECT * FROM rag_demo.chatbot_hr.policy_docs
```

Step 6: Create and Validate Vector Search Endpoint

Before we can perform Vector Search, we need a **Vector Search endpoint** on Databricks. This step

1. Initializes the VectorSearchClient
2. Defines utility functions to:
    - Check if the endpoint already exists (endpoint_exists).
    - Wait until the endpoint is fully **ONLINE** (wait_for_vs_endpoint_to_be_ready).
3. Creates a new endpoint if it doesn't exist
4. Waits for the endpoint to be ready for use

The endpoint named hr-docs-endpoint will later be used to store and search against vector embeddings of HR documents.

```python
from databricks.vector_search.client import VectorSearchClient
mport time

VECTOR_SEARCH_ENDPOINT_NAME = "hr-docs-endpoint"
vsc = VectorSearchClient(disable_notice=True)

def endpoint_exists(vsc, endpoint_name):
    try:
        vsc.get_endpoint(endpoint_name)
        return True
    except Exception as e:
        if "NOT_FOUND" in str(e) or "does not exist" in str(e):
            return False
        raise e

def wait_for_vs_endpoint_to_be_ready(vsc, endpoint_name, timeout=700, poll_interval=15):
    start_time = time.time()
    while True:
        try:
            status = vsc.get_endpoint(endpoint_name).get("endpoint_status", {}).get("state", "")
            print(f"Status: {status}")
            if status == "ONLINE":
                print(f"☑ Vector Search endpoint '{endpoint_name}' is ready.")
                break
        except Exception as e:
            print(f"[WARN] Failed to get endpoint status: {e}")

        if time.time() - start_time > timeout:
            raise TimeoutError(f" Timeout: Endpoint '{endpoint_name}' was not ready after {timeout} seconds.")
        time.sleep(poll_interval)
```

CHAPTER 8   LAKEHOUSE AI AND RETRIEVAL-AUGMENTED GENERATION (RAG)

```
# Create endpoint if needed
if not endpoint_exists(vsc, VECTOR_SEARCH_ENDPOINT_NAME):
    print(f" Creating Vector Search endpoint: {VECTOR_SEARCH_
    ENDPOINT_NAME}")
    vsc.create_endpoint(name=VECTOR_SEARCH_ENDPOINT_NAME, endpoint_
    type="STANDARD")
    time.sleep(5)  # Allow time for provisioning to start
else:
    print(f" Vector Search endpoint '{VECTOR_SEARCH_ENDPOINT_NAME}'
    already exists.")

# Wait for it to be ready
wait_for_vs_endpoint_to_be_ready(vsc, VECTOR_SEARCH_ENDPOINT_NAME)
```

After running the cell, if you click Compute in the left navigation and go to Vector Search, you will find the hr-doc-endpoint index as depicted in Figure 8-3.

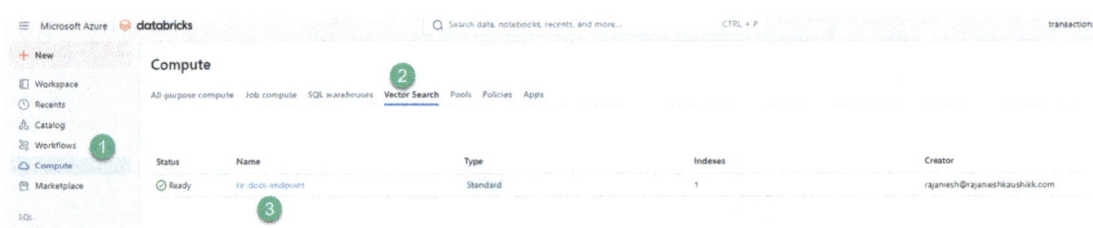

Figure 8-3. *Vector Search view showing the recently created Vector Search database*

Step 7: Create and Sync Vector Search Index

In this step, we prepare our HR documents for semantic search by

1. **Enabling Change Data Feed (CDF)** on the Delta table to support change tracking for index updates

2. **Checking if the Vector Search index already exists**

CHAPTER 8   LAKEHOUSE AI AND RETRIEVAL-AUGMENTED GENERATION (RAG)

3. **Creating the Vector Search index** using `create_delta_sync_index` if it does not exist
   - The index uses the `content` column for generating embeddings.
   - The `doc_id` field is used as the primary key.
   - The embedding model is hosted at the `databricks-bge-large-en` endpoint.

4. **Waiting for the index to become ready** using the built-in `wait_until_ready()` method

5. **Triggering a sync** to ensure all documents are indexed and searchable

Once complete, our data is stored in a searchable format optimized for vector-based semantic retrieval.

```
from databricks.vector_search.client import VectorSearchClient
import time
# Configuration
catalog = "rag_demo"
db = "chatbot_hr"
table = "policy_docs"
index = "policy_vector_index"
VECTOR_SEARCH_ENDPOINT_NAME = "hr-docs-endpoint"
EMBEDDING_ENDPOINT_NAME = "databricks-bge-large-en"
source_table_fullname = f"{catalog}.{db}.{table}"
vs_index_fullname = f"{catalog}.{db}.{index}"
vsc = VectorSearchClient(disable_notice=True)
# ☑ Enable Change Data Feed (required for triggered sync)
try:
    spark.sql(f"ALTER TABLE {source_table_fullname} SET TBLPROPERTIES
    (delta.enableChangeDataFeed = true)")
    print(f"[INFO] CDF enabled on {source_table_fullname}")
except Exception as e:
    print(f"[WARN] Could not enable CDF (maybe already enabled): {e}")
    ☑ Check if index exists
def index_exists(vsc, endpoint, index_name):
```

```python
    try:
        vsc.get_index(endpoint_name=endpoint, index_name=index_name)
        return True
    except Exception as e:
        if "NOT_FOUND" in str(e) or "does not exist" in str(e):
            return False
        raise e
# ☑ Create index if it doesn't exist
if not index_exists(vsc, VECTOR_SEARCH_ENDPOINT_NAME, vs_index_fullname):
    print(f"[INFO] Creating index {vs_index_fullname} on endpoint {VECTOR_SEARCH_ENDPOINT_NAME}...")
    vsc.create_delta_sync_index(
        endpoint_name=VECTOR_SEARCH_ENDPOINT_NAME,
        index_name=vs_index_fullname,
        source_table_name=source_table_fullname,
        pipeline_type="TRIGGERED",
        primary_key="doc_id",
        embedding_source_column="content",
        embedding_model_endpoint_name=EMBEDDING_ENDPOINT_NAME
    )
# ☑ Wait for index to be online and pipeline to complete
print(f"[INFO] Waiting for index {vs_index_fullname} to be ready...")
index_obj = vsc.get_index(endpoint_name=VECTOR_SEARCH_ENDPOINT_NAME, index_name=vs_index_fullname)
index_obj.wait_until_ready()
print(f"[☑ SUCCESS] Index '{vs_index_fullname}' is ready.")
# ☑ Optionally sync the index (usually optional if pipeline is TRIGGERED)
print(f"[INFO] Syncing index with latest data...")
index_obj.sync()
print(f"[☑] Index {vs_index_fullname} synced successfully.")
```

Once you click the Vector Search database highlighted in Figure 8-3, it will take you to the index as depicted in Figure 8-4. Once you click the index, it will provide the detailed info as shown in Figure 8-5 below.

CHAPTER 8 LAKEHOUSE AI AND RETRIEVAL-AUGMENTED GENERATION (RAG)

Figure 8-4. Vector Search index

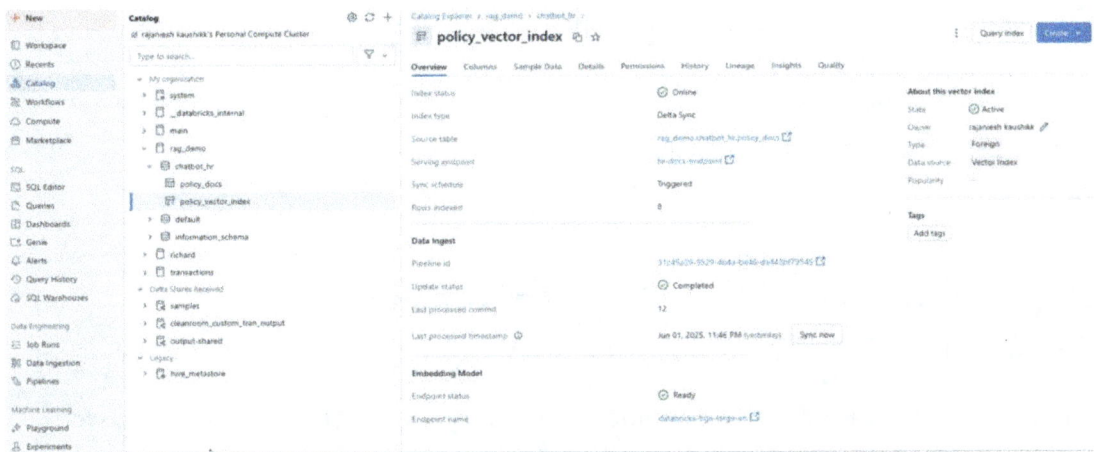

Figure 8-5. Detail view of the Vector Search index

Step 8: Perform Semantic Search on the Vector Index

In this step, we run a semantic search query using the vector index we created earlier.

- We provide a natural language question related to HR policy (e.g., *"What is the policy on parental leave?"*).

- The query is passed to the vector index hosted on Databricks Vector Search.

- The system performs **similarity search** on the indexed HR documents using vector embeddings.

- It returns the top matching documents that are most relevant to the question.

These retrieved documents will later serve as the **context** for answering the question using a large language model (LLM).

```
# Your HR chatbot query
question = "What is the policy on parental leave?"
# Perform similarity search on the HR policy index
results = vsc.get_index(endpoint_name=VECTOR_SEARCH_ENDPOINT_NAME, index_
name=vs_index_fullname).similarity_search(
    query_text=question,
    columns=["doc_id", "content"],  # HR-specific columns
    num_results=3  # More results provide better context
)
# Extract the documents
docs = results.get("result", {}).get("data_array", [])
docs
```

Step 9: Define LangChain Configuration for the HR Chatbot

Before building our Retrieval-Augmented Generation (RAG) chatbot, we need to tell LangChain how to connect all the components—like where to search for information and which language model to use to generate answers.

This is done through a configuration dictionary called `chain_config`.

What Is LangChain?
LangChain is a framework that helps you build applications powered by large language models (LLMs). It allows you to combine

- **Document retrieval** (e.g., search from a vector index)
- **LLMs** (e.g., LLaMA, GPT)
- **Prompt templates** (instructions to guide the LLM's response)

In short, LangChain takes care of connecting your **retrieved knowledge** with the **LLM output**, so you get useful, context-aware answers.

chain_config: What Each Key Means

```
chain_config = {
    "llm_model_serving_endpoint_name": "databricks-meta-llama-3-1-8b-
    instruct",
    "vector_search_endpoint_name": VECTOR_SEARCH_ENDPOINT_NAME,
    "vector_search_index": f"{catalog}.{db}.policy_vector_index",
    "llm_prompt_template": """You are an assistant that answers HR-related
    questions.
Use the following pieces of retrieved context from HR policies to answer
the question.
Some pieces of context may be irrelevant; do not use them if they are not
helpful.

Context: {context}

Answer:""",
}
chain_config = {
    "llm_model_serving_endpoint_name": "databricks-meta-llama-3-1-8b-
    instruct",  # ☑ your foundation model
    "vector_search_endpoint_name": VECTOR_SEARCH_ENDPOINT_NAME,
    # ☑ already defined earlier
    "vector_search_index": f"{catalog}.{db}.policy_vector_index",
    # ☑ your HR index
    "llm_prompt_template": """You are an assistant that answers HR-related
    questions. Use the following pieces of retrieved context from HR
    policies to answer the question. Some
    pieces of context may be irrelevant; do not use them if they are not
    helpful.\n\nContext: {context}\n\nAnswer:""",
}
```

Step 10: Constructing the Retriever Pipeline with LangChain and Vector Search

What Is a Retriever?
In a **Retrieval-Augmented Generation (RAG)** system, the **retriever** is the component that

CHAPTER 8   LAKEHOUSE AI AND RETRIEVAL-AUGMENTED GENERATION (RAG)

- Takes a user's question (like "What is the parental leave policy?")
- Searches a **vector index** (built on your HR policy documents)
- Returns the **most relevant documents or text chunks** that the LLM will use to generate its answer

This is crucial in enterprise applications because

- LLMs don't have your private HR data by default.
- A retriever brings the **right knowledge to the LLM at the right time**.

What Is a LangChain Pipeline?

A **LangChain pipeline** is a chain of modular building blocks. In this case:

1. **Retriever** (gets relevant docs from Vector Search)
2. **Formatter** (formats them into a structured prompt)
3. **LLM** (takes the prompt and generates an answer)

LangChain makes it easy to connect these components declaratively.

What Happens in This Step?

Let's break it down:

1. **Enable MLflow Tracing**
   - Tracks LangChain component calls, outputs, and helps with debugging
   - Optional but highly recommended for enterprise use

2. **Load Model and Index Config**
   - We reuse the `chain_config` you defined earlier.
   - This tells LangChain which endpoint and index to use.

3. **Create the Retriever**
   - We use `DatabricksVectorSearch.as_retriever()` to convert your Databricks vector index into a LangChain-compatible retriever.
   - It returns the top three most relevant document chunks.

4. **Format the Context**
   - LangChain needs context in a readable format to feed into your LLM prompt.
   - This step wraps each chunk like
   - Passage: Employees are entitled to 20 vacation days per year.

5. **Run the Pipeline**
   - The query flows through the retriever ➡ formatter ➡ string parser.
   - Output is a string of HR passages, ready to be used in the LLM prompt.

Why This Matters

Without this retriever pipeline:
- Your LLM has no access to HR policy data.
- It may "hallucinate" or make up answers.
- You miss out on grounding your model in **factual, authoritative documents**.

With this retriever:
- Your chatbot becomes **accurate, helpful, and trustworthy**.
- It scales across **domains**—HR, legal, compliance, support, etc.

Example Question Process

Question: "What is the parental leave policy?"
- Retriever searches your vector index for "Parental Leave".
- Finds this passage:

    ```
    "New parents can take up to 12 weeks of paid leave."
    ```

- This context is inserted into your prompt, and the LLM responds with a natural language answer.

CHAPTER 8 LAKEHOUSE AI AND RETRIEVAL-AUGMENTED GENERATION (RAG)

☑ **After This Step**

You'll connect the **retriever output to your LLM**, form a complete RAG chain, and then **log the chain with MLflow** so you can deploy it as a production chatbot.

Let's now implement this in code.

```
from databricks.vector_search.client import VectorSearchClient
from databricks_langchain.vectorstores import DatabricksVectorSearch
from langchain.schema.runnable import RunnableLambda
from langchain_core.output_parsers import StrOutputParser
import MLflow
# ☑ Enable MLflow Tracing (optional, helpful for debugging/tracking)
MLflow.langchain.autolog()
# ☑ Load the chain's configuration (from earlier cell)
model_config = MLflow.models.ModelConfig(development_config=chain_config)
# ☑ Create LangChain-compatible retriever from your HR policy vector index
vector_search_as_retriever = DatabricksVectorSearch(
    endpoint=model_config.get("vector_search_endpoint_name"),
    index_name=model_config.get("vector_search_index"),
    columns=["doc_id", "content"],  # your actual schema (no 'url')
).as_retriever(search_kwargs={"k": 3})   # top 3 most relevant chunks
# ☑ format retrieved context to insert into prompt
def format_context(docs):
    chunk_contents = [f"Passage: {d.page_content}\n" for d in docs]
    return "".join(chunk_contents)
# ☑ Execute the retriever pipeline for a sample HR question
relevant_docs = (
    vector_search_as_retriever
    | RunnableLambda(format_context)
    | StrOutputParser()
).invoke("What is the policy on parental leave?")
# ☑ Display formatted output (if in notebook)
display(relevant_docs)
```

Step 11: Building the LLM Chain to Generate HR Answers

Goal

Now that we've built the retriever to find relevant HR policy documents, the next step is to **connect it to a large language model (LLM)** via a structured prompt.

This step builds the **LLM chain** responsible for

- Accepting a question from the user
- Including the retrieved context from the vector index
- Generating a helpful, grounded answer using your configured LLM endpoint

What Happens in This Step?

Prompt Template Setup

We define a **LangChain prompt template** using

- A **system prompt** (from chain_config) that guides the LLM to act as an HR assistant
- A **user placeholder** ({question}) for inserting real-time queries

This prompt ensures consistency, tone, and clarity in the model's response.

Model Initialization

We load the Databricks-hosted foundation model using ChatDatabricks. This uses

- The LLM endpoint name (databricks-meta-llama-3-1-8b-instruct)
- Controlled settings: temperature=0.01 (for deterministic output), max_tokens=500 (for concise answers)

Testing the Chain

We test the full pipeline on a real question:

CHAPTER 8   LAKEHOUSE AI AND RETRIEVAL-AUGMENTED GENERATION (RAG)

"What is the policy on parental leave?"

The input includes an empty context for now (this will be filled automatically in the full RAG chain).

Displaying the Answer

We format the model's answer using a helper function that renders clean HTML in Databricks notebooks.

Why This Step Matters

This is where **retrieved factual knowledge meets generative intelligence**:

- The retriever ensures the model has the **right information**.

- The prompt and LLM ensure it generates a **clear, user-friendly answer**.

Together, they enable your chatbot to provide **precise, non-hallucinated responses** grounded in company policy.

☑ What's Next?

In the final step, you'll combine

- The **retriever**

- The **prompt**

- The **LLM** ... into a complete RAG pipeline that you can **log and serve with MLflow**

```
from langchain_core.prompts import ChatPromptTemplate
from databricks_langchain.chat_models import ChatDatabricks
from langchain_core.output_parsers import StrOutputParser
from IPython.display import display, HTML
def display_txt_as_html(text: str):
    """
    Nicely formats plain text as HTML for Databricks notebook display.
    """
    html = f"<div style='white-space: pre-wrap; font-family: monospace; font-size: 14px;'>{text}</div>"
    display(HTML(html))
```

```python
# ☑ Build prompt using the context from your config
prompt = ChatPromptTemplate.from_messages([
    ("system", model_config.get("llm_prompt_template")),  # Template from
    chain_config
    ("user", "{question}")  # Actual HR user query
])
# ☑ Load the LLM using your configured Databricks endpoint
model = ChatDatabricks(
    endpoint=model_config.get("llm_model_serving_endpoint_name"),
    extra_params={"temperature": 0.01, "max_tokens": 500}
)
# ☑ Example question to test the prompt/LLM chain
test_input = {
    "question": "What is the policy on parental leave?",
    "context": ""  # Will be filled in when connected to retriever later
}
# ☑ Run the pipeline
answer = (prompt | model | StrOutputParser()).invoke(test_input)
# ☑ Show the result (if using notebook)
display_txt_as_html(answer)
```

Step 12: Enable MLflow Autologging for LangChain

Before we run our chatbot pipeline, let's turn on **MLflow autologging** so that every step of our LangChain execution—retrieval, prompt construction, model inference, and output—is tracked automatically.

1. import MLflow
2. MLflow.langchain.autolog()
3. import MLflow
4. MLflow.langchain.autolog()

Step 13: Building the Full RAG Chatbot Pipeline with LangChain, Vector Search, and Databricks LLM

This step brings together all the previous components into a cohesive end-to-end LangChain pipeline. The goal is to enable a chatbot that retrieves relevant HR policy passages and generates humanlike answers using a foundation model.

Chain Configuration

We begin with a configuration dictionary that defines

- **LLM Model Endpoint:** A Databricks-hosted foundation model like `meta-llama-3`
- **Vector Search Endpoint:** The previously created Vector Search service
- **Vector Index:** The Delta table index that stores embedded HR policy content
- **Prompt Template:** An instruction template to guide the LLM when generating answers using retrieved content

Retriever Component

The **retriever** is a core part of the RAG architecture. It performs a similarity search over the vector index to fetch the most relevant chunks of HR policy documents based on the user's query.

Only the most relevant passages (top three) are selected, which balances performance and quality of answers.

Context Formatter

Since the retriever returns raw document chunks, we format these into plain-text passages. This formatted context is inserted into the LLM prompt so the model can "read" the relevant HR content before generating an answer.

Prompt Template and LLM

Using LangChain's `ChatPromptTemplate`, we define a conversational prompt that includes

- A **system message** instructing the model to focus on HR-related context only
- A **user message** placeholder where the actual HR query will go

We also configure the foundation model (served via Databricks) with parameters such as a low temperature for deterministic results and a maximum token limit.

User Query Extraction

The chatbot expects input as a list of messages (like [{role: user, content: "..."}]). To make this compatible with LangChain's routing, we extract the latest user query from this list.

Full LangChain RAG Chain

This is the complete chain, orchestrating all steps:

1. Extract the user query from messages.
2. Retrieve the top relevant HR passages.
3. Format the context.
4. Insert the context and question into the prompt.
5. Pass the prompt to the LLM.
6. Parse the result into plain text.

This modular, declarative setup makes it easy to extend or swap components in production.

Run an Example Query

We test the chain using a realistic HR query (e.g., about parental leave). The chain runs all components and returns the generated answer.

Display the Answer

We format the LLM's response using a simple HTML helper function to make it more readable in a notebook environment.

☑ Summary

At this point, you've built and tested a production-grade LangChain pipeline that

- Retrieves documents using **Databricks Vector Search**
- Generates answers with a **hosted foundation model**
- Uses modular components for retriever, formatter, prompt, and LLM
- Can be served via **MLflow** or embedded in a front-end app

This is the core architecture behind modern **RAG-based enterprise chatbots**.

```
# 1. Chain config
chain_config = {
    "llm_model_serving_endpoint_name": "databricks-meta-llama-3-1-8b-
    instruct",
    "vector_search_endpoint_name": "hr-docs-endpoint",
    "vector_search_index": "rag_demo.chatbot_hr.policy_vector_index",
    "llm_prompt_template": """You are an assistant that answers HR-related
    questions. Use the following pieces of retrieved context from HR
    policies to answer the question. Some
  pieces of context may be irrelevant; do not use them if they are not
    helpful.\n\nContext: {context}\n\nAnswer:""",
}
# 2. Retriever
from databricks_langchain.vectorstores import DatabricksVectorSearch
vector_search_as_retriever = DatabricksVectorSearch(
    endpoint=chain_config["vector_search_endpoint_name"],
    index_name=chain_config["vector_search_index"],
    columns=["doc_id", "content"],
).as_retriever(search_kwargs={"k": 3})
# 3. Formatter
def format_context(docs):
```

```
        chunk_contents = [f"Passage: {d.page_content}\n" for d in docs]
        return "".join(chunk_contents)
# 4. Prompt + model
from langchain_core.prompts import ChatPromptTemplate
from databricks_langchain.chat_models import ChatDatabricks
from langchain_core.output_parsers import StrOutputParser
prompt = ChatPromptTemplate.from_messages([
    ("system", chain_config["llm_prompt_template"]),
    ("user", "{question}"),
])
model = ChatDatabricks(
    endpoint=chain_config["llm_model_serving_endpoint_name"],
    extra_params={"temperature": 0.01, "max_tokens": 500}
)
# 5. Extract question
from operator import itemgetter
from langchain_core.runnables import RunnableLambda
def extract_user_query_string(chat_messages_array):
    return chat_messages_array[-1]["content"]
# 6. Final RAG chain
chain = (
    {
        "question": itemgetter("messages") | RunnableLambda(extract_user_
        query_string),
        "context": itemgetter("messages")
                    | RunnableLambda(extract_user_query_string)
                    | vector_search_as_retriever
                    | RunnableLambda(format_context),
    }
    | prompt
    | model
    | StrOutputParser()
)
# 7. Run example
chat_messages_array = [
```

```
    {"role": "user", "content": "What is the parental leave policy?"}
]
response = chain.invoke({"messages": chat_messages_array})
# 8. Output nicely (optional)
from IPython.display import display, HTML
def display_txt_as_html(text: str):
    html = f"<div style='white-space: pre-wrap; font-family: monospace; font-size: 14px;'>{text}</div>"
    display(HTML(html))
display_txt_as_html(response)
```

Summary

In this chapter, you explored how Lakehouse AI transforms Databricks into a powerful platform for building, deploying, and governing machine learning (ML) and generative AI solutions at scale. You learned that Lakehouse AI eliminates traditional silos between data engineering and AI/ML development by embedding intelligent tools—such as MLflow, Vector Search, Feature Store, and Unity Catalog—directly into the Lakehouse architecture.

At the heart of the chapter is **Retrieval-Augmented Generation (RAG)**, a key design pattern that improves the factual accuracy, transparency, and business relevance of large language model (LLM) outputs. RAG enhances LLM output accuracy and trust by grounding responses in current enterprise data. This approach is particularly valuable in domains like healthcare, finance, and law, where hallucinations and outdated responses can lead to critical errors.

You explored how to construct RAG pipelines using Delta tables for document storage, embedding models such as BGE and GTE for vector representation, and Databricks Vector Search for fast, semantic retrieval. You also saw how Unity Catalog governs access to AI assets and tracks data lineage, ensuring compliance and security across every stage of the ML life cycle.

Additionally, you learned about **prompt engineering** and **guardrails**—two essential techniques for shaping large language model (LLM) behavior. Prompt templates standardize communication with the model, while guardrails ensure safety, consistency, and compliance in generated outputs.

Real-world use cases demonstrate how these tools work together to solve practical problems, such as summarizing clinical notes in healthcare, detecting fraud in finance, and generating personalized recommendations in retail.

Together, Lakehouse AI and RAG provide a foundation for building AI-native applications that are not only intelligent and scalable but also **governed, explainable, and enterprise-ready**.

CHAPTER 9

Conclusion and Next Steps

As we reach the final chapter of this book, it's time to reflect on the key concepts you've explored and prepare for what comes next in your machine learning (ML) and Databricks journey. From setting up your Lakehouse environment to deploying real-time AI applications, you've built a solid foundation not only in ML techniques but also in implementing them responsibly, securely, and at scale using modern data architectures.

This chapter summarizes core learnings, highlights trusted resources for continued growth, and provides practical advice to help you apply what you've learned in real-world scenarios. Whether you're a data engineer, ML practitioner, or analytics leader, this chapter will help you chart your next steps and integrate these practices into your workflows.

The goal here isn't just to close a book—it's to open the door to production-ready machine learning with impact.

Learning Objectives

By the end of this chapter, you will be able to

- Recap and synthesize the critical concepts, tools, and workflows introduced throughout the book.
- Identify authoritative resources, communities, and platforms to deepen your Databricks and ML expertise further.
- Apply key principles from this book to structure your real-world machine learning projects.
- Evaluate different directions for career growth and technical advancement based on the foundations you've developed.
- Plan actionable next steps—whether deploying your first end-to-end ML solution or contributing to a production-grade AI system.

CHAPTER 9   CONCLUSION AND NEXT STEPS

Recap of Key Concepts

Throughout this book, you have progressively built, optimized, and operationalized machine learning (ML) solutions using Databricks and the Lakehouse Architecture. From your very first notebook to deploying advanced Retrieval-Augmented Generation (RAG) pipelines, each chapter deepened your expertise while reinforcing earlier lessons. This was not just a collection of independent modules but a deliberate progression designed to simulate real-world challenges and workflows that data professionals face every day.

The following recap distills the foundational knowledge and practical skills that will guide your future work in machine learning (ML) engineering, model governance, and AI deployment. By reflecting on the core takeaways from each chapter, you'll reinforce the cumulative nature of your learning and see how technical fluency, governance, collaboration, and real-time operationalization are interconnected pillars of modern data science. Whether your focus is technical leadership, hands-on development, or AI strategy, this refresher provides a coherent summary of your journey. It prepares you for the fast-paced future of data-driven innovation.

Getting Started with Databricks

You began your journey by exploring Databricks as a unified data and AI platform, understanding how it dramatically simplifies infrastructure complexity while supporting highly scalable analytics pipelines. This exploration included a critical understanding of the Lakehouse Architecture, which merges the transactional consistency of traditional data warehouses with the flexibility and cost-effectiveness of data lakes. This convergence was not just a conceptual framework—it became the bedrock of every subsequent workflow in the book.

Your initial hands-on tasks involved provisioning compute clusters with autoscaling and fault-tolerant capabilities, managing workspace folders that support collaborative development, and authoring interactive notebooks. These foundational exercises demonstrated how Databricks bridges the gap between data engineering and machine learning teams, providing a single environment for experimentation, governance, and deployment. Whether writing SQL queries or Python-based transformation logic, you experienced firsthand the power of a unified development environment.

Additionally, you examined how authentication and workspace security policies shape access to resources, enabling safe collaboration across different roles and responsibilities. You learned to configure identity federation, workspace permissions, and cluster access controls, ensuring data and model security from day one.

Delta Lake was introduced as the backbone of the Lakehouse. Its support for ACID transactions, schema evolution, and time travel made it more than a storage format—it became a version-controlled, fault-tolerant data layer that ensured consistency between your development and production environments. The benefits of these features became clear as you used them to power feature pipelines, enable reproducible experiments, and support real-time inference scenarios.

Industry Insight: A global logistics company could use Delta Lake to ingest real-time shipping manifests and track international freight operations. In this scenario, versioned Delta tables allow data scientists to analyze delivery performance over time, identify bottlenecks, and train models that forecast delivery delays—all without duplicating or corrupting the source data.

Practical Use Case: In a high-compliance industry such as pharmaceuticals, how could Delta Lake's time travel feature support auditing and data reproducibility in clinical ML trials??

Introduction to Machine Learning and Lakehouses

With platform fundamentals in place, you turned to core machine learning (ML) techniques: supervised, unsupervised, and reinforcement learning. You didn't just learn definitions—you worked hands-on with algorithms in Databricks notebooks, translating textbook concepts into practical workflows. For instance, you applied Linear Regression to predict housing prices, used K-Means Clustering to segment customers based on purchasing behavior, and explored policy optimization in basic reinforcement learning settings.

You gained experience designing datasets with clearly defined targets and features, transforming raw data into structured inputs that aligned with each ML task. Throughout these exercises, performance metrics such as RMSE for regression, recall, precision for classification, and AUC-ROC curves became essential tools in model evaluation. You practiced building pipelines that output not just predictions but quantifiable measures of model reliability.

To support robust model development, you implemented train-test splits and k-fold cross-validation, minimizing overfitting and enhancing generalization. These steps reflected a best-practice mindset—ensuring that your models could perform well not just on test data but in production settings under new data conditions.

The Lakehouse environment proved especially advantageous in this phase. With faster data access, built-in governance, and seamless support for both SQL and Python, you were able to iterate rapidly on model design while maintaining enterprise-grade data controls. Unified access to Delta tables meant that your feature engineering steps remained reproducible and traceable.

Industry Insight: A financial institution aiming to flag fraudulent credit card activity can leverage supervised learning in the Lakehouse. The unified platform enables real-time inference directly on transactional data, allowing risky transactions to be intercepted within milliseconds while ensuring compliance with audit trails and governance protocols.

Learning Types Comparison Table 1-1

Learning Type	Description	Common Use Case
Supervised	Learns from labeled data	Fraud detection, churn modeling
Unsupervised	Identifies hidden patterns	Customer segmentation, clustering
Reinforcement	Learns by trial and error	Robotics, recommendation engines

Data Preparation and Management

You dedicated significant effort to preparing and managing data, an area that consistently determines the success or failure of machine learning initiatives. Leveraging Databricks' integrated tools, such as Auto Loader and Structured Streaming, you learned to construct resilient ingestion pipelines that accommodate both static historical datasets and dynamic, high-velocity data streams. Whether processing CSV logs from an ecommerce site or sensor data from IoT devices, you saw firsthand how to streamline data collection at scale.

Once ingested, data quality became the next critical focus. You practiced cleaning operations to handle null values, resolve data type mismatches, and apply imputation strategies. You applied normalization techniques to rescale numerical fields and encoding methods to make categorical values model-ready. You also implemented time-based partitioning to optimize read/write performance and to support time-series modeling use cases.

Advanced preparation techniques included deduplication, fuzzy matching for inconsistent string fields, and automated data profiling to catch anomalies early. These skills are especially crucial in real-world settings, where raw data is often messy and inconsistent. Feature consistency and transformation logic were maintained across pipelines to reduce training-serving skew and ensure model reproducibility.

Crucially, Unity Catalog emerged as the governance backbone for these pipelines. With Unity Catalog, you can manage dataset access via role-based permissions, audit lineage for every transformation, and maintain schema consistency across teams. This became particularly important when collaborating in multiuser environments or when publishing datasets for consumption by other departments.

Industry Insight: In healthcare, modeling for patient readmission risk requires access to protected health information (PHI). Unity Catalog ensures that only authorized personnel can access sensitive columns while maintaining full lineage tracking for compliance with HIPAA regulations. Simultaneously, the same infrastructure supports robust modeling pipelines using de-identified views for general research and experimentation.

Implementation Consideration: How would you structure Delta Lake tables and Unity Catalog policies to support both exploratory analysis for data scientists and locked-down, production-grade access for model inference workflows in a regulated environment??

Building ML Models with MLflow

MLflow introduced structured workflows for experiment tracking, reproducibility, and life cycle management. You learned how to log training parameters, capture metrics such as accuracy or loss, store generated artifacts like models and visualizations, and register final outputs in a unified, searchable registry. These steps made it easy to organize complex experimentation cycles and ensured that results could be reproduced and understood long after the initial training run.

The MLflow Model Registry played a central role in bridging the gap between experimentation and deployment. You practiced registering models, assigning version tags, and promoting them across stages such as "Staging," "Production," and "Archived."

This model life cycle management system provided both structure and traceability, supporting CI/CD workflows and allowing you to roll back models if performance regressed.

In addition to the UI, you utilized MLflow's REST APIs and Python client to automate many of these steps, enabling integration into broader pipelines or custom applications. Comparing different training runs using experiment dashboards helped you make data-informed decisions when selecting the most robust model.

Industry Insight: In a telecom setting, a team of data scientists may simultaneously build churn prediction models based on customer usage patterns, support tickets, and payment history. MLflow enables them to track all experiments centrally, compare strategies across versions, and reuse the best-performing model as a foundation for the next iteration, ensuring collaborative progress.

Implementation Tip: When reviewing model experiments, include annotations or tags explaining why specific parameter choices were made. These notes offer critical context during team reviews and model audits, especially when transitioning a model to production.

AutoML and Model Optimization

Databricks AutoML helped you benchmark multiple models quickly and interpret their performance using generated notebooks. These notebooks didn't just show model outputs—they offered full transparency into the preprocessing steps, feature engineering logic, training configuration, and evaluation methodology. This blend of automation and insight turned AutoML into both a productivity enhancer and an educational resource.

You used AutoML to experiment with various model types across classification and regression tasks. By comparing outputs in leaderboards and analyzing charts such as ROC curves and residual plots, you developed an intuitive sense for how model complexity interacts with data characteristics. These visualizations became a quick and accessible way to understand trade-offs.

Beyond automated modeling, you expanded into manual customization. You performed hyperparameter searches using grid and random search strategies and explored regularization techniques such as L1 and L2 to improve generalization. Stratified folds and time-series-aware splits enabled robust validation that more accurately reflected real-world use cases.

Your model diagnostics skills also matured. You learned how to identify overfitting by monitoring validation loss divergence, recognize underperforming features through importance plots, and eliminate data leakage through thoughtful feature selection. These strategies helped fine-tune input pipelines for better predictive performance.

You also explored the implications of model interpretability. While models like Gradient Boosting and neural networks can offer high accuracy, you saw cases where simpler models, such as logistic regression, are favored due to their explainability, regulatory compliance, or stakeholder trust.

Industry Insight: In ecommerce, teams may rely on AutoML to generate a baseline recommendation model trained on user clickstreams and purchase data. However, for edge cases such as cold-start users or multilingual shoppers, data scientists may transition to manual tuning and domain-specific feature engineering for optimal personalization.

Strategic Consideration: What indicators should guide a team to shift from AutoML prototypes to fully customized modeling? Consider factors such as prediction consistency, regulatory constraints, feature drift, or evolving business KPIs.

Deploying Models

The deployment chapter turned your ML pipeline into a full-stack application capable of powering live business operations. You learned how to deploy models as REST APIs using Databricks Model Serving and examined a range of deployment patterns—from batch-scoring workflows that run nightly predictions to real-time APIs that serve low-latency inference requests.

A key focus of this phase was operational resilience. You examined strategies for autoscaling infrastructure based on workload intensity, implemented logging mechanisms to capture inputs and outputs for debugging and compliance purposes, and configured alerting systems to detect anomalies in production behavior. Model observability tools helped you detect data drift, prediction errors, or latency spikes in real time, enabling you to maintain reliable service-level agreements (SLAs).

You also integrated model delivery into CI/CD pipelines. By using Git-based version control and MLflow's model registry APIs, you can automate the promotion of models across staging and production environments. You practiced rollback scenarios, deployed shadow models for canary testing, and learned how to manage concurrent versions without introducing downtime.

Business Application: In fraud detection, every millisecond matters. A financial institution might deploy a real-time scoring API that flags anomalous credit card transactions as they occur. The solution must scale instantly to handle peak traffic during shopping seasons while maintaining sub-second response times. With Databricks Model Serving, you implemented this scalable, governed, and auditable deployment architecture.

Deployment Modes Quick Review

Mode	Use Case	Tooling
Batch	Nightly churn predictions	Workflows + Delta
Real-Time	Fraud detection, recommendations	Model Serving

Responsible AI and Governance

You examined the growing field of Responsible AI, using SHAP and LIME to demystify the black-box nature of machine learning models. These tools allowed you to generate visual explanations for individual predictions and understand the overall influence of features on model behavior. SHAP values, for example, broke down each prediction into additive contributions from every input feature, providing interpretable insights even in complex models like gradient-boosting machines. LIME, by contrast, approximated local behavior through simpler surrogate models, helping nontechnical stakeholders grasp the rationale behind predictions.

You also explored the broader challenge of algorithmic fairness, identifying hidden biases in datasets and quantifying their impact using metrics such as the disparate impact ratio and statistical parity difference. To address these issues, you applied data balancing strategies, such as oversampling underrepresented classes or using reweighting schemes to counteract historical bias. Additionally, you experimented with fairness constraints in model training to mitigate inequality while maintaining predictive power.

Documentation practices played a vital role in promoting transparency. You created model cards that captured metadata, including intended use, known limitations, ethical considerations, and performance breakdowns across demographic groups. These resources supported internal reviews, cross-team communication, and regulatory preparedness.

Industry Insight: A loan approval model that uses a ZIP code might inadvertently encode racial bias due to geographic segregation. With SHAP and fairness audits, a financial institution can pinpoint this issue and either remove the feature, re-engineer it, or apply fairness constraints to reduce its discriminatory impact before deployment.

Audit Readiness Check: If your organization were audited under emerging AI transparency laws (such as the EU AI Act), could you produce documentation that explains the model's decisions, tracks its data lineage, and quantifies fairness across protected groups? If not, where would you begin building that capability?

Lakehouse AI and Retrieval-Augmented Generation (RAG)

You finished the book by entering the frontier of generative AI, a domain transforming enterprise applications through intelligent, data-aware assistants. Using the Retrieval-Augmented Generation (RAG) design pattern, you built AI systems that bridge the strengths of large language models (LLMs) and enterprise-specific knowledge. Rather than depending solely on static, pretrained data, these systems retrieve and inject real-time, relevant information into prompts—ensuring grounded, fact-based answers.

You learned to create embeddings from documents using state-of-the-art models like BGE, E5, or GTE, then store and index them using Databricks Vector Search. These embeddings translated complex enterprise text—from policy manuals to technical FAQs—into semantically searchable formats. Vector Search enabled you to match natural language queries to the most relevant snippets, even when there was no keyword overlap.

You integrated these pipelines with large language models such as GPT or LLaMA, combining structured retrieval with fluent natural language output. This significantly enhanced response accuracy and reduced hallucinations, making your AI systems more trustworthy in high-stakes environments such as finance, law, and healthcare.

Crucially, you governed this entire process using Unity Catalog, which controlled access to embedding tables, vector indexes, and the LLM endpoints themselves. This governance ensured security, compliance, and traceability across every step of the RAG pipeline.

Applied Scenario: A legal department indexes thousands of contracts and NDAs stored in Delta format. When asked, "What is our liability cap with Vendor X?" the RAG pipeline retrieves matching clauses, supplies context to the LLM, and generates a plain-language answer with document citations—reducing hours of manual review to seconds.

Pipeline Management Insight: Use LangChain or Prompt Flow in conjunction with MLflow to orchestrate and track every component of your RAG pipeline—from embedding generation to vector retrieval to LLM prompting. This layered observability is essential for debugging, auditing, and improving future iterations of your AI systems.

This comprehensive recap serves not only as a reflection but as a refresher toolkit. You've built a full-stack ML skillset: data pipelines, model training, monitoring, governance, and even generative AI. You are now ready to apply these practices in production environments where scale, trust, and agility matter.

In the next section, we'll review trusted resources and learning paths to continue building on this momentum.

Resources for Further Learning

As you continue your journey beyond this book, having access to high-quality resources is crucial for deepening your expertise and staying current in the rapidly evolving fields of machine learning and data engineering. This section highlights curated learning paths, documentation, courses, community platforms, and tools that can help you reinforce and expand what you've learned in this book.

Official Databricks Resources

The most authoritative and up-to-date material on Databricks comes directly from the source. These resources offer product documentation, quickstarts, best practices, and ongoing updates:

- **Databricks Documentation**: Comprehensive documentation across compute, MLflow, Delta Lake, Unity Catalog, and workspace configuration
- **Databricks Academy**: Self-paced courses and certifications, including the Data Engineer Associate, Machine Learning Professional, and Lakehouse Fundamentals
- **Databricks YouTube Channel**: Live demos, webinars, and technical deep dives featuring platform updates and use cases
- **Databricks Blog**: Articles from engineers and partners showcasing real-world use cases, architecture guides, and solution accelerators

Books and Technical References

Supplement your knowledge with books that cover foundational and advanced machine learning, data architecture, and applied AI:

- *Designing Machine Learning Systems* by Chip Huyen: Focuses on real-world ML system design and deployment.

- *Feature Engineering for Machine Learning* by Alice Zheng: Deep dive into feature selection, extraction, and transformation.

- *Machine Learning Engineering* by Andriy Burkov: Practical guidance on the end-to-end ML life cycle.

- *Streaming Systems* by Tyler Akidau: Core concepts behind real-time processing using tools like Apache Spark.

- *Data Management at Scale* by Piethein Strengholt: Ideal for understanding metadata, data governance, and modern architectures.

Online Courses and Certifications

If you're aiming to specialize or validate your expertise, these learning platforms offer well-respected programs:

- **Coursera**: ML and data science courses by Stanford (Andrew Ng), DeepLearning.AI, and Google Cloud

- **edX**: Data engineering and AI programs from universities like Berkeley and MIT

- **Databricks Academy**: Certifications for data analysts, engineers, and ML professionals

- **Fast.ai**: A highly practical course focusing on getting models to work quickly with minimal computation

CHAPTER 9　CONCLUSION AND NEXT STEPS

Communities and Forums

Peer learning and troubleshooting are easier when you're part of an active knowledge community:

- **Databricks Community**: Forums, notebooks, and troubleshooting discussions
- **Stack Overflow**: Use the [databricks], [mlflow], and [delta-lake] tags to find common implementation questions.
- **LinkedIn Groups**: Follow thought leaders in AI, ML, and data engineering.
- **GitHub Projects**: Explore open source notebooks and implementations.
- **Meetups and Conferences**: Attend Spark + AI Summit, local ML meetups, or PyData events.

GitHub Repositories and Templates

Hands-on practice is crucial for mastery. Reuse and contribute to repositories that focus on

- End-to-end ML pipelines using MLflow and Delta Lake
- RAG pipelines and LLM orchestration with LangChain
- Experiment tracking and lineage with Unity Catalog
- Real-time feature engineering with Spark Structured Streaming

Start by reviewing the companion repository linked to this book's GitHub page at www.apress.com/ISBN.

By leveraging these resources, you can build on your existing skills, troubleshoot complex scenarios, and stay current with Databricks and broader machine learning practices. In the next section, we'll explore how to apply what you've learned to your own projects and professional goals.

Next Steps in Your ML Journey

With a solid foundation in the Databricks Lakehouse platform and modern machine learning techniques, you're now ready to move beyond theory and into applied innovation. This section offers practical guidance for translating your skills into real-world outcomes and continuing to grow as a data professional.

Build and Operationalize Your Own Projects

The best way to reinforce what you've learned is to build end-to-end machine learning solutions. Choose a domain that interests you—finance, healthcare, retail, telecom—and identify a problem where data can drive decisions. Then:

- Use Databricks to ingest and clean raw data with Delta Lake.
- Train baseline models with AutoML and refine them using MLflow.
- Create reproducible pipelines with Feature Store and orchestration tools.
- Deploy your model as a REST endpoint with built-in observability.

Start small, then iterate. Real-world model deployment involves continuous improvements and cross-functional feedback. Tools like Unity Catalog, MLflow Registry, and Databricks Jobs will help you manage the entire life cycle.

Join or Lead a Data Project Team

Whether you're a data scientist, engineer, or analyst, contribute to or initiate a collaborative AI project. These experiences hone your communication, architecture, and leadership skills. You might

- Lead a POC to introduce RAG-based knowledge assistants at your company.
- Contribute feature pipelines to an existing production machine learning (ML) platform.
- Own the monitoring and retraining strategy for a deployed use case.

Working in a team brings in operational, regulatory, and business considerations that go beyond the code. It's also the fastest way to learn enterprise ML.

Contribute to Open Source and Community

Many of the tools you learned—like MLflow, Delta Lake, and LangChain—are open source. Join their communities:

- Raise issues, fork repos, or submit pull requests.
- Share notebooks and tutorials based on your work.
- Help others by answering questions on Stack Overflow or GitHub.

You'll reinforce your understanding while helping shape the tools used by professionals around the world.

Seek Feedback and Reflect on Impact

Before scaling up any solution, take time to measure impact and solicit feedback:

- Are the model's predictions actionable and trustworthy?
- Does your deployment align with the company's privacy and governance policies?
- Have you clearly documented assumptions, limitations, and model behavior?

Reflective practice transforms technical skills into responsible, scalable, and valuable contributions.

Plan Your Career Growth

Whether you're looking to specialize or broaden your scope, use your current progress as a launchpad:

- Data scientists can explore ML Ops, generative AI, or domain-specific modeling.
- Data engineers can focus on real-time data pipelines or platform governance.

- Analysts can integrate machine learning (ML) models into business intelligence (BI) workflows or learn predictive analytics.

Certifications, conferences, mentorship, and cross-team collaboration will accelerate your trajectory.

By applying these next steps, you'll transform your learning into action and begin to shape the future of AI in your organization. In the final section, we'll summarize key takeaways and close the book with a forward-looking perspective.

Summary

As you close this book, reflect on how far you've come. From setting up your first Databricks cluster to deploying a Retrieval-Augmented Generation (RAG) pipeline with full governance, you've developed a comprehensive skill set that spans the entire machine learning life cycle.

You've learned not just how to build and train models but how to manage data pipelines, apply responsible AI practices, operationalize deployments, and ensure security and compliance—all within the Databricks Lakehouse platform.

Key Takeaways

- Databricks Lakehouse combines the scalability of data lakes with the reliability of data warehouses, enabling seamless analytics and machine learning (ML) workflows.

- Delta Lake, MLflow, Unity Catalog, AutoML, and Model Serving form a unified toolkit for full-life cycle machine learning (ML).

- Clean, well-governed data pipelines are foundational for reproducible and ethical machine learning.

- MLflow enables rigorous experiment tracking, model versioning, and deployment management.

- Model interpretability, fairness, and audit are not optional; they are necessary for responsible AI.

- Retrieval-Augmented Generation (RAG) workflows enhance large language model (LLM) applications by grounding responses in verifiable enterprise knowledge.

- Governance and collaboration—enabled by Unity Catalog and platform-native tooling—are key to scaling enterprise AI.

Looking Ahead

In the coming months and years, machine learning workflows will become more composable, governed, and accessible. Tools will evolve, but the principles you've mastered here—from feature engineering and reproducibility to audit readiness and user trust—will remain core to your practice.

Final Words

You are now equipped to drive AI innovation in real-world environments. Whether you're joining an MLOps team, launching your own AI startup, or becoming a go-to technical lead in your organization, the tools, workflows, and patterns in this book will continue to serve you.

Call to Action

As you move forward, start applying what you've learned immediately. Identify a real challenge, build a minimal ML pipeline, and iterate with governance, monitoring, and impact in mind. Share your results, seek feedback, and continue to grow.

The machine learning journey doesn't end here—it scales. Lead it with responsibility and purpose.

Index

A

ABAC, *see* Attribute-based access control (ABAC)
ACID, *see* Atomicity, consistency, isolation, durability (ACID)
Adaptive learning systems, 348
Adaptive query execution (AQE), 24
AI, *see* Artificial intelligence (AI)
Apache Kafka, 112, 115
Apache NiFi, 116
AQE, *see* Adaptive query execution (AQE)
Area Under the Curve-Receiver Operating Characteristic (AUC-ROC), 207
Artificial intelligence (AI), 13–15
    adoption, 335
    governance practices, 343
    lakehouse (*see* Lakehouse AI)
    responsible, 430, 431
    workflows, 23
Atomicity, consistency, isolation, durability (ACID), 10
Attribute-based access control (ABAC), 138
AUC-ROC, *see* Area Under the Curve-Receiver Operating Characteristic (AUC-ROC)
Automated machine learning (AutoML), 428, 429
    advanced configuration, 242–244
    benefits, 216, 217, 221, 222, 224, 225
    challenges and limitations, 222, 223
    configuring experiment, 227, 228
    data partitions, 244
    data preprocessing, 218, 219
    dataset, 225, 226, 239, 241
    definition, 215, 216
    deployment, 221
    evaluation and ranking, 220
    experiment results, 228
    experiment types and configurations, 240
    feature engineering, 219
    fraud detection, 218
    hyperparameter tuning, 220, 230
    join features, 245, 246
    leaderboard, 229
    loan defaults
        data application, 254
        deployment and testing, 256
        evaluation, 255
        overview, 254
        prediction, 255
    ML task, 226, 227
    model optimization, 231–237
    model selection, 219, 220
    performance metrics, 230
    prediction type, 242
    prerequisites, 238
    Python API
        evaluation and deployment, 251
        loading and testing, 252, 253
        retrieving, 251, 252
        running, 251
        usage, 251

INDEX

Automated machine
  learning (AutoML) (cont.)
    registration, 250
    reviewing experiment, 247–249
    scenarios, 238
    schema and prediction target, 241
    SHAP, 230
    trained models, 248, 249
    use cases, 217
AutoML, see Automated machine
  learning (AutoML)
AWS Glue, 116
Azure Data Factory, 116
Azure Event Hubs, 112

B

Batch deployment, 266–268, 273
Batch inference, 301
Batch ingestion
  challenges, 108, 109
  consolidated Delta tables, 145
  CSV file, 142, 143
  DBFS, 142
  definition, 108
  goals, 141
  handling and cleaning
    cleaned data, 153
    create directory, 149
    generate sample data, 150
    goals, 148
    handling missing values, 151
    prepare output directory, 149
    QuantitySold values, 152
    Spark DataFrame, 151
    update missing values, 152, 153
    validate data loading, 151
    verify missing values, 152
  implementation, 109, 110
  JSON file, 143
  query Delta tables, 145
  Spark DataFrames and Delta
    tables, 144
  verify consolidated data, 145
Batch vs. streaming ingestion, 114, 115
Bayesian optimization, 176
Beeswarm plot, 360, 361, 364, 370
Biased sampling, 340
Binary classification model, 355, 357
Buffering techniques, 113
Business criticality, 266
Business intelligence, 22

C

Centralized metadata management, 16
ChatDatabricks, 413
Cloud-based deployment
  benefits, 285
  considerations and challenges,
    285, 286
  definition, 283
  methods, 283–285
  scenarios, 286
Cloud integrations
  cloud-native services, 18, 19
  dynamic workloads, 19
  ecosystems, 17
  scalability, 18
  storage, 18
Cloud vs. edge deployment, 278
Clusters
  autoscaling, 24, 25
  definition, 28
  dynamic workloads, 12
  features, 28, 29

INDEX

misconfigured/static, 12
performance metrics, 26
preconfigured environments, 13
resource optimization, 13
streamlined management and monitoring, 13
CNNs, *see* Convolutional neural networks (CNNs)
Collaborative notebooks
challenges, 11
communication tools, 11
multi-language support, 12
Compliance, 16, 378
audit trails, 26
and governance, 281, 282
logs, 26
Compound AI systems, 345, 347
Container-based deployment, 284
Continual learning, 348
Convolutional neural networks (CNNs), 169, 170
Credit scoring models, 234
CRM, *see* Customer relationship management (CRM)
Customer churn prediction model, 232
computational requirements, 174
data characteristics, 173
data type, 174, 175
interpretability *vs.* accuracy, 174
problem identification, 173
Customer relationship management (CRM), 122

D

Data augmentation, 233
Data balancing strategies, 430
Databricks

AI and machine learning integration, 13-15
assigning roles to users, 41
auto loader, 116
automating repetitive tasks, 46
AutoML (*see* Automated machine learning (AutoML))
batch processing, 141-145
business use cases and industry applications, 4
career growth, 436, 437
clean environment, 47
cloud integrations, 17-19
cloud-native and open by design, 3
cloud provider, 33-35
cluster usage optimization, 44
collaboration, 3, 45
components
clusters, 28, 29
jobs, 29
notebooks, 27, 28
workflows, 29, 30
compute clusters, 12, 13
compute tab, 32
configuring clusters, 38, 39, 50, 51
configuring workspace, 37, 38
cost and performance optimization, 23-25
data ecosystem integration, 4
data landscape, 1
data life cycle platform, 2
data project team, 435
data sources, 42
definition, 1
delta sharing, 19-21
deployment (*see* Model deployment)
deployment regions, 38
feedback and impact, 436

441

INDEX

Databricks (*cont.*)
    flexibility and scalability, 2
    GitHub repositories and templates, 434
    governance and security, 4
    guidance, 435
    high-performance embedding models, 383
    interface, 30–32
    job tab, 32, 33
    keyboard shortcuts, 44
    knowledge community, 434
    lakehouse architecture, 5–11, 348
    locate resources, 31
    logging, 48
    monitoring and logging capabilities, 25–27
    monitoring jobs and clusters, 46
    navigation, 47
    notebooks, 11, 12, 51–54
    online courses and certifications, 433
    open source and community, 436
    organize workspace clarity, 43
    personas support, 3
    portal, 36
    projects, 435
    real-time analytics and AI-driven discoveries, 3, 4
    registering account, 35–37
    resources, 432
    search and filtering tools, 45
    security and governance, 15–17
    starter warehouse configuration, 51
    structured streaming, 112
    technical references, 433
    unique proposition, 5
    user access and roles, 40–42
    worker types, 40
    workloads, 21–23
    workspace deployment, 42
    workspace setting, 49
    workspace view, 31
Databricks file system (DBFS), 142, 199
Data cleansing
    data types, 123, 124
    missing values, 119
    normalization and scaling, 127–130
    outlier detection and handling, 125–127
    removing duplicated records, 121–123
    row/column removal, 120, 121
    time-series data, 120
    and transformation, 130, 131
Data drift, 263
Data encryption, 17
Data ingestion
    definition, 108
    methods
        batch, 108–110
        streaming, 111–114
    tools, 115–118
Data lakehouses, 55, 346, 347
Data lakes *vs.* data warehouses, 5, 6
Data lineage tracking, 139, 391
Data preparation
    delta tables, 387
    and management, 426, 427
Data preprocessing, 218
Data quality, 426
Data schema mismatches, 309–311
Datasheet, 342
Data streaming, 22
Data transformation
    best practices, 135
    cloud-based solutions, 133
    definition, 132
    governance and catalog integration, 134, 135

integration platforms, 132, 133
ML tools, 134
open source libraries, 132
tools, 133
Data volume, 266
DBFS, *see* Databricks file system (DBFS)
Debugging, 26
Decision trees, 61, 169, 337
Delta Lake, 10, 22, 23, 25, 226, 425
Delta sharing, 4
definition, 19
fine-grained access control, 20
growing demands, 21
interoperability, 20
real-time access data, 20
security and compliance, 21
suppliers, 21
Delta tables, 386–391
Dendrogram, 89
Density-based spatial clustering of applications with noise (DBSCAN), 89
Dependency management, 306, 307
Dependency mismatches, 308

E

ECOA, *see* Equal Credit Opportunity Act (ECOA)
Ecommerce platform, 9, 13
EDA, *see* Exploratory data analysis (EDA)
Edge deployment, 271–273, 302
EHRs, *see* Electronic health records (EHRs)
Elbow method, 96–99, 105
Electronic health records (EHRs), 395
Embedded deployment, 302, 303
Embedding models, 381, 386, 387

Embedding space, 382
Enqueue messages, 319
Ensembling techniques, 234
Enterprise ecosystems, 318
Enterprise-grade data controls, 426
Enterprise-grade governance, 378
Environment packaging, 261
Equal Credit Opportunity Act (ECOA), 344
Error-correction algorithms, 113
Estimated arrival times (ETA), 112, 113
ETA, *see* Estimated arrival times (ETA)
ETL, *see* Extract, transform, load (ETL)
EU AI Act, 343
Explainability techniques, 336
Explainable AI (XAI), 335
Exploratory data analysis (EDA), 341
Extract, transform, load (ETL), 22

F

Fair Lending laws, 344
Fairness-aware algorithms, 342
Feature engineering, 58
AutoML, 219
model accuracy, 231
File compaction, 25
Fine-grained access control, 16
Foundation models, 345, 347
Fraud detection algorithms, 15
Fraud detection system, 218
Fuzzy matching, 122

G

General Data Protection Regulation (GDPR), 343
Generative AI, 349, 350, 379
Generator, 382

INDEX

GDPR, *see* General Data Protection Regulation (GDPR)
Google Cloud Dataflow, 117
Governance
    catalog integration, 134, 135
    components, 282
    data organization, 139, 141
    RAG pipelines, 391, 392
    requirements, 281
    responsible AI, 430, 431
    security, 4, 15–17
Gradient boosting, 168, 169, 232, 429, 430
Grid search, 176
Guardrails, 392–394

H

Hallucination, 380
Handwriting recognition, 233
Hierarchical clustering, 88, 89
HIPAA, 344
Historical bias, 340
Hybrid deployments
    advantages, 291
    challenges, 291, 292
    patterns, 290
    scenarios, 292
    workloads, 289
Hyperparameters, 175
Hyperparameter tuning
    advantages, 176, 177
    AutoML, 220
    definition, 176
    example, 177–179
    MLflow and Hyperopt, 191–194
    model accuracy, 232
    objective function, 179
    spam detection system, 177

I, J

Image recognition, 23
Indexing, 388
Integration, 262
    error handling and resilience, 321
    message queues, 319
    mobile applications, 319, 320
    monitoring, 322
    performance optimization, 321
    requirements, 279, 280
    REST APIs, 318
    secure API access, 320
    versioning, 321
    webhooks, 319
Interquartile range (IQR), 125–127

K

K-means clustering, 62, 85, 88, 91, 168, 425

L

Lakehouse AI, 385, 431, 432
    benefits, 377–379
    components, 374
    concept, 373, 374
    features and capabilities, 375–377
    See also Retrieval-augmented generation (RAG)
Lakehouse architecture, 2, 424
    advantages, 426
    benefits, 6
    characteristics
        data duplication, 9, 10
        data formats, 8, 9
        data silos, 7, 8
        data storage, 7
        data versioning and time travel, 11

high-performance queries, 10
transactional capabilities, 10
unified solution, 8
data platforms, 345
limitations, 7
LangChain, 384, 387, 390
definition, 408
full RAG chain, 417
MLflow autologging, 415
pipeline, 410
prompt template, 413
Language generation, 383
Large language models (LLMs), 373, 374, 379, 431
chain, 413, 415
challenges, 349
context, 408
enterprise workflows, 349
formats, 396
generative AI, 379
prompt template, 417
retail, 397
traditional function, 380
Latency tolerance, 266
Learning types, 426
Life cycle management, 263
Lifelong learning, 348
LIME, *see* Local interpretable model-agnostic explanations (LIME)
Lineage tracking, 16
Linear regression, 59, 61, 70, 77–81, 85, 168, 169, 336, 425
LLaMA 3, 383
LLMs, *see* Large language models (LLMs)
Loan default risk prediction
binary classification model, 355, 357
create dataset, 351–355
goals, 350

MLflow, 362, 363
new model version and interpretability, 366–371
problem statement, 350
SHAP, 357–362
unity catalog metadata, 364, 365
workflow, 351
Local interpretable model-agnostic explanations (LIME), 281, 338, 339
Logistic regression, 168, 169, 235
Log transformation, 129
Looker, 22

M

Machine learning (ML)
bias, 340–342
capabilities, 22
concepts, 55, 56
data, 57
data transformation tools, 134
deployment patterns, 429
documentation and explanations, 349
emerging technologies and architectures, 345–347
evaluation metrics, 59
examples, 57
fairness and accountability, 342, 343
features, 58
goals, 423
implications and compliance, 343, 344
MLflow, 14, 160, 427, 428
(*see also* MLflow)
models, 58, 59
overfitting and underfitting, 60
performant models, 335
preconfigured libraries, 14
real-time and continual learning, 348

INDEX

Machine learning (ML) (*cont.*)
    real-world examples and use cases, 64, 65
    registered models, 365
    runtime, 238
    simplified deployment, 14, 15
    structured predictions, 349
    techniques, 425
    training and testing, 59
    types, 60–63
Mean Squared Error (MSE), 71, 77
Measurement bias, 340
Message queues, 319
Min-Max scaling, 128
Mistral, 383
Mixtral, 383
ML, *see* Machine learning (ML)
MLflow, 14, 22, 339, 344, 384
    algorithm
        comparison, 170–172
        computational requirements, 169
        data types, 170
        importance, 167
        interpretability *vs.* accuracy, 169
        problem, 168
        size and data quality, 169
    artifact structure, 275
    autologging, 415
    building ML models, 427, 428
    checklist, 304
    classification model, 186
    components, 160–162, 297
    creating databricks notebook, 165
    definition, 162
    deployment challenges, 294, 296
    end-to-end process, 259
    environment reproducibility, 298, 299
    experiment tracking, 165, 166, 230, 385, 392
        artifacts, 190
        importance, 189
        logging parameters and metrics, 189
        recording, 189
        visualization, 190, 191
    integration, 375
    interpretation metrics, 187
    loading and preparing data, 165
    loading registered model, 167
    loan default prediction
        accuracy, 203–205
        confusion matrix, 208–211
        creating and uploading data, 199
        DBFS, 199
        experiment setting, 201
        F1-score, 207
        goals, 198
        load and display data, 200
        load and make predictions, 202
        precision, 206
        PySpark, 200
        reasons, 207
        recall, 206
        recommendations, 207
        register model, 202
        training, 201
        validation accuracy, 211–213
    logs, 186, 187, 298
    log SHAP artifacts, 362, 363
    model registry, 303, 304
    models, 163, 164
    model signatures, 309
    patterns, 300–303
    philosophy, 300

predictions and evaluation
  metrics, 186
principles, 296
projects, 163
Registry, 164, 166
tracing, 410
tracking, 162, 163
train and log model, 166
viewing experiments, 188
Mobile applications, 319, 320
Model accuracy
  data augmentation, 233
  ensembling, 234
  feature engineering, 231
  hyperparameter tuning, 232
  removing outliers, 233
Model-agnostic interpretability, 337
Model cards, 342
Model deployment
  alerts, 325
  churn prediction, 293, 294
  components, 261–264, 293
  concept, 260
  considerations, 274–292
  customer churn and service, 327–332
  dashboards, 325
  definition, 259
  dependency management, 306, 307
  environment reproducibility and
    dependency challenge, 305
  external integration patterns, 318–322
  factors, 277
  goals, 260
  hybrid, 274
  life cycle, 296
  market product, 264, 265
  MLflow's approach (*see* MLflow)
  model life cycle and updates, 326, 327
  monitoring and alerting setting,
    323, 324
  monitoring life cycle, 325, 326
  strategies, 265–274
  troubleshooting, 307–318
  validating environments, 306
Model drift, 322
Model optimization, 231, 428, 429
  accuracy, 231–234
  performance tuning, 235–238
Model performance
  issues, 180
  metrics
    accuracy, 180, 181
    calculation, 185
    F1-score, 183, 184
    false positives *vs*. negatives, 184
    precision, 181, 182
    recall, 182, 183
    requirements, 184
Model selection, AutoML, 219
Model serialization, 261
  definition, 275
  formats, 276
  MLflow model artifact structure, 275
  skl2onnx library, 276
Model-specific methods, 336
MSE, *see* Mean Squared Error (MSE)
Multimodal learning, 345, 347

N

Naïve Bayes, 170
Natural language processing (NLP), 23
NDAs, *see* Non-disclosure
  agreements (NDAs)
Networking, 313–316
Neural networks, 59, 61, 169, 429

INDEX

NLP, *see* Natural language processing (NLP)
Non-disclosure agreements (NDAs), 390
Normalization techniques, 426
Notebooks, 27, 28

O

Online fraud detection system, 377
Online serving, 269
On-premises deployment
    advantages, 288
    challenges, 288, 289
    hosting models, 287
    types, 287
    use case/organization demands, 289
Operational resilience, 429

P

Partial dependence plots (PDPs), 338, 339
PCA, *see* Principal component analysis (PCA)
PDPs, *see* Partial dependence plots (PDPs)
Performance degradation, 316, 317
Performance optimization strategies
    benefits, 235
    caching, 237
    data processing, 236
    feature selection, 236
    machine learning, 234
    model complexity, 235
    scaling infrastructure, 237
Petabytes, 2
PHI, *see* Protected health information (PHI)
Photon Engine, 24, 25
Polynomial regression, 77–81

Post-hoc methods, 337
Power BI, 22, 23
Prediction frequency, 265
Prediction quality, 323
Principal component analysis (PCA), 62, 219
Prompt engineering
    context, 393
    definition, 392
    example, 393
    template, 392
    testing, 394, 395
Prompt flow, 384
Protected health information (PHI), 427
PyTorch, 14, 22, 23

Q

Query, 389

R

RAG, *see* Retrieval-augmented generation (RAG)
RAG-based enterprise chatbots, 418, 419
Random Forest, 81–85, 168, 173, 175, 194–198, 234
Random Forest Regressors, 168
Random search, 176
RBAC, *see* Role-based access control (RBAC)
Real-time API serving, 301
Real-time deployment, 269, 270, 273
Real-time learning, 348
Recommendation systems, 23, 263
Reinforcement learning, 62, 63, 425
Representation bias, 340
Resource constraints, 311–313

Responsible AI, 430, 431
REST API integration, 318
Retrieval-augmented generation (RAG), 349, 424, 431, 432
   architecture and components, 381–383
   challenges, 395
   concept, 373
   definition, 380, 381
   delta tables and vector search, 386–391
   enterprise retrieval techniques, 380
   examples, 395
   finance, 396
   governance, 391, 392
   healthcare, 395
   model and tooling options, 383–385
   prompt engineering and guardrails, 392–395
   retailers, 397
   vector search, 397–420
Retriever, 382, 410–412, 416
Risk-mitigation strategy, 281
Role-based access control (RBAC), 4, 15, 37, 41, 45, 136–138
R^2 score, 72, 77

S

Semantic Kernel, 390
Semi-structured data, 7, 8
Serverless inference, 284
Service-level agreements (SLAs), 429
Shapley additive explanations (SHAP), 174, 230, 281, 337, 357–362, 364, 368
SHAP waterfall plot, 358, 359
Shared assets, 378
Shared metadata model, 138
Silhouette score, 103–106
SLAs, *see* Service-level agreements (SLAs)
SMOTE, *see* Synthetic minority over-sampling technique (SMOTE)
Societal inequalities, 340
Spam detection system, 185
Streaming ingestion
   challenges, 111
   definition, 111
   goals, 146
   implementation, 111–114
   process and save streaming data, 147, 148
   real-time data streams, 146
   register and query streaming data, 148
   schema and load streaming data, 147
Structural discrimination, 340
Structured data, 7, 8
Supervised learning, 60, 61, 425, 426
   building and training model, 69, 70
   evaluation, 71–73
   features and target, 68
   goals, 66
   libraries, 66
   loading dataset, 67
   predicted price with residual, 75
   results, 73–77
   training and testing sets, 68, 69
Support vector machines (SVM), 168
Synthetic minority over-sampling technique (SMOTE), 207

T

Tableau, 22
Target variable, 352
TensorFlow, 14, 22
Terabytes, 2

INDEX

Term frequency-inverse document frequency (TF-IDF), 219
TF-IDF, *see* Term frequency-inverse document frequency (TF-IDF)
TPE, *see* Tree-structured Parzen estimator (TPE)
Traditional systems, 9
Transformation logic, 113
Transparency checklists, 343
Tree-structured Parzen estimator (TPE), 179
Trigger model inference, 319
Troubleshooting checklist, 317, 318

U

UI, *see* User interface (UI)
Unified batch processing, 22
Unified workload management, 23
Unity catalog, 4, 15, 17, 339, 344, 374, 376, 385, 391, 392, 427
    assign permissions, 156
    best practices, 139, 141
    create schema, 155
    create user groups, 156
    creation, 155
    data lineage, 136
    goals, 154
    load and data standardization, 154
    metadata, 364, 365
    organizations, 138, 139
    problems, 136, 137
    querying standardized data, 155
    save data, 155
    validate permissions, 157
    verify table organization, 156

Unstructured data, 7, 8
Unsupervised learning, 61, 62, 425
    age parameter in clustering, 99–102
    clustering, 87
    customer bases, 85
    customer behavior, 94
    customer segmentation chart, 92
    dataset, 88
    elbow method, 96–99
    example, 85
    goals, 85
    interpretation clusters, 93–96
    K-means clustering, 91
    loading dataset, 86
    plotting data, 87–90
    Silhouette score, 103–106
    3D visualization, clustering, 102
    visualize clusters, 91, 93
User interface (UI), 375

V

Vector, 381
Vector search, 376, 379, 383, 386–392
    create and sync index, 404, 405, 407
    create and validate endpoint, 402, 404
    create catalog and schema, PySpark, 399, 400
    database, 404
    full RAG chatbot pipeline, 416–420
    install libraries, 398
    LangChain configuration, 408, 409
    LLM chain, 413, 415
    load HR policy data, 400–402
    restart Python kernel, 399
    retriever pipeline, 410–412

semantic search, 407, 408
verify HR policy data, 402
Vendor lock-in, 3

W

WCSS, *see* Within-cluster sum of squares (WCSS)
Webhooks, 319
Within-cluster sum of squares (WCSS), 96, 98

X, Y

XAI, *see* Explainable AI (XAI)
XGBoost, 14, 173–175, 232, 234, 355

Z

Zero business value, 259
Z-ordering, 25

GPSR Compliance

The European Union's (EU) General Product Safety Regulation (GPSR) is a set of rules that requires consumer products to be safe and our obligations to ensure this.

If you have any concerns about our products, you can contact us on

ProductSafety@springernature.com

In case Publisher is established outside the EU, the EU authorized representative is:

Springer Nature Customer Service Center GmbH
Europaplatz 3
69115 Heidelberg, Germany

www.ingramcontent.com/pod-product-compliance
Lightning Source LLC
LaVergne TN
LVHW081345060526
838201LV00050B/1717